1 SAMUEL

Saul and the Witch of Endor by Gustave Doré

BERIT OLAM
Studies in Hebrew Narrative & Poetry

1 Samuel

David Jobling

David W. Cotter, O.S.B.
Editor

Jerome T. Walsh
Chris Franke
Associate Editors

A Michael Glazier Book
THE LITURGICAL PRESS
Collegeville, Minnesota

A Michael Glazier Book published by The Liturgical Press

Cover design by Ann Blattner

1 2 3 4 5 6 7 8

Library of Congress Cataloging-in-Publication Data

Jobling, David.
 1 Samuel / David Jobling.
   p. cm. — (Berit olam)
 "A Michael Glazier book."
 Includes bibliographical references and index.
 ISBN 0-8146-5047-3 (alk. paper)
 1. Bible. O.T. Samuel, 1st—Criticism, interpretation, etc.
I. Title. II. Series.
BS1325.2.J55 1998
222'.4306—dc21   97-52050
                       CIP

For my dear friends in the Bible and Culture Collective,
and for Catherine

CONTENTS

ACKNOWLEDGMENTS

My gratitude goes first to my immediate family, Esther Cherland and Rebekah Jobling, who have borne all the things that families have to bear during the producing of a book. I thank them for their encouragement and their patience with my absences from them (including my absences of mind). Two other groups who are for me like families have also played a role and paid a price. My relationship with colleagues and students at St. Andrew's College I experience as a daily miracle of Christian community and effective collaboration. They have respected and supported the intellectual journey I take in this book even when I have gone in strange directions. One of my great discoveries at St. Andrew's has been how research and teaching can and must nourish each other. My courses on 1 Samuel in 1993 and 1994 were a decisive factor in the shaping of a lot of fragmentary material into a book, and I especially thank the students in those courses.

The other "family" is the Bible and Culture Collective. Through my association with them, almost a decade long, collaborative professional work has become for me the norm, and writing things by myself and under my own name now seems exceptional and odd. So I have felt guilty when work on this book has interfered with our collective endeavor, especially in the first half of 1997. Friends, this is what I was doing when I was failing to answer the e-mail, and I dedicate the book to you in great thankfulness for our work together.

Among the many colleagues from whose work on 1 Samuel I have profited, I particularly thank Robert Polzin. While I rarely agree with him and sometimes am hard on him, he has been in many places in this book my necessary vis-à-vis, without whom it would have been much harder for me to think through my own ideas. He was also a genial host at Carleton University where one of my chapters had its first outing.

I thank Danna Fewell for a careful reading of the penultimate draft and many helpful suggestions. I also thank John Havea, her student at Perkins School of Theology, for using the manuscript in a course he was teaching, and giving me the benefit of that. And I thank Danielle Duperreault, who as a member of the 1 Samuel class long ago made her mark on my reading of Hannah, for her assistance in the closing stage of the book's preparation.

The many people who have helped me will not begrudge my giving special mention to two. Gary Phillips also read the penultimate draft, but that is a drop in the bucket of what I and my book owe to him. Long before we came together in the Bible and Culture Collective he was my collaborator. I begin to lose count of the joint presentations we have done in various settings, earning us the name (among others) of "the Bert and Ernie of postmodern biblical studies" (so Carole Fontaine). Gary is the one to whom I show my work at every stage, though I shudder to think of the time he meticulously spends on it and the cost to his own work. And I am well aware of other colleagues who could say the same. Gary, it's great that you help us to write *our* books, but we are longing to see *yours!*

When I was starting work on the book, St. Andrew's enabled me to hire Catherine Rose as a "student assistant." Colleague rather than student, collaborator rather than assistant, she has entered deeply into the texture of the book. In many places I have benefited from the conversations we had, and the broadness of concept that I hope the reader will find here owes much to her. And, as I duly acknowledge in appropriate places, she is the co-author of Part IV. I am alone responsible for the final presentation, but she did much of the research, especially on Matthew Arnold, and she and I together have presented at conferences, and elsewhere published, work preparatory to Part IV. Catherine, to you too I give the book—it was yours already.

Parts of this book make use of material I have published elsewhere. For permission to reuse journal articles I thank the publishers and editors of the following journals: *Bulletin of the Canadian Society of Biblical Studies, Journal of Biblical Literature, Scandinavian Journal of the Old Testament, Semeia.* For permission to reuse material from published books I thank E. J. Brill, The Pilgrim Press, and Sheffield Academic Press. In all cases the material in question has been thoroughly reworked for this book.

Excerpts from Donald Barthelme's *The Dead Father* are quoted by kind permission of the publisher, Farrar, Straus and Giroux.

Part I

THE READER AND THE BOOK

The numbers in square brackets throughout this book, whether in the text or in footnotes, indicate cross-references. The numbers refer to other pages in this book where the reader will find further material on the topic under discussion.

Chapter 1

SAMUEL'S BOOK, MY BOOK, ME, AND YOU: AN AUTOBIOGRAPHICAL ESSAY ON METHOD

Any finished work tells implicitly the story of how it came to be. This book tells its story rather explicitly, but it was only near the end of the writing that I realized this.

Consciously I had three main aims. The first was to test the possibility of organizing a book on the Bible according to Terry Eagleton's "triptych of . . . class, race and gender,"[1] the guiding categories of recent ideological criticism. These categories have, in fact, given shape to my book, for Parts II, III, and IV deal respectively with class, gender, and race. The second aim was to read 1 Samuel *as a book,* that is, as having some sort of completeness in itself. The issue here is that 1 Samuel is part of a much larger narrative. It continues a story, and its own story will be continued. It seems to me, though, that a book of the Bible, as we have it, is a literary thing that commands authority—commentaries are written on it, study groups study it, and so on. My aim has been to exploit the tension between reading 1 Samuel in itself and reading it as part of something larger. Out of this tension I have, I believe, offered a completely new interpretation of its closing chapters. My third aim was to come to terms with 1 Samuel as a historical document in a double sense, as coming out of some setting in ancient Israel, and as being itself a piece of historiography, a telling of a past. My conviction has grown, in the course of the writing, that what we have in 1 Samuel (and the larger narrative to which it belongs) is a national autobiography, developed over a long time and out of an acute anxiety about how Israel's present is related to its past.

---

[1] *The Ideology of the Aesthetic* (Oxford: Basil Blackwell, 1990) 5.

3

These were my conscious aims. The surprise that the book sprang on me when I had almost finished it was that while I had been pursuing these aims *it* had taken the shape of an autobiography—an intellectual autobiography of my own to answer to Israel's autobiography. The book unfolds in a sequential way as a record of my development as a biblical scholar over more than twenty-five years. This discovery shapes the following introductory remarks. As I sketch what I do in each of the parts and chapters of this book I shall sketch also the dominant methods that I use and how these fit into a developing pattern. It is a pattern that comes from meditation on my own journey, but I believe it has much in common with the experience of others and may provide you with a way of reading the recent history of biblical studies. In any case I believe that we should be more explicit about our individual identity as scholars and the specific issues that shape our writing. I shall pursue this thought later, in my discussion and use of psychoanalytic method [20–24, 282–305].[2]

My story has three stages that correspond in a rough and ready way to decades.

The 1970s: Structuralism and Feminism

Structuralism and feminism came to me at the same time, and I see them as the two parents of all that has followed. They shaped each other in ways I hardly understood then, since they seemed to belong to different worlds. Structuralism has a certain priority not for any

---

[2] In this chapter I try to provide a discussion of method sufficient for the reader to understand this book. It is not intended as a full account of the methods of biblical study that I mention, nor do I provide extensive references. For these I refer readers above all to The Bible and Culture Collective, *The Postmodern Bible* (New Haven: Yale University Press, 1995). As a member of the collective that wrote that book I share its critical understanding of and attitude toward the different methods, and toward the question of method in general. Other resources are available. See especially Gale A. Yee, ed., *Judges and Method: New Approaches in Biblical Studies* (Minneapolis: Fortress, 1995); Janice Capel Anderson and Stephen D. Moore, eds., *Mark and Method: New Approaches in Biblical Studies* (Minneapolis: Fortress, 1992); Steven L. McKenzie and Stephen R. Haynes, eds., *To Each Its Own Meaning: An Introduction to Biblical Criticisms and Their Application* (Louisville: Westminster/John Knox, 1993). More generally on methods of literary criticism see Irena Makaryk, ed., *Encyclopedia of Contemporary Literary Approaches* (Toronto: University of Toronto Press, 1994).

chronological reason but because it generated my first publications in the mid-1970s. I did a good deal of feminist writing at the same time, but it was not published beyond the bounds of resource packages for church use.

Structuralism. I think it has become futile to debate whether I am a structuralist or whether anyone is any more. If being one entails believing that all human meaning can be reduced to binary oppositions (life/death, present/absent, and so on) I no longer am a structuralist, though I still find binary analysis often indispensable. But arguments over such points tend to lose sight of the main philosophical issue. I agree with Peter Caws that structuralism—whether we use the word or not—stakes a major philosophical claim, nothing less than a new theory of why humans find the world intelligible. The short history of structuralism has not provided nearly enough time for this claim to be adequately tested.[3] So I remain involved in the debate. I have tried to reclaim the word "structuralism" while shedding some of the positivist baggage it has often carried. I see continuing value even in some of its much-maligned technical terminology.[4] But in this book I neither insist on the word nor make use of the terminology. Rather, I emphasize the two great things that structuralism has taught me, and which determine all my writing. The first is an insistence on the *system* of meaning in the text. The text gives expression to a set of relationships between different elements, relationships of both form and meaning. Various names have been given to this underlying and generating system. Daniel Patte, for example, calls it the text's value system (a term that stresses ethical and theological dimensions).[5] I often refer to the "logic" of the text. What is the text getting at, and how can we express this in a comprehensible patterned way? This is a question I am always trying to answer.

The second legacy of structuralism, closely related to the first, is that I seek clues to meaning primarily on a *large* textual scale. I give priority to the question of what 1 Samuel means *as a whole*. Mine is a deductive method. This puts me at odds with the prevailing trend in the narrative study of the Bible, which looks for meaning in the literary arrangement of shorter sections and builds up the meaning of the

---

[3] Peter Caws, *Structuralism: The Art of the Intelligible* (Atlantic Highlands, N.J.: Humanities Press International, 1988) 2–4.

[4] See David Jobling, "Structuralist Criticism," in Yee, *Judges and Method* 91–118; Bible and Culture Collective, *The Postmodern Bible* 91–118.

[5] E.g., *The Religious Dimension of Biblical Texts: Greimas's Structural Semiotics and Biblical Exegesis.* Semeia Studies (Atlanta: Scholars, 1990) 66.

whole inductively from these smaller-scale analyses. I do not regard this as simply a matter of taste. I think that my method is more appropriate to the sort of literature the Bible is.

I see the Bible performing a function close to that of myth as understood by Claude Lévi-Strauss—who, among the structuralists, has had the strongest influence on me. According to him, myth deals with a society's defining beliefs and with fundamental contradictions in its system of belief. The work of myth is to give a sense that these contradictions have been resolved—though they are in principle beyond resolution—and thus to make existence tolerable for the society.[6] I do not equate biblical narrative with myth, since that term is best kept for the products of societies where the sense of history is much less developed than in Israel. But when the past is viewed from a sufficient distance and for the purpose of explaining the present, as I believe is the case with the Bible, historiography functions very like myth. Lévi-Strauss insists that a society's mythic record can only be understood as a total system comprising many particular myths. In the case of the Bible the total system means the whole narrative, and eventually the whole canon.

Part II of this book (chs. 3–5) bears the closest resemblance to structuralism. Much of chapters 3 and 4 is based on two earlier, explicitly structuralist essays[7] in which I dealt in a Lévi-Straussian way with two contradictions in Israel's understanding of its past. In Chapter 3 the contradiction is between divine and human government—YHWH as king versus a human king. This contradiction gets expressed primarily in terms of judgeship and kingship as opposed systems of government, and it is the work of 1 Samuel to accomplish the transition from one system to the other in a satisfying way. The contradiction in Chapter 4, less fundamental but still severe, is between the inherently dynastic nature of monarchy and the memory that Israel's monarchy is not traced from its first king. How could kingship legitimately pass from the house of Saul to the house of David?

In these chapters another consequence of my assumptions becomes particularly clear. Myths are characterized by an iron necessity at the level of *plot*. The stories *must* achieve certain narrative resolutions since the society's very existence depends on their doing so. The consequence is that character becomes subordinated to plot, so that mod-

---

[6] *Structural Anthropology,* translated by Claire Jacobson and Brooke G. Schoepf (New York: Basic Books, 1963) 206–231.

[7] *The Sense of Biblical Narrative: Structural Analyses in the Hebrew Bible II.* JSOT.S 39 (Sheffield: JSOT Press, 1986) 44–87; *The Sense of Biblical Narrative: Structural Analyses in the Hebrew Bible I.* JSOT.S 7 (2nd ed. Sheffield: JSOT Press, 1986) 12–30.

ern literary notions about the coherence and development of character cannot be expected to apply in any straightforward way.[8] Specifically I argue that Samuel and Jonathan are rendered incredible as characters by the urgency of the plot function they must perform [69–70, 98–99].

In these chapters, 3 and 4, as I investigate what is going on in the larger narrative context I undermine the status of 1 Samuel as a "book." The text I read in Chapter 3 is Judges 2–1 Samuel 12, and in Chapter 4 it is 1 Samuel 13–2 Samuel 7. 1 Samuel gets parceled out into these other literary units. Pondering this fact that I was writing a book on 1 Samuel but not treating it as a unit made clear to me the need for an introductory discussion of the different ways in which the biblical narrative can be divided up, and the impact of these divisions on our reading. This is what I offer in Chapter 2. It then occurred to me that some other work I had drafted, which I present here as Chapter 5, was essentially a structural analysis of 1 Samuel *as a unit*. This chapter proposes an understanding of 1 Samuel based on a single structural feature (and contains the only diagram in my book!). 1 Samuel, I suggest, generates quite unexpectedly, but with startling precision, a "third way" of government, an alternative to both judgeship and kingship. Lévi-Strauss would call this a "mediation" of the contradiction. I take it to be the product, probably at an unconscious level, of Israel's sense that neither judgeship nor kingship fully satisfies its need for an acceptable theology of government.

Feminism. The feminist part of my development comes to clearest expression in Part III (chs. 6–8), which is devoted to different kinds of feminist reading. All of my professional work has been in theological seminaries, and it began at the exact moment when a lot of denominations were beginning to ordain women and the number of women seminarians was increasing exponentially. The issue of feminism and the Bible was urgent, and I became deeply involved in it because it plainly entailed issues of justice, because the questions became increasingly pressing in the classroom and, I ought to add, because feminism opened up wide areas of research for a young scholar.

I was an enthusiastic proponent of feminist work on the Bible from the outset, and never drawn to any male resistance or backlash. I do not know all the reasons. It had a lot to do with the colleagues and comrades involved. Also, I have been a one-person Hebrew Bible department in my seminary, so that if *I* did not facilitate feminist discussion of the Bible it would not happen. All along the way I have had to deal with the issue of my status as a male scholar doing feminist reading. My work has met with a fair amount of rejection from some

---

[8] For extensive treatment of the issue of character in the Bible see *Semeia* 63.

women feminist scholars, but there have been more who have supported it. These battles go on. I do not see how a responsible biblical scholar can avoid participation in so crucial an area as feminist criticism. Through my readings, such as the ones here, I try to work out appropriate ways for a male to participate.

In the 1970s we worked mostly with a feminist hermeneutic of *recuperation.*[9] Though the negative could not be avoided, there was a great thirst in the seminary for the recovery of *positive* elements from the biblical tradition—positive images of women, positive metaphors for God drawn from female experience. These positive elements had to be rescued from a tradition of male interpretation that had obscured and ignored them. This meant that a sharp line of division was drawn between a relatively positive Bible and an almost wholly negative tradition of biblical interpretation. The culmination of this approach was Phyllis Trible's *God and the Rhetoric of Sexuality.*[10]

Nevertheless, the negative was bound to reassert itself. People began to ask whether negativity to women and the female was merely in the interpretation or whether it was not constitutive also of the Bible itself. During a feminist workshop in the late 1970s a Christian feminist who took a negative view of the Bible asked me why I *wanted* the Bible to portray women positively. I recall this now because the same unsettling question arose again in the writing of this book, and I shall take it up near the end of the book when I have completed my feminist readings [306–307]. By 1980 I was asking, in response to the most celebrated chapter of Trible's book,[11] how so very patriarchal a society as Israel could publish, as its major myth of origins (Genesis 2–3), something that Trible read as essentially a feminist tract.

The story of biblical feminism after 1980 is of course long and complex. For me the important line of development has been feminism's coming critically to terms with other currents in a more broadly defined ideological criticism, and I shall resume this story in a moment.

I begin the specifically feminist part of the book with a reading of the character Hannah in 1 Samuel 1–2 (Chapter 6). My approach here reaches back to the biblical feminism I first knew in the 1970s, the hermeneutic of recuperation. I reclaim Hannah from a tradition of interpretation that has failed to take her measure. She has been seen as a victim, a typical biblical barren woman who must wait for a divine

---

[9] See Bible and Culture Collective, *The Postmodern Bible* 245–247.

[10] *God and the Rhetoric of Sexuality.* Overtures to Biblical Theology (Philadelphia: Fortress, 1978).

[11] *God and the Rhetoric of Sexuality* 72–143.

miracle to give meaning to her life. I see her as a bold initiative-taker who makes good things happen that without her would not happen, and who knows what she is doing.

If this approach seems now a little old-fashioned, that is itself a sign of the varied ways in which feminist biblical scholarship has developed since the 1970s. Such simple raising of the profile of biblical women has not lost its importance, but it has been augmented with other feminist strategies. In Chapter 7 I respond to the imperative within feminism for an interdisciplinary approach.[12] I also follow a critical and suspicious current in feminism as I look at the role women play in the career of David. His wives Michal and Abigail, like Hannah, take bold initiatives, but *their* initiatives are appropriated into a narrative strategy that is anything but pro-woman. Their energy is wholly channeled into the boosting of David's career, and no importance is ascribed to them beyond this. In this chapter I also follow the recent trend to see feminism in the context of a more comprehensive system of gender construction. Under the rubric of gender I take up David's relationship not only to his women but also to Jonathan, concluding that Jonathan is made to serve David's ends in just the way that women do, only more so.

It would be too optimistic to claim that attention to feminist issues has by now become routine in biblical studies, but it ought to be, and progress has been made in that direction. As one (certainly not the only) way of responding to and boosting this trend I offer in Chapter 8 a comprehensive survey of the women in 1 Samuel, making use of a variety of reading strategies. I offer no corresponding survey of the male characters because our current situation in interpretation does not permit such facile symmetries. The women characters have been neglected in the history of interpretation. My focusing specifically on them is a gesture of ongoing commitment and thanks.

The 1980s: Poststructuralism and Ideological Criticism

In this second stage the complexity of the methodological issues is much greater than in the first. Poststructuralism and ideological critique are related to structuralism and feminism, but they raise more

---

[12] Mieke Bal, *Murder and Difference: Gender, Genre and Scholarship on Sisera's Death*, translated by Matthew Gumpert (Bloomington, Ind.: Indiana University Press, 1988) 135–138.

troublesome questions of definition, and many people prefer alternative terminology.[13]

In the 1970s I experienced feminism and structuralism as being
scarcely related to each other at all. The latest outrages of Paris intellectuals against the world of humane letters seemed not of large significance for debates on the ordination of women or styles of feminist
preaching. But by the 1980s deep connections began to be seen. Poststructuralism and ideological criticism became increasingly engaged
with each other, often conflictually.

The theoretical issues could, indeed, become overwhelming. In the
mid-1980s I took a year's sabbatical leave, and one of my tasks was to
write an article for *Semeia* in which I would summarize all these issues.
I anticipated two or three months' work. In the event I was driven to
despair by what seemed the impossibility of giving any shape to the
article. (At one point I sent an SOS to a colleague across the Atlantic to
see if he could help me out of the morass). I did not get the article finished even in the eight months that I found myself devoting to it. This
is part of what I eventually wrote:

> In trying to write [this piece], I have encountered, to an extent quite be-
> yond my previous experience, a "writer's block," and have been per-
> suaded that the only way of overcoming it is to write it into the paper
> itself. I perceive two main causes (which . . . tend to compound each
> other). The first is a vertigo in the face of the endless theoretical propos-
> als. . . . The second is the threat of bad faith for anyone who tries to be
> a male feminist, a rich advocate of the poor, an American socialist—an
> existence increasingly oxymoronic. . . . The "block," I conclude, comes
> from my own implication in the scene which I am trying to interpret.
> The fragments of theory which prove so hard to integrate are fragments
> of myself and my professional identity. The effort to control the frag-
> ments, to process them into a "finished" essay, leads to an ever more
> desperate drifting "out of control."[14]

Producing that article, finding some sort of way through the conceptual and ethical thicket, was my baptism of fire. It was the precondi-
tion for writing this book, or anything else of value.

Poststructuralism. This term indicates a development out of but
beyond structuralism. Structuralism sees human products as formed

---

[13] See Bible and Culture Collective, *The Postmodern Bible* chs. 3 and 7.

[14] "Writing the Wrongs of the World: The Deconstruction of the Biblical Text in
the Context of Liberation Theologies," *Sem* 51 (1990) 82. Though this issue of *Semeia*
is dated 1990 my article was completed in early 1987.

by the complex interaction of semiotic systems, systems of signs. Poststructuralism, as I understand it here, agrees that human products express underlying systems of signs and can be so analyzed, but it insists that these systems cannot, as the early structuralists supposed, be reduced to a few systems (or even one), the analysis of which will provide complete understanding. Instead, entering into the world of signs both *unravels* and *explodes* our sense of the meaning of human products, indeed the meaning of "meaning" itself.

These two metaphors—the unraveling and the explosion of meaning—indicate a double impulse in poststructuralism, two crucially different angles from which to view it. The unraveling we call *deconstruction*. The emphasis here is that meaning systems cannot finally be logically grounded. They can always be traced back to the arbitrary preference for one term of a binary opposition over the other—absence over presence, clarity over obscurity, etc. But the system-makers are at great pains to cover their tracks, to give their systems the *appearance* of logical grounding. Jacques Derrida's typical procedure in his rereading of the western philosophical tradition is to expose both the arbitrariness and the track-covering. As it relates to the reading of a text deconstruction does its work by seeking the points of hesitation or contradiction, the points where the text's failure to close the circle of meaning is most apparent. No human product, literary or otherwise, is exempt from this kind of undermining of its claim to truth.

The explosion goes under different names, such as the "free play" of signs or "unlimited semiosis." This point of view has its most important precursor in the founder of American semiotics, C. S. Peirce, and is now represented by semioticians like Umberto Eco. They see binary systems as completely inadequate to account for the way people create and communicate meaning. Human sign systems exist in uncontrollable variety, and they are in fluid and fecund interaction with each other. The words in a text, for example, belong to many sign systems simultaneously, and they can be brought into new relations, productive of new meaning, with an unlimited number of other systems.

Another important term used in this connection is "intertextuality." The definition of "text" on which this word is based is very broad, capable of including almost any kind of human product. In this book I mostly use "intertextuality" in the sense of reading two literary texts together, using each as a lens for reading the other. There is no limit to the possible "intertexts" for a given text, and the results are unpredictable, just as when we introduce two people to each other we cannot fully predict what they will talk about. But the process is not arbitrary: we try to introduce people we think will find each other interesting and have valuable things to discuss.

Ideological criticism. By this term I refer to readings of the Bible that come out of political engagement on behalf of human liberation. I choose the term because it implies engagement at the level of theory, in alliance with practice. Some people, though, would deny that the term "ideological criticism" necessarily implies an option for the disempowered. What *they* understand by ideology is the conceptual structure that undergirds *any* political expression. They thus construe ideological criticism in a neutral way as the analysis of any political practice from any point of view. Such usage has recently been very much to the fore in the reading of the Bible, and of 1 Samuel particularly [291]. But systems of power have an interest in concealing, not revealing, how they work. Their ideological "analysis" will be ideological obfuscation. Authentic ideological analysis always positions itself on the side of the disempowered.

For me, as for many others, engagement with feminism was the point of entry into ideological criticism. Ideological criticism as I practice it, therefore, not only entails feminist criticism but continues somewhat to privilege it: it is in this mode that my feminist engagement continues.[15] But it became clear in the 1980s that gender, important as it was, needed to be joined to other political questions and critical categories, particularly race and class, and that these categories needed to be kept in a dynamic interaction rather than in separate compartments. Attention to issues of race is something I have learned more slowly since my seminary work has not pressed them on me to the extent it has the issues of gender. As to class, it is difficult to enter into serious conversation about it in a North America that imagines itself classless (though it is easier in Canada than in the United States). My insight here has been deepened by revisiting my own upbringing in an English working-class family striving desperately for upward mobility (the Margaret Thatcher pathology).

Several emphases of ideological critics are important for understanding this book. First, they deny the possibility of a neutral political stance and call us to declare and critically analyze our own locations.[16] Second, they draw lines of connection between the object of study—in this case the text of 1 Samuel—and the political location of those doing

---

[15] In one of the most influential recent books on method in biblical studies feminist criticism in particular stands for ideological criticism in general. See Danna Nolan Fewell, "Reading the Bible Ideologically: Feminist Criticism" (McKenzie and Haynes, *To Each Its Own Meaning* 237–251).

[16] For an extensive treatment of the issues see Richard J. Bernstein, *The New Constellation: The Ethical-Political Horizons of Modernity/Postmodernity* (Cambridge, Mass.: M.I.T. Press, 1992).

the studying, making us look for ways in which our political location may predispose us to a certain view of issues arising in the Bible or in ancient history. Third, they emphasize the need for interdisciplinary research, forcing us to ask whether our insistence on disciplinary boundaries is not merely a protection of the centers of power that we have set up for ourselves.[17]

A fact of crucial importance for understanding recent developments in biblical studies is that people reading the Bible out of engagement in *different* liberation struggles differ not only on particular points of interpretation but on the fundamental question of whether the Bible is, from their point of view, "part of the problem" or part of the solution. There are some broad tendencies. Black theology and Third World liberation readings tend to see the Bible as a charter for liberation: when it is read aright it reveals a god who sides with the poor. Gay and lesbian readings, and to an increasing extent feminist readings, on the other hand, tend to see the Bible primarily as complicit in the structures of oppression. However, as the debate develops there emerge many exceptions and middle positions, so that such generalizations are of diminishing value. These tensions are felt particularly in the seminary. The contradiction is never absent from my classroom between enabling students to gain power *over* a Bible that has been used to oppress (and often abuse) them and to find power *in* the Bible for their ministerial work.

Poststructural ideological criticism in this book. Poststructuralism and ideological criticism have developed very much in awareness of each other, and their relationship is among the most sharply debated issues of recent times. Some politically engaged readers reject poststructuralism wholesale, claiming that its refusal of any kind of grounded meaning must lead to political indifferentism or nihilism, but others see poststructuralism as collaborating in political struggle by breaking down the theories on which power structures are based. I take the latter view, and bring the two currents into close relation with each other.[18]

Deconstruction, the identification of points where the text's system of meaning fails to achieve the coherence it seems to aim at, is a technique I

---

[17] In addition to Bal (n. 12 above) see Terry Eagleton, *Literary Theory: An Introduction* (Oxford: Basil Blackwell, 1983) 194–217.

[18] See "Writing the Wrongs of the World." Marxism was already an important ingredient in the development of structuralism; see Claude Lévi-Strauss, *Tristes Tropiques*, translated by John and Doreen Weightman (New York: Atheneum, 1975) 57–58; Fernando Belo, *A Materialist Reading of the Gospel of Mark*, translated by Matthew J. O'Connell (Maryknoll, N.Y.: Orbis, 1981).

use in various ways throughout the book. It operates already in Part II, for example in my analysis of the failure to achieve a consistent portrayal of Samuel. More specifically I identify 1 Sam 8:1-3 as what deconstructive critics call an "aporia," a moment when the strain in the text becomes unavoidably apparent [62–64]; I show that the text's attempt to use these verses to forge a narrative link between judgeship and kingship is desperate and finally futile. This discovery then points the way to an understanding of the text's fundamental contradiction.

It is in Part IV (chs. 9–10), however, that poststructuralism and ideological criticism, and their interconnectedness, come into focus. We (I and Catherine Rose, with whom I collaborated on Part IV) use the category of race as a way of reading the Philistines in 1 Samuel, but we do not see the discourse of race as functioning independently. Rather, we find it to be in complex interaction with the discourses of class and gender, so that eventually the categories cease to be separable. We present 1 Sam 18:17-29 as a particularly dizzying combination of race, class, and gender issues [227–232].

My becoming aware of the interdependence of the ideological categories in 1 Samuel had a decisive impact on the shape of my book. I very much wanted to keep the tripartite structure based on class, gender, and race, but I was not sure that the term "class" was appropriate for what I cover in Part II, the transition from judgeship to monarchy. From our contemporary perspective it is natural and necessary to see such a transition in class terms. The movement of a society from less to greater political centralization always redraws the class map and creates new classes. But the biblical account of the transition, with the exception of a few passages (of which 1 Sam 8:11-18 is the clearest), effaces these class dynamics. What the reading of the Philistines (Part IV) made clear to me was that issues of class, though overtly absent for the most part, are in fact being covertly processed through the discourse of race. Israel's relationship with the Philistines turns out to be more a class than a race issue. This discovery enabled me to go back and recognize how class issues were also being dealt with in the guise of gender issues (Part III). I concluded that ideological analysis did provide the tripartite structure of the book with a solid foundation, but only when applied in this complex way.

Chapter 9 shows ideological criticism and intertextuality in collaboration. We heed the imperative to keep ancient and modern ideologies in critical relationship by approaching the issue of the Philistines from a non-biblical perspective. We start with the question: Why, for the last several centuries, have some Europeans chosen to call others "Philistines"? Why, with the whole range of biblical terminology to choose from, has *this* term seemed to fill the bill? Only when we have answered this question do we turn to the biblical Philistines, and we allow the answers we have found to shape the way we read the Bible. Intertextually, the "text" of the modern European discourses (particularly, but not only, Matthew Arnold's *Culture and Anarchy*) becomes the lens through which we read the biblical text. We conclude that the treatment of Philistines, both ancient and modern, has to do with an *anxiety about otherness*—the despising and marginalizing of the Other combined with the impossibility of establishing one's difference from the Other.

The 1990s: New Historicism and Psychoanalysis

This most recent stage of my story is the most difficult on which to gain perspective, since these are issues with which I and others are most immediately struggling; hence my discussion here will be a bit more extensive.

New historicism. Throughout my career a debate has been going on over the status in biblical studies of historical questions. Who wrote it, when, where, for whom? What, in that context, did the author mean by it? Up to the 1970s most academic biblical scholars either considered their work done when they had answered these questions or—in the case of scholars working in religious settings—felt that they could move directly from these historical judgments to questions of the relevance of the Bible for the present. While this is still essentially the position of many scholars there has recently been major change in the field. Some scholars, while retaining a primarily historical approach, have refined their methods far beyond the asking of such simple questions. Others, a greater number, have downplayed the importance of historical questions in favor of other kinds of questions they want to put to the text.

My career as I have so far described it has been caught up in the reaction against the dominance of historical approaches. Structuralism and poststructuralism specifically affirm the importance of "synchronic" (or system) questions, as against "diachronic" (or process) ones. However, I have recently been coming to see that these issues, and my own history, cannot be understood in such simple binary terms. Part of the reason why I first embraced structuralism was to free myself from the historical criticism that had dominated my training as a student, but now my other commitments will no longer permit me to maintain an extreme ahistorical position. Feminism and ideological criticism demand attention to historical questions as much as—in a sense more than—traditional historical criticism does. I am having to rethink the question of history.

For politically engaged readers the necessity of historical questions stems above all from our own embeddedness in history. The Bible is a political reality in the present, and so are the methods we use to read it. It is because we are aware of *our* embeddedness in present history that we interrogate the Bible about *its* embeddedness in past history. A single historicity binds past and present, for example in the varied uses of the name "Philistine." Only by a thorough immersion in the problems of the relationship between *our* present history and *our* Bible (that is, the variegated presence of the Bible in our culture) can we approach responsibly the problem of the relation between *past* history and the *past* existence of the biblical text. One of the reasons why feminists and ideological critics have been suspicious about synchronic methods is that an unconcern with past history can easily go along with a neglect of political issues in the present.[19]

My attention to history in this book begins with my very decision to introduce issues of method in this autobiographical way, which enables me to show how the methods I use are embedded in the recent history of biblical scholarship. Throughout the book I continue to pay attention to the historicity of all our reading of the Bible.

My approach to *ancient* history is a double one, in line with the double historicity of 1 Samuel. On the one hand it emerged as a book at some particular point in time. On the other hand it purports to tell the history of a yet earlier time. We know very little in detail of either of these times, but we know a good deal in general terms or, I would rather say, in systemic terms. We have considerable understanding of the "mode of production" in Israel at different times in its history, and this understanding is vital for the reading of the biblical text.

In Chapter 7 I shall discuss the concept of mode of production in some detail [144–146]. Suffice it to say here that it refers to the system that governs all the activities of a society—the production and distribution of goods, the promulgation of laws and beliefs, the practices of religion, and so on—and the ways in which these activities are interrelated. To begin with the later history, the history of 1 Samuel as a book, I see the narrative to which it belongs (the Deuteronomic History: see below) as the result of a very long process of development. We cannot

---

[19] *The Postmodern Bible* stopped short of doing an adequate job on this issue. We have no chapter on "new historicism" or the like, though our Chapter 7 on "Ideological Criticism" is quite closely related.

say with any precision when the present form (or rather forms) of the narrative crystallized, but we can be certain that it was during the time of Israel's subjection to one of the great empires of postexilic times, whether Persian or Greek. This sort of imperial system we refer to as a *foreign tributary* mode of production. The material producers (mostly the peasants) are subject to "a two-tier form of the tributary mode of production," needing both to service the native Israelite elite and to deliver tribute to the imperial overlord.[20]

Turning to the more ancient history that 1 Samuel purports to recount, we have to be even more agnostic about details. So far as the interactions between characters are concerned I read entirely for what the text may tell me about the point of view of its postexilic creators, and not at all in the hope of finding out anything about the eleventh century B.C.E. But at the level of mode of production it is quite another story. The primary theme of 1 Samuel is Israel's transition to monarchy. Such a transition certainly occurred at some time in history and constituted a critical shift in Israel's mode of production (from a relatively egalitarian *familial* or *household* mode to a *native tributary* mode in which the peasants were subject to taxation by their Israelite rulers). So while we cannot know to what extent, if any, 1 Samuel puts us in touch with real characters and detailed events we do know that it constitutes postexilic Israel's most important recorded response to a major systemic transition in its ancient past.

This new sort of historical work, the kind that concentrates on a thick description of social systems rather than on a sequential narrative record of history, provides input that is directly usable in ideological criticism. It will have an important part to play in my reading of the text.[21]

---

[20] Norman K. Gottwald, *The Hebrew Bible in Its Social World and in Ours.* Semeia Studies (Atlanta: Scholars, 1993) 369.

[21] A recent interchange between William Dever and Keith Whitelam helps focus these very complicated issues (Dever, "The Identity of Early Israel: A Rejoinder to Keith W. Whitelam," *JSOT* 72 [1996] 3–24; Whitelam, "Prophetic Conflict in Israelite History," *JSOT* 72 [1996] 25–44). Dever calls into question the work of some recent "minimalist" biblical historians, including Whitelam, who claim—as he understands them—that there is almost nothing we can know about the early history of Israel. Dever retorts that recent developments in archaeology have, on the contrary, enabled us to write a reliable history of Palestine in the twelfth and eleventh centuries. I believe the quarrel is a false one. (The signs of a rapprochement are actually quite clear in both essays; see pp. 19, 41.) Dever is working more as an archaeologist, Whitelam more as an ideological critic, and these roles tend to produce mutual suspicion. What Whitelam is rejecting is not the possibility of writing

I take up historical concerns in my feminist section as I look at a variety of feminist approaches to the issue of Israel's transition to kingship and its impact on women [146–150]. Even scholars whose interests are mainly literary prove unwilling to ignore the historical questions, and their findings are strikingly convergent with those of scholars whose orientation is mainly historical. The battles between historical and literary critics that have loomed so large for a generation appear to have little relevance to these feminist readers. The sort of historiography that I review in this chapter, especially in the work of Carol Meyers, is of the systemic kind, squarely based on archaeology and comparative anthropology.

My book ends with two sorts of comprehensive account of 1 Samuel, and it is in the first of these (Chapter 11) that I sum up what I have to say about historical issues. I develop the idea of 1 Samuel and the surrounding narrative as *national autobiography,* forged out of long wrestling with the memory of the past and subject to constant revision up to a late date. The implicit decision to hold on to the past, to continue to interrogate it, is a significant one, since we know that other roads were available and were taken—for example by Ezekiel, Qoheleth, and the "P" parts of the Pentateuch—in the same postexilic context [256].

In order to give a name to the distinctive postexilic voice that speaks in 1 Samuel I have retained the term "Deuteronomic," and continue to speak of "the Deuteronomic History." The latter term refers to the sequence of books Joshua, Judges, Samuel, and Kings in the Jewish Bible (with, in most accounts, Deuteronomy included as a prologue). "Deuteronomic" refers to the ideological point of view from which this history (as well as some other literature, especially the book of Jeremiah) was created. I retain this language against the advice of friends with whom I usually find myself in agreement, who believe that we ought to treat the whole narrative from Genesis to Kings as a single entity and feel that to name a part of that narrative "Deuteronomic" is to fall back into an outmoded and unacceptable kind of historical criticism. I can only reply that I *do* find the Deuteronomic literature dis-

---

a history along Dever's lines but rather certain outmoded assumptions in the writing of history. The history of Palestine has been written as "the history of Israel" to the neglect of other peoples who lived there. Also, history-writing in this tradition has hoped to use the Bible much too directly as a source and has tended strongly to want to maximize the historical truth of the biblical record. Whitelam is right to criticize this tradition, but I believe that Dever would do so too. Both are interested in the new systemic kind of history, though from different perspectives.

tinctive within the Bible. (My conclusions in this book would not, for example, carry over to Genesis–Numbers.) But I do not necessarily buy into any particular developed form of the Deuteronomic hypothesis (for example that there was a preexilic edition of the History). I use the terminology only in the general way defined in this paragraph.

The Deuteronomists' view of history is tragic, and their decision to continue to grapple with history is a brave one. The past is lost, and because it is lost adequate models for the present cannot be developed out of it. This tragic sense of a lost past centers in 1 Samuel since what is most deeply sensed as lost is some ideal state of affairs that preceded the monarchy. But the loss is so profound that it entails the partial loss of national memory. The ideal state of affairs cannot even be conceived, only sensed as lost. Chapter 11 consists of various ways of trying to grasp the tragedy, mostly through the lenses of some very diverse intertexts—an Anglo-African novel of the 1890s and an American one of the 1970s, and two theoretical texts from the 1990s—that also bring back into view, but from new angles, issues of class, gender, and race.

It is by reference to this historical situation that some problematic features of 1 Samuel are, I believe, best to be explained. The book is noted for a profusion of narrative problems: doublets, *non sequiturs*, inconsistent presentation of characters, and so on. In addition, its Masoretic Hebrew and Septuagint Greek forms differ much more than in most biblical books. Traditional historical critics have seen these features as symptoms of an unusually complex literary prehistory. They have often responded by concentrating on this prehistory at the expense of the book's final forms, seeing 1 Samuel as a collection of diverse materials put together by an unusually clumsy hand. I reject this approach, but I agree with the historical critics that the symptoms exist and need to be explained.

I experience 1 Samuel as a book that does not have its subject matter under control, that struggles with everything it has to say. I put this down to the relationship in which this text stands to the past out of which it emerges, and for which it must account. 1 Samuel struggles with contradictions in the tradition it receives *because these are still contradictions within the mindset that receives them.* The community creating and living by this text was not of a single mind about what the past had bequeathed them.

1 Samuel is literarily unstable and fragmented, then, because the sense of past out of which it was created was unstable and fragmented. The versions we receive are possible tellings of the story. Disagreements within a version or between versions are to be read as points of hesitation over the meaning of the past. These hesitations

are there for us to read precisely as hesitations. No single version of Saul's rise to kingship satisfies, so conflicting stories demand to be told. When the Hebrew and the Greek do not agree on an important question (for example, who was the aggressor in the war in 1 Sam 4:1 [219, 223]), our task is not to decide which version is right (it is hard to give any sensible meaning to such a task), but to ask what the hesitation might signify.

The uncertainty climaxes, as I have said, in the ways that the transition from judgeship to kingship is remembered/forgotten. 1 Samuel is more unstable and fragmented than the books around it because it is the book that deals with this transition head on. Judgeship and kingship meet in 1 Samuel like two continental plates that as they distort each other leave a narrative landscape marked by every kind of thinly covered geological irregularity.

Psychoanalytic criticism. The metaphor from geology, highlighting the question of how we relate the text's surface to its depths, provides a suitable transition to my last methodological area. I recall the seminal effect on me of a famous passage from the autobiography of Lévi-Strauss, whom I have acknowledged as the greatest influence on the structuralist side of my development. He links geology and psychoanalysis with Marxism: "All three demonstrate that understanding consists in reducing one type of reality to another; that the true reality is never the most obvious; and that the nature of truth is already indicated by the care it takes to remain elusive."[22] The more you resonate with this quotation, the more you will enjoy this book!

In the field of literary criticism there has recently been a major renewal of interest in psychoanalysis. Psychoanalysts, beginning with Freud, have always been interested in literature but they have tended to use it to exemplify some existing analytic system. Such one-way traffic between psychoanalysis and literature, where literature raises all the questions and psychoanalysis has all the answers, does not come close to realizing the full potential of psychoanalytic method and is fortunately becoming less fashionable. Newer models try to be open to *all* the unconscious processes at work—at the level of narration and character, between text and interpreter, between interpreters.[23] Two quotations from Mieke Bal suggest the scope and tone of these endeavors. "The different positions of analyst and patient are unevenly

---

[22] Lévi-Strauss, *Tristes Tropiques* 57–58.

[23] Shoshana Felman, *Writing and Madness [Literature/Philosophy/Psychoanalysis]* (Ithaca, N.Y.: Cornell University Press, 1985); Mieke Bal, "Psychopoetics," *Poetics* 13 (1984) 241–260.

distributed among text and reader or critic."[24] In other words, the work of analysis passes both ways; the reader is also being analyzed. Even more radically (this time in relation to visual, rather than literary, art), "Whether the motivation originates in the painter's irretrievable psyche or in the viewer's unacknowledged response is utterly beside the point."[25] The *source* of psychological insight in the process of interpretation, Bal is saying, may not be determinable. Unconscious processes do not follow customary ideas of cause and effect.

The Bible has had its share of old-style psychoanalytic readings, and there is still a place for them.[26] But such readings, useful as they may be, leave unexploited major parts of the potential of the methods. Let me illustrate this with a brief discussion of a work that deals with 1 Samuel, John Sanford's Jungian reading of Saul.[27] Sanford believes that Saul, by the time of his death, achieves "individuation," his individual Self finally breaking the bounds of egocentrism. This is the positive outcome of Saul's tragedy, and it exemplifies the psychological value of literary tragedy. I like the level at which Sanford's book is written—accessible to a wide audience and closely in touch with the therapeutic dimension of analysis. The problems I raise are two. First, psychoanalytic reading need not be, nor is it best, directed at the literary *character*. We are not dealing with real life, where the analysand is a human individual. Sanford deals with Saul as if he were a real person. But psychoanalytic theory undermines the unity, taken for granted in most forms of criticism, of the literary "character."[28] For example, a psychoanalytic reading may relate the interplay between the characters in a text to psychic processes of the narrator, the author, or perhaps, in the case of the Bible, the community that lives by the text.

My other problem with Sanford has to do with a specific decision he makes about how to read Saul's story. Noting the Bible's tendency to give multiple accounts of each step in Saul's career—the king-making, the rejection, etc.—Sanford says, without further explanation, that he has simply chosen the alternative that seems best for his purpose.[29]

---

[24] "Psychopoetics" 244.

[25] *Reading "Rembrandt": Beyond the Word-Image Opposition*. The Northrop Frye Lectures in Literary Theory (Cambridge: Cambridge University Press, 1991) 359.

[26] I particularly commend David Halperin's recent Freudian treatment of Ezekiel: *Seeking Ezekiel: Text and Psychology* (University Park, Pa.: Pennsylvania State University Press, 1993). See my review in *Religion* 25:392–394.

[27] *King Saul, the Tragic Hero: A Study in Individuation* (New York and Mahwah, N.J.: Paulist, 1985).

[28] Cf. my earlier discussion of character in relation to myth [6–7].

[29] *King Saul* 4.

This results in his ignoring, for example, the asses story in 1 Samuel 9–10 and the account of Saul and the Amalekites in ch. 15. This decision seems to me to squander one of the main strengths of psychoanalytic method, namely its stress on the significance of the small detail. In individual psychotherapy (which always offers a tempting analogy) the analyst is particularly interested in the patient's different tellings of "the same" story! Of what, the psychoanalytic critic will ask, is this tendency of 1 Samuel to say everything twice a symptom?

I anticipate that psychoanalytic criticism is one of the main areas where big changes will occur in biblical studies in the coming generation and major advances will be made.[30]

Let me give some examples of how I attend in this book to processes I take to be unconscious. At the level of verbal detail (the "Freudian slip") I shall ask why 2 Sam 21:8 refers to Saul's daughter Michal when it obviously "means" his other daughter Merab [184]. At the story level my reading of Hannah will pivot on a piece of vital information—that the sons of Eli are corrupt priests—at first withheld from the reader but then belatedly provided (2:12-17) [135–136]. Coming upon this information constrains the reader to go back and read Hannah's story in a quite different way. I surmise that the narrator's procedure expresses hesitation between revealing and concealing how radical is the initiative "he" ascribes to the character Hannah. Again the analogy with the couch is tempting—the patient "forgets" something vital, and later "remembers" it at an inappropriate moment.

The phenomenon I explore in Chapter 5 happens at a still deeper level. The Deuteronomic text seems by some automatic process to discover a "third way" of government mediating between the extremes of judgeship and kingship, and at some later time the creation of the canonical book 1 Samuel isolates this third way and makes it much more visible. No theory yet exists for understanding such a process. It arises out of Israel's communal psyche as it comes to terms with the past. I observe it, and discuss it as best I can.

---

[30] More broad-ranging psychoanalytic readings of the Bible have begun to appear. Bal, in reading the Samson story, works at the level of the individual character, but her treatment is very different from Sanford's mimetic approach. The construction of so unlikely a character as Samson expresses—as it tries to alleviate—male anxiety. See Mieke Bal, *Lethal Love: Feminist Literary Readings of Biblical Love Stories* (Bloomington, Ind.: Indiana University Press, 1987) 37–67. Ilona Rashkow's intertextual reading of Genesis and Freud is another important contribution: *The Phallacy of Genesis: A Feminist Psychoanalytic Approach* (Louisville, Ky.: Westminster/John Knox, 1993).

It is at the end of the book that I make my most far-reaching psychoanalytic suggestions, in my second comprehensive view of 1 Samuel (Chapter 12). Here I introduce the crucial concept of "transference." I use this term in the same way that Jane Gallop does: to trace the ways in which the dynamics *in* the text are reproduced in the interpretation *of* the text.[31] In addition to Gallop's own work on Jacques Lacan, a classic demonstration of this method is Shoshana Felman's reading of Henry James's *The Turn of the Screw,* where she shows that the interpretive options critics have adopted in reading James's story parallel the belief options available to the characters in the story.[32]

In this sense a profound transferential relationship exists between the Bible and the story of psychoanalysis itself. Freud's discovery of psychoanalysis is a story of one who framed his conflict with his father in biblical terms, who identified himself with Joseph the interpreter of dreams, and so on. Thus we should not anticipate that psychoanalysis will emerge unchanged from being employed in the interpretation of the Bible. In analyzing the Bible it is inevitably analyzing its own foundations.[33]

My introduction of transference spells the end of any remaining pretense that I might keep the discussion of psychoanalytic method at arm's length from the question of myself as reader. As Gallop shows in her work on Lacan, the transferential reading has to be a reading of the self. If my work as a biblical scholar is governed by motives of which I am myself partly or wholly unconscious I need to know this. My recent discovery of Michel Serres, a French theoretician with whom I share a background in mathematics, has made me confront, for example, my need for my biblical readings to be like mathematical demonstrations. There is nothing necessarily good or bad about this need, but it has to be brought to consciousness. Again, the experience on which I have based this chapter, of my book's organizing itself as a record of the stages of my career, forces me to confront the work of the unconscious.

The need for professional readers of the Bible to be self-analytic in our work is made the more urgent by the enormous impact the Bible has on our culture, its immense potential for good or ill.[34] If I remain unconscious

---

[31] *Reading Lacan* (Ithaca, N.Y.: Cornell University Press, 1985). I am not concerned with how closely this use of the term corresponds to its meaning in the classic Freudian system.

[32] *Writing and Madness* 141–247.

[33] See Bible and Culture Collective, *The Postmodern Bible* 187–195.

[34] "The Bible, of all books, is the most dangerous one, the one that has been endowed with the power to kill" (Mieke Bal, *On Story-Telling: Essays in Narratology,*

of my motivation I am the more likely to do foolish and even dangerous things with the Bible. As I have worked in theological seminaries I have become convinced that internalized biblical scenarios play a role in the way a person practices ministry and in the very decision to become a minister. Using transference, I have developed a pedagogical method for enabling students to reflect on the biblical passages to which they instinctively turn in certain situations as a way of coming to terms with their own motives and practices in ministry. Such work brings us to the boundary between biblical studies and therapy, the last, perhaps, of the many boundaries I would like to breach. Psychoanalysis is, after all, a practice of healing before it is a literary method.

In Chapter 12, therefore, I try to come to terms with my reasons for writing this book. I try to explain to myself what has in effect been a bondage to 1 Samuel. I have been working on this biblical book for two decades, and it has elicited from me far more published work than any other. But my work in Chapter 12 is not merely a self-analysis, which readers might find of limited interest. I present it also as a way of reading the text. If to read 1 Samuel is to read myself, then to read myself is to read 1 Samuel. Beginning from a verse of 1 Samuel with which I intensely identify, I attempt in transferential terms an extensive paralleling of the text with major currents in its interpretation. This leads to a suggestion for how we might read the whole of 1 Samuel.[35]

Doing the Right Thing

Beyond what I have offered here there will be very little separate methodological discussion in this book. I have tried to keep reflection on method and reading of the text as close to each other as possible. I try to raise methodological issues out of the text and to do things with

---

edited by David Jobling [Sonoma, Cal.: Polebridge Press, 1991] 14). Bal is referring among other things to the South African Apartheid regime.

[35] A precursor to this work is an essay of mine on Gerd Theissen's psychological reading of Paul ("Transference and Tact in Biblical Studies" in Timothy K. Beal and David M. Gunn, eds., *Reading Bibles, Writing Bodies*. Biblical Limits [London and New York: Routledge, 1997] 208–218); see Theissen, *Psychological Aspects of Pauline Theology*, translated by John P. Galvin (Philadelphia: Fortress, 1987). I try to show that Theissen's treatment of Paul's conversion represses a methodological "conversion" of Theissen's own about which he both wishes and does not wish to speak, and that this tells us much about what is happening in current biblical studies.

the text that focus the issues. Of course I shall not work all the time with one or another precisely defined method. Different methods work together. For example, my old-fashioned recuperative feminist reading of Hannah (ch. 6) depends crucially on an exegetical move that is deconstructive or psychoanalytical.

Methodology in biblical studies is in ferment. Distinctions are important to make sometimes, but they are hard to maintain, for there are links everywhere. To give a sense of this ferment I have deliberately stressed the interconnectedness of the methods more and more as the book progresses. When readers reach Part V they will experience a kaleidoscopic effect as now one approach comes into view, now another. This corresponds to my own experience as I have tried to describe it, of the explosion of meaning, the uncontrollability of method. Our situation as readers is just as fragmented and unstable as the text of 1 Samuel.[36]

Another reason for this strategy is to make clear my refusal of any methodological orthodoxy. I say this in response to scholars like Robert Alter and Frank Kermode who, in defining the proper scope of a "literary" approach to the Bible, consider the methods I use inappropriate at best (their actual list of suspects includes feminist, ideological, psychoanalytic, deconstructive, and Marxist criticism).[37] Such attempts to establish a new orthodoxy, a "right" way of reading the Bible as literature, give currency to a view of what is going on in biblical studies and in literary criticism generally that is a travesty. I shall not here repeat the critiques of this school—of its methods and its pretensions to authority—that others have effectively made.[38] Rather I will try to show its inadequacy in practice through my readings. I find the new orthodox narratology to be a "narrowtology" in response to which

---

[36] Many parts of this book are based on published essays in which I follow with some clarity and consistency a limited range of methods. Some readers may find interest in comparing those essays with what they have turned into here.

[37] *The Literary Guide to the Bible* (Cambridge, Mass.: Harvard University Press, 1987) 5–6. See also Meir Sternberg, *The Poetics of Biblical Narrative: Ideological Literature and the Drama of Reading* (Bloomington, Ind.: Indiana University Press, 1985), especially p. 50.

[38] Bal, *On Story-Telling* 59–72; Bal, "Literature and Its Insistent Other," *JAAR* 57 (1989) 373–383; Burke O. Long, "The 'New' Biblical Poetics of Alter and Sternberg," *JSOT* 51 (1991) 71–84; David M. Gunn, "Reading Right: Reliable and Omniscient Narrator, Omniscient God, and Foolproof Composition in the Hebrew Bible" in David J. A. Clines, Stephen E. Fowl, and Stanley E. Porter, eds., *The Bible in Three Dimensions: Essays in Celebration of Forty Years of Biblical Studies in the University of Sheffield* (Sheffield: Sheffield Academic Press, 1990) 53–64; David Rutledge, *Reading Marginally: Feminism, Deconstruction and the Bible*. Biblical Interpretation Series 21 (Leiden: E. J. Brill, 1996) 102–110.

I aim for an "uncircumscribed" reading. This joke on "uncircumcised" will become clear in Chapter 12, where I respond most directly to the new orthodoxy. I do so (in line with my principle of letting the theoretical issues emerge from reading the text) by tracing in 1 Samuel itself the contours of the issues that divide me from other "literary" readers.

The title of Spike Lee's movie "Do the Right Thing" asserts the urgency of the ethical imperative—its *greater* urgency—in a situation of ethical vacuum or chaos. Within the methodological ferment I have tried to write an ethically responsible book, a book that insists on the question of what we scholars are doing when we write about the Bible in North America at the end of the millennium. I have had to reimagine what kind of thing a biblical book is and what kind of act it is to write a book about one of these old books.

I am guided in my readings by Mieke Bal's criteria of "plausibility, adequacy, and relevance."[39] For plausibility I have the least concern, at least *a priori*. A reading may seem plausible at first to very few people, maybe only to the one who reads. But its plausibility may grow, especially if it fits the experience of an emergent reading community, a community that is becoming more socially and politically visible. I do not shun inconsistency: why should my text be less conflicted and rifted than the text I am reading? The interesting question is, *why* do I find myself wanting to say different and even contradictory things about the same text: what is it about the text that causes this?

Adequacy is a forbidding term. If we were to take it literally, a reading would be adequate only if it took into account every aspect of the text and of other readings of the text. But it is important to retain the term as a limiting point for our readings. We never achieve adequacy, but we go on trying to. Remaining vulnerable to the question of adequacy keeps us from the laziness of "anything goes." It obliges us to think constantly about the place of our readings within the range of readings, within the conflict of interpretations. In a sense the whole discussion of method boils down to forming the habit of thinking through what one is doing as part of doing it.

Relevance is for me the most immediate criterion. I write from my own location, and I make no effort to detach myself from it in the name of scholarly objectivity. Much of what I have written I have worked through with students and colleagues, and it would not be the way it is if it emerged from a different context. I work in a small Christian theological seminary in a rural area of Canada. It is extremely feminist

---

[39] *Lethal Love* 13.

(half the faculty and three quarters of the students are women), and politically very left. My people are keen to read the Bible and to do so closely and subtly. They lose interest if the discussion slips far away from their experiences and concerns, but they respond amazingly to any invitation to exercise their imagination and artistic skill in reading these texts. I have wanted to write a book worthy of them more than I have wanted to write one to satisfy my professional colleagues.

Still, these criteria can be reconciled to each other only approximately, and no set of criteria can fully comprehend what it means to do the right thing in my situation. The same questions endlessly recur. Are my readings so much the product of my setting that they lack effectiveness in other settings? Has my setting enabled me to identify significant aspects of the text and its interpretation that have been neglected? Are old allegiances to some sort of standards—academic, religious, or political—still blocking my access to things that really matter in the text?

Of such questions only you, my known or unknown reader, can finally judge. I have tried to keep my relationship to you always in mind. Sometimes I shall make heavy demands on you, particularly in Chapters 3 and 4 where I establish a foundation for the rest of the book. These chapters are long and their argumentation intricate, and it is hard to wean myself from the old objectivist rhetoric of structuralism. I hope that there and throughout the book I have given adequate guideposts.

I offer my readings passionately because I feel them passionately, but at the same time I want them also to stimulate your readings, which will be different. I often leave my readings unfinished, or barely sketch possible alternatives to them, so that there will be work for you to do. Can these two aims be brought together? How can I passionately feel the rightness of my readings and yet leave you the same freedom that I claim for myself? It is a paradox. It is the paradox of all teaching. Regardless of the extent to which your readings may agree with mine, I trust that they will engage with mine rather than circumvent them. And I hope you will be persuaded (if you are not already) that we should not read so influential and so dangerous a book as the Bible except in full acknowledgment of the unfamiliar and urgent ethical imperatives laid upon us by the various New World Orders that compete for our allegiance.

In the last analysis I have, like any other writer, no choice. Having done the best I can, I deliver over to you the First Book of Samuel, along with the immense history of its interpretation including mine, for you to do the right thing with it where you are.

Chapter 2

WHAT, IF ANYTHING, IS 1 SAMUEL?

1 Samuel is a book of the Bible and so belongs to a class of literary objects that is familiar to us, that we take for granted; but central to my treatment throughout this book will be the recognition of how *artificial* a piece of literature 1 Samuel is. Any piece of literature is an artifice, but 1 Samuel is so in some special ways. In this chapter I shall look at the implications of the creation of this biblical book, and at an alternative framework in which its contents might be (and perhaps in ancient times were) read.

Books and Books: The Division of the Biblical Narrative

The Jewish Bible (the Masoretic Text, or MT) begins with a long, continuous narrative running from Genesis to Kings. At an early time this was broken into nine "books," but "1 Samuel" is not one of the nine, for in the MT "Samuel" is a single book including what we now call 1 and 2 Samuel. The division of Samuel into two first occurred, so far as we know, in the Greek Septuagint translation (LXX).[1] The LXX also inserted between Judges and 1 Samuel the book of Ruth (which the MT placed elsewhere). The Christian traditions have on these points followed the LXX.

1 Samuel is part of the literary sequence we know as the Deuteronomic History [18–19], but the canonical book divisions came much

---

[1] It should be noted that the LXX has no books called "Samuel"; what we call 1–2 Samuel and 1–2 Kings are there the four books of "Kingdoms."

later than the creation of the History itself, so that it is problematic to organize a study of the Deuteronomic History according to the canonical books as, for example, Robert Polzin does in his multi-volume work.[2] On the basis of intrinsic analysis of the History a set of divisions quite different from the canonical book divisions has been proposed. Martin Noth, who first put forward the hypothesis of the Deuteronomic History, suggested that certain passages in it function as theological summaries, reflecting from time to time on where the story stands, recalling what has happened, and anticipating what is to come.[3] Noth's suggestion was later refined by Dennis McCarthy.[4]

The summary passages that immediately concern us are Judg 2:11-23, 1 Samuel 12, and 2 Samuel 7. There is no reason why these summaries may not be taken to define an alternative set of "books" to the canonical ones, including a "book" that runs from Judg 2:11 through 1 Samuel 12 and another that extends from 1 Samuel 13 through 2 Samuel 7. I shall, in fact, base much of my work on these two hypothetical "books," and so they need names. Judges 2:11–1 Samuel 12 I shall call "The Extended Book of Judges,"[5] and 1 Samuel 13–2 Samuel 7 I shall call "The Book of the Everlasting Covenant."[6]

The Difference it Makes

How one divides the larger narrative makes a big difference to how one reads the material in 1 Samuel. I will argue this at length in the following chapters, but as a foretaste I take an example from Lyle Eslinger. In his reading of the first part of 1 Samuel he adopts a theory of

---

[2] *Moses and the Deuteronomist: A Literary Study of the Deuteronomic History. Part One: Deuteronomy, Joshua, Judges* (New York: Seabury, 1980); *Samuel and the Deuteronomist: A Literary Study of the Deuteronomic History. Part Two: 1 Samuel* (San Francisco: Harper & Row, 1989); *David and the Deuteronomist: A Literary Study of the Deuteronomic History. Part Three: 2 Samuel.* Indiana Studies in Biblical Literature (Bloomington, Ind.: Indiana University Press, 1993).

[3] *The Deuteronomistic History.* JSOT.S 15 (Sheffield: JSOT Press, 1981) 4–11 and passim.

[4] "II Samuel 7 and the Structure of the Deuteronomic History," *JBL* 84 (1965) 131–138.

[5] Consistently with his hypothesis Noth sees the Bible's coverage of the time of judges as extending into 1 Samuel. See *Deuteronomistic History* 47–53.

[6] With intentional play on the name of this series. The justification for these names will appear in chs. 3 and 4.

reading according to which the reader is entirely under the control of the narrator, who gives instructions in the narrative about how to read it. What makes this mode of reading interesting, and not merely mechanical, is that the instructions are not always easy to spot, so that the reader is required to participate in an active way. But the reader who follows the instructions will in due course discover that they are, in fact, complete and unambiguous.[7] I am not sympathetic to this theory of reading, but let us for present purposes play the game Eslinger's way. What the reader must know is *where* in the text the instructions are to be found. Eslinger is clear on this point. He reads "from the context of 1 Sam 1–12," a decision "no more or less arbitrary" than other possibilities.[8] So his reader is one who began to read at the beginning of 1 Samuel.

An example of the exegetical difference this makes is found in 1 Samuel 4. Who is to blame when Israel is defeated by the Philistines and forfeits the Ark of the Covenant? Eslinger is tremendously insistent that it is the fault of Hophni and Phinehas (and, more ambiguously, of Eli) and *not* any fault of the people as a whole. The dutiful reader will therefore speculate about whether the punishment fits the crime and worry theologically about a god who punishes the many for the sins of the few.[9]

I certainly agree that a reader who began to receive instructions at 1 Samuel 1 will be perplexed over this matter. He will later be completely baffled by the ceremony of national repentance in which Samuel leads the people in 1 Samuel 7. If the people have been guiltless in the war, of *what* are they repenting?[10] But the reader of the Extended Book of Judges, who began to read at Judg 2:11, was immediately provided (Judg 2:11-19) with a different and quite explicit set of instructions [43–45]. Such a reader will not be surprised at YHWH's wrath against *Israel* in 1 Samuel 4, for she will be familiar with this wrath as an essential part of the theological dynamic of Judges and will know of plenty of faults of the people—especially in Judges 17–21—that justify the wrath. Nor will she be surprised that it is the *Philistines* who are the agents of YHWH's wrath, since they have never been dealt with ac-

---

[7] This theory is very close to that of Meir Sternberg, *The Poetics of Biblical Narrative: Ideological Literature and the Drama of Reading* (Bloomington, Ind.: Indiana University Press, 1985).

[8] Lyle Eslinger, *Kingship of God in Crisis: A Close Reading of 1 Samuel 1–12*. Bible and Literature Series 10 (Sheffield: Almond, 1985) 136.

[9] *Kingship of God* 134–135.

[10] Eslinger's own embarrassment with this passage is obvious: *Kingship of God* 234–235.

cording to the rules laid down in Judg 2:11-19. As a judge, Samson ought to have defeated the Philistines. But the subjugation formula, which in other judge stories sums up the defeat of the enemy (see Judg 3:30, 4:23, etc.), was omitted from the Samson story. The reader may well be puzzled that these dynamics are taking so many chapters to play out, but she will surely let out a cry of recognition when she comes to 1 Samuel 7, which returns to the scenario envisaged in Judg 2:11-19 and includes the long-awaited subjugation formula: "So the Philistines were subdued" (7:13). Such a reader, in contrast to Es-linger's reader, will conclude that the defeat in 1 Samuel 4 was due in part to national sin, though the sin of the priests certainly complicates matters.

Here, then, are two readings of 1 Samuel 4 that are quite different, and the difference lies not in reading method (for I accepted Eslinger's rules for the sake of argument). The different readings are due simply to different ways of dividing the biblical narrative.

The Power of the "Book"

Polzin shares my assumption that the canonical books are later than the Deuteronomic History. "I recognize . . . that the division of the text into books is itself artificial and must have taken place much later than the composition of the History. Nevertheless, by whatever process this division took place . . . this process, by and large, has recognized and remained faithful to the structural plan of the History that I assume existed in the original composition."[11] Polzin recognizes the artificiality of the divisions but denies any implication of arbitrariness. He claims that the beginning of each book, including 1 Samuel, functions as a summary of the major issues of the book.

Joel Rosenberg takes a position apparently similar to Polzin's in his treatment of "1 and 2 Samuel" in *The Literary Guide to the Bible*. He claims that "the Masoretic parceling of books," whereby a long narrative work was divided into what we know as the "books" of the Bible, "gives Samuel a beginning and end *that most fully accord* with the shape of [the] larger argument."[12] One should note that Rosenberg is less insistent than Polzin, for elsewhere he hints that other divisions of

---

[11] *Samuel and the Deuteronomist* 230.

[12] "1 and 2 Samuel," *The Literary Guide to the Bible,* edited by Robert Alter and Frank Kermode (Cambridge, Mass.: Harvard University Press, 1987) 123; my emphasis.

the larger narrative would have been possible and perhaps as good: 1 Samuel 1–7 could be put with Judges, or 1 Kings 1–2 with Samuel.[13] But the similarity is misleading, for Polzin and Rosenberg are referring to *different* book divisions and to different canons of Scripture. Rosenberg sees the beginning of our "1 Samuel" as an appropriate beginning for the single Masoretic book of Samuel (our 1 and 2 Samuel together), while Polzin (at least in the passage quoted) definitely has *1* Samuel in mind.[14]

Rosenberg might conceivably be right that the canonizers chose the most apt points of division. Polzin might even be right that the creators of the Deuteronomic History included in their work summary anticipations of what was to come and spaced these at convenient "book" length from each other.[15] Perhaps an argument could be devised that would make them both right. But one has to be suspicious. The alternative possibility, which I affirm, is that the canonical books exercise a power over our reading, authorizing some ways of reading over others. The canonical books come to us as given. We are familiar with where they begin and end and so tend to devise arguments that they begin and end in the right places. It is this sheer givenness of the biblical books, I suggest, that makes us pass over without comment statements, like those of Polzin and Rosenberg, that require critical examination.

We write a lot of books whose topic, even whose title, is "1 Samuel." As we do so it is hard to avoid asserting at some level the *rightness* of beginning to read at 1 Samuel 1 and stopping at 1 Samuel 31. Many of these books are, like this one, constrained by being part of a series on the books of the Bible. There are, to be sure, works that take as their topic some literary object *not* coterminous with 1 Samuel,[16] and so disturb our tendency to let canonical tradition decide into what bits we divide the Bible for the purpose of study. But I surmise that authors who let the canon define the scope of their book get more contracts, and sell more copies, than those who do not. The canonical books tend to define academic courses in theological schools or elsewhere, and a course on 1 Samuel will tend to favor as its textbooks those that are on

---

[13] Ibid. 122, 138.

[14] Though elsewhere he will suggest that the Song of Hannah (1 Samuel 2) and the Song of David (2 Samuel 22) form a frame for the Masoretic "Samuel" [166–169].

[15] But contrast Peter D. Miscall, *1 Samuel: A Literary Reading* (Bloomington, Ind.: Indiana University Press, 1986) 11: "There is no overview like Joshua 1 or Judges 2 that tells us in advance what the book is to be 'about'."

[16] For example Eslinger, *Kingship of God* on 1 Samuel 1–12, or Fokkelman, *Crossing Fates* on 1 Samuel 13 to 2 Samuel 1.

1 Samuel. So an industry develops that privileges books that take a biblical book as their topic. The implications of the canon extend even into economics!

Canonical Issues

In this section I shall say more about the pressures of the canonical divisions on the way we read.

The beginning and end of 1 Samuel. As I shall argue in more detail, the canonical division exerts a tremendous pressure on scholars to read the beginning of 1 Samuel as a new beginning—to read it *forward* rather than *backward*.[17] The reading of the book has been dominated by the assumption that the beginning of 1 Samuel coincides with the beginning of a new phase of Israel's story—the rise of the monarchy—with a corresponding suppression of the question of its continuity with what went before. We are led to link Hannah, for example, more with the women who follow her than with those who precede her. I shall turn on its head Polzin's claim that the canonizers who set the division between Judges and Samuel revealed 1 Samuel 1 as a "natural" introduction to what follows. My view is that the canonizers wielded great power over subsequent reading precisely by *making* 1 Samuel 1 into an introduction. This decision has specific effects, which we shall consider.[18]

If the beginning of 1 Samuel has been overemphasized as a beginning, its ending has been underemphasized as an ending. This is presumably because of the influence of the Jewish canon, which makes no division at this point. I shall take the paradoxical position of subverting unexamined effects of meaning that are due to overemphasis on the beginning, while trying to create new effects of meaning by emphasizing the placement of the ending. But on both sides of the paradox I shall be looking for new meaning through the questioning of old assumptions and habits.

The book of Judges. A canonical book division affects the reading of the books on both sides of the boundary. The point of division, in the Jewish canon, between Judges and Samuel probably affects our reading of Judges even more than of Samuel. It contributes massively to a

---

[17] See Walter Brueggemann, "I Samuel 1: A Sense of a Beginning," *ZAW* 102 (1990) 33–48.

[18] Miscall, *1 Samuel* 8, problematizes "the space between Judg. 21:25 and 1 Sam. 1:1" in a most useful way.

negative assessment of the period of the judges. The last five chapters of Judges paint a picture of anarchy and attribute the anarchy to Israel's lack of a king. The effect of the Extended Book of Judges is quite different. It carries us beyond the time of anarchy to the triumphant vindication of judgeship in Samuel's deeds (1 Samuel 7) and words (1 Samuel 12).

The beginning of the canonical book of Judges likewise contributes to a negative assessment of judgeship. Judges 1:1–2:10, which deals with Israel's failure to eradicate the Canaanites and complete its occupation of the Promised Land, belongs more naturally to the book of Joshua, since it ends with a second report of Joshua's death (Judg 2:8-10, cf. Josh 24:29-31).[19] But the book of Joshua needs to give the impression of triumphant conquest, so the accounts of an *incomplete* conquest are excluded from it and attached to Judges. In contrast to the Extended Book of Judges, then, the canonical book of Judges gets dumped on from both ends. At the beginning the dark side of the conquest traditions is added to it, while at the end the vindication of judgeship in Samuel is taken away from it.

This so tendentiously conceived book has recently come into its own. Current biblical scholarship is marked by an immense desire for the book of Judges! One prominent witness to this is the recent book *Judges and Method*,[20] which is intended as a primer for students on the newer interpretive methods in biblical studies. Out of all the books of the Jewish Bible Judges was selected for this purpose. Such a choice would have been inconceivable even ten years ago. Whatever the reason for this popularity [169–170], I wonder whether, had the past bequeathed to us the Extended Book of Judges instead, it would have satisfied our desire in the same way.

The book of Ruth. There is another canonical issue to which I shall frequently revert, and which requires brief comment here. This is the presence of Ruth between Judges and 1 Samuel in the LXX and Christian canons. Almost all scholarly treatments ignore Ruth and read 1 Samuel as taking up the story from the end of Judges. Due no doubt to my own classical training in biblical criticism, I was very slow to recognize the canonical importance of Ruth. There are several reasons for ignoring it. First, it appears in the Jewish canon at quite another place, so that in the MT Judges and Samuel are adjacent. Second, many schol-

---

[19] Not only should Joshua die in his own book but much of the material in Judges 1 is actually repeated from Joshua: see Josh 15:63, 16:10, etc.

[20] Gale A. Yee, ed., *Judges and Method: New Approaches in Biblical Studies* (Minneapolis: Fortress, 1995).

ars explicitly or tacitly base their work on the Deuteronomic History, which does not include Ruth. Third, perhaps the very words that link Ruth to the time of the judges—"In the days when the judges ruled" (Ruth 1:1)—also suggest that it is parenthetical to the main narrative sequence, for they evoke the time of the judges as very long ago.[21]

Despite all this, we cannot ignore Ruth. It is as canon that the Bible has been and is read; it is as canon that it exercises its unique cultural power.[22] The part played by canonical *sequence* in this exercise of cultural power needs further study, but it is hard to believe that it is not pivotal for the way a canon enters consciousness and habit. Sequence is likely to be of even greater significance for the Christian canons, which (including the New Testament) purport to tell *one* story from beginning to end, than for the Jewish canon. Canonically, any Bible that defines 1 Samuel as a book at all (i.e., the LXX and Christian Bibles) precedes it not with Judges but with Ruth.[23] This is why I shall make substantial reference to Ruth in a number of places.

My Assumptions and Procedure

What, if anything, is 1 Samuel? The title of this chapter is borrowed from Stephen Jay Gould, who shows in an altogether different context (evolutionary biology) that whether something is significantly a "thing" is a matter of where you draw the lines.[24] For those in the Christian canonical tradition 1 Samuel is a biblical book, a most potent thing. But in the Masoretic canon 1 Samuel is not a thing, though it is half a thing.

---

[21] For these issues see David Jobling, "Ruth Finds a Home: Canon, Politics, Method" in J. Cheryl Exum and D. J. A. Clines, eds., *The New Literary Criticism and the Hebrew Bible.* JSOT.S 143 (Sheffield: Sheffield Academic Press, 1993) 125–139.

[22] Yet there has been very little serious examination of canons as literary works. The work of Northrop Frye is the most obvious exception; see Northrop Frye, *The Great Code: The Bible and Literature* (London: Routledge & Kegan Paul, 1982), especially pp. 105–138. See also Gabriel Josipovici, *The Book of God: A Response to the Bible* (New Haven and London: Yale University Press, 1988).

[23] This is strictly true only up to the fifteenth century C.E., when it became common to divide Samuel into two even in Hebrew Bibles. Despite the Jewish canon the rabbis often write about Ruth as if it were between Judges and Samuel. (I shall look at a prime example [231]).

[24] Stephen Jay Gould, "What, If Anything, Is a Zebra?," *Hen's Teeth and Horse's Toes: Further Reflections in Natural History* (New York and London: Norton, 1984) 355–365.

In the intrinsic organization of the Deuteronomic History hypothesized by Noth and McCarthy it is not any kind of a thing at all.

My initial reason for working with the Noth-McCarthy divisions was not that they are better than the canonical ones but simply that they are different. They help to defamiliarize for us the familiar biblical books. They also provide a worthy test of claims, like those of Polzin and Rosenberg, that the canonizers made divisions at the most appropriate places. It will be clear, though, that in this book I am treating the Noth-McCarthy divisions as more than a convenient alternative. I see in them a valuable contribution precisely to the *literary* study of the Bible. I find them to correspond well with my own sense of the quasi-mythic structures of the narrative, particularly as regards the issue of government (Part II). So I take seriously the possibility that they did serve as working divisions in a pre-canonical (Deuteronomic) but otherwise essentially identical text.

In that case the canonical divisions represent a tendentious revision of the Deuteronomic work. I shall for this reason confine my use of the term "Deuteronomic" so far as possible to the pre-canonical stage. I assume that our texts developed over a long period, with the canonical divisions coming particularly late. My procedure in the next part of the book (Part II) will be to read the text first at the Deuteronomic stage, the stage of the Extended Book of Judges and the Book of the Everlasting Covenant, before going on to read the canonical 1 Samuel by contrast. I invite you to imagine a time when nothing was known of the canonical book divisions, when the narrative summaries were accepted as providing a useful division of the Deuteronomic work. I do not and cannot know where, when, and especially if such a situation existed. But this does not take away from the usefulness of my strategy. I hope that my reading may give plausibility to my suggestion about history (and even be a contribution to the ongoing study of the Deuteronomic History). In any case it will provide a powerful lever for opening up the received text of 1 Samuel to our reading.[25]

2 Samuel 21:1-14: A 1 Samuel Outtake

2 Samuel 21:1-14 tells the story of Rizpah, a secondary wife of Saul. The marriage obviously took place during the time of 1 Samuel, but 1

[25] It is noteworthy that such eminent literary readers as Eslinger and Fokkelman make a major division after 1 Samuel 12. See n. 16 above.

Samuel fails to tell us about it. The passage tells of another, seemingly major incident in Saul's career about which 1 Samuel is silent: he "had tried to wipe out" the Gibeonites (2 Sam 21:2).

Some reading strategies reviewed in the last chapter—poststructural, ideological, psychoanalytic—programmatically read texts for what they significantly omit. From this point of view the "thing" that 1 Samuel is is constituted by its omissions as well as by its inclusions. "Reading" the omissions usually has to be a work of imagination, of asking oneself what the text might have, or ought to have, included. But 2 Samuel 21 actually identifies for us some omissions from 1 Samuel and therefore demands our attention. I shall pursue the implications of the Rizpah story at appropriate points.

Part II

CLASS: THE POLITY OF ANCIENT ISRAEL

PROLOGUE

In this part of the book I shall examine 1 Samuel's treatment of the theme of government in Israel. The first half of 1 Samuel deals with this theme in three clear phases: the establishment of Samuel's leadership, which is also the reestablishment of judgeship (chs. 1–7); the establishment of Saul's kingship (chs. 8–12); and the rejection of Saul's kingship (13:1–16:13). I include the anointing of David (16:1-13) as part of the third phase since it does not, as a reader might expect, inaugurate the kingship of David as a new phase. 1 Samuel is not at all about the reign of David. Rather, the whole latter half of the book surprisingly covers the completion of *Saul's* reign, a reign we had assumed to be over, or virtually over. Even when Saul dies at the end of the book the reign of David is not immediately in view. The Philistines are in the ascendant, and government in Israel (as it has been in the past and will be again in the future) is in the hands of foreigners.

In the previous chapter I defined two Deuteronomic "books" that constitute a division of the History different from the canonical book division, namely the Extended Book of Judges and the Book of the Everlasting Covenant. The theological summaries that mark off these "books" (Judg 2:11-23, 1 Samuel 12, 2 Samuel 7) are concerned above all with the question, "What form of government is appropriate for Israel?" It is the theme of government, therefore, that gives shape to the Deuteronomic History, or at least the part of it in the vicinity of 1 Samuel.[1]

---

[1] "The Book of Samuel has been called the Biblical *Politeia*. The Book of Judges deserves the same designation" (Martin Buber, *Kingship of God*, translated by Richard Scheimann [New York: Harper & Row, 1967] 84). This reference suggested to me the title for this part of my book.

This being the case, it is appropriate and even necessary to begin by looking at the Deuteronomic "books." The canonical definition of 1 Samuel, I claim, distorts the Deuteronomic treatment of government, and the way to remedy the distortion is to read the Extended Book of Judges and the Book of the Everlasting Covenant. I shall do this in Chapters 3 and 4 respectively. In a book about 1 Samuel, obviously, I must give most attention to the canonical book, but I shall need to dwell at considerable length on the material outside it (much more on the book of Judges than on 2 Samuel 1–7), since without this context the dynamics of 1 Samuel and the significance of its creation as a separate book cannot be understood. As I suggested earlier, it is only at this macro-textual level, embracing nearly sixty chapters of the Bible, that we can work out the structure of the narrative [5–6]. You will experience these chapters as a long journey but I hope you will agree at the end that the journey was necessary. This is the only part of the book in which I treat the text in a sequential way, and these admittedly heavy chapters will provide a necessary matrix for everything else I shall have to say.

In Chapter 5 I shall reread the theme of government, but asking this time what understanding emerges if we focus precisely on 1 Samuel and its canonical placement. (I shall give attention here to the implications of the insertion of Ruth, in some canons, between Judges and 1 Samuel.) The result is surprising. 1 Samuel is, in an obvious way, "The Book of Samuel and Saul," covering exactly the combined lifetime of these two characters. As a book of transition from judgeship to kingship it is also a book of transitions from one generation of leaders to another. Pursuing the theme of generational transition leads to an alternative possibility for government, different from both judgeship and kingship and perhaps expressing a fundamental discontent with both, in which leadership in Israel passes between surrogate fathers and sons.

Chapter 3

1 SAMUEL 1–12 IN THE EXTENDED BOOK OF JUDGES

The Deuteronomic Extended Book of Judges (Judg 2:11–1 Samuel 12) presents a sort of debate over the merits of governmental systems. It has two aims: to present judgeship as a divine dispensation and as in some sense an ideal, and to explain how it gave way to kingship. These goals are pursued by two contradictory strategies. From one point of view the book chronicles a fall from an ideal and tries to assign blame for this fall. From another it tries to persuade itself that there really was no fall, that kingship can be brought within the ideal. I shall detail these strategies when I come to 1 Samuel 8–12.

The Extended Book of Judges falls into two parts. The first, immensely long, follows judgeship from its beginning, through many vicissitudes, to its high point in 1 Samuel 7. 1 Samuel 8–12 then records the transition to kingship. For ease of presentation I shall subdivide the first part into two, after Judges 16. Up to Judges 16 the treatment of judgeship follows a fairly even course, giving the reader frequent points of orientation. Thereafter the familiar landmarks disappear, and the reader waits a long time for guidance as to what is going on.

Judges 2:11–16:31: The First Judge Cycles

Analysis of the text. The period of rule by judges in Israel is programmatically inaugurated by Judg 2:11-19, which summarizes the period as a series of repetitions of the following cyclical scheme:

  1. Israel falls into apostasy against YHWH.[1]
  2. A foreign oppressor dominates Israel for a time.
  3. Israel appeals to YHWH.[2]
  4. YHWH attends to the appeal and sends a judge to save Israel.[3]
  5. The judge defeats the oppressor.
  6. During the judge's lifetime Israel remains faithful to YHWH and is safe from external threat.

After the judge's death apostasy is renewed and a new cycle begins.

Several aspects of the theory need to be underscored. First, the judges are to be chosen by YHWH. Israel does not go looking for a leader; it appeals to YHWH, who sends one. Second, each judge is to be an exemplary leader throughout his or her life, able to keep Israel safe and faithful to YHWH. Finally, it is of the greatest importance to note that rule by judges corresponds only to points 4 to 6 in the cycle. Points 1 to 3 constitute a *gap* during which no judge is in place. These gaps are integral to the judge system as Judg 2:11-19 conceives it.

The cycles thus announced begin in Judg 3:7[4] and are evident, through six repetitions, as far as ch. 16. The following are the six judges (often referred to as "major judges") with the section corresponding to the judgeship of each. (In each case I have identified as the "gap" the material belonging to points 1–3.)

Othniel	Judges 3:7-11[5] (gap 3:7-9a)
Ehud	Judges 3:12-30 (gap 3:12-15a)

[1] After the death of a judge or, at the beginning of the period, after the death of Joshua.

[2] Robert Polzin questions whether Israel's appeal to YHWH is to be construed as repentance and insists that Israel's faithlessness continued unbroken through the whole of Judges (*Moses and the Deuteronomist: A Literary Study of the Deuteronomic History. Part One: Deuteronomy Joshua Judges* [New York: Seabury, 1980] 155–156, 159, 162, and elsewhere). I believe that repentance is integral to the theory though in particular cases the sincerity of the repentance may be doubted.

[3] I shall not enter into discussion of what a judge actually was and did, or of the fact that the figures we refer to as "judges" are rarely so called in the text (for these matters see the commentaries, and the Judges volume in this series). Some of the issues involved will arise in the course of my discussion, but in general I mean by "the judges" the people who led Israel in the period of the judges, doing all the things—judging, teaching, fighting—that are part of leadership.

[4] The intervening material, 2:20–3:6, continues the Deuteronomic theological comment but takes up other issues.

[5] This first cycle exhibits the cyclical pattern with greater clarity even than Judg 2:11-19.

Deborah   Judges 4–5 (gap 4:1-3)
Gideon   Judges 6:1–8:32 (gap 6:1-10)
Jephthah Judges 10:6–12:7 (gap 10:6-16)
Samson   Judges 13–16 (gap 13:1)[6]

However, a reading of these cycles makes it clear that they do not entirely correspond to the theory. The rule that YHWH chooses the major judges is broken in the case of Jephthah (10:18–11:11). The later judges cease to be exemplary leaders. Gideon not only goes astray but leads Israel astray (8:24-27). This theme of the faithless judge continues probably in Jephthah and certainly in Samson, whose selfishness and incontinence threaten to thwart YHWH's purpose. A correlate of these failures is the growth of internecine conflict in Israel. The theory of the judges (2:11-19) anticipates no such conflict, but it appears in the judge cycles almost from the beginning and grows in intensity (5:15-17, 7:24-8:3, 12:1-6; cf. also 15:9-13). The judge cycles show, then, great and growing departures from the theory.

The six judge cycles up to Samson do not include quite all of 3:7—16:31. My table above omits 3:31, 8:33–10:5, and 12:8-15. Much of this extraneous material tells of a different group of judges: Shamgar (3:31), Tola and Jair (10:1-5), and Ibzan, Elon, and Abdon (12:8-15). These have often been called "minor judges" because the accounts of them are so much shorter than those of the major judges. The rest of the extraneous material consists of a single long passage, 8:33–9:57. It tells how Abimelech, a son of the judge Gideon, briefly reigned as king after his father's death. I shall return shortly to both these kinds of extraneous material.

The problem of continuity. The most remarkable and problematic aspect of the judge theory, though the text makes no comment on it, is that it contains no provision for continuity of leadership. After each judge, as initially after Joshua, there is neither a successor in place nor a procedure for getting one. In fact there is no expectation that Israel will ever have a leader again. The sequence of events through which a new judge will eventually appear is set in motion only by Israel's apostasy. If no sin, then, it seems, no leader.

The alternative scheme of minor judges looks like an attempt to grapple with this problem of continuity. The notice for each minor judge begins with "after him," implying that there is no gap; each holds office in continuity with his predecessor, whether this be a major or another minor judge. The concern for continuity is perhaps underlined by

---

[6] The appeal to YHWH is missing from this cycle.

the fact that the sequences of minor judges get longer each time—one judge in 3:31, two in 10:1-5, three in 12:8-15.

The issue of continuity arises in another important way in the judge cycles themselves. Each judge through Gideon meets and defeats a single enemy, of whom we then hear no more; but in the last two cycles (Jephthah and Samson) the Philistines emerge as oppressors who persist from cycle to cycle, whom neither judge fully overcomes.[7] This continuity of threat perhaps calls for continuity in leadership.

Finally, the account of Abimelech's kingship (8:33–9:57) brings into the debate a form of national leadership that preserves continuity by definition. When a king dies his son becomes king.[8] But to achieve this continuity the divine initiative in choosing Israel's leaders must be given up.[9]

Continuity, it seems, has become the central issue of contention in the debate over leadership that is going on in Judges. So important is this issue that the possibility is entertained, quite early in the judge cycles, of abandoning judgeship for kingship. In view of the fact that this transition *will* be completed in 1 Samuel we need to take a long look at the experiment with kingship in Judges 8–9.

Israel's first experiment with kingship.[10] Kingship arises as an issue even before Abimelech, in the account of the judgeship of his father Gideon. This gives a keen point to Abimelech's name, for it means "my father is king"! After his victory over the Midianites, the Israelites approach Gideon with an offer of hereditary rule (8:22). Gideon refuses the offer and specifically rejects the hereditary principle (v. 23). He does so on the ground that human monarchy contradicts the kingship of YHWH, but the gloss is taken off this pious declaration by the following passage (vv. 24-27) in which Gideon makes, from the spoil taken from the Midianites, a religious object that

---

[7] The mention of them in 10:7 is mysterious, for they play no further part in the Jephthah cycle. Samson's failure to overcome them fully agrees with 13:5: "It is he who shall *begin* to deliver Israel from the hand of the Philistines."

[8] It is of interest that beginning with Gideon there is a concern with the generational relationships of the judges, their parents and/or children (so Jephthah and Samson, as well as the minor judges Jair, Ibzan, Abdon). Nothing in the judge theory leads us to expect this interest in heredity, but it anticipates hereditary kingship.

[9] It is interesting that there is no suggestion of divine initiative in the rise of the minor judges. There too, perhaps, it is traded for the assurance of continuity.

[10] For a fuller treatment of this topic see my *The Sense of Biblical Narrative: Structural Analyses in the Hebrew Bible II.* JSOT.S 39 (Sheffield: JSOT Press, 1986) 66–84.

becomes the cause of apostasy for all Israel, and particularly for Gideon and his family.

In v. 28 we get the closing formula for Gideon's judgeship—subjugation of the Midianites, rest for the land (cf. 3:30). But before the notice of his death (8:32) we are told of Gideon's[11] many wives and sons. We learn more particularly of one son, Abimelech. Abimelech's mother is Gideon's *pîlegeš* (v. 31), in distinction from his "wives" (v. 30). Scholars have come to realize the inappropriateness of the traditional "concubine" as a translation of *pîlegeš*. The meaning may rather be (and particularly in this case seems to be) "wife living in her father's, not her husband's house" [170–172]. Nonetheless an issue of legitimacy is raised, since the status of Abimelech's mother comes to bear negatively on his claim to leadership (9:18).

A new judge cycle seems to begin at 8:33, and verses 33-34 recount Israel's apostasy in the usual way. But v. 35 adds a surprising new sin to the catalogue: failure to "exhibit loyalty" to Gideon's family. What such loyalty would consist of is not yet clear (presumably the subsequent story in ch. 9 provides the answer), but the verse begs the question why there should be *any* obligation to the surviving family of a judge.

As the new chapter opens Abimelech plots with his kin in Shechem to become ruler. The words he uses are revealing: "Which is better for you, that all seventy of the sons of Jerubbaal rule over you, or that one rule over you?" (9:2). This implies that Gideon's seventy sons are exercising some form of rule. The story thus assumes the hereditary principle; Abimelech simply suggests that *mon*archy would be its most appropriate form. Having killed (as he supposes) his seventy "legitimate" brothers, Abimelech assumes monarchical rule (v. 6; cf. v. 22). But one of the seventy, Jotham, has survived (v. 5). After Abimelech has been made king Jotham tells his famous fable (vv. 7-15, with interpretation in vv. 16-20), which rejects not only Abimelech's kingship but all kingship, suggesting that kings are parasites on the productive members of society.[12] Jotham flees and disappears from the story (v. 21). Thereafter Abimelech's reign does not prosper, and ends disastrously.[13]

---

[11] Hereabouts Gideon sometimes appears under his alternative name of Jerubbaal. See the commentaries for the problem of the double name.

[12] Jobling, *The Sense of Biblical Narrative II* 71–77; also Martin Buber, *Kingship of God*, translated by Richard Scheimann (New York: Harper & Row, 1967) 75.

[13] In my fuller reading I suggest that the Gideon-Abimelech story contains many other indications that monarchy is the major issue, from the names of the characters to the statement that Gideon and his brothers "resembled the sons of a king" (8:18). It deals with all the problems posed by the multiplicity of royal offspring: primogeniture, legitimacy, usurpation, palace intrigue focused on the king's wives.

To determine what this story is saying about monarchy we have to look at a passage in Deuteronomy (sometimes called "the law of the king") that is essential background to all consideration of monarchy in the Deuteronomic History:

> *When you have come into the land that the* LORD *your God is giving you, and have taken possession of it and settled in it, and you say, "I will set a king over me, like all the nations that are around me," you may indeed set over you a king whom the* LORD *your God will choose.* One of your own community you may set as king over you; you are not permitted to put a foreigner over you, who is not of your own community. Even so, he must not acquire many horses for himself, or return the people to Egypt in order to acquire more horses, since the LORD has said to you, "You must never return that way again." *And he must not acquire many wives for himself,* or else his heart will turn away; also silver and *gold he must not acquire in great quantity for himself.* When he has taken the throne of his kingdom, he shall have a copy of this law written for him in the presence of the levitical priests. It shall remain with him and he shall read in it all the days of his life, so that he may learn to fear the LORD his God, diligently observing all the words of this law and these statutes, neither exalting himself above other members of the community *nor turning aside from the commandment,* either to the right or to the left, so that he *and his descendants* may reign long over his kingdom in Israel. (Deut 17:14-20; I emphasize parts that are important for my discussion.)

According to this formulation Israel might at any time after entering its land seek from YHWH a king, and receive a king of YHWH's choice. There are indeed conditions, but with one exception they are laid upon the king himself (he is to be moderate in his behavior, and so on). The only condition laid upon Israel is that the king must be an Israelite, but this condition is illogical since it is YHWH who chooses the king. It is specified that any such kingship would be hereditary (v. 20).

In 1 Sam 8:5 Israel will take up its option to ask for a king, but it will not be doing so for the first time. It does so already in Judg 8:22. Is the offer of kingship to Gideon legitimate in the terms laid down in Deuteronomy 17? Gideon's rule is to be hereditary: this agrees with Deut 17:20. An apparent problem is that the king must be *of YHWH's choice.* But the people might argue that they *are* requesting a king of YHWH's choice since YHWH chose Gideon to be national leader. They

---

See *The Sense of Biblical Narrative II* 69, 86. These matters are not unfamiliar to Israel, according to the later parts of the Deuteronomic History, but they are not relevant to our reading up to 1 Samuel 12.

simply want to ratify Yнwн's choice at a different level. The people's proposal is, then, legitimate. It is Gideon's pious refusal that is at odds with the law of the king.

However, despite his refusal, the story proceeds as if Gideon had *accepted* the kingship. His subsequent behavior casts doubt on the seriousness of his refusal, for in 8:24-27 he *acts like* a king, and, in the terms of Deuteronomy 17, like a *bad* king. He accumulates as much gold as he can (Deut 17:17b) and as a result turns aside from Yнwн's commandment (Deut 17:20a). A little later he "multiplies wives for himself" (vv. 30-31; Deut 17:17a).

How could this monarchical experiment legitimately come to an end? For monarchy *is* dynastic, and once in there is no obvious way out.[14] Judges does not deal with this issue at the surface level; it does not raise the question of succession to Abimelech or even trouble to tell us if he had children. But I believe it does deal with the problem—at a mythic if not an intentional level—through the character Jotham.

Jotham is not just a name attached to a fable; he is a character in the narrative, and he alters its dynamics. He is the rightful heir to Gideon's kingship, certainly after Abimelech's death and perhaps (if there is doubt about Abimelech's legitimacy) already before. Jotham's survival seems at first sight to constitute a problem, for we are left with a surviving king and a worthy one. More profound consideration, however, reveals Jotham not as a textual embarrassment but as a solution to the problem of how to get out of a monarchy once it has begun. Jotham in effect abdicates his claim, brings to an end Israel's first monarchical experiment, and restores judgeship simply by disappearing! Moreover, as he disappears he delivers in his fable a powerful theoretical rejection of monarchy as such.

Judges 8–9 is in a bind. It seeks to convey an antimonarchical message through the story of a proto-monarchy that came to grief. But even a bad monarchy is intrinsically permanent! The solution is what I want to call the "worthy refuser." The paradoxical message of Jotham's fable of the trees is that anyone worthy of kingship would be worthy enough to refuse it, while anyone not worthy enough to refuse it will be a bad king.[15] The overloaded character Gideon is made to play both

---

[14] Even recent history tells us something of the tenacity of monarchies, discredited though they may seem to be (I am thinking of pretenders to the throne of Russia or the restoration of monarchy in Spain). I will later discuss the tenacity of the house of Saul [102–103].

[15] Compare Groucho Marx's quip that he wouldn't want to belong to any club that would accept him as a member.

these roles: he speaks the classic words of the worthy refuser in 8:23 but goes on to play the role of the unworthy accepter. The true "worthy refuser" in the story is Jotham himself. He does not solve the problem at the level of logic, for no such solution is possible, but he solves it impressively in narrative terms. As a rightful king and worthy to be a king he withdraws from the story, leaving in his place his words— words that scorn kingship and praise its worthy refusers!

It is important to note how the narrator of Judges 8–9 identifies the voice of the antimonarchical Jotham with his own voice. This is seen most clearly in Jotham's statement that the people have not done right by Gideon (9:16b), for the narrator has already said just the same thing in his own voice (8:35).[16] The rest of the Abimelech story confirms this negative assessment of the monarchical experiment, which ends in disaster. Previously Israel's experience with kings had been with the kings of foreign nations, and it had been bitter. Now Israel has had an equally bitter experience with kings of its own.

Judges 17–1 Samuel 7: The Last Judge Cycles

The reader who reads beyond Judges 16 is likely soon to suppose that the judge cycles ended there, though she will perhaps be puzzled that there was no statement to that effect. The theory was wearing thin as the stories diverged from it more and more. The cycles were growing wearisome, and presumably could not go on forever. Even though kingship had been repudiated as an option the need for continuity of leadership was coming more and more to the fore, especially given the presence of a persistent enemy, the Philistines.

At any rate, after ch. 16 the familiar landmarks cease to appear. Israel falls into many bad ways in chs. 17–21 but not explicitly into apostasy against YHWH. There are no judges and no foreign enemy appears, not even the Philistines. Startlingly, given Israel's experience with kings, a nostalgia for kingship soon begins to punctuate the story (17:6, 18:1, 19:1, 21:25). But the persistent reader of the Extended Book of Judges will come eventually—shortly after the Philistines *do* reappear— to 1 Sam 4:18. There she will learn that Eli the priest, about whom she has been reading for several chapters, was a *judge* who judged Israel for the standard forty years! If that brief notice fails (as well it might) entirely to convince her that the judge cycles are still contin-

[16] See Polzin, *Moses and the Deuteronomist* 174.

uing, all doubt will be stayed by the account of Samuel's judgeship in 1 Samuel 7.

Judgeship in parody and apotheosis. The reader, suddenly forced to come to terms with an "Eli cycle" extending from Judges 17 to 1 Sam 4:18, will find that it can all be made to fit in a looking-glass sort of way. The national falling away after the death of Samson is convincing enough even without "the Baals and the Astartes." But the sequence of foreign oppression, cry to YHWH, appearance of the judge, and the judge's defeat of the enemy, is all delightfully muddled. Eli enters the scene not as a judge meeting a need but as an effete priest in a corrupt system. His career is simply a continuation of the national apostasy, of the abuses that mark the end of Judges (I shall later examine some interesting links between the Elide priesthood and Judges 17–21). Is there a cry to YHWH? Well, there is one in Judg 21:2-3 and it brings a solution to the immediate problem—but the solution is worse than the problem since it entails wholesale rape. The real cry to YHWH, the one that will set Israel's history back on track, is Hannah's (1 Sam 1:10-11) [131–135]. But it is not in response to these cries that Eli appears (though he is present at Hannah's cry and makes a fool of himself over it). The irony is made complete by the Philistines; instead of Eli's being "raised up" to defeat them it is his corrupt regime that brings them back from their long absence to defeat *him* (1 Samuel 4)!

If in Eli judgeship is parodied at every turn, in Samuel it is vindicated and completed. The Samuel cycle, formally speaking, extends from 1 Sam 4:19 through 1 Samuel 7. There is a problem in that Samuel has had an earlier career, in 1:1–4:1, as apprentice priest and prophet. (I shall return to these categories in a moment.) But even there judgeship was strongly suggested by the parallels drawn between Samuel's birth and Samson's [171–172].

All six points of the judge cycle can easily be demonstrated in 4:19–7:17. 1 Samuel 4:19–7:2 is the gap between Eli and Samuel (points 1-3 in the cycle) while 7:3-17 brings Samuel back as judge (points 4-6). There is a measure of narrative strain in the treatment of the gap, since much of the evidence for the first three points has to be read retrospectively from 7:3-6, of which I give the text:

> (3) Then Samuel said to all the house of Israel, "If you are returning to the LORD with all your heart, then put away the foreign gods and the Astartes from among you. Direct your heart to the LORD, and serve him only, and he will deliver you out of the hand of the Philistines." (4) So Israel put away the Baals and the Astartes, and they served the LORD only. (5) Then Samuel said, "Gather all Israel at Mizpah, and I will pray to the LORD for you." (6) So they gathered at Mizpah, and drew water and

poured it out before the LORD. They fasted that day, and said, "We have sinned against the LORD." And Samuel judged the people of Israel at Mizpah.

Given the complexity of the narrative currents in this part of 1 Samuel, the narrative strain is really remarkably slight. The analysis is as follows:

1. "Israel falls into apostasy against YHWH." This first element is probably the hardest to work out. What happens after Eli's death is not Israel's apostasy, since the text goes in other directions. However, in the section quoted Samuel charges that this interval *has* been a time of apostasy, and Israel accepts the charge (note the very close parallels to Judg 3:7, 10:10, etc.)

2. "A foreign oppressor dominates Israel for a time." Again it is Samuel's speech that makes this clearest; "deliver you out of the hand of the Philistines" (7:3) is the standard language for foreign oppression. I shall consider later in just what sense Israel has been under the domination of the Philistines. But the loss of the ark to the Philistines might well stand as a metonym for foreign oppression, and the "twenty years" for which Israel was without the ark (7:2) are reminiscent of the length of foreign oppression in the judge cycles (Judg 3:8, etc.)

3. "Israel appeals to YHWH." In 7:6 Israel addresses YHWH in a clearly repentant fashion. It is a slight anomaly that the appeal comes *after* the appearance of the judge-deliverer and at his instigation, since in the regular cycle the judge appears after the appeal, but again we can refer to 7:2 where we learn that "the house of Israel lamented after YHWH." This is similar to the "cry to YHWH" in the typical judge cycle, and even if the very unusual Hebrew verb used here does not suggest repentance[17] Samuel still perceives the people as repentant in 7:3.

4. "YHWH sends a judge." The only problem here is Samuel's earlier career. It is in 7:3 that he first appears *in the role of judge.*

5. "The judge defeats the oppressor." Samuel's defeat of the Philistine oppressor could not be more explicit (7:3, 7-14). Note especially the formula that the Philistines were "subdued" (7:13; cf. Judg 3:30, 11:33, etc.)

6. "Israel remains faithful to YHWH during the judge's lifetime and suffers no external threat." The subjugation of the Philistines lasts "all the days of Samuel" (1 Sam 7:13). There is also internal peace, assum-

---

[17] The verb is *nhh*. The LXX translators may well have had a Hebrew text that read *pnh*, with the sense of "repent," but in such cases text-critical method directs us to prefer the more difficult reading.

ing that "Amorites" (7:14) refers to non-Israelites living in the land. "Samuel judged Israel all the days of his life" (7:15) suggests that he maintained Israel's faithfulness to YHWH.

Other discourses of government. Besides judgeship, other forms of government are referred to in this section of the text either as actually in place or as hypothetical possibilities. The narrative in Judges 17–18 is about *priestly* leadership, though at the domestic and tribal levels, not the national. The priesthoods involved are heterodox, and the whole story exemplifies the national confusion at this time. The subsequent story in Judges 19–21 does not make priesthood much of an issue, but it does mention the legitimate national priesthood. In 20:27-28 the Israelites make an oracular inquiry at the Bethel sanctuary, and the priest there is the same Phinehas, grandson of Aaron, with whom YHWH made an everlasting covenant of priesthood in Num 25:10-13.

As we move into 1 Samuel the opening chapters suggest a situation in which Israel's national life revolves, in the absence of other leaders, around the central sanctuary and its priests. The links with the end of Judges are strong but confusing. They have to do with both priestly lineage and location. As to lineage, Eli's priesthood seems to be in legitimate descent from Aaron since 2:27-36 sees his house as having been in an everlasting covenant with YHWH.[18] Another small indication is the recurrence of the name "Phinehas" as one of Eli's sons.

The issue of location is confusing since the stories link priesthood with two different places, Shiloh and Bethel (which means "house of God"). Eli's priesthood is at the shrine in Shiloh (1:3), which houses the ark of God (3:3), Israel's most sacred religious object, but in Judg 20:27-28 Phinehas and the ark are located not at Shiloh but at Bethel. The story in Judges 19–21 does refer to Shiloh. There is an annual YHWH festival there (Judg 21:19), which fits well with the annual festival repeatedly referred to in 1 Samuel 1–2; but Shiloh has no priestly authority in Judges 19–21, and it is the scene of a mass rape (Judg 21:16-24). However, immediately before this story we were told that "the house of God *(beth-el)* was at Shiloh" (Judg 18:31)!

This is thoroughly confusing and creates unclarity about Eli's priesthood.[19] How has the shift occurred from Bethel to Shiloh, a place

---

[18] Based on descent from "your ancestor in Egypt" (v. 27). This must be Aaron, who was chosen by YHWH in Egypt (Exod 4:14-16), though not actually as priest (this happened in the desert, in Exodus 28–29). The priestly genealogies in the rest of the Bible (e.g., 1 Chron 6:3-8) do not, however, include Eli.

[19] See especially Peter D. Miscall, *1 Samuel: A Literary Reading* (Bloomington, Ind.: Indiana University Press, 1986) 9–10.

certainly less hallowed by tradition (Gen 35:1-15) and perhaps of evil repute? We might suggest that Eli's priesthood is being parodied just as his judgeship is. The entire message about leadership by priests, both in Judges 17–21 and in 1 Samuel 1–4, is that it is ineffectual or worse.

Eli's sons, Hophni and Phinehas, are evil priests who cheat the worshipers (2:12-17) and exploit the women temple servants (2:22). The reader has the sense of being still in the ethical ambience of Judges 17–21: "everyone doing what is right in their own eyes" seems now to extend to the very priestly leaders of Israel. On account of these offenses of his sons the priesthood of Eli's house is rejected by God. The rejection is announced in 1 Sam 2:27-36 and carried out in 1 Samuel 4 as part of the story of Israel's war against the Philistines. When Israel is defeated, the ark is captured and Eli's sons are killed (4:11).[20] Their death "on the same day" is the sign verifying the truth of the prophecy of the fall of Eli's house (see 2:34). The news of the loss of the ark also kills Eli (4:18). A coda to the story tells of the birth of a son posthumously to Phinehas (4:19-22). This child's name seals the prophecy: Ichabod, "Glory gone."[21] Thus is the curtain drawn on leadership by priests.

The other national leader to appear in the early part of 1 Samuel is, of course, Samuel himself. The story technique whereby his rise in stature at the temple is interwoven with the fall of Eli's sons (1:24–3:19) leads the reader to suppose that Samuel will become a priest and found the new priestly house that is to replace Eli's. However, Samuel's career takes a quite other turn. He becomes established as a *prophet* (3:20–4:1), in which role he exercises leadership in Israel. At his next appearance (ch. 7) this role gives way, as we have seen, to that of judge, but Samuel's prophetic role will reappear in ch. 9 and in other parts of 1 Samuel.

Though there are no kings between Judges 17 and 1 Samuel 7 the discourse of *kingship* is not absent. The narrator whose voice we hear in Judges 17–21 finds the national situation so appalling, the lack of government in the gaps between judges so dangerous that kingship looks like a good or even necessary alternative. It was because "there

---

[20] It is perhaps surprising that the picture is not completed with an account of the destruction of Shiloh. The narrative books never mention this event, though it is a vivid memory in Jer 7:12, 14; 26:6.

[21] The reader may suppose that this son fulfills another part of the prophecy, that there will be one survivor of Eli's house to lament its ruin (2:33). This proves not to be so. It is Abiathar (22:20-23) who fulfills this prophecy.

was no king in Israel" that "all the people did what was right in their own eyes" (17:6, 21:25). This point of view, though, is expressed only in the narrator's asides (also 18:1, 19:1); there is nothing about kingship in the stories being told. This narratorial voice "forgets" what the narrator of 8:33–9:57 said (through Jotham) about kingship. This voice implies that it is time Israel took up its option (Deuteronomy 17) to seek a king from YHWH.

It will be some time yet before Israel does so: 1 Samuel 1–7 goes in other directions. Still, these chapters are not quite empty of references to kingship. In 2:10 Hannah's song ends with: "The LORD . . . will give strength to his king, and exalt the power of his anointed," and according to 2:35 the "faithful priest" who will replace Eli's house "shall go in and out before [YHWH's] anointed one forever." In other words, this new priesthood will be part of a coming monarchical system, and priesthood and monarchy will be coeternal.

For some commentators these explicit references to monarchy are the tip of an iceberg. They find a great wealth of other monarchical allusion in the opening chapters of 1 Samuel.[22] Thus Polzin reads the story of Hannah as a "parable" in which Hannah's demand for a child parallels, and provides anticipatory commentary on, Israel's later demand for a king.[23] I do not want to reject this reading simply because my own reading of Hannah is so very different [131–142], but I can find no plausibility in it, and I wonder whether Polzin would have proposed it if he had not decided *a priori* that the beginning of 1 Samuel is the beginning of a new stage in the Deuteronomic History. He needs to find at the beginning of 1 Samuel a programmatic introduction to what follows, and he finds it through his parable.[24]

Even the two explicit references in ch. 2 create problems for the monarchist reading. 1 Samuel 2:10 stands in diametric ideological opposition to the rest of Hannah's song, which celebrates social

---

[22] See especially Polzin, *Samuel and the Deuteronomist: A Literary Study of the Deuteronomic History. Part Two: 1 Samuel* (San Francisco: Harper & Row, 1989) 22–39, 44–49; Lyle Eslinger, *Kingship of God in Crisis: A Close Reading of 1 Samuel 1–12.* Bible and Literature Series 10 (Sheffield: Almond, 1985) 99–112.

[23] See especially Polzin, *Samuel and the Deuteronomist* 25–26. Polzin entitles the whole chapter "Hannah and Her Son: A Parable."

[24] See my earlier comments, and recall especially Miscall's statement that 1 Samuel has no overview introduction [31–33]. No more am I persuaded by Polzin's claim that the references to Eli's "throne" (1:9; 4:13, 18) are royal allusions (*Samuel and the Deuteronomist* 23, 44, and elsewhere). Rejecting Polzin on this point is Frank Anthony Spina, "Eli's Seat: The Transition from Priest to Prophet in 1 Samuel 1–4," *JSOT* 62 (1994) 67–75.

transformation for the benefit of the poor and oppressed. The song's values are egalitarian, not monarchist.[25] 1 Samuel 2:35 certainly anticipates monarchy and suggests enthusiasm for it, but by the same token it sets a major question mark against monarchy, for the message of the whole passage, 2:27-36, is that YHWH can and will annul even "everlasting" covenants. The covenant of priesthood with Phinehas was clearly stated in Num 25:13 to be permanent. Indeed, the original promise of permanence is recalled even in the act of bringing the covenant to an end: "The LORD the God of Israel declares: 'I promised that your family and the family of your ancestor should go in and out before me forever'; but now the LORD declares: 'Far be it from me'" (1 Sam 2:30)! This startling discovery, that everlasting covenants are not necessarily so, adjusts our entire theoretical notion of kingship and creates a precedent that will weigh heavily in the later treatment of the royal houses of Saul and David.[26]

Though leadership by priests disappears as an option after 1 Samuel 4, the theme of the fall of the house of Eli reappears in 14:3, 18-19; 21:1-9; 22:6-20. It is intertwined with the fall of the house of Saul, confirming at the narrative level the mythic parallel of two "everlasting" covenants that have been rescinded. It seems, then, that the narrative's entire interest in priesthood lies in the way it frames the discourse of monarchy.

If priesthood functions to provide oblique comment on monarchy, so, perhaps, does prophecy. Israel's traditions bind kingship and prophecy tightly together. The later parts of the Deuteronomic History will include innumerable stories involving prophets and kings; their main point is that prophets criticize and attempt to restrain kings on YHWH's behalf. (2 Samuel 12 provides a good example.) But there is also a need for prophets to be involved in the making of kings (e.g., 2 Kings 9), and at other critical moments of royal decision-making (e.g., 2 Kings 22:14-20). Samuel's establishment as a prophet readies the reader for the ambiguous role he will later play in the rise of monarchy.

Rule by foreigners is also a form of government in Israel. Indeed, it is the form of which the creators of the Bible have by far the fullest and most immediate experience. In 1 Samuel 1–7 Israel is threatened with Philistine rule.

---

[25] Because of the gender dimension I reserve for later a lengthier discussion of Hannah's song [166–169, 173].

[26] There is one other piece of "monarchic" discourse that deserves mentioning, namely the confusion between Samuel's name and Saul's. In 1:28 Hannah refers to Samuel as *šāʾûl* (= "Saul," meaning "given" or "lent") to YHWH [68, 111].

The judge theory deals with rule by foreigners in a simple way. It is the result of Israel's apostasy and it ends after Israel repents. To the extent that 1 Samuel 1–7 restores the logic of the judge cycles it contains the Philistines within this simple view. Samuel gets rid of them as a judge gets rid of any other national enemy (cf. also 1 Sam 12:9-11). But the Philistines are an enemy who cannot be thus contained. Already they have persisted as an enemy from one judge cycle to another, but the problem will become much worse. Samuel's expulsion of the Philistines from Israelite territory for his lifetime (7:13) will in the subsequent chapters be quickly revealed as fictional, for they will soon be back. Israel's experience of the Philistines necessitates some new way of theorizing about foreign rule. The judge theory is not adequate to the task.

It is interesting to read 1 Samuel 4, particularly v. 1, in relation to this problem of how to relate the Philistines to the theory. The Masoretic Hebrew reading makes the Israelites the aggressors in the war ("Israel went out to battle against the Philistines"). In this reading the war is one of national resistance to foreign domination such as all the judges have waged. This fits with the Philistines' claim that the Israelites have up to now "served" them (4:9). Despite the Philistines' long absence from the story (for eight chapters after Judges 16), they have—it is implied—been occupying Israel all the while. All this agrees with the judge theory (see also 1 Sam 7:3, 13-14). But the Greek text of 4:1 inserts the words "the Philistines mustered for war against Israel" before the mention of Israel. This makes the Philistines the aggressors and moves outside the framework of the judge theory. These Philistines are not the enemy sent by YHWH during the time of Israel's apostasy. They are what they will be throughout 1 Samuel: aggressors who seek to conquer Israel and eventually succeed.

These Philistines who loom so large for Israel loom large also for me in my thinking about 1 Samuel. The unexpected Other who unravel Israel's logic, they have served also to unravel my ideas about reading the Bible. I shall devote to them a whole section of this book (Part IV), and there I shall gather up the threads of the foregoing analysis.

Where Now?

Where can the story go after 1 Samuel 7, and how can it get there? In the person of Samuel judgeship is triumphant. He has comprehensively solved all of Israel's problems, both internally ("everyone doing what is right in their own eyes") and externally (the longstanding Philistine threat). Kingship, having had its moment of attractiveness, has now faded from the scene, helped on its way by another example of the evils of hereditary rule in Eli and his sons. Kingship has no remaining appeal as we reach the end of 1 Samuel 7.

Still, we know where the story must go. The brute fact of history is that Israel once upon a time ceased to be a judgeship and became a monarchy. Now is that time; now that transition must be told. But how can the transition be told in a plausible way? The historians are faced with a contradiction that is irreducible in principle but must be resolved if any coherent account is to be given of Israel's past.[27] We can express it as follows:

1. Human monarchy is alien to the religion of YHWH, but
2. Israel became a human monarchy under YHWH.

Let us pause at this point to imagine the narrators' options. There is no more powerful tool for getting at the dynamics of biblical narrative than to ask: How could the story have been different, and what difference would it have made?

One option would have been to make the transition to kingship immediately after what is now the end of Judges. Then a king could have arrived to clean up an anarchic mess, and the reader's doubts about Gideon and Abimelech might have been lost in the euphoria. But this, it seems, would not do. For some reason the mythic work requires that kingship emerge not at judgeship's nadir but at its zenith. The work of recounting the transition must be done at this very moment when it seems the hardest.

On one point, at least, the reader feels confident. The next words after 1 Samuel 7 must surely be "Then Samuel died and was buried" (cf. Judg 12:7, etc.) Samuel's life is over. Not only has he reached the appropriate end of a judge's life, but his whole life has been narratively accounted for. We have been told that he judged Israel, and kept the Philistines at bay *all his days* (7:13, 15). Keeping him alive now would be at the cost of getting into hopeless contradiction with these affirmations in ch. 7.

Still, let us, in considering the options, keep even this question open for a moment. If Samuel lived on, how might kingship come? Obviously by the people proposing to him what they proposed to Gideon: "Rule over us, you and your son and your grandson also" (Judg 8:22). But we know nothing (yet) of any son of Samuel.[28]

---

[27] This is a fundamental mythic contradiction in Lévi-Strauss's sense [6–7].

[28] The Gideon story neatly introduced a son of Gideon just before the people's proposal (see Judg 8:20); so will the Samuel story, though altogether less neatly.

Assume, on the other hand, that Samuel will now die. Israel will then be faced yet again with the problem of the gap between judges. But suppose—the possibility is just on the edge of thought—that Samuel has been so very great a judge that he has prepared Israel at last to meet the challenge of this freedom. This time, perhaps, Israel will not turn from Yhwh, but will live in faithfulness with no human mediator. How could that story be told . . . ?

Coming back to reality, the next major option would be to relate the transition to kingship and to lay the responsibility for it on the people. After Samuel's death, unable to face its consequences, Israel takes up its Deuteronomic option and asks Yhwh for a king. Such a choice will reflect poorly on them. Uniquely surrounded by the blessings a righteous judge brings, why must they *now* have a king and become "like the nations" whom the judges have so comprehensively defeated? But, to make the best of a bad job, this is probably how the transition will have to be told.

What actually happens includes aspects of several of these scenarios, but it is different from any of them.

1 Samuel 8–12: Israel Becomes a Monarchy

To deal with its problem 1 Samuel 8–12 adopts two strategies. On the one hand it presents the coming of kingship as a bad thing and lays blame for it. On the other hand it suggests that kingship is not necessarily a bad thing, that it can be incorporated into the logic of judgeship. These strategies are incompatible, and the narrative work is, as we anticipated, intensely problematic. These chapters are among the densest in the Bible. After summarizing the story I shall deal with each of the two strategies in turn.

A summary of the story. 1 Samuel 8–12 falls into five acts, with a prologue in 8:1-3. In the prologue the aged Samuel appoints his sons judges. This proves to be a disaster, for the sons are corrupt. Act I (8:4-22) tells how the people ask Samuel for a king. Samuel opposes the request but Yhwh instructs him to grant it. Act II (9:1–10:16) tells the long story of how Samuel, on Yhwh's instructions, privately anoints Saul to be king. In Act III (10:17-25) Samuel calls a national gathering at which Saul is selected by lot and proclaimed king by Samuel. Act IV (10:26–11:13) is complex. It mainly tells how Saul defeated the Ammonites and rescued the people of Jabesh-Gilead (11:1-11), but there is a frame story (10:26-27, 11:12-13) that tells about Saul's generous treatment of some people who disapproved his election as king.

The final act (V) covers 11:14–12:25. It has its setting in Gilgal, where Samuel assembles the people after the Ammonite war to "renew the kingship" (11:14). This act consists almost entirely of a speech by Samuel (ch. 12) in which he theologically ratifies the kingship and brings it within the framework of Israel's covenant with YHWH. The speech never mentions Saul by name and barely acknowledges his presence. It is a theoretical discourse about monarchy.

Laying the blame. In these chapters kingship arrives in Israel. Indeed it arrives several times over, in the various anointings and kingmakings, and the reader may well ask why all this repetition is necessary. But by the end of ch. 12 it is a kingship nobody wants—Samuel, YHWH, and the people of Israel all agree that the demand for a king was bad. (Saul's opinion is not asked.) 1 Samuel 12:16-19 is the climax: Samuel says that the people have acted wickedly, YHWH ratifies this judgment by supplying a miracle, and the people declare that "we have added to all our sins the evil of demanding a king for ourselves." But the three parties have reached this point of agreement from different directions.

Samuel is for the most part staunch in his opposition to kingship. In chs. 8 and 12 he is consistently so. The people's original request "displeases" him (8:6), and he warns them of the harm that will come from a king (8:11-18). In ch. 12 he accepts the transition as a *fait accompli*, but he still wants to convince the people that they have made a bad choice. He argues the case first by defending his own record as judge (12:3-5) and then by defending judgeship as a system (12:6-11).

The Samuel of the middle chapters, 9–11, is not so consistent. In 10:18-19 he reaffirms the view that to desire a king is to reject YHWH, and later in the same scene (v. 25) he repeats his warning about the perils of kingship (cf. 8:11-18) and even deposits in the archives a document stating his position.[29] It is also significant that Samuel makes no move to appoint a king even after YHWH has told him to do so in ch. 8. In ch. 9 it is YHWH who takes the initiative.

On the other hand, except in the parts of ch. 10 just referred to, Samuel accepts Saul as king and sometimes shows a real enthusiasm for him (9:22-24; 10:7, 23-24; 11:14). A rather different note is struck when Samuel assumes *authority* over the newly anointed king, especially in 10:8. This begins a narrative line that continues beyond ch. 12, and I shall explore it in the next chapter.

---

[29] The NRSV translations, *"ways* (of a king)" (8:9) and *"rights and duties* (of the kingship)" (10:25), convey different impressions of Samuel's intention, but they are in fact alternative translations of the same single Hebrew word. (The difference between "king" and "kingship" does not seem important.)

The attitude of *the people* is not complicated. Prior to their repentance in 12:19 they do not waver in their demand for a king, and only a few express dissatisfaction with *Saul* as king (10:27).

Much the most puzzling attitude is that of YHWH. He consistently reads the people's demand for a king as rejection of himself (8:7-8; 10:18-19, cf. 12:18). He instructs Samuel to warn the people of the evils of a king (8:9). Yet he insists on letting the people have their way (8:9, 22). He takes the initiative in finding a king (especially in ch. 9, and also in the use of the sacred lot in 10:19-21). Though the people eventually admit their error, YHWH will not even then reverse the decision to have a king.

YHWH seems to want to make sure that the people get a *good* king, and Saul does start out well. But Saul's subsequent failure casts doubt on YHWH's benevolent intentions. Certainly in the one promise that he makes about Saul's future career, that Saul will save Israel from the Philistines (9:16), YHWH is incorrect—whether from ignorance or insincerity we cannot say.[30] All in all it is hard to be enthusiastic about the role YHWH plays in Israel's transition to kingship.

When a story achieves a resolution none of the characters want, we expect it to seek a culprit. This story is no exception. By a quite extraordinary maneuver it lays the blame mainly on Samuel.

The obvious option, which I sketched earlier, would be to blame the people, but this is evidently unacceptable. The Deuteronomic historians are perhaps not ready to lay such a burden of guilt on their ancestors. But I believe there is a much profounder reason. Any attempt to blame the people would lead to utterly intolerable conclusions about the actions and attitudes of YHWH. The text, however, gives clear indications of pursuing this option up to a point. Indeed, if we could ignore 8:1-3 (and a few words in v. 5) we would say that this was the option chosen. Let us for a moment do so, since it will help us clarify the situation. The people take up the option that Deut 17:14 allows them, to ask YHWH for a king. They see that Samuel is old, and after their long experience of judgeship they are not prepared to face the consequences of his death. Not even Samuel has solved the fundamental problem of continuity.

It is to Samuel himself that the people bring their request. For the Deuteronomic historians this has a definite advantage. By letting the last judge also be the kingmaker they achieve a comforting sense of continuity between judgeship and kingship. But Samuel, not surprisingly,

---

[30] I will return to the question of why Israel needs saving from the Philistines, Samuel having defeated them already.

does not like the people's request. He sees in it a rejection of himself and everything he has striven for. Still, he dutifully takes it to YHWH.

YHWH's response to the people's request is self-contradictory. YHWH first states that the people have rejected him *but not Samuel* (8:7), and then instantly retracts this by saying to Samuel, "Just as they have done to me . . . *they are now doing to you*" (v. 8). This symptom of confusion has not been sufficiently attended to by commentators. It is a signal that YHWH is torn in two.

What I think is happening can be expressed as follows. Hearing his own words from Deut 17:14 spoken back to him by the people, YHWH himself borrows Gideon's words from Judg 8:23! YHWH agrees with the righteous judge—as Gideon in that moment was—rather than with his own words through Moses. He espouses not just Gideon's words but the whole implication of the Gideon-Abimelech story. To shift from judgeship to kingship leads to disaster.

In rejecting judgeship—Samuel and all he stands for—the people have indirectly rejected YHWH, who is the provider of judges. But YHWH seems dissatisfied with this way of putting it. He wants to see the people's request as a *direct* uncomplicated rejection of himself. So he stumbles over his words. Worse, having gotten into this fix he stubbornly insists that the people must have their way even when they cease to want it. YHWH passes from confusion to petulance and punitiveness. He is punishing the people for reminding him of words of his own that he wanted to forget!

This "divine" dilemma is happening, of course, in the mind of the Deuteronomic historians. It is not possible to save YHWH from this dilemma, for it is simply one manifestation of the fundamental contradiction within which the historians work [58]. Israel's history can be made coherent only on the assumption that YHWH gave permission for a form of government of which he disapproved. But this does not make theological sense.

There is no remedy, but there is the possibility of obfuscation. Can any of the blame be shifted elsewhere? The only available fall guy is Samuel. It is to this need to shift the blame, I suggest, that we owe the presence of 1 Sam 8:1-3 in our Bible. As we now read the story of Israel's turn to kingship, beginning with these verses, the first actor is neither the people nor YHWH, but Samuel. Israel's kingship stems from an action of Samuel, his attempt to make his sons judges in Israel.

In many years of rereading I have never been able to rid myself of my initial sense of the absurdity of these three short verses. To do what he does Samuel must first of all, at the cost of extreme narrative inconsequence, be kept unnaturally alive after ch. 7. Then he must be made responsible for the utter bathos of 8:1-3. The greatest of judges, at the moment of triumph for him and his office, so far forgets the nature of judgeship as to try to make it hereditary.[31] If his understanding of judgeship were not enough to deter him, could he not be warned by the memory of Abimelech, or by his own personal memory of the sons of Eli, that hereditary leadership brings no good?

To the extent that such a statement is even meaningful Samuel acts here completely "out of character" [69–70]. His action is no more coherent with what we otherwise know about him than are Hannah's words about kingship (2:10) with what we know about her [167–169]. Samuel is old. Perhaps we are invited to think of him, like Solomon, as blotting a perfect record in the infirmity of age (1 Kings 11:4). He is old, he worries what will happen after he dies, he tries to solve the problem himself. Such a line of thought might save for the text some plausibility. Better, though, simply to accept that the narrative is under intolerable pressure. It is more than ironic that the stalwart foe of kingship should become its cause. But the text is at the end of its resources.

The people and YHWH reap the benefits of blaming Samuel. The people are let almost entirely off the hook. Their request for a king is now prompted not only by Samuel's age but also by the bad leadership they are getting: "You are old, and your sons do not follow in your ways" (8:5).[32] YHWH also gains, since Samuel's resistance to the people's request is robbed of its theological force. It can now be read as pique at not getting his own way in the matter of his sons. When YHWH says "they have not rejected you" (8:7) he might now mean "it is not your ridiculous attempt to make your sons into judges that the people are rejecting." Attention is diverted from YHWH's—and the historians'—dilemma.

In telling the story this way the historians have not only preserved some plausibility for their narrative. At a deeper level they have also redrawn the mythic map. I noted earlier that having the last of the judges also be the kingmaker allows a comforting sense of continuity between two systems that are really antithetical. But the story goes even further by making judgeship into the *effective cause* of kingship. The last and greatest judge tries, in a sense, to turn judgeship into

---

[31] Buber refers to "the delinquency of Samuel himself in relation to the antidynastic temper of the judgeship (I Samuel 8:1-5), a delinquency not yet sufficiently recognized in its significance for the Samuelic crisis" (*Kingship of God* 76).

[32] "The scene [8:1-3] has been invented to explain the people's demand for a change in the form of government" (John van Seters, *In Search of History: Historiography in the Ancient World and the Origins of Biblical History* [New Haven: Yale University Press, 1983] 251).

kingship by making it hereditary. As a direct result he does turn judgeship into kingship. 1 Samuel 8:1-3 enables the transition from judgeship to kingship by making judgeship self-destruct!

So much for the *text's* blaming of Samuel. This work that the text begins is enthusiastically continued by a number of the recent literary readers.[33] They interpret Samuel's action in 8:1-3 as self-seeking and go on to read his subsequent career in the same way. Samuel's retrospect on his own career (12:2-5), read in a certain way, can be made to fit particularly well into this interpretation. These verses seem to me to be a part of his justification (continuing into 12:6-11) of judgeship *as a system*, but it is possible to read them as Samuel's acting up for having been thwarted, or even as an indication that he has not yet abandoned the hope that his sons may succeed him (see 12:2).

The thing for which commentators chiefly blame Samuel, however, is obstructing YHWH's will. Once YHWH has decided to give the people a king no one should gainsay him. In this sort of reading the question of the *merits* of YHWH's will remains unasked. The blaming of Samuel can be taken to great lengths. Polzin, for example, doubts that Samuel was accurately reporting YHWH's words when he delivered his warning to the people in 8:11-18. Maybe Samuel was "interpreting" to his own advantage, for YHWH would surely not be so inconsistent as to warn the people of the consequences of their request after he has decided to grant it.[34] So the burden of divine consistency is conveniently loaded onto Samuel (who, after all, is just a self-server). I believe I am as suspicious as the next person, but I confess that at this point my suspicion is drawn not to the faithfulness of Samuel's reporting but rather to the motives of the commentator.

This kind of reading avoids the real issues. It arises in part (at the risk of belaboring the point) from reading 1 Samuel as a new beginning, but it arises even more from a refusal to take a position on the most important question the text is putting to us, namely whether Israel's shift to kingship *was* a disaster. This is the question that the text has been struggling with at least since Gideon and Abimelech, and we need to keep it at the center of our attention. What we make of Samuel or any other character will depend on how we answer this prior question.

---

[33] Polzin (e.g., *Samuel and the Deuteronomist* 104–108) represents an extreme. But see also Eslinger, *Kingship of God* 260–262, 270–272; Meir Sternberg, *The Poetics of Biblical Narrative: Ideological Literature and the Drama of Reading* (Bloomington, Ind.: Indiana University Press, 1985) 94–98.

[34] *Samuel and the Deuteronomist* 82, 86–87.

The whole notion of Samuel's obstructing YHWH overlooks the fact that the two are in ideological agreement. They agree that the people's request for a king is wrong and ungrateful. They agree in disagreeing with "the law of the king" in Deuteronomy 17. Samuel repeats this agreed position in 10:19 and 12:16-20, and there is no reason to dispute his claim to speak in those places in YHWH's voice. The only point at which Samuel and YHWH differ in these chapters is that Samuel is determined to stop the disaster from happening if he can. Samuel wants to dissuade YHWH from doing what they both know to be bad.

To provide some context let us compare the scene with a quite different one. In Exod 32:9-10 YHWH, driven to fury by the episode of the Golden Calf, announces to Moses his intention of destroying Israel and making Moses' descendants into a new chosen people. Moses employs all his argumentative resources to dissuade YHWH from this course, and eventually wins. I have not read any commentary that castigates Moses for "obstructing the divine will" in this matter! This is perhaps because the commentators find nothing to admire in YHWH's plan of action in Exodus. They are glad Moses won the argument since their own very existence as Jews or Christians was at stake!

Samuel attempts to dissuade YHWH from just such a disastrous course. I read the way I do because I (and the reading communities of which I am a part) see as little to admire in YHWH's intention in 1 Samuel 8 as in Exodus 32. Mine is a pro-Samuel reading because it is an antimonarchical reading. Regardless of where the text stands—and I hope I have shown that it does not stand in one single place—*I* regard Israel's turn to kingship as a disaster in its real historic effects. You the reader will have to decide whether this taking of a position leads me astray or into a deeper understanding of what is going on in 1 Samuel.

Kingship incorporated into judgeship. Assigning blame for a disaster is not, however, the only narrative strategy in 1 Samuel 8–12. The other strategy is to suggest that there was no disaster. Though kingship makes some difference to Israel's national life, at the most basic level nothing has changed since kingship can be subsumed under the logic of judgeship. This gets expressed in part through the theoretical discourse of ch. 12, but mainly through the portrayal of Saul. In the following sections I will outline a variety of ways in which the logic of kingship is subsumed, in these chapters, under the logic of judgeship.

The speech of Samuel in 1 Samuel 12 has another function than to convict Israel of fault in seeking a king. Even more importantly, it evokes a covenantal understanding of Israel's whole history. Samuel brings the history of judgeship into the context of a sacred history governed by the conditional covenant, a history inaugurated by the rescue from Egypt and given its meaning by the covenant-making at Sinai

(12:6-8). YHWH's faithfulness to Israel in the time of the judges is of a piece with his covenant faithfulness from the beginning. The rest of the chapter then expressly draws the new kingship into this conditional covenant (12:13-15, 20-25; the technique of putting the people's repentance between these passages is very effective). Israel now has a king, but Israel with its king stands in exactly the same relationship to YHWH that it always did. "If" is still the operative word. If Israel, with its king, is faithful, it will prosper; if not, not.

My discussion to this point has hardly touched on the other major character in the account of Israel's turn to kingship, namely the king! This neglect of Saul is due to the text's own strategy of keeping theological discussion of kingship separate from accounts of the actual king. I have up to now been speaking almost entirely of ch. 8, before Saul appears, and of ch. 12, which ignores him.[35] In this section I shall deal mainly with chs. 9–11, and shall argue that the depiction of Saul remains mostly within the framework of judgeship.

(1) The text is insistent that Saul is chosen, like a judge, by YHWH's sole initiative. In one account Saul comes to Samuel as YHWH's chosen (9:16-17), in the other he is chosen by the sacred lot (10:20-22). Of course YHWH's choosing the *first* king does not negate the hereditary nature of kingship (and Deut 17:15 requires that the choice be YHWH's). But it is significant that in 1 Samuel 8–12 YHWH makes no commitment to Saul's *descendants* (contrast Deut 17:20).

There is in fact no hint of the theme of heredity in the account of Saul's rise. Through ch. 12 he has neither wife nor son and the issue of succession is not raised. The significance of this omission can be seen from the immediately following ch. 13. There Saul already has a grown son, and 13:13-14 tells us that YHWH, prior to the events of ch. 13, had intended Saul to found a dynasty! All these matters have been deferred until ch. 13, I suggest, as part of a strategy that excludes the hereditary principle in kingship from the theological work of chs. 8–12. The Saul of chs. 8–12 is less than a king.

(2) Saul's military activity is very much that of a judge. In 11:1-11 he faces a foreign incursion and responds by issuing the call to the tribes to assist him in repelling it. This is exactly the judge pattern. This incident forms part of a debate in chs. 8–12 about the nature of warfare. When the people in 8:20 demand a king who will "go out before us and fight our battles" the words suggest *offensive* warfare, such as kings engage in, rather than the wars of national liberation of the

---

[35] The lack of interest in Saul is revealed in a particularly striking way when he is not mentioned even in connection with his war against the Ammonites (12:12).

judges.[36] But when YHWH refers to warfare in 9:16 he does so entirely in the language of the judge stories: "He shall save my people from the hand of the Philistines."[37] Even when the scope of Saul's activity is extended to something apparently more permanent and general, the judge language is still kept: "save them from the hand of their enemies all around" (10:1, LXX).

The debate is concluded by Samuel, who lays special stress on the military issue. In 12:12 he suggests that it was only when faced with a military threat, from the Ammonites, that the people demanded a king. Samuel here adjusts the story a little, since when the people asked for a king "to fight our battles" (8:20) there was no specific threat. But his point is that the judges have proved adequate to deal with Israel's military needs, right up to his own defeat of the Philistines (12:11). Judgeship easily wins the military debate.

(3) A prominent aspect of Saul's relationship to the judges is the stress laid on his personal characteristics. When Samuel hints to Saul of his coming elevation Saul pleads his lowly origins (9:21), and this directly recalls Gideon's response to *his* call (Judg 6:15). The parallel underscores the divine freedom in the choice of Saul: YHWH does not choose as humans might. But this link with Gideon is double-edged. The Saul who begins like Gideon will end like Abimelech, pleading to be put to death (Judg 9:54; 1 Sam 31:4)![38] By contrast with his lowly origins, Saul's handsomeness and stature are mentioned when he first appears (9:2) and again in 10:23. Physical prowess as a positive recommendation is found sometimes in Judges: Samson's mission could hardly have been accomplished without his preternatural strength, and Jephthah is a "mighty warrior" (Judg 11:1).

(4) The Saul of these chapters also avoids the bad ways of a king as these have been defined in Deut 17:16-17, in the depiction of Gideon and Abimelech, and in Samuel's warning in 1 Sam 8:11-18. He does not acquire military capability, or wealth, or women. He does not behave as a tyrant, but forgives his enemies (11:12-13).

---

[36] Recall the textual issue in 4:1 over the difference between offensive and defensive warfare [57].

[37] Note also the reference to the "cry to YHWH" in the same verse.

[38] Along a quite different line, the question of Saul's origin raises ominous possibilities. His provenance from Gibeah calls to mind the hideous events related of that town in Judges 19–21. In the most literal way Saul is a product of the anarchy of the time of the judges. He must be the offspring of the rape-marriages by which Gibeah and Benjamin were repopulated! Just as the book of Ruth stands in for the missing birth story of David [106–109], so Judges 19–21 accounts for Saul's origin. The contrast between the two kings could hardly be more effective.

(5) For the most part Saul is under Samuel's authority. This is seen above all in ch. 12 when Samuel simply sidelines Saul and keeps the reins of national power firmly in his own hands—even announcing that he himself will continue to guide the nation in the future (12:23). In 11:7 he *accompanies* Saul to the war against the Ammonites. Even in the exploit by which he is to prove himself Saul, it seems, cannot manage alone.[39]

In contrast to all these points Saul does in chs. 9–11 begin to assert himself as king, but only to a very slight extent. There is a striking difference between 10:8 and 10:7 [85–88]. In 10:8 Samuel addresses the new king as an underling, simply ordering him about, but in 10:7 Samuel allows Saul the freedom of a king: "do whatever you see fit to do." There is, besides, a compelling moment at the conclusion of the Ammonite war. Seeking a judgment on an important matter (the fate of Saul's opponents), the people turn to Samuel, but it is Saul who renders the judgment. His words are those of a king who has taken power. Kingship is already breaking free of the unnatural theological constraints imposed on it, and will continue to do so as we read beyond ch. 12.

One narrative possibility after 1 Samuel 7 would have been the death of Samuel and the beginning of a new judge cycle, and though the story moves in a quite different direction 1 Samuel 8–12 does seem to take the shape of a judge cycle. It does so, though, in a curiously double way. Along the more obvious trajectory (ch. 11) the people (a portion of them) fall under Ammonite oppression, send out an appeal (cf. the "cry to YHWH"), and find a deliverer in Saul. There is nothing about apostasy in this story but otherwise Saul functions as an ordinary judge in an ordinary judge cycle.

The other trajectory is more interesting. Israel (after Samuel's quasi-death) falls into apostasy *by asking for a king.* YHWH does in fact characterize the request as apostasy in exactly the terms familiar from the judge cycles: "forsaking me and serving other gods" (8:8). The punishment must then be kingship itself, perceived as oppressive (8:11-17).[40] Especially striking is the allusion to the cry to YHWH at the end of Samuel's warning: "And in that day you will cry out because of your king . . . but YHWH will not answer you" (v. 18).

---

[39] We should recall also the confusion of identity between Samuel and *šā'ûl* (Saul) in 1:28 [56, 111]. Perhaps the people who asked for Saul did not need to— they already possessed, in Samuel, the one "asked for"!

[40] In a similar way Abimelech's kingship could be thought of as the punishment in the new judge cycle that seems to be beginning in Judg 8:33-34.

Samuel and the Limits of Character

Nowhere is the narrative strain in chs. 8–12 clearer than in the presentation of the character Samuel. The development of character in biblical narrative, I have suggested, is tightly constrained by the necessities of plot [6–7]. This applies to Samuel in an extreme degree. Here I gather up the threads from the preceding sections and examine Samuel's plot functions a little further. Even up to 1 Samuel 7 he has lived two not fully consistent lives, in chs. 1–4 and ch. 7. From being a temple servant and then a prophet he has to turn into the greatest of the judges so that judgeship can end on a positive note. The latter agenda would be best served by letting him die in ch. 7, but the text has other needs that require his survival. This makes nonsense of ch. 7, according to which he keeps the Philistines at bay and judges Israel all his days (7:13, 15). The Philistines come back soon after ch. 7 (by implication as soon as 9:16), and what meaning can his "judging" have when a king has replaced him?[41]

Living on, Samuel plays multiple roles. Because he is the *last* of the judges it is for him to enact the transition from judgeship to kingship and thus to supply an appearance of continuity between the two systems. More than this, he must be the *effective cause* of the coming of kingship, though this means stepping out of character and contradicting everything for which he has stood and will stand. He must even be an enthusiastic supporter of Saul's kingship, a role to which I can do full justice only in later chapters [87, 119–121]. Yet while he lives he must also continue to represent and struggle for the old order that is passing, trying to maintain that order even if it means resisting YHWH's will. All these roles he plays in chs. 8–12, and later he will have still others.

Like Jotham before him and Jonathan after, Samuel is obliged by the exigencies of the plot to become a paradoxical character who provides the only means of solving a narrative problem that his very existence creates or aggravates. Jotham created a problem by surviving as legitimate heir to Israel's proto-kingship, but as heir he could solve the problem by repudiating the kingship, by in effect abdicating [49–50].

---

[41] Van Seters (*In Search of History* 353) agrees with my view of Samuel as "the last of the victorious judges," and also notes the discrepancy with Samuel's later career (though rather weakly, it seems to me). He is very much in touch with the logic of the text when he goes on to remark, "The author . . . really regards 'the days of Samuel' as closed at the end of chap. 7 but must have a new situation of need to account for the rise of Saul."

Jonathan will have an analogous role in achieving the impossible transition from Saul to David [98–99]. So with Samuel. As a surviving judge ("all the days of his life," 7:15) he seems to make the beginning of kingship impossible, but at the same time he is the only one who can begin it.

Given the variety of contradictory roles that Samuel must play, can we expect any sort of coherence in his character as it is presented to us? Can we apply psychological measures and other standards of character portrayal that we have internalized as readers in the Western literary tradition? In one sense I would say "no," and this seems to me to render pointless the assessments (usually negative) of Samuel by some recent commentators. But in a more profound sense I want to answer "yes." The search for psychological coherence in a character like Samuel, though it is doomed to failure, remains of vital importance *because it is a search for psychological coherence in the biblical text, in the community that created it to live by, and ultimately in ourselves as culturally shaped by the Bible.* The rifts in a character like Samuel are rifts in what we might call "the biblical unconscious,"[42] which has fed our own unconscious. So a thorough psychological study of Samuel as the Bible presents him, though it could not be based on a mimetic understanding of character, is much to be desired. It would need to include his early life, the childhood abuse he suffered [306–307], and his precocious rise to national leadership. I have not done such a study; it is one of the things I leave to you. In a certain sense, though, this whole book is a psychological study of "Samuel," as the name not of a character but of a large piece of the biblical tradition.

A Lost Ideal?

Judgeship versus kingship. I have traced in this chapter how the Extended Book of Judges deals with the issue of government in Israel. This book, which covers the entire period of judgeship in Israel, comes to a double conclusion. It decides that judgeship was good and that it represented the will of YHWH during this period, but it also comes to accept kingship as another expression of the will of YHWH, and strives to bring the two dispensations into a single view.

---

[42] By analogy with Fredric Jameson's "political unconscious." See Fredric Jameson, *The Political Unconscious: Narrative as a Socially Symbolic Act* (Ithaca, N.Y.: Cornell University Press, 1981).

Recent critical response to the complexity of the Deuteronomic History has tended to use the method of redaction criticism. Especially in 1 Samuel 8–12 scholars think of an editor bringing together a pro- and an antimonarchical source.[43] The fundamental problem with this view is its assumption that there was once a time when people—the creators of the hypothetical sources—found the issue of government in Israel simple, so that they could give one or another simple account of it. I do not believe the issues were ever simple.

Another approach sees the text, however it came into being, as achieving a theological reconciliation between judgeship and monarchy. An excellent example is the work of Dennis McCarthy,[44] who uses historical tools with a fine critical sense and holds the theological achievement of the editors in high respect. This piece influenced me greatly when I first began to work on these texts. I now believe, however, that a resolution or balancing of such a profound contradiction as exists in Israel's view of monarchy did not and could not occur. It is not a balanced view that the Extended Book of Judges achieves. Its conclusion is heavily weighted on the side of judgeship.

More satisfying is the account of Buber. Though, like the redaction critics, he sees the text as a combination of preexisting pro- and antimonarchical books,[45] and at times speaks like McCarthy of an editorial "balancing" of points of view, he goes a good deal further when he speaks of "two antithetical parts (being) true simultaneously."[46] Best of all, he locates the text's creation in the urgent debates of the postexilic situation, when Israelites were occupied with the question: What do the old traditions about monarchy mean now that the monarchy is no more? In this context, the final form "had to succeed and did succeed."[47]

"Success," however, is too optimistic a word. The Extended Book of Judges is certainly an extraordinary performance. It talks around the Lévi-Straussian contradiction magnificently, and it gives the sense of a resolution achieved. But it does not really account for what kingship is, so that more theological work remains to be done, work that will call this first "resolution" into question. We will find (see my next chapter) that the resolution can be achieved only at the expense of

[43] Norman K. Gottwald, *The Hebrew Bible: A Socio-literary Introduction* (Philadelphia: Fortress, 1985) 312 and bibliography, 635–636.

[44] "The Inauguration of Monarchy in Israel," *Interp.* 27 (1973) 401–412.

[45] E.g., *Kingship of God* 68.

[46] Ibid. 83.

[47] Ibid. Also excellent on the exilic context is Robert G. Boling, *Judges: Introduction, Translation, and Commentary.* AB 7 (Garden City, N.Y.: Doubleday, 1975) 278; he sees a debate whose terms are "monarchy," "tribal confederation," and "Mosaic ideal."

splitting Saul into two and of separating monarchy in general from Davidic monarchy.

In a quite different sense the Extended Book of Judges does not account for what *judgeship* is either, and this will be the focus of my concluding remarks in this chapter.

The God of the gaps. "Something has been attempted . . . but it has failed." This is Buber's judgment on Israel's turn to monarchy.[48] Both within the Bible and in a long tradition of its interpretation the time before the rise of the monarchy has been regarded as an *ideal* time. Israel's relation to YHWH then was a right relation, as it never was after. But what was the nature of this ideal? What specific content can we give to it?

An ideal premonarchical time must include the time of the judges along with the time of Moses and Joshua, so rule by judges ought to be presented as somehow an ideal form of rule. But at this point, it seems to me, the narrative depiction of the time of the judges (my Extended Book of Judges) very largely fails us. We cannot perceive the judges as embodying an ideal because the text tells us almost nothing about *how* they ruled. They "judged Israel" for long periods, but virtually nothing is said of these periods. Nearly all the recorded incidents in the judges' lives relate to their calling and their wars.[49] One possibility is that the major judges express an ideal in that each one recapitulates the story of Israel's salvation, the passage from bondage to freedom experienced archetypically in the exodus. But after the exodus we get *some* indication of how Moses and Joshua governed Israel. There is simply no hint of how the judges governed. Perhaps what was ideal about the judges was that under their rule nothing happened—which may not be a bad ideal!

Buber raises a different possibility, an intriguing one, namely that the ideal is to be found not in the rule of the judges but in the gaps between them. These gaps give the impression of being a theological contrivance. The larger biblical tradition about a judge period gives no hint of systemic discontinuity and seems to assume a continuous sequence like that of the minor judges.[50] But Buber sees the gaps as essential. For him the ideal is no human government at all, "a commonwealth for which an invisible government is sufficient."[51] The possibility of this

---

[48] *Kingship of God* 83.

[49] Only with Deborah and Samuel do we get any sense of ongoing judicial activity: Judg 4:4-5; 1 Sam 7:15-17.

[50] See 1 Chron 17:10 (the parallel 2 Sam 7:11 should probably be read accordingly); 2 Kings 23:22; Isa 1:26; Ruth 1:1.

[51] *Kingship of God* 75 (cf. 59–60, 64–65).

ideal is expressed "by the fact of the pause, for a time, between *shophet* [judge] and *shophet* . . . a fact which was inseparable from the institution of the judgeship. . . ."[52]

Buber's suggestion certainly concurs with what I have called the judge theory. After the death of a judge (just as initially after the death of Joshua) there is no provision for continued leadership. Israel comes under the direct rule of YHWH, whatever this may mean, and is freed from all human systems of government. A new judge arises only if Israel falls away from YHWH, which in fact it always does; but so important is the ideal of "invisible government" that it is renewed when each judge dies. Perhaps this time Israel will get it right.

Buber's suggestion seems to me of great importance, and it will be the basis for my further exploration of these issues, but it does not get us any farther in giving any positive content to the ideal. If in the accounts of the careers of the judges there are very few depictions of ideal government, in the gaps there are none.

"Not done in Israel." Any evocation of the premonarchical time as an ideal in the Extended Book of Judges is achieved mostly by negative means: by showing the evils of the other possibilities. Israel's experience with Eli's sons and with Samuel's places any kind of hereditary leadership in a bad light. Samuel sets out the evils of kingship in an unusually explicit way in 1 Sam 8:11-18.[53]

This brings us to the important concept of "that which is not done in Israel." In 2 Sam 13:12 Tamar speaks of rape (or perhaps incest, or both?) as "not done in Israel," conjuring up a national ideal in which certain evils have no place. Judges 19:30 is similar: also in reference to rape—in this case turned into murder—the Levite asks if such a thing as the treatment of his wife has ever happened in Israel before. Might we read 1 Sam 8:11-18 as a listing by Samuel of things that are "not done" in some such ideal Israel? I shall return to this question in a moment, from a new angle.

The egalitarian society. A powerful recent trend in scholarship gives political precision to Buber's ideal, and it is a trend of which, given the political aims of my book, I take particular notice. Norman Gottwald sees premonarchic Israel as, in its theoretical self-understanding and to a large extent in practice, an egalitarian society.[54] Emerging largely as a result of revolt against the Canaanite city-states and their kings, Israel

---

[52] Ibid. 83 (cf. 76–77, 84).

[53] More mildly, Deut 17:16-17 alludes to evils into which kings *might* fall.

[54] Norman K. Gottwald, *The Tribes of Yahweh: A Sociology of the Religion of Liberated Israel 1250–1050 B.C.E.* (Maryknoll, N.Y.: Orbis, 1979).

determined to be a radically different kind of society. Gottwald's theory has been accepted in principle by many other scholars, including, from a feminist perspective, Carol Meyers [146–147].

As Gottwald freely admits, the biblical text gives limited support to his view; there are few indications of such an egalitarian society. But there are some. Judges 5, though its ancient poetry is hard to interpret, includes much to suggest a peasant revolt against a stratified, statist economy.[55] Jotham's fable (9:7-15) strongly suggests an ethos of "from each according to his/her ability." 1 Samuel 1–12 adds to these indications not only the warnings of Samuel against forced labor but also the reversal of unequal social and political relationships in the Song of Hannah.[56] These four passages from the Extended Book of Judges—Judges 5; 9:7-15; 1 Sam 2:1-10; 8:11-18—though they are insufficient to determine the ethos of the whole book are cumulatively impressive in giving some sense of reality to Israel's ancient ideal. These indications of an ideal society dovetail with "what is not done in Israel." In "Israel," Samuel implies, no individual can make others work for him. In "Israel," according to Jotham, unproductive parasites are not tolerated.

Israel and the nations. Another indicator of ideal Israel is that it is not "like the nations." This form of words is repeatedly used in relation to the possibility of kingship—one of the first things to say about having a king is that it would conform Israel to the nations round about (Deut 17:14; 1 Sam 8:5, 20). But again this is only a negative indication, not developed in the text as a positive ideal. There is little about how non-monarchical Israel works out its existence in ways different from its monarchical neighbors. At most we can perhaps pick up a few hints: "Israel" does not exact tribute (Judg 3:15) or drive people to starvation (6:1-6).

The only respect in which the issue of Israel and the nations *is* consistently stressed in the Extended Book of Judges is in Israel's need for *political independence*, its need not to be occupied or dominated by any of the nations. But this seems a quite commonplace aspiration, not something that would make Israel in any way ideal. Gottwald's Israel likewise fights fiercely for independence. But Gottwald goes on to the subsequent question: Independent to what end? To be in what way different?

In not pressing this question, in asserting the need for independence as an end in itself, the biblical text invites the conclusion that the

---

[55] It is important to note that only in the Deborah cycle is Israel in conflict with indigenous Canaanite kings. The other judges face external enemies.

[56] See Gottwald's own reading, *Tribes* 534–540.

only thing keeping Israel from its ideal is its subjugation to foreigners. Yet it also carefully rules out such a conclusion! Through the logic of the judge cycles the text insists that foreign domination comes from the failure of the ideal, not vice versa. The fugitive ideal is not, it seems, political separation and independence as a nation among nations. The ideal is to be in some sense not a "nation" at all.

Conclusion. I break off here with the provisional conclusion that the postexilic Israel whose consciousness the biblical text expresses has forgotten its founding ideal but continues to be haunted by it. At the end of the book I will resume this discussion of a lost ideal and give a particular sense to this "haunting" [273–281]. The Extended Book of Judges evokes an ideal that, with the exception of a few notable passages, is almost vacuous, whether in Buber's or in Gottwald's terms. But this has not prevented the sense of an ideal past from persisting into later generations of Bible readers, and even into our own day.

In his treatment of Deuteronomy to Judges Polzin sees in Judges a complete breakdown of the ideological certainties that were encouraged and explored in Deuteronomy and Joshua.[57] The unpredictability of YHWH in Judges prevents any ideology from finding a grounding. Polzin's discussion is profound, and adds a dimension to my analysis. Part of the reason why Israel cannot get in touch with, cannot "get a fix on" its ideal is precisely YHWH's unpredictability. For YHWH's radical freedom is an intrinsic part of Israel's ideal![58] YHWH's unpredictability is the correlate of the radical human freedom that haunts Israel.

Gabriel Josipovici provides another helpful angle.[59] Like most recent readers he experiences the book of Judges negatively. (For him it marks the "faltering" of the narrative rhythm that uniquely characterizes the Bible.) But he interestingly refers to Judges as "an attempt to revert to an Edenic world,"[60] and suggests that its message is "we cannot return to Eden simply by doing what is right in our own eyes."[61] The ideal with which Israel has to live consists of doing what is right in the eyes of an unpredictable and invisible ruler. On the other hand

---

[57] Polzin, *Moses and the Deuteronomist* 146–204; for a useful summary see pp. 210–212.

[58] There is a harsh reminder of this in 1 Sam 6:19–7:2. The Philistines cannot hold onto the ark, the symbol of YHWH's presence, but this does not mean that Israel can simply "have" it either.

[59] *The Book of God: A Response to the Bible* (New Haven and London: Yale University Press, 1988) 108–131.

[60] Ibid. 125.

[61] Ibid. 126.

it is utterly lost by doing what is right in one's own eyes. But where is the line that separates these options?

Having lost touch with its historical ideal, postexilic Israel has trouble answering the questions posed by its present experience and cannot adequately explain to itself how the present emerged from the ideal past.[62] This is the plight of the Deuteronomic historians.

I shall later ask what it is about this plight that inhibits Israel from presenting its past in class terms in an adequate way [103–104]. And at the end of the book I shall look further (with help from Jacques Derrida) at the negative, tragic aspect of the historians' plight [274–278]. For now I simply underscore the pathological symptoms of that plight. Unable to grasp their ideal past in a positive way, they turn it into an anti-ideal. This is what happens in Judges 17–21, where the narrator paints a picture of Israel's unique freedom—and wants at any price to free Israel from it! The Israel of these chapters, far from being ideal, does exactly those things that are "not done in Israel" (19:30). Then in 1 Sam 8:1-3 judgeship is made responsible for the coming of kingship—the ideal is blamed for the fall!—and in the next book of the Deuteronomic History, to which we now turn, a different ideal will be substituted for the one that has been lost.

[62] At the risk of trivializing, let me retell a joke from Douglas Adams that gets the point: "'It's at times like this . . . that I really wish I'd listened to what my mother told me when I was young.' 'Why, what did she tell you?' 'I don't know. I didn't listen!'" (*The More Than Complete Hitchhiker's Guide* [New York: Wing Books, 1989] 52).

Chapter 4

1 SAMUEL 13–31 IN THE BOOK OF
THE EVERLASTING COVENANT

One of the indications that there is a major break after 1 Samuel 12 is the fewness of the narrative threads left untied at that point. Let us review them.

Once again we expect Samuel to die. The reason he outlived his first natural death, in ch. 7, was apparently to get kingship started. This he has now done. After he has delivered his valediction in ch. 12, what more can there be for him to do? Yet his closing words (12:23) indicate that he will still live on as teacher and intercessor. The reader wonders how this will work out.

Saul will presumably continue to be king. He has made a good start, but we wonder, in view of Samuel's dire predictions in 8:11-18, whether this will continue. A few other questions linger about Saul and his office. Is he the "anointed" referred to in 2:35? Will the prediction of 9:16 be fulfilled, that Saul will deliver Israel from the Philistines? The Philistines have been out of the picture since Samuel defeated them in ch. 7. Will they come back? The ways in which these questions will be answered will thwart the reader's expectations and confirm the sense of a cleft between the Extended Book of Judges and the Book of the Everlasting Covenant.

There is one other leftover narrative thread, one so thin and frayed as to be hardly a thread at all. In 10:8 Samuel ordered Saul to precede him to Gilgal, where after "seven days" Samuel would offer sacrifice. Has this been forgotten? Surely much more than a week must have passed between the events of 10:8 and ch. 13. Or was the expectation of 10:8 fulfilled when Saul and Samuel were together at Gilgal in 11:14-15 and sacrifice was offered? This thread has in fact been neither tied up nor forgotten. It is a measure of the tenuousness of the narrative connection that direct continuity between ch. 13 and what preceded it hangs by just this thread. . . .

The Everlasting Covenant

The name of the series to which this book belongs is *Berit Olam*, "Everlasting Covenant." "Covenant" is a key term in both the Jewish Bible and the New Testament (the word "testament" is a synonym for "covenant"). The adjective "everlasting," though, points to the fact that there are covenants that are not everlasting.

Everlasting covenants in the Bible are often referred to as "unconditional." They are of a type opposite to the conditional type of covenant to which Samuel appealed in ch. 12. YHWH's covenant with the people Israel, established through Moses, is almost invariably presented under the sign of the conditional, the "if." This is the covenant that is operative throughout the Extended Book of Judges, right up to its very last verse (12:25, "If you do wickedly"). The next piece of the Deuteronomic work, to which we turn in this chapter, has as its theme the establishment of an unconditional, everlasting covenant.

God enters into a number of everlasting covenants in the Jewish Bible—with the new humanity after the flood (Genesis 9), with the descendants of Abraham (Genesis 17), with the priestly house of Phinehas (Numbers 25). But the everlasting covenant perhaps most central to Israelite consciousness (and, through the theology of Jesus as Messiah, to Christian consciousness) is the one with the house of David.

This is why I call 1 Samuel 13–2 Samuel 7 the Book of the Everlasting Covenant. The end point, 2 Samuel 7, is the classic narrative expression of the everlasting covenant with David's house (e.g., "established forever," v. 16). But the appropriate starting point is not so clear. Why should we attach the Deuteronomic summary in 1 Samuel 12 to what precedes rather than what follows? Most of the Deuteronomic summaries (2 Samuel 7, for instance) have a prospective and well as a retrospective function. But 1 Samuel 12 hardly does, and it conspicuously does not look forward to *hereditary* kingship. So I take 1 Samuel 13 as the beginning of the new "book."

The correctness of this choice is strongly confirmed by the fact that the very first issue taken up in ch. 13 is the lastingness (or otherwise) of Saul's kingship. The key verses are 13:13-14. According to how we translate v. 13 (see below) YHWH had, or might have, "established [Saul's] kingdom forever." This precise form of words belongs to the technical vocabulary that will be used in 2 Samuel 7 for the promise to David. In fact, however, Saul's kingship "will not continue" by reason of a cultic offense of which Samuel has declared Saul guilty. The promise that David will receive at the end of the Book of the Everlasting Covenant is expressly denied to Saul at the beginning.

1 Samuel 13:1–16:13: The Rejection of Saul

There are two accounts of Saul's rejection, one in 1 Sam 13:8-15, the other in 1 Samuel 15. 1 Samuel 13–15 is often entitled "the rejection of Saul," and this makes sense because Saul's rejection is the most important topic. But there is other material in these chapters. Most of it concerns Saul's son Jonathan (13:2-4, 16, 22; 14:1-46), with whom I will deal later [93–99]. I concentrate here on the two rejection passages, providing only summary accounts of the other material as it is relevant to my purpose. In fact I choose to define the section as 13:1–16:13, since the account of the anointing of David in 16:1-13 is necessary for understanding Saul's rejection.

The first rejection account. There is a preamble in 13:1-7 that ominously prepares for Saul's fall. It begins with the formal notice of his reign (v. 1), confirming our sense that the reign had not really begun in chs. 9–12. This regnal notice is not quite the first in the Bible. The first was Abimelech's in Judg 9:22, which was very brief, mentioning only the length of his reign (which was also brief). The brevity no doubt indicated a lack of enthusiasm about this king.

Saul's notice is a bit more expansive in form, including his age at accession as well as the length of his reign. This still does not indicate great enthusiasm: most of the later regnal notices will also include at least the king's capital city. Did Saul have a capital? Was it the disgraceful Gibeah?[1] But what is really alarming about 13:1 is that it fails to give even the information it is formally designed to give. Where Saul's age ought to be the text simply leaves a gap, and most readers agree that there must be another gap in the statement of the length of his reign. This is given as "two years," which seems impossibly short. Scholars surmise that something like "twenty-two" was intended.

Most commentators blandly tell us that the numbers have "dropped out" (so NRSV note), as if there were something innocent about the process. What we are dealing with here are the vital statistics of the first

---

[1] 10:26, cf. Judges 19–21.

king of Israel to be chosen by YHWH and anointed in his name! If they were wanted, they would be there; if they had gotten lost they would have been found again. We will never know, but we may suspect. Did someone decide that these data should not be part of Israel's memory, that they should be consigned to oblivion? The sorry state of 13:1 is an initial marker of the direction Saul's fortunes will soon take.

1 Samuel 13:2-7 tells of a military campaign that, after initial success, turns against Israel and Saul. The enemy are the Philistines! This is a point of decision in the text. 1 Samuel 9:16, the prediction that Saul will save Israel from the Philistines, is remembered and assumes significance, while 7:13, the record of Samuel's defeat of the Philistines, is forgotten. In the event 9:16 will prove untrue. The Philistines will be a major factor in Saul's reign to its very end, but he will conspicuously fail to save Israel from their hands. His failure is adumbrated already in this report of the first campaign.

Next comes the first account of Saul's rejection (13:8-15). Most recent translations (like NRSV) translate the actual words of rejection along these lines: ". . . you have not kept the commandment of YHWH. . . . YHWH *would have* established your kingdom over Israel forever, but now your kingdom will not continue" (vv. 13-14). This would mean that Saul was set a test on which the permanence of his dynasty depended, and he failed it.[2]

But there is no real warrant for "would have." The Hebrew is the simple past tense, "established." It is true that Hebrew has no separate way of expressing such modal meanings as "would," "might," etc., and uses the simple tenses when it intends a modal meaning. So "would have" is a valid translation. But it is not a necessary one. There is no reason why we should not simply read, "Just now YHWH established your kingdom over Israel forever. But now your kingdom will not continue." This would mean that when YHWH established Saul as king he made with him an everlasting covenant.

Logically speaking, regardless of what 13:13-14 may intend, it is the latter translation that expresses the truth of the matter. What else is YHWH doing in making someone a king than entering into a covenant with his dynasty? This is how Deut 17:20 sees kingship, and how the Gideon-Abimelech stories see it. This dynastic aspect of monarchy, as we noted, was carefully repressed in the theological work of 1 Samuel 8–12, but it has not taken long to resurface! The NRSV translation

---

[2] A change in the Hebrew vowels would allow the translation, "If you had kept the commandment of YHWH . . . then YHWH would have established your kingdom over Israel forever." In this case the sense of a test is even stronger.

amounts to a sort of theological nonsense: it says in effect, "If you had done thus and so you would have entered a relationship with no 'ifs'."

The latitude in the translation corresponds to uncertainty in the theology. We have here identified, I believe, the major theological work of the Book of the Everlasting Covenant. Monarchy is inherently dynastic. If YHWH approved Israel's monarchy, why then do its later kings not trace their descent from its first king? Why Davidides, not Saulides? Did YHWH swear an everlasting covenant with Saul? If so, how could it be annulled? If not, was Saul's kingship real, was YHWH "for real" in approving it?

In the previous chapter I identified a contradiction[3] in the deep structure of the Extended Book of Judges:

1. Human monarchy is alien to the religion of YHWH, but
2. Israel became a human monarchy under YHWH.

In the Book of the Everlasting Covenant we have found an equally basic contradiction:

1. Monarchy is inherently dynastic, but
2. Israel's monarchy is not traced from its first king.

The great number of different ways the text will try to resolve this contradiction is an indicator of its irresolubility in principle. But the textual work has to be done: the impression must be created that the contradiction has been resolved.

Samuel announces that Saul is rejected because he sinned against YHWH, but the charge cannot be made to stick, or only on the flimsiest grounds.[4]

This is where the slender thread joins 13:8 to 10:8. According to 10:8 Samuel was coming to Gilgal to offer two kinds of sacrifice, "burnt offerings" and "sacrifices of well-being," and Saul was to wait seven days in Gilgal for Samuel's arrival. Upon his arrival, Samuel would offer the sacrifices and tell Saul what to do next. Before we can understand 13:8-12 we must look again very closely at 10:8.

To begin with, it begs the question of what is to happen if Samuel is late. "Wait seven days until I come" is not strictly meaningful. What is needed is, "If I come within seven days, then . . . ; if not, then . . . ." In the absence of other indication Saul ought to be released after seven days from whatever obligation he was under.

---

[3] This is a contradiction of the kind on which Lévi-Strauss bases his study of mythology [6–7, 58].

[4] David M. Gunn, *The Fate of King Saul: An Interpretation of a Biblical Story.* JSOT.S 14 (Sheffield: JSOT Press, 1980) 33–40, reaches a conclusion similar to mine though he does not refer to 11:14-15.

Next, what is the obligation? It is hard to say. Later the text may seem to say that Saul was obliged *not to offer sacrifices on his own account*, but this is a big jump to make on the basis of 10:8 alone. If we follow this line of thought it takes us first to 11:14-15. These verses go a long way toward satisfying the expectations of 10:8. Samuel, Saul, and the people are together at Gilgal, and they offer "sacrifices of well-being." Everything is in place except the burnt offering. But 13:8-12 seems to disregard 11:14-15 and refer directly back to 10:8. Saul and the people at Gilgal wait seven days. Samuel does not come. Saul collects the material for both kinds of sacrifice. He offers the burnt offering, and instantly Samuel arrives. The reader suspects a setup here. If only Saul had offered first the sacrifices of well-being. By the time he was finished, Samuel would have arrived!

"You have not kept the commandment of YHWH your God" (13:13). For this claim by Samuel to carry any conviction at all, the "commandment" must be understood as follows: "Thou shalt not, as unauthorized personnel—even as a king—offer the burnt offering. If authorized personnel are unavailable, wait as long as it takes." If this is what the commandment means, the text fails to say so! And why should Saul not reply that, having been frustrated in his attempt to follow Samuel's instruction in 10:8, he had fallen back on Samuel's more general command in 10:7 and followed his own best judgment?

Yet Saul appears to know that what he did was wrong or irregular. "I only did it because I was absolutely forced," he says (v. 12). How did he know, how was he supposed to know, that he was unauthorized to perform a certain kind of sacrifice? This whole line of interpretation is quite unsatisfying, and I shall propose another, but only after looking at the second rejection account.

The second rejection account. The story in ch. 15 can be more briefly summarized, since this time it is clear what Saul did wrong. The chapter begins with an oracle of YHWH that Samuel delivers to Saul. Saul is to settle an old score for YHWH by exterminating the Amalekites. Saul has good success in this task, but the reader easily spots that in disposing of the fruits of victory (vv. 8-9) Saul has not followed the letter of v. 3. He has not fully exterminated the Amalekites. YHWH also has noted this, and tells Samuel that he has "changed his mind" about making Saul king (v. 11).

Samuel goes to Saul and finds him in a mood of self-congratulation; he believes he has done what YHWH wanted (vv. 13, 15, 20-21). Samuel delivers YHWH's verdict (see v. 16) and fills it out amply. He crushes Saul's justification of his actions and delivers an announcement of rejection (vv. 26, 28) even more powerful than the one in 13:13-14. Again Saul confesses his fault (vv. 24-25, 30) and desperately seeks a reconciliation with Yhwh and with Samuel; but in the final words of the chapter the narrator repeats in his own voice Yhwh's "change of mind" about making Saul king.

Though there is no uncertainty here over what Saul did wrong, the question surely arises of whether the punishment fits the crime. Saul meant to do Yhwh's will and thought he saw a way of doing it that would give Yhwh even more honor. Why waste the animals when the best of them could be offered to Yhwh? Why not make an example of Agag to show what Yhwh does to his enemies? Both Agag and the animals would have finished up just as dead. Again the reader is sufficiently dissatisfied to look for a different level of understanding.

"Samuel grieved over Saul" (15:35, cf. 16:1; the term is one often used for mourning a death). This grief is perhaps surprising, since in delivering the messages of rejection Samuel has shown little sympathy for Saul. On the other hand, in 15:11 Samuel was angry over Yhwh's change of mind, which suggests that he opposes the rejection of Saul. He does distinctly soften toward Saul *after* he has delivered the message of rejection, agreeing at least to help Saul save face (15:30-31). I shall shortly suggest a reason for Samuel's grief.

The narrator tells us also that Samuel and Saul part forever after this scene (v. 35). The form of words is worth comment: "Samuel did not see Saul again until the day of his death." One takes this to refer to Samuel's death (since he died first), with the meaning "Samuel never saw Saul again." But a more pointed reading is possible, "Samuel did not see Saul again until the day of *Saul's* death," anticipating Saul's calling up of Samuel's spirit on the eve of Saul's death in battle (ch. 28).[5]

The anointing of David. In both the rejection accounts Samuel has made reference to Saul's successor, whom Yhwh has already chosen but whose identity remains unknown. Without delay the text moves in 16:1-13 to the identifying and anointing of this successor.

As before, kingmaking is Samuel's job, and Yhwh summons him to it in 16:1. The opening words have a surprising abruptness: "How long will you grieve over Saul, (given that) I have rejected him?"[6] This seems harsh, since Samuel has taken on the burden of announcing Saul's rejection when Yhwh seemed reluctant to do so in his own voice. There is tension here between Yhwh and Samuel. Samuel is far from willing to be part of the anointing of a new king and tries to get out of it. Yhwh has to go to some lengths to secure Samuel's compliance (vv. 2-4). Is this

---

[5] Actually they do meet again in the flesh in 19:18-24.
[6] NRSV does not have a connector like "given that," but most translations do.

just a continuation of Samuel's old resistance to kingship or has he become really attached to Saul?

Throughout the whole anointing scene YHWH pays Samuel back, in a childish and self-contradictory way, for his reluctance. Samuel tries to second-guess YHWH's choice among Jesse's sons. He judges by outward appearance. The question of whether physical attributes have anything to do with fitness for leadership has arisen with some of the judges and especially in the choice of Saul [67], and it can scarcely be said to have been resolved in any particular way. Here YHWH claims a knowledge that makes all human impressions irrelevant, and implies that Samuel is foolish to be guided by such impressions (16:7). But then YHWH chooses someone whom Samuel has not had a chance to see! Perhaps if Samuel could have seen David along with the other sons he would have got it right. The narrator, at any rate, is very taken with David's outward appearance (v. 12).

What we have here is another example of YHWH becoming irrational about the choosing of kings and Samuel taking the blame. One might go so far as to wonder whether YHWH made his decision impromptu, whether he had previously decided on Eliab or one of the others, or made no decision at all, and hit upon David simply in order to go against Samuel's preference. This would fit with the striking reluctance to *name* David. He is not named in the anticipations in 13:14 and 15:28, and in the anointing scene we are not given his name until the last possible moment (16:13b), *after* he has been anointed!

An uneven playing field. It is not possible to make a sensible comparison between the monarchies of Saul and David, for different rules apply to them from the outset. Davidic monarchy represents a *new* divine dispensation in Israel, not a continuation of the dispensation under which Saul reigned.[7]

No sin by David or his descendants can rupture the everlasting covenant: "When [David's offspring] commits iniquity, I will punish him. . . . But my covenant loyalty will not turn from him as I turned it from Saul . . ." (2 Sam 7:14-15). There could not be a clearer statement that Saul's kingship was under different rules from David's. There is a vast contrast between what counts as sin for Saul and for David. The episode with Uriah and Bathsheba (2 Samuel 11–12) seems expressly designed to demonstrate how hideous sin can be and still not turn YHWH's loyalty away from David's house. The accounts of Saul's rejection seem equally designed to demonstrate the smallness of the sin that "justifies" the rejection.

---

[7] One might suggest as an analogy the new dispensation in creation in Gen 9:1-7, as it changes the rules laid down in Genesis 1.

The contrast in YHWH's treatment of Saul and David is beautifully illustrated by a startling contradiction in ch. 15. In announcing to Saul YHWH's rejection of him Samuel states that this is YHWH's *final* word. God, after all, cannot "change his mind" (v. 29). But YHWH *has* changed his mind in v. 11, as the narrator confirms in v. 35.[8] Translations like the NRSV try to hide the contradiction by their choice of words ("regret" in v. 11, "be sorry" in v. 35). There is no warrant for these different translations: the word is the same and means the same in all three verses. One cannot escape the conclusion that the translators are simply trying to avoid the scandal of the Bible's contradicting itself.

The point, I suggest, is simply that YHWH can change his mind about Saul but not about David. YHWH's choice of Saul was not his final word, but his choice of David is. This contradiction in ch. 15 exactly reflects the basic contradiction in the Book of the Everlasting Covenant, that one everlasting covenant can be annulled in favor of another.

A deep-structural reading of Saul's rejection. What Saul does wrong, I think, is to be unable to assert himself as king. He cannot be the bearer of the new order because he cannot free himself—the text will not let him free himself—from the old order. Even after ch. 12 he continues to be less than a king. Rather than his failure (some sin or other) being the cause of his rejection, his rejection—his not being allowed to be a real king—is the cause of his failure. The text stages in Saul a mythic representation of its own ambiguity about kingship.

I return yet again to 10:7-8. It would be hard to imagine a more explicit clash of concepts of kingship than we find in these adjacent verses. On the one hand, "do whatever you see fit to do, for God is with you" (10:7)—do what seems best on your own authority. On the other hand, "wait, until I come to you and show you what you shall do" (v. 8)—do nothing without the permission of another. Verse 7 does no more than state what it is to be a king, but anyone to whom the words of v. 8 can be addressed is no king at all. Verse 7 is a tautology, v. 8 a contradiction.

---

[8] Gunn, *The Fate of King Saul* 72–73. Meir Sternberg, *The Poetics of Biblical Narrative: Ideological Literature and the Drama of Reading* (Bloomington, Ind.: Indiana University Press, 1985) 502, argues that Samuel's word in v. 29 does not carry the authority of "the lord of history" (v. 11) or "the master of narrative" (v. 35). But the contradiction is so startling that a narrator in full control of the narrative would let it stand only for the specific purpose of making a statement about Samuel's authority, and it is difficult to see why the narrator should want to do so here. This case is typical of Sternberg's procedure of resorting to subtle rhetorical argument whenever the narrator's control seems to be in question. My procedure, by contrast, is to look for the significance of the narrator's loss of control.

It may be objected that *God* can dictate even to a king. In Israel kings must heed God's word spoken by God's prophet. This raises the question of whether Samuel is speaking in YHWH's name. It is hard to give a simple answer. 1 Samuel 10:7-8 concludes a long speech of Samuel that began at 10:1 and was announced as "the word of God" (9:27). Yet we do not find the divine "I" in this speech, whereas we do find Samuel's "I" (v. 8). It is at least possible that Samuel is ordering Saul about on his own authority. This possibility becomes certainty in 13:8-15, where Samuel acts entirely on his own initiative. He alone declares that the king of Israel is in breach of YHWH's commandment. He alone announces that YHWH has rejected Saul. The situation is admittedly more complicated in ch. 15, but even there Samuel is the active agent of the rejection and YHWH only belatedly ratifies what Samuel has effectively done (16:1). The text stages a direct encounter between the judge and the king, between the old order and the new. In this encounter judgeship sets the terms and kingship accepts the terms.

I have shown the difficulty of defining any specific obligation that Saul is under in 13:8-12, the first rejection scene. I now suggest that his real obligation is simply *to do nothing without Samuel,* without Samuel's "showing him what to do" (10:8). Samuel is late. At the mythic level he is late because he is dead. He has become, as we say, "the late Samuel." He has completed his life as a judge (ch. 7). He has lived on to make a king, and he has made a king. He has delivered his valedictory.[9] Now it is time for the king to be a king, to "do whatever he sees fit, since God is with him" (10:7). This is what Saul does in 13:8-12. He judges the situation and takes action. He acts as a king acts, but his doing so brings Samuel back quick (as opposed to dead) to tell Saul that he has committed the ultimate sin, the sin that means divine rejection. And Saul admits his fault. What he feels guilty of is not a cultic blunder, but *acting at all in the absence of Samuel.* He should have waited to be shown what to do. The live king should have waited for the dead judge.

What Saul does wrong in ch. 15 is a bit different, but not much. This time his fault is to *interpret* the law of the "ban," the obligation totally to exterminate conquered peoples (e.g., Deut 7:2), instead of just obeying it. The ban belongs to the old premonarchical order. Real kings dispose of their plunder as they see fit. For example, they like to make a show of triumph over humiliated rivals (cf. Judg 1:7). Above all, they interpret laws and traditions to their own advantage and find ways of

---

[9] Chapter 12. All the other great ones who did this—Jacob (Genesis 49), Moses (Deuteronomy 33), Joshua (Joshua 23)—had the decency then to die.

justifying their actions theologically. In ch. 15, just as in ch. 13, Saul begins to act like a king. But again, when Samuel confronts him, he abjectly repents. Especially he admits he can do nothing without Samuel, and craves Samuel's continued support (vv. 25, 30).

"Though you are little in your own eyes," says Samuel to Saul, "YHWH anointed you king" (15:17, recalling 9:21). But whenever Saul gets a bit bigger in his own eyes he is rebuked, and he is not able to do anything about it. He cringes before Samuel. A real king would know how to be rid of such a "turbulent priest" who got in his way, and Saul himself will later learn the art (see 22:6-19). But in the presence of Samuel, central symbol of the old order, Saul can never assert himself.

What this means is that kingship has not begun at all, nor judgeship ended. This is the meaning not only of Saul's failure but of Samuel's living on. While he lives, the transition does not really happen. Saul cannot make it happen. He is willing to submit to the laws of the old order, and so he does not bring in a new one. Some interpreters try to get at this dynamic in terms of Saul's psychology,[10] or of the dynamics of his tragedy,[11] and I think that what is going on is translatable in such ways. But I prefer to talk first about the narrative's laying on the character Saul its own inability to achieve the transition from judgeship to monarchy.

We can now understand Samuel's unexpected grief over Saul's rejection. He could not prevent kingship but he has achieved the next best thing—a king he can control, a king who is less than a king. Samuel has won his battle with Saul, so he wants to keep Saul as a figurehead who conforms to his (i.e., judgeship's) idea of what a national leader should be. YHWH is impatient at Samuel's grief because he is still, for the old incomprehensible reasons, bent on having a real king. He is determined that Samuel will not a second time get a king he can control. This goes a long way toward explaining the kingmaking in 16:1-13, where Samuel is deprived of any real control over or even understanding of what is going on. He is needed as a functionary: continuity still requires that the last judge be the kingmaker. But this will be a new kind of king, one who is beyond Samuel's reach.

The narrative's treatment of YHWH is interesting. By making Samuel so much the agent in the rejection accounts the narrator clears the stage and lets Samuel and Saul, the old order and the supposedly

---

[10] John A. Sanford, *King Saul, the Tragic Hero: A Study in Individuation* (New York and Mahwah, N.J.: Paulist, 1985).

[11] J. Cheryl Exum, *Tragedy and Biblical Narrative: Arrows of the Almighty* (Cambridge: Cambridge University Press, 1992).

new, battle it out. Except for nudging the story along toward the kingship of David, YHWH scarcely controls the events. The issues at stake in
this mythic battle are too problematic and contradictory, I suggest, for
the events to be laid directly to YHWH's charge. When YHWH does come
directly into the action, in ch. 15, he immediately gets embroiled in a
troubling theological contradiction over whether he is capable of
changing his mind.

The narrative sequence of the rejection accounts. Repetition of the
same or similar events, such as we have in the two accounts of Saul's
rejection, highlights what comes between, in this case 13:16–14:52. Up
to 14:46 this material has to do with war against the Philistines, and it
strongly confirms Saul's rejectedness. He is humiliated, and cuts a
sorry figure in contrast to his son Jonathan [94–95].

But 14:47-52 greatly changes the picture. This passage enthuses
over King Saul and the kingly things he does. He forms an army, routs
enemies, claims the best soldiers for his own bodyguard, founds a
family. True, this is still a limited kingship. Saul has a small official staff
and just one woman (14:50)—a king will want more of both. (2 Samuel
21 attributes to Saul at least one secondary wife.) Nonetheless, this
passage shows an unexpected resilience in Saul. He is doing quite well
for a rejected king. 1 Samuel 14:47-52 demonstrates Saul's ability, after
all, to grasp kingship—at least in the absence of Samuel. These verses
counteract the expectation that the rejection accounts create, that Saul's
reign is virtually over, and prepare us for the long reign he has still
ahead of him.

1 Samuel 16:14–2 Samuel 1: Saul Lives On

At 1 Sam 16:13 Saul has been rejected and his successor apparently
put in place. Yet he lives on—endlessly, it seems.[12] This is a text that has
great trouble getting rid of its characters even when their time seems
to be up. Despite his rejection there is never a suggestion that Saul
should not continue to reign through his whole lifetime.

All through these long chapters in the second half of 1 Samuel theological work, or as I call it mythic work, is getting done. The main part
of this work is to find new ways of justifying the replacement of Saul
by David. Paradoxically, it is the narrator's unsatisfiable need to ex-

---

[12] Robert Polzin, *Samuel and the Deuteronomist: A Literary Study of the Deuteronomic History. Part Two: 1 Samuel* (San Francisco: Harper & Row, 1989) 213.

plain Saul's rejection that gives Saul narrative space in which to reign. Only after his rejection does he become a real king! He becomes a fairly bad king, though not to the extent feared in 8:11-18. He lets others fight his battles, dominates his household, persecutes a usurper in true royal style. He demonstrates royal control over the religious sector by a mass slaughter of priests (22:6-19). On the other hand, his fatal flaw of not being able to grasp and hold on to kingship sometimes reappears.

This section of text, 1 Sam 16:14–2 Samuel 1, is the longest I take at a single mouthful in this book, but this seems to me the right procedure, underscoring my insistence that we should work first on a large textual canvas. For orientation, readers should note that I organize the section around Saul's relationships with the various other actors, Samuel, David, Saul's son Jonathan, and the Philistines, and I constantly revert to the basic theological question: How can an everlasting covenant be annulled?

Saul and Samuel. Though Samuel now almost disappears from the story he has two further meetings with Saul, and they both reiterate Saul's submission to Samuel. The first is in 19:18-24, during the time when Saul is pursuing David (see below). We are surprised that David goes to Samuel for asylum since this is the only passage that suggests a relationship between the two. It is probable that the scene has been created simply to remind the reader of Samuel's continuing power over Saul. 1 Samuel 19:23-24 recapitulates in satirical fashion Saul's incorporation into a band of prophets in 10:9-13. The relationship between these two passages is underscored by the repetition of the proverb "Is Saul also among the prophets?" The earlier passage showed Saul on his way to the height of fortune; the recapitulation shows him sunk in degradation. Both passages equally show him under Samuel's sway.

The second meeting is more remarkable, for it is after Samuel's death. In ch. 28 the beleaguered Saul still needs Samuel to tell him what to do. He goes to the length of finding a medium to raise up Samuel's ghost [185–189]. But dead Samuel has nothing different to say to Saul from what he said when he was alive. In fact 28:17 alludes to, and quotes, ch. 15.

One theme worth noting in ch. 28 is Saul's zeal for YHWH. Learning perhaps from his experience in ch. 15, Saul has becomes a zealot in doing what he perceives as YHWH's will. In conformity with the law in Deut 18:10-11 he has expelled from the land all mediums and wizards (28:3). This links up in an interesting way with 2 Sam 21:2, according to which Saul "in his zeal for the people of Israel and Judah" tried to wipe out the Gibeonites. The Gibeonites were an anomaly in Israel, people who by deception avoided extermination during the conquest (see Joshua 9). Saul no doubt felt that getting rid of the anomaly would be a pious act.

His religious zeal seems, however, to be an embarrassment to the narrator, since neither of these zealous acts (28:3, 2 Sam 21:2) is recorded at the time Saul performed it. Both are recalled only in connection with later incidents, and one of the two is expelled beyond the boundary of 1 Samuel altogether.

Saul and David. The relationship between the king and his destined successor begins in harmony and even sweetness, continues in contrast and rivalry, and ends in incoherence.

Quick to get to the point, the text brings Saul into contact with David immediately after David's anointing (16:14-23). When the burdens of kingship lie heavy on Saul he seeks relief in music, and David is the one who can provide it. Saul loves David (v. 21). The "evil spirit from YHWH" that afflicts Saul (v. 14), the same evil spirit that will later inspire him to attack David (18:10-11, 19:9-10), David here has the power to quell.

The harmony does not disappear all at once. We continue to glimpse it at certain moments up to 19:7. But within the text's constraining logic—the need to account for the transition from Saul to David—the relationship must be developed in disharmony, and this is what we increasingly find in chs. 17–23.[13] A contrastive logic develops that lays the whole burden of fault on Saul. He has to be bad so that David can be good. Saul is rejected, David elected, and each new incident drives this home. Saul is shown negatively almost everywhere, but even more he is shown as frustrated. His plans to harm David are always turning out to David's advantage. A second level of contrast provides intense narrative tension. Saul is disloyal to David and tends to drive him away. David is loyal to Saul and tends to seek his presence. Hence the relationship can find no stability whether they are together or apart.

But what are Saul's options?—as always, to be or not to be a king. He can resist the usurper as kings do, or he can capitulate to him. For usurper David is, much as he may be Mr. Clean in his actions and overt intentions. What the text recounts is a battle between Saul and David with their rival royal claims—but not on a real battlefield (as in the first chapters of 2 Samuel, when the houses of Saul and David get into a good clean fight). No, this is a strange theological battlefield created by secret elections and rejections and, ultimately, by the contra-

---

[13] I omit from consideration here, and defer to the next section, all passages involving Jonathan as a third in the Saul-David relationship, namely 18:1-5; 19:1-7; ch. 20; and 23:15b-18.

dictory Deuteronomic theology. The textual action mimics the theological dilemma.

Throughout chs. 17–23 only one option seems to be available to Saul. He must resist David. In realistic fiction Saul might raise this gifted young man to the highest level in his administration, but in the text we have his insane jealousy makes him squander the gifts David so winsomely offers. This is the only kind of king Saul can be. In this bind, insanity is the text's final recourse. Saul is, or becomes, an actual madman! What shall we think about a text that can do its work only by making its central character insane? Is it kingship itself that is insane?

Each incident in David's career is expressed in terms of his rivalry with Saul. When David defeats Goliath, Saul cannot claim a share of the credit even by supplying armor, for David can do without armor (17:38-39). The women who sing victory songs zero in directly on the rivalry: "Saul has killed his thousands, and David his ten thousands" (18:7). This incident inaugurates a new theme, that of women who assist David's rise, and the theme continues in 18:17-29 as David becomes Saul's son-in-law [151–152, 227–232]. In a pattern to be often repeated, Saul tries to do David harm (he intends David to be killed in seeking the brideprice) but succeeds only in helping him. In the next chapter David's new wife becomes his ally against Saul (19:11-17). 1 Samuel 19:18-24 (the incident of Saul's prophesying) is another attempt on David's life that ends in Saul's humiliation.

In the long account of Ahimelech and the priests of Nob (21:1-9 [MT 2-10]; 22:6-23) David is the friend of priests, while Saul is their slaughterer.[14] Again Saul's intentions against David are frustrated. As the story ends Saul has lost control of the oracular ephod, and David, having possession of it, uses it to frustrate Saul (23:6-13).

The relationship that began in harmony and has developed in conflict ends in narrative incoherence. After 23:19 (with the disappearance of Jonathan) the text tries to solve the theological problem of how kingship could pass from one royal house to another by means of the characters Saul and David alone. It attempts to show Saul *both* as the rejected one *and* as willingly abdicating to David. This proves impossible to achieve.

In ch. 24 Saul is again in pursuit of David. When chance puts Saul's life in David's hands, David—in conformity with his role as the good

---

[14] The fact that Saul thus fulfills YHWH's rejection of Eli's house from the priesthood serves to focus Saul's own rejection. See David Jobling, "Saul's Fall and Jonathan's Rise: Tradition and Redaction in 1 Samuel 14:1-46," *JBL* 95 (1976) 368–369.

character—spares him: "The LORD forbid that I should . . . raise my hand against him; for he is the LORD's anointed" (v. 6). He can well afford this generosity, being himself YHWH's anointed![15] Saul, weary of trying to be a king, switches finally to his other option, capitulation to David. He joins the chorus and acknowledges David's coming kingship (24:20). In effect this is an abdication, and it provides a new sort of explanation of the transition from Saul to David. The old order legitimates the new (just as when Samuel the judge inaugurated the monarchy). In the spirit of the new harmony Saul and David address each other as "father" and "son" (24:11,16) [114, 122–123].

However, this resolution of the problem is no resolution at all, for after an important interlude in ch. 25 (to which I will turn in a moment) the story in ch. 24 has to be told all over again in ch. 26. Despite his apparent change of heart in ch. 24 Saul is yet again pursuing David at the beginning of ch. 26. There are some variations in the repetition. Saul does not repeat his abdication, but he blesses David (26:25) and invites him back to court (v. 21). Saul again addresses David as his son (26:17, 21, 25) but David does not this time call Saul father.

The verse immediately following (27:1) marks the end of a relationship that has run out of options. Despite Saul's changes of heart the only Saul David can believe in is the murderous Saul. It is not that Saul is insincere. It is that he no longer knows how he really wants to deal with David. The inclusion of the two versions of the story shows that the narrator himself no longer knows how to portray Saul. The attempt to portray him *both* as a rejected king who behaves treacherously *and* as one who is willing to accept his rejection and yield to David cannot be sustained. The problem of the transition from Saul to David simply cannot be solved in terms of the relationship between the two characters.

The story of David, Abigail, and Nabal (25:2-42), sandwiched between chs. 24 and 26, stands in an allegorical relation to these chapters.[16] In the allegory the character Nabal corresponds to Saul (lest we miss the point, Nabal's feast in 25:36 is "like the feast of a king"). This technique enables new things to be said about the relationship between Saul and David.

The allegory directs the reading of chs. 24 and 26 in a number of ways. In 25:38 Nabal dies, but some time before he literally dies his

---

[15] See Gunn, *The Fate of King Saul* 102–103, and the important discussion in Joel Rosenberg, *King and Kin: Political Allegory in the Hebrew Bible*. Indiana Studies in Biblical Literature (Bloomington, Ind.: Indiana University Press, 1986) 136–139.

[16] One obvious reason for seeing the story this way is the name "Nabal," which means "fool." It is an unlikely name for a parent to give to a real child.

heart is said to "die within him" (v. 37). This suggests that Saul's heart, like Nabal's, has already "died within him" and that it is high time for Saul too to die. The story in ch. 25, we might say, kills Saul in effigy. A central point of the story is that Nabal dies without David's having to kill him. David is preserved from killing Nabal—and hence from "bloodguilt"—by Abigail's action. This brings into focus David's sparing of Saul when he has the chance to kill him in chs. 24 and 26. Nabal, like Saul, is shown gruffly repelling David's friendly overtures: this casts Saul as himself a *nābāl*, a "fool."[17] David calls himself Nabal's "son" (25:8), recalling the father-son language in chs. 24 and 26. Abigail wishes that those who seek to do harm to David may suffer Nabal's fate (25:26). To whom can this allude other than Saul?[18]

Finally, the allegory in ch. 25 underscores the incoherence into which the Saul-David relationship falls at the end. The attempt to present Saul as a character who can announce David's coming kingship while at the same time seeking his death is, I have suggested, a failure. Chapter 25 anticipates this failure in a compelling way by distributing the contradictory aspects of Saul among two different characters. Nabal is the Saul who opposes David and seeks his life, but the Saul who foresees and accepts David's rise to power is represented by Abigail (25:28-31). The bifurcation of Saul's character, which I have traced throughout his story, is here allegorically enacted.[19]

The theological work of Jonathan. I used to think that the primary means for making the transition from Saul to David theologically plausible lay in the treatment of Saul's son Jonathan.[20] Now I would grant Jonathan a more modest place, as one means among several, but in terms of clarity and coherence he still seems to me to provide the most plausible "explanation" of the transition.

One way for a kingship to end is by abdication. Saul might simply give up his kingship to David, and we have seen how this possibility is played with in 24:20. But this possibility failed because Saul could not perform such an act sincerely. My thesis is that what Saul cannot do Jonathan, as Saul's heir, can do and does. He gives up his heirdom to David.

---

[17] Saul admits to having been a "fool" in 26:21, though the word used is a different one.

[18] See Polzin, *Samuel and the Deuteronomist* 211.

[19] As part of my feminist reading I shall later retell this story from Abigail's perspective [152–158].

[20] *The Sense of Biblical Narrative: Structural Analyses in the Hebrew Bible I* JSOT.S 7 (2nd ed. Sheffield: JSOT Press, 1986) 12–30.

To present Jonathan adequately I need to step back into the chapters preceding 16:14. He first appears in chs. 13–14 as co-commander with Saul in the war against the Philistines. The first reference to Jonathan in 13:2-4 does not identify him as Saul's son. He is successful in battle, and the text broadly hints that Saul steals the credit from him: "Jonathan defeated the garrison of the Philistines" (v. 3), but "all Israel heard that Saul had defeated the garrison of the Philistines" (v. 4)! In the briefest possible space we see here a double pattern in the relationship: (1) Saul and Jonathan are *identified* (their parallel roles in v. 2); but (2) Jonathan *replaces* Saul, as he achieves greater things (v. 3). This pattern of identification and replacement is the key to Jonathan's role throughout.

He next appears in 13:16, immediately following the first account of Saul's rejection. It is surely not an accident that this moment is chosen to identify him for the first time as Saul's son. In the rejection account the possibility of Saul's founding a dynasty is raised and denied in a single gesture: "YHWH had (or would have) established your kingdom . . . forever, but now your kingdom will not continue" (13:13-14). Jonathan is the real victim of this gesture. Saul (as it turns out) will be king for life, but his heir will never be king. Jonathan has lost his royal expectations before we knew he had them.

The reader of 13:16 may feel manipulated by this narrative trick. Learning that Jonathan is Saul's son, and recalling his success in 13:3, she may get a momentary lift at the prospect of so able an heir. But he can never be the heir, because of the rejection. The text continues to play with these feelings through the long story that follows (14:1-46). We read it knowing that Saul's house is rejected and in expectation that it may reveal the identity of the "man after YHWH's heart" (13:14) who will replace him. The text to all appearances builds up Jonathan as that man in sharp contrast to the declining Saul. But we know that Jonathan is the one person it cannot be.[21]

The preamble to ch. 14 stresses the closeness of Saul and Jonathan (13:16, 22, cf. 14:21), but the chapter itself sets them in utter contrast. In this contrast all the glory accrues to Jonathan, and Saul is made to look ridiculous. Jonathan and his servant boldly snatch a military advantage (14:1-15), but Saul, rather than pressing the advantage, hesitates burlesquely. First he needs a roll call to determine that his own son is missing from the camp (v. 17). Then, with all the signs of YHWH's approval of the battle staring him in the face, he insists on seeking con-

---

[21] For a full discussion of 14:1-46 along these lines see Jobling, "Saul's Fall and Jonathan's Rise."

firmation from the divine lot (vv. 18-19). Later, though anxious to press for victory, he allows himself to be persuaded by his priest to consult the lot again (vv. 36-37). The priest in the story (see also v. 3) is Ahijah, descendant of the house of Eli, and the reference to a rejected priestly house emphasizes the rejection of Saul's house.

Saul's frustrations continue. He imposes on his troops an oath of abstinence from food (v. 24), with disastrous results. The oath puts in jeopardy the life of Saul's son and the battle's hero, for Jonathan unwittingly transgresses it (v. 27). The hungry troops cannot fight well (vv. 28, 31). When they finally do eat, Saul—ever pious—delays yet again in order to build an altar (vv. 32-35). And when he consults the sacred lot about whether to pursue the Philistines the procedure will not work because Jonathan's offense has not been expiated (vv. 36-42). When we reach the final scene Saul has become quite pathetic. Unable to get an answer from God, he allows his will to be balked by the people, who will have none of his plan to put Jonathan to death (vv. 44-45). The closing verse suggests that a great chance for overwhelming victory has been missed (v. 46).

Saul's loss is Jonathan's gain. His resolution and prompt action, attended by signs of divine approval, are in sharp contrast to Saul's hesitation and fumbling after divine guidance. As 13:2-4 already hinted, it is Jonathan who is effectively fighting Saul's battles (see 9:16). Saul's belated attempt to share the credit fails to impress the people, who are well aware who was the real hero of the day (14:45).

The pattern of identification and replacement between Saul and Jonathan is already well established in chs. 13–14. After first asserting the closeness of father and son, these chapters later set up a contrast between Saul and Jonathan, who receives such marks of divine approval and such acclaim of the people as befit a king. The puzzle for the reader is to understand what is achieved by this. Why build Jonathan up as the heir apparent who succeeds where his father fails? Why tantalize the reader with clues that this is the man after YHWH's heart? The answer to these questions emerges, I believe, after David comes on the scene.

When I read the account of Saul's conflict with David (1 Samuel 17–23) I omitted the passages in which Jonathan appears. To these passages I now turn: 18:1-5; 19:1-7; ch. 20; 23:15b-18. My procedure is justified by the fact that these Jonathan passages are so independent of their context. The rest of chs. 17–23, with the single exception of 22:8, gives no hint that Jonathan even exists. The Jonathan passages employ a narrative strategy quite different from the rest of chs. 17–23.

According to Edmund Leach, "From [1 Samuel 18] through to 23 *every* reference to Jonathan serves to emphasize his role identification with David. This equation implies that David ultimately replaced Jonathan as Saul's 'rightful' successor."[22] To the identification-replacement pattern between Saul and Jonathan, which continues in these chapters, is added a similar pattern between Jonathan and David. Jonathan oscillates between close identification with David and an emptying of himself into David, a readiness to be replaced by David as Saul's heir.

Rather in the way that the first judge cycle (Judg 3:7-11) presents the cycle in its bare bones, so the first Jonathan passage (18:1-5) concisely says everything that needs to be said. The other Jonathan passages will simply ring the changes on these themes. 18:1-5 follows immediately on David's defeat of Goliath and reintroduction to Saul, and expounds his relationship to Jonathan in a beautifully structured way:

> 18:1   Jonathan establishes *identification* with David: "Jonathan loved him as his own self."
>
> 18:2   Saul confirms the *identification* of Jonathan with David by adopting David: he "would not let him return to his father's house."
>
> 18:3-4 Jonathan makes David his *replacement* by handing over to him his own clothes and weapons.
>
> 18:5   Saul confirms the *replacement* of Jonathan by David, making David his general as Jonathan previously was.

The pattern could not be exhibited more effectively. But what does it mean?

When we last took leave of Jonathan in ch. 14 he was at the high point of his fortunes, to the extent that the reader seemed invited to see in him the "man after YHWH's own heart" who would replace Saul. If Jonathan has the stature of a king, then 18:4 must be read as an abdication. It is the *royal* garments and the *royal* weapons that he hands over to David.[23] David is now king not only in the secret counsels of YHWH (16:1-13) but also by the abdication in his favor of the one worthy and ready to be king. Taken together, 14:1-46 and 18:1-5 have a significance that runs ahead of the narrative presentation. The kingship has in effect already passed from Saul to David by the mediation of Jonathan. The remaining Jonathan passages serve merely to reinforce this.

In 19:1-7 Jonathan's double role-identification is very clear. Saul tries to enlist him on his own side against David (v. 1a), but his identification with David is at once reaffirmed (v. 1b), and he warns David of Saul's intentions (vv. 2-3). For the time being, however, Jonathan's

[22] *Genesis as Myth and Other Essays* (London: Jonathan Cape, 1969) 67.

[23] Julius Morgenstern, "David and Jonathan," *JBL* 78 (1959) 322.

identification with David does not break his unity with his father: "Saul listened to the voice of Jonathan" (v. 6). The two act as one in restoring David to his place as Saul's adopted son (v. 7, cf. 18:2). These observations are confirmed by some features of style. First, the seemingly unnecessary attachment of "father" and "son" to the proper names in 19:1-4 (e.g., "Saul's son Jonathan") stresses their identification at the moment when it seems in doubt. Second, the repetition of the name "Jonathan" at the end (four times in vv. 6-7) makes clear the importance of his mediating role.

Even more than ch. 14, ch. 20 belongs to Jonathan. He is present throughout, sometimes in David's, sometimes in Saul's company. In vv. 1-23 he is with David. During Saul's absence at Ramah (see 19:23-24) Jonathan is presented unmistakably as a king. David enters his "presence" and we think of the royal presence of Saul that David enters and leaves (16:21, 22; 17:57; 19:7). Jonathan speaks with the authority of a king: "You shall not die" (20:2) exactly balances Saul's "He shall not be put to death" (19:6) The role identification between Saul and Jonathan is tremendously strong at the beginning: "Behold, my father does nothing either great or small without disclosing it to me" (v. 2). Verses 4-11 display great subtlety. Even while acting as king, Jonathan strongly affirms his identification with David (v. 4) and allows himself to be enlisted as mediator. David at first seems to accept the identification of Jonathan with Saul, regarding the son as the father's plenipotentiary (v. 8b) and adopting the attitude of a suppliant (v. 8a). But David's hints that Jonathan might act against his interests elicit a forceful denial: "Far be it from you!" (v. 9).

Verses 12-23 move entirely in the identification-replacement pattern of Jonathan and David. Jonathan's abdication is clear: "May the LORD be with you, as he has been with my father" (v. 13). He appeals to David for loyal treatment after David has become king. In this section we witness perhaps the sharpest collision between Jonathan's two identifications, with Saul and with David. It is just when he has most clearly "become king" that he most clearly "abdicates"!

In 20:24-34 Saul is back at court and Jonathan is with him. Saul questions Jonathan about David (v. 27); he is suspicious about the Jonathan-David identification. Jonathan, disingenuously exploiting the Saul-Jonathan identification, replies that David petitioned him as if he were a king, acting as Saul's deputy (v. 28). But Saul is not to be bluffed. "You have chosen the son of Jesse to the shame of your mother's nakedness," and while David lives "neither you nor your kingdom shall be established" (vv. 30-31). This is the only time the specific vocabulary of kingship *(mlk)* is ever used in direct connection with Jonathan. Saul here assumes that his kingship is dynastic and that Jonathan is his heir.

Pointedly not picking up on this hint that he is to succeed Saul, Jonathan falls into his accustomed role of mediation (v. 32). Saul rejects this mediation not by word but by deed. In one of the most revealing verses (33) of the whole narrative Saul tries to impale Jonathan as he previously tried to impale David (18:11; 19:10)—and from this Jonathan deduces that his father seeks *David's* life! The identification of Jonathan and David is total: an act directed at one is an act directed at the other.

The last brief passage, 23:15b-18, provides a neat counterpoint to ch. 20. Reversing the roles of 20:1, Jonathan goes to David as to a king. In v. 17 he sees himself as paired with David in David's coming glory: "I shall be second to you." But identification is swallowed up in the unambiguous statement of replacement: "You shall be king over Israel."

Jonathan offers the most compelling example of a narrative strategy I have already identified in Jotham and Samuel. Like them he is a character who by his mere existence aggravates a problem, but who becomes the necessary means for solving that problem [49–50, 69–70]. He is heir to the throne, so that David, in order to become king, will have to replace not only a legitimate monarch but also a legitimate heir. But in all his appearances Jonathan moves the story toward its goal of transferring power to David. Jonathan's identification with Saul, as Saul's heir, provides him with the royal authority to abdicate. His identification with David enables the emptying of his own heirdom into David. And when his job is done, he abruptly disappears: after 23:18 we do not hear of him again until the notice of his death in ch. 31.

It is hopeless to try to explain Jonathan through standard categories of narrative character.[24] He represents the extreme case of character being emptied into plot [6–7]. His attitudes and actions lack any normal motivation. He is the heir, and the heir does not normally champion the cause of an upstart against his own. It is not a matter of someone demonstrating a human virtue to an extreme degree[25] but of someone acting without reason against his own interests. Nor can it simply be that Jonathan "saw which way the wind was blowing" and acted in his own long-term interests, for on more than one occasion he could have allowed David to be killed simply by doing nothing.

---

[24] I will later offer an alternative reading of David and Jonathan that will nuance this statement [161–165].

[25] "In the figure of Jonathan, the Old Testament has a real nobleman of high sensibility" (Hans Wilhelm Hertzberg, *I & II Samuel: A Commentary*, translated by John S. Bowden. The Old Testament Library [Philadelphia: Westminster, 1964] 172).

Jonathan knows the divine plan and acts in accordance with it. The other principals, Saul and David, also in some sense know where the narrative is going because it has been revealed to them (Saul in his rejection, David in his anointing). Jonathan receives no revelations, and yet he knows. Mysteriously, the divine plan is open to him. In 23:17 he speaks as a prophet: "The hand of my father shall not find you; you shall be king over Israel, and I shall be next to you" (cf. 20:13-16). Jonathan knows because it is theologically necessary that he know. Without his mysterious knowledge he could not fulfill his narrative role.

Saul and the Philistines. Foreign domination is also a form of government in Israel [56–57]. In the judge theory rule by foreigners is the consequence of apostasy, so that it seems like an externalization of Israel's broken relationship to YHWH. On the other hand foreign domination calls forth YHWH's compassion, makes him open to Israel's "cry."

The Philistines come on the scene as a new kind of enemy, breaking the logic of judgeship. Samuel, indeed, seems to submit them to that logic when he defeats them in ch. 7. But they quickly return as a threat, and Saul's major task as king is to save Israel from the Philistines (9:16). The complete occupation of Israel by the Philistines at the end of 1 Samuel—as well, of course, as the death of Saul and his sons—is therefore the ultimate expression of Saul's failure. Israel has again been "delivered into the hands of the Philistines." Even the victories over the Philistines that Israel enjoys during Saul's time are ascribed to the heroism of others, Jonathan and David.

Aside from 14:47, which preserves a startlingly different memory of a Saul who carried all before him, the Philistines in their every appearance assist the narrative's movement toward David's kingship. It is by his successes against the Philistines (chs. 13–14) that Jonathan is built up to the point at which he can "abdicate" in David's favor. Saul's attempt to use the Philistines to destroy David misfires and makes David stronger (18:20-29). The Philistines recognize David's prominence early in the story (21:11). They refuse his help in their final battle with Saul (ch. 29), from which, whatever the outcome, he could have gained no credit in Israel.

Where Saul fails to defeat the Philistines, David will eventually succeed in 2 Samuel. This contrast provides yet another "explanation" of the transition from Saul to David—an explanation that has often been favored by historical critics. David became king only when Saul's house was extinct at the hands of the Philistines, and he established his rule by defeating the Philistines.

Too many explanations. How could the everlasting covenant with Saul be annulled in favor of an everlasting covenant with David? We have now completed our review of the ways in which the second half of 1 Samuel gets at this question. No single satisfactory reason can be given since the contradiction allows no final resolution, so many different reasons are offered. Psychoanalysis provides an analogy in its concept of "overdetermination." A psychic phenomenon is overdetermined when it can be explained in a number of different ways, and the multiplicity of explanations becomes itself a psychological problem.[26] The transition from Saul's monarchy to David's is overdetermined. Fragments of various "explanations" are everywhere to be found.

The military explanation is the most readily available: the Philistines beat Saul, David beat the Philistines. But this is not a *theological* solution, and it gets turned on its head—Saul's failure to defeat the Philistines is seen as an effect of his rejection rather than a cause of it. Another approach that is hinted at is that David received the right of succession when he became Saul's son-in-law. Some ancient monarchies may have had this principle of succession, but it will not do as an explanation here since the text assumes kingship to pass from father to son.[27] Yet another possibility is that Saul lost the kingship because he became mad and incapacitated, because he could not hold onto the allegiance of Israel or even of his own family. But this only displaces the problem to another level. Why did these things happen, and why once they happened could not the kingship pass to Saul's son?

Saul's relationships with other characters provide, as we have seen, other elements of explanations. Saul cannot become a real king because he cannot shake free of the premonarchical order embodied in Samuel. Saul might abdicate in favor of David, but this proves narratively impossible to achieve. The most consistent and impressive effort at an explanation is in the work around the character Jonathan. If Saul cannot abdicate, his heir can.[28]

Finally, though, it all comes down, as it must, to the paradox of ch. 15. Power passes from Saul's to David's house because God can change his mind about Saul but not about David!

---

[26] See J. Laplanche and J.-B. Pontalis, *The Language of Psycho-analysis,* translated by Donald Nicholson-Smith (New York and London: W. W. Norton & Company, 1973) 292–293.

[27] See Jobling, *The Sense of Biblical Narrative I* 17–18.

[28] It is helpful again to compare Jonathan to Jotham in Judges 9 [49–50]. Like Jotham, Jonathan is the heir; like Jotham, he abdicates. He almost becomes, like Jotham, a "worthy refuser" of kingship, but unlike Jotham he does not reject kingship as such. His abdication is in favor of another king, not in favor of a return to the old order.

The End of Saul (1 Samuel 31, 2 Samuel 1). Saul's death is recorded in 1 Samuel 31. The manner of it (31:4) pointedly recalls the death of Israel's first king, Abimelech (Judg 9:54). Abimelech's death brought to an end Israel's proto-monarchy. Does Saul's death likewise mark the end of monarchy in Israel? The text is careful to specify that Saul's sons, his natural heirs, die with him. The reader knows, of course, that David is waiting in the wings. Still, the parallel with Abimelech is compelling, and I will later find ways in which the text backs up this hint that monarchy in Israel might have ended with Saul.

As David completes the account of Saul's and Jonathan's death with his great lament in 2 Sam 1:19-27 the reader looks for him now to take over of the kingship, to complete the narrative current begun with his anointing (16:1-13) and confirmed by the predictions of Jonathan, Abigail, and even Saul himself. But at this moment David does not look at all well positioned to do so. The Philistines are in full control and David is most ambiguously related to them, still nominally in their service but involved in double dealing with them. Are there to be more vicissitudes before the new everlasting covenant is established?

2 Samuel 2–7

David duly arrives at the kingship, and the everlasting covenant, and there are not really many vicissitudes. He becomes king first of Judah and then of all Israel. He begins to act like a king, especially in the multiplying of wives (2 Sam 3:2-5; cf. Deut 17:17, Judg 8:30-31). Familiar themes reappear. Without anyone overtly telling them, the characters somehow know that David's kingship has been promised by YHWH (Abner, 3:9-10; all of Israel, 5:2). David is kept from bloodguilt in 3:28-29 as in 1 Samuel 25. The climax comes in 2 Samuel 5–7. David takes Jerusalem, builds a palace, acquires even more women and children, and brings the ark of God to Jerusalem. He arrogates to himself just the sort of priestly function that got Saul into trouble. Finally, YHWH enters formally into the covenant with David's house.

However, this narrative takes two turns that ought to astonish the reader. The Philistines virtually disappear, while the house of Saul reappears.

The Philistines. Given the situation at the end of 1 Samuel we anticipate that, before David can enter his glory, he will have to deal with massive opposition from the Philistine conquerors. In fact they are scarcely a factor. They do not reenter the story until David is well established, and the account of warfare with them is even then quite brief (2 Sam 5:17-25). Where have they been since 1 Samuel 31? Why, given their supreme position, have they stood aside during the time of conflict between Saul's and David's houses?

The only possible conclusion is that the Philistine domination is merely a correlate to the decline of Saul. Once Saul is dead the theme of foreign domination disappears as a serious option in the text's political debate. The Philistines become merely a cipher in Israel's internal struggle. We see this particularly clearly in 2 Sam 3:18. Abner, who was Saul's commander but is now trying to persuade Saul's party to go over to David, "recalls" a promise of YHWH to David that the reader does not remember having been made: "Through my servant David I will save my people Israel from the hand of the Philistines. . . ." Of course this is the very promise made to *Saul* in 1 Sam 9:16! David has obviously inherited it along with everything else. But what for Saul was a lifelong losing battle David will achieve with scarcely an effort.

The house of Saul. Nothing in 1 Samuel prepares us for the "long war between the house of Saul and the house of David" (2 Sam 3:1) that occupies most of chs. 2–4. We feel a fitting sense of closure in the apparent death of all the males in Saul's family in 1 Samuel 31, and this closure is confirmed by David's lament in 2 Sam 1:19-27. We may, indeed, recall Jonathan's request in 1 Sam 20:14-15 that David remain loyal to any survivor of Jonathan's house, but this request seems to belong to a different narrative trajectory, and in fact this trajectory will not be resumed until the Book of the Everlasting Covenant is over, when in 2 Samuel 9 David takes care of Jonathan's lame son. By then he can perform an act of loyalty without any suggestion of a threat to his position.

The appearance of a previously unknown son of *Saul* is a different matter. The reader feels his sense of closure violated by the appearance of Ishbaal in 2 Sam 2:8, and this occurrence blows to the winds one of the best "explanations" of the transition from Saul to David, that Saul's house had no male survivors. There is also some appearance of narrative trickery. In 1 Sam 14:49 Saul is said to have three sons, and three die with him in 31:2. However, these lists do not agree: Ishvi in 14:49 is replaced by Abinadab in 31:2. Ishvi, who is not said to die, might at a pinch be the Ishbaal of 2 Samuel (but where did Abinadab spring from?)

One might see here a reminder that monarchies, once begun, are hard to get rid of [46–50]. But the main effect is that the account of David's final triumph is brought down from the theological heights— the inevitable rise of YHWH's anointed in 1 Samuel—to a piece of power politics that descends to the sordid (e.g., 2 Sam 3:22-30). The specter is conjured up in Israel's tradition that David's right to the kingship was merely the right of conquest. The narrative line of the promise to David is compromised, or at least loses its gloss. Even a reader who to this point has been carried along by the promise theme may now ask whether the establishment of David is not ultimately the result of an injustice against the house of Saul.

In both these cases, the Philistines and the house of Saul, it is as if the Deuteronomists, having done their best theological work in the chapters up to 2 Samuel 1, are now taking a breather before the grand climax in 2 Samuel 7. But they lose thereby some of their labor, for they make their earlier achievement seem less plausible.

A Substitute Ideal?

I concluded the previous chapter with a section entitled "A Lost Ideal?" [70–76]. This section reaches directly back to that one. 1 Samuel 12, I argued, incorporates kingship into the logic of judgeship. In a similar but converse way 2 Samuel 7 incorporates judgeship, in fact Israel's premonarchical traditions in general, within the logic of dynastic kingship. 2 Samuel 7:6-11a places the covenant with David in direct continuity with Israel's past, first with the exodus (v. 6, cf. 1 Sam 12: 8), then with the judges (vv. 7-11a).[29] Judgeship is subtly put down for its failure to deal with foreign oppression (v. 11, cf. v. 1), but it is still accepted as a dispensation of YHWH out of which David's kingship has legitimately emerged. David rules in the interests of the whole nation (v. 10). The eternity of the royal house parallels the eternity of Israel (vv. 24, 26). The only past form of leadership not invited to this celebratory party is *Saul's* kingship (v. 15).

The effect of the Deuteronomic "books," the Extended Book of Judges and the Book of the Everlasting Covenant, is simply to juxtapose two dispensations, judgeship and dynastic (Davidic) kingship. Both are from YHWH; both are good in their time. They are in continuity with each other, and each is in continuity with Moses. Any sense of a significant transition is played down, or rather it is redefined as the shift from monarchy's false start in Saul to its proper fulfillment in David. Hidden from view is the possibility of any fundamental incompatibility between the two orders, between the conditional and the unconditional covenant.

---

[29] I take v. 7 to be a reference to the time of the judges even though the text oddly says "tribes" (the parallel in 1 Chron 17:6 has "judges"). In any case the judges are referred to in v. 11.

The incompatibility cannot, however, really be hidden. In my analysis in this and the previous chapter I have drawn attention to many signs of narrative strain in the accomplishment of this theological work. One sign that I have not stressed, but that aptly highlights my point, is how Samuel's speech in 1 Samuel 12, in contrast to almost all the other Deuteronomic summaries, lacks a real forward-looking element. Samuel fails to adumbrate the dynamics of dynastic kingship.

Let us return, then, to Israel's "lost ideal." In the Book of the Everlasting Covenant there are no attempts to flesh out that ideal of Israel's premonarchical past. There are no more sketches of an egalitarian order such as we found in Judges 5 and 9, 1 Samuel 2 and 8. The Book of the Everlasting Covenant is future- rather than past-oriented. The rule of the house of David is a *new* ideal to which all the previous dispensations were looking forward. Nothing of value in the past has been lost; all has been fulfilled.

I present this whole part of my book (Part II) under the heading of "class." But we have found in the biblical text very little that, from our contemporary perspective, we recognize as class discourse. Is this because our categories are anachronistic, so that we are looking for the wrong things? I do not believe so. As anthropological evidence clearly shows, any transition to kingship, or to some other greatly heightened degree of state centralization, increases social stratification and creates new classes [146–149]. And we know that the Deuteronomic tradition is capable of generating what we easily recognize as class discourse, not only in the four passages just mentioned but in the impressive social legislation of Deuteronomy, as well as on rare occasions in the later part of the Deuteronomic History, such as the account of Naboth's vineyard in 1 Kings 21.

What is it, then, that prevents the Deuteronomists from giving any effective class analysis of the transition from judgeship to kingship? I believe the problem lies in their attempt to make a new, substitute ideal out of *just one kind of kingship* while at the same time theoretically rejecting other kinds. They resolve their own ambiguity over kingship by saying that there is one kingship of David and another of Saul. In the later parts of the History they will likewise claim that there is one kingship of Judah in the south and another kingship of Ephraim in the north. But this will not work. Kingship is kingship, a specific system of government with specific social effects. By trying to have it both ways the Deuteronomists disqualify themselves from any effective sociopolitical critique of monarchy.

Chapter 5

A READING OF GOVERNMENT IN
THE CANONICAL 1 SAMUEL

We have completed our long journey through a vast portion of the Deuteronomic History. We have read there a monumental and endlessly complicated debate over what would be the most appropriate government for Israel.

In the two preceding chapters I disregarded the canonical book divisions. Now I turn to the canonical book 1 Samuel. The process of canonization, subsequent to the Deuteronomic work, has produced a book whose boundaries do not coincide with the beginnings or ends of the Deuteronomic "books" or even with their natural subdivisions. My thesis here is that the Deuteronomic mythic work gets very much recast by the canonical creation of 1 Samuel. In particular the reader is encouraged to frame the terms of the debate over government otherwise than the Deuteronomists did. The "canonical unconscious" is different from the "Deuteronomic unconscious" in surprising ways.

The Beginning and End of 1 Samuel

There were two stages of canonization. The first, which produced the Masoretic Jewish canon, gave us the beginning of our 1 Samuel but not the end. In the Jewish canon our 1 Samuel is only the first half of a single book of Samuel. The second stage, which produced the Greek and eventually the Christian canons, defined 1 Samuel as a book.[1] At this second stage Ruth was inserted between Judges and 1 Samuel.

---

[1] Though with a different name in the LXX, "1 Kingdoms." I use "1 Samuel" for convenience.

I shall discuss first the beginning of 1 Samuel, including an extended comment on the impact Ruth has on our reading of 1 Samuel, and then turn to the ending of the book.

The beginning of (1) Samuel. At the first (Masoretic) canonical stage, 1 Samuel 1 is made into the beginning of a very long book that extends to the threshold of the reign of Solomon. The character Samuel, whose birth story begins this book, casts a long shadow forward, far beyond his own much prolonged life. He gives his name to virtually the whole account of the reign of the two kings he anointed, Saul and David. On the other hand, he ceases to point backwards. The time that henceforth will be canonically registered under the name of "Judges" is over before Samuel arrives. Readers are encouraged to see Samuel not as a judge and a vindicator of judgeship but as inaugurating the process that leads to the monarchy of David.

Along with this effect on our reading of the character Samuel goes an equally strong encouragement to read judgeship and kingship in a certain way. The book of Samuel follows immediately upon the words, "In those days there was no king in Israel; all the people did what was right in their own eyes" (Judg 21:25). The reader of the book of Samuel not only anticipates that it will press quickly toward monarchy but also expects this change of government to be for the better. Anything would be better than the world depicted at the end of Judges! Furthermore, the reader is nudged toward understanding "In those days" as applying to *the whole epoch* of the judges rather than simply to Judges 17–21. The last words of Judges become a blanket judgment on judgeship as a system.

The same pro-monarchical logic that created the last verse of Judges also determined the point of division between Judges and Samuel. It is a logic that tends to forget that seeking a king is rejection of YHWH, and to forget also the bad experience Israel had with Gideon and Abimelech. It remembers instead the shortcomings of judgeship and looks back to Deuteronomy 17 as positive permission for kingship.

The impact of Ruth. At the second canonical stage nothing changes about the view forward from the beginning of what is now 1 Samuel, but the view backward is different since what now immediately precedes is not Judges, but Ruth. The presence of Ruth tends to make the beginning of 1 Samuel even more into a beginning, and to confirm the tendency to read it as the beginning of monarchy. Both the opening and the closing words of Ruth confirm this tendency. The opening, "In the days when the judges ruled," makes that time seem remote, a separate era from that of the books to follow. The closing, the very last word, is "David." I like to ask my students when David is first mentioned in the Bible. The answer is that it depends on what you mean by the Bible! The Jewish canon creates a sort of "messianic secret" around David; it seems reluctant to name him and does so only at the last possible moment (1 Sam 16:13 [84]). The LXX and Christian canons, on the other hand, long anticipate his appearance by naming him already in the book of Ruth. Ruth, we can even say, functions as a quasi-birth story for David,[2] a highly positive one, just as the account of Gibeah at the end of Judges functions as a highly negative quasi-birth story for Saul [67].

Ruth is a harvest story that moves from dearth to plenty. In its place in the Christian canon it becomes also a story of the move from judgeship to kingship. Hence judgeship is put on the side of dearth, kingship on the side of plenty. "In the days when the judges ruled, there was a famine in the land." This opening sentence of Ruth is in complete agreement with the closing sentence of Judges, which it immediately follows. The two sentences together convey the message that there was a famine in the land because there was no king in Israel. But by the end of Ruth there *is* a king in Israel, or at least the announcement of one. In fact the inclusion of Ruth and the creation of 1 Samuel result in a series of books that end respectively with (a) the urgent need for monarchy (Judges), (b) the announcement of the coming of David, founder of the "true" monarchy (Ruth), and (c) the resolution through Saul's death of the problem of an alternative monarchy to the true one (1 Samuel).

To define the issue even more sharply, Ruth offers a sort of canonical alternative to 1 Samuel. The two books achieve exactly the same journey: from "the days when the judges ruled" to "David." Before the reader of the LXX-Christian canon even hears of Samuel or Saul she knows that the ground covered by their joint story can be—has been—covered without them, much more briefly, simply, and pleasantly. Instead of the dark theological intricacies of conditional and unconditional covenants in 1 Samuel we have a sweet pastoral story that passes from famine to plenty, from death to birth.

This notion of Ruth as canonical alternative, or short-cut, is perhaps the tip of an iceberg, and I shall develop it briefly. Ruth alludes (in 4:12) to the story of Tamar and Judah in Genesis 38. What gives point to the allusion is not just the general theme of fertility but the fact that both stories provide genealogical information linking Judah to David. When one thinks of these two stories, Ruth and Genesis 38, a word that comes readily to mind is "intrusive." Genesis 38 famously intrudes into the

---

[2] Jacob Neusner entitles his book on the midrash on Ruth "The Mother of the Messiah" (*The Mother of the Messiah in Judaism: The Book of Ruth.* The Bible of Judaism Library. [Valley Forge, Pa.: Trinity Press International, 1993]).

Jacob-Joseph story, the story of the descent into Egypt. Historical critics tend simply to bracket it out from the reading of the "main" story.[3] Ruth is intrusive at the canonical level: it has been inserted into the Deuteronomic story of Israel.

These intrusions have analogous effects. Ruth suggests an alternative reading of the transition from judgeship to kingship, one that ignores the issues involved in the Mosaic, conditional covenant. Genesis 38, coming immediately after Joseph's journey into Egypt (37:36), suggests an alternative to the entire canonical "salvation history," which is centered on Israel's going down to Egypt and returning from there. In Genesis 38 Judah's story develops in Canaan. There his children are born. Why does his story ever need to leave Canaan? Judah does, in fact, continue to be an actor in the account of the going down to Egypt (Gen 43:1-10, etc.) But it is completely impossible to reconcile this role with ch. 38.[4]

Genesis 38 and Ruth together belong to a view of the past, centered on the tribe of Judah, that need not include Israel's being in Egypt at all. David is from Judah, and his triumph establishes the dominance of his tribe, so from a Davidic perspective it is Judah's story that is the founding story, the story that defines identity. Genesis 38 and Ruth, these sections that intrude into the salvation history and the Deuteronomic History, imply that we could do without exodus, conquest, Moses, and all the elaborate (conditional) theology and make do perfectly well with a canon that consisted of Genesis up to ch. 38 and then jumped straight to David via Ruth. These sections help evoke an alternative, indigenous past consisting of the first ancestors, the dimly-remembered judges, and the genealogy of David's house.[5] This same sense of the past is implied in the early chapters of 1 Chronicles, which see real history as beginning when "the LORD . . . turned the kingdom over to David"

---

[3] In reaction against this tendency literary readers seek ways of showing how it is integrally related to the main story. See for example Robert Alter, *The Art of Biblical Narrative* (London: Allen & Unwin, 1981) 3–12.

[4] See David Jobling, "Ruth Finds a Home: Canon, Politics, Method," in J. Cheryl Exum and D. J. A. Clines, eds., *The New Literary Criticism and the Hebrew Bible.* JSOT.S 143 (Sheffield: Sheffield Academic Press, 1993) 131–132.

[5] To Genesis 38 and Ruth we should perhaps add Judg 1:1-21. This passage is also concerned with the Judahite genealogy, and it is intrusive in the sense that it belongs to the material that intrudes between the two accounts of the death of Joshua, in Josh 24:28-31 and Judg 2:6-9 [34]. When Danna Fewell read a draft of this book she pointed out that Genesis 38, Judges 1, and Ruth all ambiguate the notion of "ethnically pure" lineage and point to an indigenous population whose descent is traced via women. She went on to suggest that my "alternative past" is the women's version of Israelite history. I reserve judgment on this suggestion since

(10:14). Anything before this is presented only as genealogy, in which pride of place belongs to Judah.[6]

From the perspective of the Davidic "winners" putting Ruth before 1 Samuel makes the latter superfluous, even dispensable. For them the less complex—and more Davidic—account of the past is much to be preferred.

The end of 1 Samuel. Much scholarly attention has been given to the beginning of 1 Samuel, but very little to its ending. The end point is usually seen as no more than a convenient point of division somewhere near the middle of the Masoretic book. Some readers prefer to make the division after 2 Samuel 1 so as to link David's lament there with the account of Saul's death in 1 Samuel 31.[7]

I shall turn in a moment to the specific question of 2 Samuel 1. More broadly, I have already suggested that important things change between 1 Samuel and the opening section of 2 Samuel [101–103]. Unexpectedly the Philistines disappear and the house of Saul reappears. The end point of 1 Samuel highlights these changes and has other striking effects. The end of 1 Samuel sees Israel without a king except in promise. Saul and his heirs are dead and David is in limbo.

At the end of 1 Samuel Israel seems to be back, in fact, to where it was at the end of Judges—"no king in Israel"! This observation is supported by the general similarity between the stories in Judges 20–21 and 1 Samuel 30—they both have an anarchic "Cowboys and Indians" feel, and they both tell of the mass abduction of women. There is also a very curious numerical coincidence in these stories. David divides his force of six hundred into groups of four hundred and two hundred (1 Sam 30:10) while exactly the same number of Benjaminite survivors are divided into exactly the same subgroups (Judg 20:47, 21:12).

The reader passing hurriedly from 1 Samuel to 2 Samuel in eager expectation of David's reappearance may fail to notice how ambiguous David's situation has become.[8] Compromised as he is by his association with the Philistines, can he be sure that he will be greeted with enthusiasm even by his former partisans? Like Saul in the first stage of

---

I shall later argue that the Davidic ideology exploits the powerful initiatives of women, including Ruth, to serve purely patriarchal ends [150–160, 173–175].

[6] 1 Chronicles 2–4. Despite the parsimony of the narrative allusions in these chapters the Genesis 38 story rates two full verses (2:4-5)!

[7] So J. P. Fokkelman, *The Crossing Fates (I Sam. 13–31 & II Sam. 1). Narrative Art and Poetry in the Books of Samuel*, Volume II. (Assen and Maastricht: Van Gorcum, 1986).

[8] I shall later make this ambiguity the basis for my new reading of the end of 1 Samuel [234–240, 286–288].

his career (up to 1 Samuel 12), David at the end of 1 Samuel has no sons (though he does have wives). Does he have what it takes to be a dynast? Before we are far into 2 Samuel, David's sons will spring up like weeds (2 Sam 3:2-5).

In respect to David the division after 1 Samuel 31 has a different effect, I suggest, even from a division after 2 Samuel 1. In 2 Samuel 1 David already steps out of ambiguity to take center stage. He is the one to whom messages of state are delivered, the one to speak the official eulogy on the fallen royal house. The narrator seems to crown David as soon as Saul is dead, even if it takes the Israelites a little longer to do so.

The other important issue at the end of 1 Samuel is the Philistine domination. This would seem to be a real obstacle to any rapid narrative movement toward kingship for David. That the Philistines do not, in fact, present an obstacle is one of the big surprises I have identified at the beginning of 2 Samuel.

In summary, the reader who pauses to look around at the end of 1 Samuel will ask whether David's royal prospects are still on track. At a deeper level she may ask whether Israel will resume being a monarchy at all, or continue in its familiar role of subservience to foreign occupation. In asking this latter question she will be in touch, I believe, with a deep stratum of 1 Samuel, a stratum where dynastic monarchy as such is in question. The rest of the chapter will excavate this stratum.

The Book of Samuel and Saul

The creation of 1 Samuel, with just the beginning and ending that it has, alters the impact of both the Deuteronomic History and the Jewish canon. It creates *a time between* judgeship and dynastic kingship, a time of transition from one to the other, but different, perhaps, from either.

Judges and 2 Samuel present the two main options in a generally negative way. I have already argued that our book of Judges has been organized to highlight what is negative and to marginalize what is positive about the judge system [33–34]. But is 2 Samuel negative about dynastic kingship? Surprisingly, if we take it as a whole, it is more negative than positive.[9] At least it takes much of the gloss off David's rule. It might be possible to stomach the sordid wars between the houses of Saul and David (2 Samuel 2–4) if, as ch. 7 claims, these are necessary to

---

[9] This is the general conclusion of Robert Polzin, *David and the Deuteronomist: A Literary Study of the Deuteronomic History. Part Three: 2 Samuel.* Indiana Studies in Biblical Literature (Bloomington, Ind.: Indiana University Press, 1993).

bring about unparalleled benefit for Israel. But where is the benefit in the latter part of the book? The effect of dynastic kingship, on the showing of 2 Samuel 9–20, is that Israel must bother itself with the unseemly behavior of the king's sons rather than with important national issues.

1 Samuel is created as a space between these negatives. What is this book, exactly, and how does it assess Israel's options for government?

If one wanted to give 1 Samuel a descriptive name, a subtitle, the first that would come to mind, surely, is "The Book of Samuel and Saul." In the most precise way the book begins with the birth of Samuel and ends with the death of Saul (so precisely that it even lops off 2 Samuel 1). It focuses the reader's attention on the relationship between these two characters, on the transition from one to the other.

A famous interpretive problem in the very first chapter of 1 Samuel suggests that in some mysterious way these two characters share a single identity. The person who names a child in the Bible very often gives an explanation of the name based on an etymology (so, for example, many times in Genesis 29–30). This is what Hannah seems to be doing in 1 Sam 1:20, but in explaining the name "Samuel" by saying that she "asked" YHWH for the child she uses a verb, *š'l*, that is actually related to the name "Saul," not "Samuel"! In 1:28 she uses the same verb when she says that Samuel is "given" (or "lent") to YHWH, and this time the form of the verb that she uses is *šā'ûl*—identical with the name of the future king! Who then is the leader "asked" of YHWH by Israel? Is it Saul, Samuel, or in some sense both?

Samuel is the last judge, Saul the first king. But these functional characterizations are problematic, for Samuel is already more than a judge, while Saul is not yet a real king. Samuel is associated with a potpourri of leadership categories. He succeeds a priest and arrogates to himself priestly functions, he is a prophet who delivers oracles and leads a prophetic band, he makes and unmakes kings. Saul teeters on the verge of kingship, but his kingship is less than real since it is not allowed to develop into a dynasty. He often acts much more like a judge, and twice we find him joining a band of prophets. As they are created in the text of 1 Samuel these are anomalous leaders, liminal figures who perhaps want to direct our attention to some option different from judgeship *or* kingship.

A Third Way of Government

I want to suggest a quite new way of looking at leadership in 1 Samuel. Samuel and Saul, though their combined lifetimes define the scope of the book, are not the only leaders found in it. At the beginning we enter upon a scene in which Israel is somehow under the leadership of the priest-judge Eli. At the end we leave a scene in which David has been announced as the successor to Saul. The four leaders are held together by the following pattern of surrogate fatherhood and sonship:

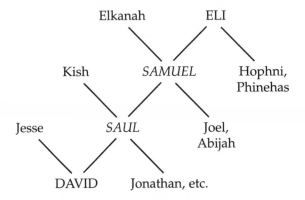

The top-left to bottom-right diagonals represent natural fatherhood-sonship, and the central top-right to bottom-left diagonal (in upper case) represents surrogate fatherhood-sonship. Through three transitions in leadership we see the following pattern. The leader has natural sons who play a significant role in the story, but he adopts the next leader as a surrogate son. This surrogate son has (obviously) a natural father who plays some role, though a subordinate one, in the story.

This scheme exactly defines 1 Samuel and is almost unique to this book. Certainly there is nothing like it in either Judges or 2 Samuel. Another, albeit cumbersome, subtitle suggests itself: "The Book of Surrogate Fatherhood and Sonship Among National Leaders."

I shall explore this pattern at length. It constitutes a form of leadership succession that avoids the main problems of both judgeship and dynastic kingship. The leader in place adopts in his lifetime a successor who will take over at his death. In contrast to judgeship this assures continuity of government. In contrast to dynastic kingship it allows for YHWH's free choice of each leader. Why could Israel not simply continue to govern itself in this way?

In fact this system is not entirely unique. It is a reversion to the principle of succession from Moses to Joshua (see Num 27:18-23), and the reader of the biblical narrative is constrained to ask whether a great deal of trouble might not have been avoided by YHWH's appointing a successor to Joshua in the same way! The other biblical example of surrogacy is the succession of Elisha to Elijah (2 Kings 2)—though there are kings in place, Elijah and Elisha are national leaders from the text's point of view.

To look at 1 Samuel in terms of the surrogacy pattern is to focus sharply on the processes of transition from one leader to another, and this is what I shall be doing. I shall be looking at the literary creation of the relationships between Eli and Samuel, Samuel and Saul, Saul and David, how these relationships are given definite qualities—practical, emotional, and so on. What goes on between the old leader and the new?

To do this effectively it will be necessary to filter out extraneous issues, issues that arise from the necessities of various other threads of plot—the issues, in fact, with which we have been dealing in the last two chapters. For example, the relationship between Samuel and Saul is loaded with extensive baggage by the necessity of achieving the transition to monarchy. Still, there may be elements of the relationship that escape this necessity.

Rather than working sequentially through 1 Samuel I want to work toward the Samuel-Saul relationship, which is the pivotal one for the whole book. I shall first present (or review) what happens in the other generations (Saul-David and Eli-Samuel), in order to sharpen my reading of the transition from Samuel to Saul.

Saul and David. As my earlier reading indicated, the pressure of the text's other theological programs is here particularly powerful [90–99]. Saul *must* be at enmity with David against David's will. Events in general *must* tend to favor David and disfavor Saul. Jonathan, Saul's natural son, *must* stand in a particular set of relations with both Saul and David. These are the main filters through which the surrogacy data have to be observed. I shall build from the Saul-David accounts a checklist of features of the surrogacy pattern that I will later use for purposes of comparison.

In the surrogacy system (see the diagram) there are four functional male roles: old leader, new leader, new leader's natural father, old leader's natural son(s). Here these roles are played by Saul, David, Jesse, and Jonathan, but the family constellation extends in this case to include Michal, Saul's daughter.[10]

---

[10] Michal's sister Merab scarcely becomes a character. Alice Bach notes that "David . . . becomes a surrogate son to Saul." She sees 1 Samuel as "a taut chain of fathers and sons, tensions of male power" ("The Pleasure of Her Text," in eadem, ed., *The Pleasure of Her Text: Feminist Readings of Biblical & Historical Texts* [Philadelphia: Trinity Press International, 1990] 37). Bach stresses Oedipal conflict between fathers and sons (real or surrogate) rather than the positive features of succession that I am trying to discern. She deals also with my theme of mediation of the relationships by

1. Language. What we are looking for here is simply the use of "father" and "son." David calls Saul "father" (24:11) and Saul several times calls David "son" (24:16; 26:17, 21, 25). David also refers to himself as Nabal's son (25:10), and I have suggested above that Nabal stands for Saul.

2. Acknowledgment of the succession. In 23:17 Jonathan states that Saul has already acknowledged that David will be king, and in the following chapter (24:20) Saul makes this acknowledgment directly to David. The first case may be a reluctant bowing to the inevitable, but in the second Saul, despite his powerful enmity toward David, expresses a somewhat enthusiastic recognition of David's leadership qualities.

3. The new leader's natural father. At issue here is the process of separation between natural father and son that frees the son for the surrogate relationship. In David's first appearance, the anointing scene, Jesse does not even count him among his sons! Samuel invites *all* the sons to the sacrifice (16:5), but Jesse does not bring David and has to be prompted by Samuel to remember him at all (v. 11). Eliab's later words (17:28) confirm the impression that David is treated more as a servant, a sheep-boy, than as a son. Shades of Cinderella. Thus there is a lot of distance between this father and son from the outset.

In the subsequent narrative Saul directly commands Jesse to yield his son (16:19, 22) and then will not permit David to "return to his father's house" (18:2). There is no reason to think that Jesse is reluctant to let his son go. His profit from David as Saul's servant will likely more than offset his loss of a sheep-boy.

During the time that he is at enmity with David, and pursuing him, Saul many times refers to David pejoratively as "the son of Jesse" (so does Nabal in 25:8). Saul's avoidance of the hated name of David is psychologically understandable, but why should the patronymic "son of Jesse" be pejorative? Perhaps Saul in these places recalls David's natural father in order to distance himself from David. His use of "the son of Jesse" certainly stands in striking contrast to "my son David" (24:16, etc.)[11]

4. The old leader's natural son. Here more than anywhere the relationships are overdetermined by the special theological work required

---

women and her work in fact implies a feminist critique of the surrogacy pattern [191–194].

[11] For a full discussion of the estrangement between David and Jesse see Joel Rosenberg, *King and Kin: Political Allegory in the Hebrew Bible.* Indiana Studies in Biblical Literature (Bloomington, Ind.: Indiana University Press, 1986) 174–176.

of Jonathan. Jonathan's sole function is to enable the transition of power to David. This function drives a wedge between Saul and Jonathan since Saul looks to Jonathan to be his successor (20:31). Jonathan's relation to David becomes the occasion for Saul's sharp reproach (20:30-34, cf. 22:8).

Still, the estrangement between father and son is not due entirely to David. Even before David comes on the scene (chs. 13–14) the impression of distance between Saul and Jonathan is much stronger than the impression of closeness. Saul sees Jonathan as a rival, a threat. He is even ready to put him to death (14:44). The text's failure to identify Jonathan as Saul's son when it first introduces him (13:2-3) nicely indicates this distance between them.

5. The role of women. David becomes Saul's son-in-law. This cements the surrogate relationship in a specific way. The son-in-law theme is common in folktales, and in some leadership systems the son-in-law is actually the successor [100]. In popular usage the son-in-law is a "son" ("You're not losing a daughter, you're gaining a son"). Like her brother Jonathan, Michal loves David and assists him. But their marriage is aborted when Saul takes Michal away from David and gives her to someone else (25:44). The son-in-law relationship therefore fails. In 2 Samuel the marriage proves a failure also in personal terms (2 Sam 6:20-23). In this case, then, there is ambiguity about how the son-in-law motif might relate to surrogacy.

In 25:43 David marries a woman called Ahinoam, which is the name also of Saul's wife (14:50). The text does not say directly that David takes Saul's wife. There are several points, however, that make us speculate whether this is not the implication. First, in 2 Sam 12:8 YHWH says to David, "I gave . . . your master's [i.e., Saul's] wives into your bosom."[12] Second, it is striking that the formulae used to identify the two Ahinoams—by patronymic in 14:50 ("daughter of Ahimaaz"), by place of origin in 25:43 ("Ahinoam of Jezreel")—do not rule out their being the same person. Third, 25:43 follows immediately upon the story of David, Abigail, and Nabal, which I have suggested functions as an allegory of the relationship between Saul and David [92–93], and in which David takes the wife of Nabal, the character who stands for Saul. This introduces an entirely less savory way in which a woman may mediate between generations of leaders. I shall later connect it with the negative impact that monarchy has on the lives of women [160].

---

[12] Jo Ann Hackett, "1 and 2 Samuel," in Carol A. Newsom and Sharon H. Ringe, eds., *The Women's Bible Commentary* (Louisville, Ky.: Westminster/John Knox, 1992) 92.

General comments. Beyond these specific features we need to get a more general sense of the Saul-David relationship. Saul's attitude to David rapidly turns to enmity, jealousy, and sheer rage, as the theological program requires, but at beginning and end we get a different impression. In 16:14-23 David appears as a real help to Saul when he suffers under the burden of leadership—certainly a more congenial "son" than the Jonathan of chs. 13–14. And at the end Saul comes to realize David's qualities and even to reach some contentment about his succession (chs. 24 and 26), though this does not lead to a reconciliation (27:1).

Given all the other things that are going on in the story, it is hard to make definite statements. But features compatible with the surrogacy pattern do seem to be preserved in the Saul-David relationship.[13]

Eli and Samuel. This is the least developed of the surrogate relationships, and it can be covered quite briefly.

1. Language. Eli calls Samuel "son" (3:6, 16).

2. Acknowledgment of the succession. Eli does not specifically acknowledge Samuel as his successor though he does acknowledge YHWH's call to Samuel (3:8).

3. The new leader's natural father. Samuel is physically removed from his natural father Elkanah at a much earlier age even than David. Elkanah seems quite uninterested in Samuel and tends to be absent at key moments in the story.

4. The old leader's natural sons. Eli becomes estranged from his sons (2:22-25), not only because of their wickedness but also because of his inability to influence them (2:25; cf. somewhat differently 3:13). In 4:17-18 it seems to be more the loss of the ark than his sons' death that precipitates Eli's own death. Samuel has no direct relationship to Eli's wicked sons, Hophni and Phinehas, but it is their failure that opens the way for him, as we see from the artful intertwining of their career with his (2:11-26). To some extent he directly replaces them, as he becomes a functionary at the Shiloh shrine.

5. The role of women. The mediation of the Eli-Samuel relationship by a woman is quite different from the son-in-law pattern we found with Saul and David, but it is even more pivotal. The mediator is Hannah, whose position is diametrically opposite to that of Michal—mother of the new leader rather than daughter of the old. As I shall argue more fully, the initiative whereby Samuel becomes a leader and Eli's successor comes entirely from Hannah [134–135]. Eli's surrogate fatherhood

---

[13] For another view of this relationship, through the eyes of Rembrandt, see [268–273].

is strongly confirmed by the fact that Samuel can be said to have been born as a result of the initial encounter between Eli and Hannah (1 Sam 1:9-18; Eli's role has a faint resemblance to the role of the divine being in annunciation scenes).

General comments. It is not clear whether Eli feels any warmth for Samuel. Romantic Sunday School readings of 3:1-18 can mislead: there are no terms of endearment other than the repeated "My son." In fact, Eli calls down a curse on Samuel in 3:17, and we must ask whether Eli is not complicit in the abuse of Samuel—not only the night and morning of terror in ch. 3 but also Samuel's forcible separation from home and parents at a very young age. It is revealing that Eli is absent from the passage that mentions Samuel's precocious national leadership during Eli's lifetime (3:19–4:1a). Perhaps to achieve this position Samuel has had to distance himself from his mentor.

Of the three generations this is the one in which a definite apprentice relationship most clearly exists between the old and the new leader.

Samuel and Saul. I shall develop some of the points at much greater length here, since this is the key relationship in 1 Samuel.

1. Language. Samuel and Saul never call each other "father" and "son," but in the account of their first meeting (9:1–10:16) there is some highly suggestive play with these words, especially "father." Consider first the following passage, which comes after Samuel has predicted that Saul will attach himself to a prophetic band "and be turned into another man" (10:6):

> When all who knew him before saw how he prophesied with the prophets, the people said to one another, "What has come over the son of Kish? Is Saul also among the prophets?" A man of the place answered, "And who is their father?" Therefore it became a proverb, "Is Saul also among the prophets?" (10:11-12)

Both words, "son" and "father," occur in this passage. The question "And who is their father?" is awkwardly placed, since it separates "Is Saul also among the prophets?" from the note that these words became a proverb. Such awkwardness usually means that the intrusive material has some special importance. The question of who is the father of the band implies the question of who is *Saul's* father, since Saul has become a member of the band. The LXX, in fact, reads not "Who is their father?" but "Who is *his* [i.e., Saul's] father?" The implied answer is Samuel, especially since in the reprise of this incident (19:18-24) Samuel is said to be "at the head" of the prophetic band. Samuel has become the prophetic "father" of "the son of Kish" (this is perhaps what it means to "be turned into another man").

This suggestion is strengthened by the account of Saul's return home, which follows immediately (10:14-16). It is surely very striking that it is not his father Kish who meets and questions him, but an uncle—even though it was his father who sent him on his journey. Since there seems to be no point to this substitution at any other level we may take it to imply distance between father and son. Kish does not appear in the story again.

Finally, though it is hard to see a clear link, this sequence recalls a question attributed to Kish earlier, "What shall I do for/about my son?" (10:2). We are told specifically that Kish asks this question because he is "worrying" about Saul. Yet Kish is not worried enough even to meet Saul on his return. Perhaps distance between the two characters is confirmed by the extraordinary distance the text places between Kish and his own question, which is introduced as Samuel's prediction of what two anonymous men whom Saul will meet will report Kish as having said!

2. Acknowledgment of the succession. This feature gets swallowed up in the dynamics of the Deuteronomic debate over judgeship and kingship. Samuel must be the kingmaker, which obviously implies acknowledging Saul's succession, but the acknowledgment has to be grudging since Samuel is reluctant to be succeeded by a king. The clearest statement of the acknowledgment is in 12:1-2.

3. The new leader's natural father. On the relation of Saul to his father there is nothing to add to point 1 above. Samuel is not brought into any relationship to Kish.

4. The old leader's natural sons. Again the dynamics of judgeship and kingship distort our view. I have suggested that the introduction of Samuel's sons as unworthy leaders (8:1-3) is the text's desperate ploy for laying the blame for kingship on Samuel [62–64]. The historians were obliged to provide Samuel with bad sons and the precedent of Eli and his sons lay ready at hand. Once they have provided the occasion for the people's request for a king the text will take no further interest in Samuel's sons. For example, there is no interplay between their failure and Saul's rise, such as we found between Eli's sons and Samuel. The most we can say for present purposes is that the old leader's sons do appear in the story and that the new leader becomes a substitute for them: "your sons do not follow in your ways; appoint for us, then, a king" (8:5).

5. The role of women. There is no woman who plays in the creation of the Samuel-Saul relationship such a powerful mediating role as those of Michal and Hannah in the other two generations. But there are two important avenues we need to explore. The first takes us again to the story of Samuel's first meeting with Saul in 9:1–10:16. Readers have noted in this story an allusion to the type-scene of "women at the well."[14] When Saul arrives in Samuel's town he meets women who have come out to draw water (9:11-13). In like circumstances Abraham's servant (Genesis 24), Jacob (Genesis 29), and Moses (Exodus 2) also met a woman or women. In each of *those* cases the woman/women turned out to be daughter(s) to a prominent person, and a marriage resulted. There is no suggestion that the women in 1 Samuel 9 were Samuel's daughters or that Saul married one of them. Still, the allusion to the type-scene is unmistakable. Perhaps it betokens a *failure* of mediation in the Samuel-Saul relationship. A natural connection might have sprung up between them but did not.

The other avenue carries us much farther afield. There is a woman who powerfully mediates the relationship between Samuel and Saul, one whose function is mediation in the most literal sense: the Medium of Endor (ch. 28). Narratively she enters the story much too late to mediate the transition of leadership from Samuel to Saul. This belatedness could be another marker of the *failure* of mediation in this generation, but I believe that the medium is a narrative mediator in a much more profound sense than we have seen so far. She focuses the question of whether it is possible to achieve mediation between the present and the past. Later we shall read her story in detail and draw from it far-reaching conclusions about Israel's relationship to its past [185–189, 303–305].

General comments. The Deuteronomic work creates a particularly opaque filter through which to view the relationship between Samuel and Saul, but the surrogacy angle, I believe, enables us to reread the dynamics of the relationship in interesting ways and to give a more satisfying account of it than we could before. The dominant theme of my earlier reading was that, after making Saul king, Samuel assumes a continuing authority over him. Because of Samuel's role as maker and breaker of kings this often comes across as an alienating kind of authority. Already in the anointing scene Samuel begins to tell Saul what to do (10:8), and the following episode of the prophetic band (vv. 9-12), especially when read with 19:18-24, looks like Samuel asserting dominance over Saul. In the rejection scenes Samuel simply cows Saul with the force of (what he presents as) the divine judgment.

Nevertheless, there is something unsatisfying about this reading. It fails to do justice to the warmth that Samuel expresses towards Saul.

---

[14] See Alter, *Art of Biblical Narrative* 60–61; Polzin, *Samuel and the Deuteronomist: A Literary Study of the Deuteronomic History. Part Two: 1 Samuel* (San Francisco: Harper & Row, 1989) 93.

Already in 9:1–10:16 Samuel gives Saul special honor at the feast (9:22-24) when YHWH has not instructed him to do so. His words in 10:24 could scarcely express greater enthusiasm for Saul. In ch. 15 he expresses such regret over Saul's rejection that YHWH rebukes him for it (16:1).

It is interesting to test the limits of a reading in which Samuel's power over Saul is the power of *tutelage*.[15] Samuel instructs Saul as the master does the apprentice. "I will instruct you in the good and right way," Samuel says to Israel in 12:23. How better to exercise this function than as advisor to the new king? In such a reading, extricated from the Deuteronomic agenda, Samuel is a strict instructor, not patient with failure but deeply attached to his pupil.

Samuel's first instruction to Saul (10:8) reads easily as the words of a master to an apprentice, and the incident of the prophetic band is most naturally understood in terms of a master's tutelage (cf. especially the relation between Elijah and Elisha in 1 Kings 19:19-21, 2 Kings 2:1-18). It is also worth recalling that in 1 Sam 11:7 Samuel and Saul lead Israel *together*. Shorn of the heavy theological baggage, what happens in 13:8-15 is that Samuel rebukes Saul for no other cause than disobeying his instructions (recall that Samuel makes no direct appeal to YHWH's authority). Teachers set their pupils difficult and even unfair tests just to see what they will do. It is in this vein that Samuel arranges to be a bit late.

Even in ch. 15, where YHWH gets into the picture and the theological stakes are high, it is possible to read a story of Samuel's instructing Saul in the finer points of the Law. But Samuel's course of instruction is now violently interrupted. The student he has worked with so long is suddenly consigned to oblivion, and Samuel, perhaps, will have to begin again with a new apprentice. It is no surprise that he is upset and, in the following scene of David's anointing (16:1-13), reluctant and alienated from YHWH.

1 Samuel 19:18-24 creates difficult problems however we read it. It contradicts 15:35, which says that Samuel and Saul never met again. And Samuel's way of dealing with Saul's intention to murder David

---

[15] In an unpublished paper ("Sex in the Messianic Age: David's Relationships as Fore Play?") Walter Deller suggests "that Samuel's role vis-à-vis Saul is as his 'liminal instructor' and that Saul's 'failure' is intimately bound up with Samuel's inability to let go of Saul to be the person/role he needs to be—i.e. Samuel's failure to enact his role to completion." I agree with this. What Deller means by "liminal instructor" is the instructor of a novice in a rite of passage. For me the "passage" involved is not only Saul's but, more importantly, Israel's passage from the old order to the new.

seems almost jocular: he puts Saul into prophetic trance, giving David time to escape. A "tutelage" reading may help. Samuel's *new* pupil, David, looks to him for help. Samuel's rejected pupil, Saul, on seeing Samuel again, cannot avoid falling back into the old pattern of apprentice. The technique of recalling the beginning of Saul's career when he first joined Samuel's prophetic band (10:9-13) compellingly supports this reading.

The final scene is the posthumous appearance of Samuel to Saul in ch. 28. Even more than in ch. 15 Saul is *in extremis*. He hopes that even death may not have broken his bond with his teacher; and to a degree his hope is justified: Samuel's ghost does at least appear. Saul, most revealingly, responds to the ghost's request for an explanation with the words, "I have summoned you *to tell me what I should do*" (v. 15). Samuel here shows no warmth; his response to Saul is fully governed by the theological agenda. But it is exactly in the terms of ch. 15 that he responds, and perhaps it is not wrong to catch here an echo of the regret he expressed in that chapter. At any rate both 19:18-24 and 28:3-25 preserve a strong undercurrent of the relationship of Samuel to Saul as still that of master to learner.

Assessment of the surrogacy pattern. In arguing that 1 Samuel—precisely 1 Samuel—shows an unexpected coherence based on a surrogacy pattern of leadership I have, of course, read the data in such a way as to make the hypothesis as plausible as I can. Let us now try to assess what has been achieved.

The firmest basis for the hypothesis is the macro-structure from which I began. My diagram [112] *does* summarize 1 Samuel, so far as its major male characters are concerned, extraordinarily well. This fit not only suggests but demands that we see how far the surrogacy pattern can account for details, whether it can assert itself through the more or less opaque screens of the other things that are going on in the text.

Samuel, Saul, and less clearly Eli accept and acknowledge the succession of the next leader. But this is not to say much; it is really the minimum requirement for the hypothesis. The language of "father" and "son" provides more significant support,[16] but this language is neither very prevalent nor, perhaps, very remarkable,[17] and the full weight of the hypothesis certainly cannot rest on it.

---

[16] Note that in another example of surrogacy Elisha calls Elijah "father" (2 Kings 2:12).

[17] When I was growing up in the north of England it was normal for any mature male to address me as "son."

What is most striking about the way the pattern is worked out in 1 Samuel is the regularity with which the male characters other than the leaders are brought into the action. We need to speculate whether dealing with these characters is in some way essential to the system. I begin with *the new leader's natural father.* In a surrogacy system a process of separation of the new leader from his natural father would be necessary. The father would have to give up family expectations for the good of the nation. But what are we to make of the apparent indifference to their sons that is common to the fathers in all three generations—Elkanah, Kish, and Jesse? All these men seem to be or become distanced from their sons (the most complicated case is that of Kish, who expresses concern for Saul but then just disappears). None of them express any sense that honor is being done to their sons, and hence to themselves.

Perhaps this literary creation of distance is a way of averting the problem of the natural father's powerful rights, in a patriarchy, over his son. What would happen if he were to assert those rights? It is intrinsic to the system, of course, that the surrogate father is a person of power, so that the natural father would likely not get far if he tried to assert his rights. This is most clearly suggested by Saul's peremptory removal of David from Jesse. But why not avoid the potential conflict altogether, the text seems to suggest, by making the fathers involved indifferent to what becomes of their sons?

Another possibility that would be worth exploring is along psychological lines. Is there a tendency for men whose fathers are indifferent to them to demonstrate the precociousness and ambition out of which leaders are made?

The converse issue is that of *the old leader's natural son(s).* This relationship is apt to be particularly distorted in a text whose main overt work is to account for the transition to kingship. Heredity is in the air; the merits of leaders' sons as leaders are under scrutiny. We need to keep such potential distortion in mind as we look for indications of how accounts of the surrogacy system deal with this relationship.

In a well-functioning surrogacy system the leader's natural sons would have no expectations and their father would not be allowed to entertain any on their behalf. This does not, however, rule out the envy, ambition, and nepotism that tend to find their way into any system. 1 Samuel is very clear that in the first two generations the natural sons, Eli's and Samuel's, are *proven* bad leaders. The implication, it seems to me, is that even as the text is pressing on toward kingship it is acutely aware of kingship's main problem, that a hereditary system may provide bad leaders. Perhaps it is at the same time reaching out toward the possibility of a different system that avoids the problem. This gives plausibility to my surrogacy hypothesis.

The third generation, however, departs from such a simple pattern. Far from being bad, Jonathan is almost preternaturally good (though not necessarily in ways that would make him a good leader). But this ought not to make us question the conclusions we drew from the earlier generations, since Jonathan simply could not do his necessary theological work if he were a bad character. A definite distance exists between him and his father Saul from very early in their story, before David even appears.

In all three generations, therefore, something is amiss between the leader and his natural sons. Is there something about "the precociousness and ambition out of which leaders are made" (to repeat the phrase I used a moment ago) that tends to make them bad fathers?

In each generation there is significant mediation by a woman, but it is worked out very differently in each case. In the Eli-Samuel generation the mediation is by the new leader's mother. The Saul-David generation is a mirror image of this, with mediation through the old leader's daughter (the son-in-law pattern). Another possibility that is at least hinted at is that David steals Saul's wife. The Samuel-Saul generation is quite different. After an abortive hint at the son-in-law pattern (ch. 9) mediation comes at (or even after) the last moment, through the Medium of Endor. For now let this summary suffice. There is considerably more to say on this theme, but it is best left for my survey of the women of 1 Samuel [191–194].

Of all the features we have looked at, the one that seems most intrinsic to the surrogacy system is the relationship of *instruction* between the old and the new leader.[18] Instruction of Samuel by Eli is implied in the terms of Samuel's dedication to temple service (see especially 1 Sam 3:1). It is altogether absent from the relation of Saul to David, but the reasons are understandable. I have tried to show how this category of instruction can provide a very plausible reading of the whole relationship of Samuel to Saul.

Conclusion. I began this chapter by suggesting that the chief literary effect of the creation of the book called "1 Samuel" is the carving out of a space, literary but also theological or mythic, between judgeship and dynastic kingship. I have now suggested that what most fills that space is the assertion of a third way, a system of government different from both the others. This third way is first of all a formal structure suggested by the shape of the book, but it acquires real content in some of the particular features of the book. It gains further substance

---

[18] This is evident between Moses and Joshua, e.g., Exod 17:10, 14; Deut 31:7-8; 34:9, and between Elijah and Elisha.

from comparison with relationships elsewhere in the Bible, between Moses and Joshua and between Elijah and Elisha.

I am not aware that anyone before me has recognized surrogacy as structurally defining 1 Samuel. I do not propose, and tend not to believe, that anyone at any stage of the production of 1 Samuel consciously thought of surrogacy as a system. What I rather suggest (and I shall discuss this much more fully at the end of the book) is that the later generations of Israel, endlessly reimagining and agonizing over the past, meditating on the inadequacies of the models the past offered for each new present, unconsciously recognized or created this third way and framed it in a "book." No such system of leadership succession ever actually existed in Israel. Its "existence" is textual and canonical, not mimetic in the sense of reflecting any known history.[19]

I have identified and tried to explain the relative absence of *class* indicators in 1 Samuel [103–104]. Does the surrogacy pattern add anything to a class analysis? A surrogacy system does not in principle require the sharp class division of a statist, monarchical system. Someone lacking class privilege could advance through his merits,[20] though there might be class constraints on who was well positioned to do so. At first sight this "rags to riches" possibility is not developed in 1 Samuel. The surrogate sons come from prosperous families.[21]

However, this may be too hasty. We must beware of applying in a doctrinaire way our own class categories. For example, David and Samuel are *younger* sons of their natural fathers, and Saul is from a weak clan in a weak tribe (9:19). These may be systemic disadvantages as important as those we associate with class. The account of David's becoming Saul's son-in-law has elements of a rags-to-riches fantasy [231–232]. At the very least we can say that the surrogacy pattern expands the horizons of a class reading of 1 Samuel.

I offer my surrogacy hypothesis for what it may be worth. If it were to achieve nothing else, it has at least given us the opportunity to study a series of relationships unique in the Bible. But I believe it does much more. In her book *Death and Dissymmetry* Mieke Bal proposes a "countercoherence" for the book of Judges. By this she means a new prin-

---

[19] It has occurred to me that such a system may have had an afterlife within Judaism in patterns of rabbinic succession, but to pursue this would exceed my competence.

[20] Or her merits! Surrogacy is to all appearances a male system but there is no intrinsic reason why it needs to be.

[21] Kish is called "a man of wealth" (9:1). Jesse, like Kish, looks like a farmer and rancher on a large scale (see 17:17-18). Elkanah's unusually long genealogy (1:1) implies, like Kish's (9:1), social prominence.

ciple of organization against which the prevailing principle of organization can be measured point by point and opened up to critique.[22] The surrogacy pattern precisely fits this definition of countercoherence. It emerges from the text as a means for critically examining the existing "coherences" of judgeship and kingship, and offers a pattern of government that might be an improvement over both of them.

---

[22] *Death and Dissymmetry: The Politics of Coherence in the Book of Judges* (Chicago: University of Chicago Press, 1988) 16–21.

Part III

GENDER: HANNAH AND HER SISTERS

PROLOGUE

This part of the book takes up issues of gender. This mainly means paying attention to the presence of women in 1 Samuel, but under this category I shall also revisit the relationship between David and Jonathan.

The character Hannah is central to my reading. She is the first major character in 1 Samuel and her actions are of key importance in the way the story develops, but my reason for making her so prominent is also a personal one. When I received the greatest academic honor of my life I chose to speak about Hannah, and I wished in this book to present what I then said as intact as possible.[1] This is what I do in Chapter 6, which is for this reason quite short. My portrait of Hannah is very much within the "recuperative" feminist paradigm and is extremely positive. In fact I now consider it too positive, and will nuance it later in the book [306–307]. But it has its own logic, and in Chapter 6 I prefer to leave it alone.

The topic of Chapter 7 is the way the role of women changes as Israel shifts from one governmental system to another. In moving to issues of gender, therefore, we do not turn away from those of class. In fact, we will find here and in Part IV that the approach via gender or race makes the class issues more accessible. Many scholars have suggested that movement to a more centralized, statist political system restricts the options of women. It is of great methodological interest that different scholars have made this suggestion out of widely varied disciplinary backgrounds—on the one hand from primarily literary readings of the text, on the other hand from considerations of history and anthropology—and I shall explore the implications of this convergence.

---

[1] I refer to my presidential address to the Canadian Society of Biblical Studies; see "Hannah's Desire," *BCSBS* 53 (1994) 19–32.

The context in which we read proves to be especially important for reading the women of 1 Samuel. The effect of monarchy on women is to be seen primarily in the development of the characters of David's women, Michal, Abigail, and Ahinoam of Jezreel. But these are characters whose stories belong to the Book of the Everlasting Covenant: they begin in 1 Samuel but are completed only in 2 Samuel, so that we need to ask what is the effect of the creation of 1 Samuel on our reading of them. Likewise the women in 1 Samuel 1–12 need to be considered in the context of the Extended Book of Judges, and the canonical presence of Ruth takes on special importance in a feminist reading. Hannah proves to be a pivot point for readings in these various contexts. She is in close touch with the women of Judges (and Ruth), but the tentacles of monarchy reach back to her too—a little bit in the text, a great deal in the interpretation of it.

In connection with David and his women I take up David's relationship to Jonathan as a gender issue. The possibility that theirs was a consummated gay relationship is of such importance in our current cultural scene that it must not be ignored. I conclude that the role Jonathan plays is analogous to that of David's wives.

Chapter 8 asks what we can say about the women precisely of 1 Samuel, the canonical book. This chapter is analogous to Chapter 5, where I asked the same question about government. I look at *all* the women in the book, including some hypothetical or implicit ones, and make some general comments about the themes and structures that emerge. The most substantial reading here is of the Medium of Endor, whom I read as a very important and positive character. She is the last major woman character to be introduced, as Hannah is the first, and I now think of them as the two stout bookends of 1 Samuel rather than seeing Hannah in solitary splendor.

Chapter 6

HANNAH'S DESIRE

1 Samuel begins with a woman's story, the story of Hannah, which extends as far as 2:21. My reading of it is in four parts. In the first two parts I concentrate on the text, looking first at the character Hannah and then at the narrator. In the third part I use an intertextual method, reading the story of Hannah that is *implied* in Luke's use of 1 Samuel as a prototype for the beginning of his gospel. In the last part I turn to the modern interpretation of Hannah's story, looking at the assumptions that underlie one group of literary readings.

My overarching category is that of *desire:* how the text and its interpretation are constituted by the meeting of the desires of subjects— characters, narrator, interpreters perceived as individuals or as groups. These desiring subjects interact *with each other,* but conflicting desires interact also *within* each subject.

What Does Hannah Want?

A first reading. (1:1-8) Hannah is one of two wives of Elkanah. She is unable to have children, while Elkanah's other wife, Peninnah, has children. This situation has persisted for many years. The text refers to Peninnah as Hannah's "rival," and tells how she taunted Hannah over her childlessness. It also tells of Elkanah's effort to comfort Hannah with the words of v. 8, "Am I not more to you than ten sons?" The effort is not an impressive one. If you wish to assure someone of your love, the line "Are *you* not more to *me* than . . . ?" seems much more promising than "Am I not more to you . . . ?"! The students in one of my classes came to the conclusion, with which I agree, that the bigamist Elkanah is quite content and has every reason to be. He has "both a wife to love and a wife to make children."[1] He has no need of children from Hannah, and perhaps fears that she would cease to be attractive if she were worn out by childbearing. And he cannot understand why the two women, enjoying their several marital satisfactions, are not just as happy with the situation as he is.[2]

(1:9-11) Hannah finds her situation intolerable. She makes no reply to her rival's taunts or to her husband's reassurance. But to YHWH, at the shrine of Shiloh, she pours out her heart. She makes a vow that if YHWH will give her a son she will dedicate the son back to him, to serve at the shrine as a Nazirite. What does Hannah want? She certainly wants relief from childlessness, and to bear a son. But why exactly? She does not want to bear a son to Elkanah, for she vows away any interest Elkanah might have in their son. Maybe she suspects that Elkanah does not want a child by her. She does not want a son for herself, at least not for the maternal enjoyment of bringing him up, for this also will be cut short by her vow. Does she want to bear a son merely to show she can, with whatever improvement in marital and social status that might bring?

Her vow opens up another possibility, that what she wants is a son *in the service of YHWH,* a son being prepared for a position of leadership in Israel. Perhaps this is an ambitious woman who, having little scope herself, hopes to satisfy her ambition vicariously through her son. Perhaps she has heard how Samson, the hero and judge of Israel, was a Nazirite born to a childless woman, and hopes her son may follow in Samson's footsteps.

(1:12-20) Hannah prays close to where Eli the chief priest is standing, and he takes notice of her. Perhaps she intends him to. This man figures in her plans. He will have a role to play in the career she envisages for her son. When he accuses her of drunkenness she answers politely but boldly, "No, my lord." The very first word she speaks out loud in the story is to the chief priest of Israel, and it is "No"! She makes an impression on Eli, and gains from him a blessing: "The God of Israel grant the petition you have made to him" (1:17). The reader may detect irony in this blessing, for Eli does not know what Hannah's silent prayer was about, and has no reason to suspect that it concerned him. Following this encounter Hannah cheers up, and in due time after she returns home her wish for a son is granted.

---

[1] Jo Ann Hackett, "1 and 2 Samuel," in Carol A. Newsom and Sharon H. Ringe, eds., *The Women's Bible Commentary* (Louisville, Ky.: Westminster/John Knox, 1992) 89.

[2] On Elkanah's attitude see Marcia Falk, "Reflections on Hannah's Prayer," *Tikkun* 9 (1994) 62–63; Danna Nolan Fewell and David M. Gunn, *Gender, Power, and Promise: The Subject of the Bible's First Story* (Nashville: Abingdon, 1993) 137.

(1:21-28) At the time of the next annual Shiloh festival—after Samuel is born, but when he can scarcely be more than three months old—Elkanah assumes that the whole family will be going to the festival and that they will take the baby to the shrine to fulfill Hannah's vow. Perhaps this assumption is dictated by a desire to get back as soon as possible to the way things were before Samuel arrived! But Hannah insists on waiting till her son is weaned before taking him to the shrine. "Do what you like," replies Elkanah, "only—may YHWH establish his word" (v. 23). This is odd, since YHWH has not said anything so far in the story. It could be just a pious remark, but the reading of LXX is enticing: "May YHWH establish what comes from *your* [that is, Hannah's] mouth." Elkanah himself is establishing Hannah's word by going along with her timetable!

At any rate Hannah's firm control of events continues in the next stage of the story, Samuel's eventual weaning and dedication at the shrine. It is she who takes Samuel to Shiloh, arranges the appropriate offerings, and explains the situation to Eli. The Hebrew text does not trouble to make clear whether Elkanah was even there.

(2:1-10) On the occasion of her son's dedication Hannah sings her great triumph-song. It is noteworthy that she sings it neither when she discovers her pregnancy nor when her son is born, but at his dedication. This strongly encourages my suggestion that it is the dedication that satisfies her desire. Most of the song is a hymn of praise to YHWH as the one who delivers the oppressed by reversing social and political distinctions. It alludes to her own situation, celebrating the reversal of fortune between barren and fertile women (v. 5), but it generalizes far beyond this immediate situation, celebrating also the reversal of weak and strong, hungry and satisfied, poor and rich. The song concludes, though, with a statement that seems out of place: YHWH "will give strength to his king" (2:10). There is no king in Israel, but perhaps Hannah shares the view of the verse that, in the Deuteronomic History, immediately precedes her story, the last verse of the Book of Judges, "In those days there was no king in Israel; all the people did what was right in their own eyes" (Judg 21:25). Does Hannah look forward to the establishment of monarchy in Israel, and even hope that her son will have a role to play in setting it up? It seems hard, though, to reconcile this possibility with the revolutionary political sentiments of the rest of her song.[3]

(2:11, 18-21) Hannah assists and monitors Samuel's progress at the shrine when each year she takes him a new robe. When we last hear of her she has become the mother of a large family, a family that, we are led to believe, she owes to the priestly blessing of Eli. It is not clear that either she or Elkanah wants these children.

---

[3] I shall have much more to say about 2:10 in a later reading of the song [166–169].

A second reading. At first sight this reading of Hannah's story seems complete. You will have noticed that I omitted one section of the text (2:12-17), but this is a section that makes no reference to Hannah or her family. It deals with the priestly activities of Eli's sons, Hophni and Phinehas. But it seems to me that the intrusion into Hannah's story of this seemingly unrelated section calls in question the completeness of my first reading, and in fact makes such a difference to the story that we have to go back and read it all over again.

Hophni and Phinehas are mentioned as early as 1:3. This verse tells us nothing about them, but it does imply that all the events of Hannah's story take place while they are priests at Shiloh. We do not hear of them again until after Hannah's story has reached its climax (the dedication and the song). Only then (2:12-17) do we learn that they are wicked priests who take more than their share from the sacrifices of the worshipers at Shiloh.

The text insists that they mistreat every worshiper in the same way: "When *anyone* offered sacrifice" (2:13), "This is what they did . . . to *all* the Israelites" (v. 14). If to all, then to Elkanah and Peninnah and Hannah! This simple observation has a devastating impact on our first reading. That reading innocently accepted the facts as the narrator provided them, and the narrator did not provide this information about the wicked priests. But now we have no other choice than to read this information back into Hannah's story. In doing so we realize that year by year, as she attended the feast, Hannah experienced the rottenness of the priestly regime.

Nor have we yet heard the last of Hophni and Phinehas's misdeeds. Immediately after the end of Hannah's story we are informed that "they lay with the women who served at the entrance to the tent of meeting" (2:22). Hannah may have been aware of this sexual exploitation. Perhaps she talked to these women, came to know them. Has she herself been the object of lustful gaze, or worse, as she worshiped at the shrine? Were the story to be turned into a novel or a film no one would be surprised if Hannah became a victim of priestly lust and Samuel proved to be the result of a sordid and brutal encounter in the recesses of the tent of meeting.   ❭

This second reading posits a Hannah who understands very well what happens when "all the people," even the priests of Israel, "do what is right in their own eyes." She can respond only by doing what is right in her own eyes. Why does she want to dedicate her son to the shrine? Is it as a way of intervening in the appalling situation there, a way of protesting that what the priests are doing is "not done in Israel" [73]? Does she go further and make a connection between the national situation and her own? Does she connect the power of a priest to use the women at the shrine in whatever way he wishes with the power of any man to marry several wives and play them off against each other as he wishes? Does she look for fundamental systemic change for the benefit of her sex?

Surely I have gone too far! Perhaps. But when did I begin to go too far? At what point did I transgress the limits of plausibility? It is not easy to say. This is a story that can be read, invites being read, as making space for an imaginative answer to the question, "What does Hannah want?"

What Does the Narrator Want?

The question arises: how does Hannah's desire relate to that of her narrator?[4] It is a question that is very important in theoretical terms as well as in this particular case. In one sense Hannah, like any other character, belongs to the narrator. All that she has, or says, or is, is his (my gendering is deliberate). I the reader have no access to her except through his telling. When I read her my way am I claiming that my reading corresponds to what the narrator wanted? No, I am not. What my Hannah wants is likely not what the narrator wants her to want! Mine is a reading against the grain; yet I claim that it falls within the range of what the narrator's text *permits*.

Why does the narrator not record the misdeeds of Hophni and Phinehas when he first tells us of their priesthood (1:3)? Perhaps because such information would disturb the story of Hannah as he wants to tell it. But in that case why not withhold all mention of Hophni and Phinehas until after Hannah's story has been completely told? Why slip them in just before the last episode of Hannah's story? The narrator seems to want to hold back information from the reader but to be not quite able to. I would still have been free to pursue my line of interpretation even if all mention of the wickedness of Eli's sons had been postponed until after Hannah's story, but then I would have been going directly against the narrator's telling. As it is I can think of my telling as collaborating with the narrator's, as bringing out a tendency in his reading.[5] For I am far from supposing that the narrator does not share my enthusiasm for the character Hannah. Subsequent reading of this

---

[4] Fewell and Gunn also study the tension between the character Hannah and the narrator (*Gender, Power, and Promise* 139–140).

[5] By putting it this way I do not mean to imply that we should *never* read diametrically against what we understand the narrator to be saying!

text has often missed the narrator's enthusiasm, but it is clear to me that he makes Hannah a bold, determined, and even dominating character. Even more, by presenting her as one of Israel's poets and singers he puts her in the company of Miriam and Deborah, women who also sang triumph-songs and were leaders in Israel (Exodus 15, Judges 5)— as if her dedication of Samuel were an act of leadership on a par with the defeat of the Canaanites or even with the crossing of the Sea!

One way of expressing my divergence from the narrator's story is in terms of the categories of "private" and "public" [147–149]. The activity of the priests is a public matter, but our first impression (and also probably our expectation) of Hannah's story is that it belongs to the private, family sphere. Read in these terms the narrator's treatment of Hophni and Phinehas suggests a *hesitation* over letting Hannah operate in the public sphere. Though he implicitly links her, through her song, to women who exercised public power in Israel he seems content to tell the rest of her story in a way that suggests that she acted mainly to fulfill private needs.

For me the bottom line is that the narrator ascribes to Hannah the sole *initiative* in her story, and therefore in the ongoing story of which she is a part. As James Ackerman says, "God seems to be waiting for a human initiative."[6] All that follows as a result of this story, all that Samuel will achieve—whether the resolution of existing problems or the opening up of future possibilities—is the result of Hannah's vow and would not have occurred without her. If this be granted there are two ways in which we can relate Hannah's initiative to its consequences. One is the "God moves in a mysterious way" approach. In this view what Hannah began for reasons of her own God continued for reasons of which she had no inkling. The other approach is to give Hannah credit for knowing what she was doing, to present her as responsible for the consequences of her initiative. The narrator may prefer the first option. I prefer the second.

What Does Luke Want?

The first two chapters of the gospel of Luke are a rewriting of the beginning of 1 Samuel, including Hannah's story, and in this section I offer an intertextual reading of the impact of each story on the other.

---

[6] "Who Can Stand before YHWH, This Holy God? A Reading of 1 Samuel 1–15," *Prooftexts* 11 (1991) 3.

Overt links. The best-known link between Luke's text and 1 Samuel is Mary's song, the so-called Magnificat (1:46-55), for which Hannah's song is the prototype. But this identification between *Mary* and Hannah comes as a surprise, for in the earlier part of Luke's account it is *Elizabeth* who has been set up as the Hannah character—in her barrenness (1:7) and in the need for her son to abstain from liquor (1:15). Many readers both ancient and modern have supposed that it was *she* who originally sang the Magnificat. The splitting of Hannah into two characters, Elizabeth and Mary, continues in the splitting of Hannah's *son* into two characters, John and Jesus, the sons of Elizabeth and Mary. John is to be a Nazirite like Samuel, but it is Jesus who is dedicated at the Temple (2:22-24) and reminds his parents that that is where he belongs: "Did you not know that I must be in my father's house?" (2:49). The growing up of *both* John and Jesus is recorded in terms reminiscent of Samuel (1:66, 80, 2:40, 52, cf. 1 Sam 2:21, 26, 3:19).

Deeper links. These overt allusions by no means get to the heart of the profound and pervasive presence of 1 Samuel in Luke's account. Luke wants to tell a story of God's intervention to save God's people Israel, who are helpless to save themselves. To specify the nature of this intervention Luke draws heavily on what scholars call the David-Zion complex of traditions.[7] He sees in Jesus a new Davidic king: "The Lord God will give to him the throne of his ancestor David" (1:32, cf. 1:27, 69), and he presents the Temple and its priesthood as a center of purity, filled with people who are "righteous" (Zechariah, Elizabeth, Simeon) and who patiently await the king's coming and the nation's salvation.

One might have expected Luke to seek an Old Testament prototype in the story of David. What prompts him to choose instead the beginning of 1 Samuel? Most obvious is the need for a birth story. The Bible provides no birth story for David, but the beginning of 1 Samuel provides the next best thing, the birth story of David's *forerunner*. Samuel can be seen as standing in the same relation to David as John the Baptist stands to Jesus; as John baptized Jesus, so Samuel anointed David. But there is more to Luke's choice even than this. Samuel's birth occurs at a historical moment when *something* needs to be done about Israel, about the terrible state into which it has fallen. This fits exactly with Luke's main purpose, to tell of God's intervention to save Israel.

Luke's impact on the reading of Hannah. In choosing this prototype Luke cannot avoid tapping into deep currents of the Old Testament text,

---

[7] W. Lee Humphreys, *Crisis and Story: Introduction to the Old Testament* (Palo Alto, Cal.: Mayfield, 1979) 55–64.

some of which may flow the way he wants, others not. Luke must impose his desire on the Samuel text, and in so doing he imposes his desire on Christian readers of the Samuel text. To tell *his* story Luke borrows and processes the story of Hannah, and those of us whose expectations have been shaped by the New Testament will tend to read Hannah in terms of how Luke has redefined her. Two aspects of this process I simply mention here, intending to take them up later [165–173]. First, to read Hannah's story through the grid of Luke 1–2 is to read it *as a new beginning.* For Christian readers there is no more absolute beginning than the beginning of a gospel. Second, the Lukan grid directs us to a particular understanding of God's initiative: God acts to save Israel by the establishment of the Davidic kingship.

A third aspect I can develop at greater length here. The Lukan grid attunes us to divine rather than human initiative. Luke firmly restores what is so strikingly absent from Hannah's story: the annunciation pattern, in which God takes the initiative to bring about the birth of the hero and in which the human characters are typically filled with doubt and confusion. Luke has greatly underscored the human impossibility of his births by means of the themes of old age (Elizabeth) and virginal conception (Mary).[8] The "God moves in a mysterious way" paradigm is firmly in place, especially in the account of Elizabeth. Until she is "filled with the Holy Spirit" (1:41) she can see in the events only a personal act of kindness by God to her to relieve the social disgrace of barrenness (1:25). In contrast to the Hannah story Luke *specifies* this as Elizabeth's motive for wanting a child.

Hannah's impact on the reading of Luke. So much for Luke's imposing his desire on Hannah. Are there, conversely, symptoms in Luke's text of an inability to contain Hannah, places where she has imposed her desire on him?[9]

---

[8] It is a marker of the shift to divine initiative that both John and Jesus (unlike Samuel) are named by divine decree.

[9] Some recent contributions to the study of Luke have been very hard on him. They see him as having an iron hand in a velvet glove, imposing an ideology that serves a conservative agenda through a gentle, pleasing brand of storytelling that can even appear to be on the side of the poor and oppressed. See Gary A. Phillips, "'What is Written? How are you Reading?' Gospel, Intertextuality and Doing Luke-wise: Reading," *Sem.* 69/70 (1995) 111–147; Jane Schaberg, "Luke," in Carol A. Newsom and Sharon H. Ringe, eds., *The Women's Bible Commentary* (Louisville, Ky.: Westminster/John Knox, 1992) 275–292. I agree with these critics, and applaud them for putting to the New Testament sharp ethical questions that are long overdue. For my own part, though, I prefer not to scold Luke any more, but to let the Jewish Bible take its own revenge on Luke's manipulation of it.

We can begin by asking whether his splitting of Hannah into two is not an admission that there is more to her than a single one of *his* characters can contain. Only when they work together, it seems, are Luke's two women able to reproduce Hannah's initiative. Luke devotes a considerable section (1:39-56) to the meeting of Elizabeth and Mary, on their own initiative and in the absence of men, and makes this meeting the context of the Magnificat.

The most enticing symptom of Luke's story being shaped by Hannah's comes, however, near the end of his account. He has had to split Hannah not just into two, but into three: there is more to her than even Elizabeth and Mary *together* can match. And he gives no other name to this third character than—Hannah (in Greek, Anna)![10]

One's first impression might be that in the divvying up of Hannah, Anna gets little more than the name. Anna's story covers only three verses of Luke's text (2:36-38), verses that are in the shadow of the much longer section on Simeon (vv. 25-35). Though she is a prophet, she gets no words. Still, I think she gets a good deal more of Hannah than just her name. As a female prophet she joins a very small biblical company, including Miriam and Deborah. Long a widow, she seems free of male control. Where Hannah dedicated *her son* to the shrine, Anna has dedicated *herself*. And when she becomes aware of Jesus she hurries to alert "all those who were looking for the redemption of Jerusalem." Has not Luke, as an afterthought, or as the return of the repressed, given us here a character very like my Hannah, now grown old and long since free of Elkanah's tender mercies but still looking out for the salvation of her people?

What Do the Literary Readers Want?

The title of this section makes it seem more comprehensive than it is. I shall be dealing not with literary approaches in general but with a group of three readings of Hannah's story, those of Robert Alter, Lyle Eslinger, and Robert Polzin.[11] Different as they are, these all belong to the recent movement that, I have suggested, has established itself as a

---

[10] I acknowledge here my debt to a brilliant analysis by my student Catherine Rose of this splitting of Hannah into three.

[11] Alter, *The Art of Biblical Narrative* (London: Allen & Unwin, 1981) 82–86; Eslinger, *Kingship of God in Crisis: A Close Reading of 1 Samuel 1–12.* Bible and Literature Series 10 (Sheffield: Almond, 1985); Polzin, *Samuel and the Deuteronomist: A Literary Study of the Deuteronomic History. Part Two: 1 Samuel* (San Francisco: Harper & Row, 1989). References in this section are to these works.

new literary orthodoxy [25–26]. I shall concentrate on general tendencies in these readings, with some specific references.

"Lukan" tendencies. The tendencies I identified in the last section are readily apparent in the literary readings. Polzin (pp. 22–39) provides a clear illustration of the first and third. He reads Hannah *forward*, explaining her story almost entirely by things that happen later in the Deuteronomic History, and he stresses the *monarchical* element in her song through a comparison with the song of David in 2 Samuel 22. Eslinger (pp. 71–72, 92) illustrates the second tendency. He tries to show that Hannah's story is after all a story of *divine initiative*, since it begins with YHWH closing her womb (1:5-6). I would argue that in these respects the literary readings are closer to the assumptions of Luke than to those of the Samuel narrator. It is impossible to know the extent to which such tendencies result from the unconscious imposition of the Lukan grid, but to be aware of the grid helps us to identify the tendencies. Christians are often simply unaware of how their internalization of the New Testament constrains their reading of the Jewish Bible, and Christian scholars of the Jewish Bible need to trace and subvert this process by critical analysis.[12]

Inattention to feminist readings. Nevertheless, it is to two larger and more fundamental issues that I want to draw particular attention. First, these literary readers read without reference to any of the political contexts in which the Bible is now being read, which in the case of Hannah means feminism in particular. It quickly becomes clear when I use their work in a class full of women students that they do not employ gender as a tool of narrative analysis. To take a simple example, Polzin (pp. 23–24) parallels Hannah's vow with Jephthah's without so much as asking whether there is a difference between a father vowing a daughter to death and a mother vowing a son to Temple service.

These readers share a pronounced sympathy for Elkanah, and are at pains to present him in a positive light. Polzin (p. 30) ascribes to him a "God-centered perspective," while Eslinger (pp. 70–71) calls him "pious" and "fair in his dealings." Consider the problem of translation in 1:5. Depending on the meaning of one obscure word we may read Elkanah's action at the sacrifice in one of two ways. Either he gives

---

[12] Instead, Christian products like the Common Lectionary reinforce it. True to form, the Common Lectionary includes of Hannah's story only 1:4-20 and 2:1-10 (Year B, Proper 28), so that her song celebrates Samuel's birth rather than his dedication [133].

Hannah a *special* portion of food *because* he loves her, *though* YHWH has closed her womb (NRSV), or he gives her only the *regular* portion *though* he loves her, *because* YHWH has closed her womb (RSV). Faced with this choice the literary readers take the second option, which reflects more creditably on Elkanah (Eslinger, p. 71; Polzin, p. 19). Above all, they agree in admiring his words of "comfort" to Hannah in v. 8: Alter refers, and his comment is typical, to "Elkanah's touching effort to console his beloved wife [and his] tender devotion to Hannah" (p. 83; cf. Eslinger, pp. 75–76; Polzin, pp. 22–23).

Hannah, by contrast, comes in for criticism, for reasons that include the following: (1) ingratitude to Elkanah in going on desiring a child when he has assured her she does not need one (Polzin, pp. 22–23); (2) "making a deal" with YHWH (i.e., her vow: Polzin, p. 24); (3) reluctance or delay in paying her vow to YHWH (Eslinger, p. 86); and even (4) her "self-awareness and certitude" (Polzin, p. 24). None of the literary readers, who so often offer highly subtle insights into features of the text, sees any need for subtlety in explaining Hannah's desire for a child. They take it as a stock situation: a child will give her social status, put an end to the taunts of her rival wife, and enable her to provide for her husband what he most wishes and expects from her. No more needs to be said![13]

Gender assumptions are not the only ones governing the literary readings. Perhaps even more numbing is the assumption that the story of Hannah is a story of plain country folk. Words like "simple," "ordinary," and "humble" and expressions like "a simple, sincere country wife" (Alter, p. 84) abound. I share the assumption that Elkanah and his family were farmers. Most Israelites were. So, by background, are most of my students, but the word "simple" does not spring to mind when I think of them. The students in the class to which I referred earlier found in the literary readings the age-long contempt of urban for rural people. Of course the assumption that Hannah is "simple" determines in advance how her story is to be read. If God is going to create something out of the initiative of so simple a character it will *have* to be "in a mysterious way"! We can, though, turn this logic on its head. Perhaps the need to protect divine initiative dictates that the human characters be perceived as simple.

The omniscient narrator. The second thing the literary readers seem to me to want is a narrator who is in control of all the meaning that can legitimately be found in the text [289–290]. The word they usually

---

[13] Again Luke's reshaping of Hannah's desire through his presentation of Elizabeth (Luke 1:25) may have played a role here.

use is that the narrator is "omniscient," all-knowing. By this they mean that the narrator *claims* omniscience, for example claims to know the secret thoughts of the characters, including God. But this quickly shades over into saying that the reader is obliged to accept the narrator's claim, as when Eslinger calls the narrator "the author and finisher of our reading" (p. 75, subliminally borrowing the authority not this time of Luke but of Heb 12:2). In this view interpretation is nothing more than discovering and following the indications the narrator skillfully provides, and it is bad interpretation to move outside this framework. This is not an omniscient, but an omnipotent narrator![14]

No king in Israel. These two desires, to circumvent the claims of readings that grow out of acknowledged political commitments and to insist on strong narratorial control, are, I think, related. The literary readers betray an anxiety that in current interpretation of the Bible, if I may so put it, "all the people are doing what is right in their own eyes." In what they perceive as an anarchic situation they look for a "king in Israel," a narrator who has everything under control. In my final chapter I shall extend this parallel—between anarchy in the narrative and "anarchy" in the interpretation of the narrative—to the whole of 1 Samuel [290–292, 300–301].[15]

---

[14] Cf. Phillips on the Lukan narrator: "'What is Written?'" 125–131.

[15] The address that forms the original for this chapter has a fifth section, "What Do I Want?" (see David Jobling, "Hannah's Desire," *BCSBS* 53 [1994] 29–32). The points it includes I have to a large extent covered in Chapter 1 of this book.

Chapter 7

CONTEXTS FOR HANNAH

Most of this chapter will be taken up with the effect on the women of Israel of the transition to monarchy. We will examine this from a variety of angles, not only literary and canonical but also anthropological. We will look not only at women characters in 1 Samuel but also at some scholars' views of how the transition affected historical women. The primary conclusion will be that women suffered a diminishment of their status in the historical transition and that this corresponds, in the text, to the way the narrator coopts the energies of some women characters in the achievement of his narrative goal, the kingship of David. The narrator extends this cooption even to the character Hannah, to whom we turn later in the chapter, but some narrative currents resist the cooption and indicate that Hannah is better matched with the women of Judges than with those of 1 Samuel.

Interdisciplinary Perspectives on Women and Monarchy

Literary criticism and interdisciplinarity. In this chapter more than any other I explore the boundary between literary reading and the study of the history of ancient Israel. It is true that I pay attention to Israel's history elsewhere (notably in Chapter 11), but there my interest is in the postexilic time, the time of the production of the text. Here I venture into the time evoked in 1 Samuel, the time of the transition to monarchy.

The discipline of literary criticism is well placed to make a contribution within a radically interdisciplinary framework of research. In the last generation literary criticism has in fact been the nearest thing to a "universal" discipline, taking the lead in inviting broad interdisciplinary connections and happily drawing on every possible area of thought as relevant to the reading of texts. Thus it is that the work of such figures as Jacques Derrida, a philosopher, or Julia Kristeva, a semiotician and psychoanalyst, has been much more readily appropriated in the English-speaking world by literary critics than by philosophers and psychoanalysts! Terry Eagleton, a leading literary critic, asserts that the business of literary criticism is to put itself out of business as a separate discipline and direct its efforts into a general critique of culture.[1]

However, literary approaches to the Bible have not kept pace in this respect with literary criticism generally. The establishment of the claims of literary criticism as a valid approach to the Bible has been one of the great changes in recent biblical studies, but there has developed a would-be new orthodoxy in the literary study of the Bible that in a calculated way puts tight limits on what literary methods are "appropriate" to the Bible. I have styled the results as more a "narrowtology" than a narratology [25–26, 288–296]. I believe that a broad interdisciplinary context is necessary if the literary study of the Bible is to be of real usefulness to the different kinds of people who read the Bible.

The reason why I choose this chapter to highlight these issues is that the need for methodological fluidity has been argued most powerfully by feminists. Feminists espouse a radically critical form of interdisciplinarity as a way of breaking down the disciplinary boundaries male academics have set up.[2] It is therefore appropriate to use my "Gender" section as a place to broaden the relatively narrow literary approaches I myself have followed up to this point in the book. There has been a notable variety in the methods used by feminist readers to deal with the transition from judgeship to kingship in Israel, and a notable convergence in their results. As a reader you will experience here, therefore, a sharp and deliberate change in my mode of discourse as I move to ground not typically covered in literary readings of the Bible.

Mode of production. I begin with a term that its proponents claim has interdisciplinary implications on the broadest scale. This term, "mode of production," belongs to Marxist political theory.[3] It denotes the total system by which a society produces and consumes things—

---

[1] *Literary Theory: An Introduction* (Oxford: Basil Blackwell, 1983) 204.

[2] Mieke Bal, *Murder and Difference: Gender, Genre and Scholarship on Sisera's Death,* translated by Matthew Gumpert (Bloomington, Ind.: Indiana University Press, 1988) especially 135–138.

[3] For the following discussion see my "Feminism and 'Mode of Production' in Ancient Israel: Search for a Method," in David Jobling, Peggy L. Day, and Gerald T. Sheppard, eds., *The Bible and the Politics of Exegesis: Essays in Honor of Norman K. Gottwald on his Sixty-Fifth Birthday* (Cleveland: Pilgrim, 1991) 239–251.

not just material goods but ideas, laws, literature, and everything else. It includes *both* the forces of production with which the society works— not just raw materials but also human physical and mental powers— *and* the relations of production, the social (especially class) relations that determine who works and who enjoys the products of work.

A society does not simply happen upon a set of arrangements by which to organize itself. It also, especially when there are unequal classes of producers and exploiters, produces laws that fix the arrangement and (very important) creates ideologies that show the system to be the best possible one, indeed to be a part of the natural order of things. In ancient societies this ideological work was done largely through theology: the system under which people live is shown to be the will of the gods. The regime can maintain the mode of production much more efficiently by getting people to believe in it at this fundamental level than by imposing it through laws or sheer force (though these means are always available as a backup).

Mode of production is thus a very comprehensive concept, and classic Marxist theory posits the existence of only a few basic modes (though with a great deal of local variation) in all human history. Which of these modes are relevant to the study of ancient Israel?

Marx defined an "Asiatic" mode, more usefully renamed by others the "tributary" mode, of which Israel's monarchy is probably an example. The tributary mode of production is based mainly on agriculture. The agricultural producers are legally free peasants (as opposed to slaves) but the land they work belongs in theory to the state (the king) and the peasants owe tribute in kind—understood as rent or tax—to the state. They also owe other kinds of tax, notably in the form of forced labor on state projects (see 1 Sam 8:11-18). The exploiting class consists primarily of state officials, of whom there are many because these societies are heavily bureaucratic.

The mode of production in premonarchical Israel is much less clear. Marxist theory offers inadequate options, but recently a "household" or "familial" mode of production has been proposed that probably fits the bill.[4] These terms indicate a social arrangement of people living in small communities connected relatively loosely with structures

[4] Marshall Sahlins, *Tribesmen.* Foundations of Modern Anthropology (Englewood Cliffs, N.J.: Prentice-Hall, 1968) especially 75–81. "Could this not serve as a most adept description of *early Israel?*"—so William G. Dever, "Unresolved Issues in the Early History of Israel: Toward a Synthesis of Archaeological and Textual Reconstructions," in David Jobling, et al, eds., *The Bible and the Politics of Exegesis* 347 n. 20 (Dever's emphasis).

beyond their community, with each household able to provide for almost all its needs—and with little incentive to produce beyond its needs. This is very compatible with Gottwald's picture of egalitarian Israel [73–74]. The anthropological data make it clear that monarchies are typically formed by the imposition of central control on such looser and more egalitarian societies.

How can discussion of mode of production illuminate the roles of women? In the household mode the work of both women and men is closely integrated in the ways that extended families provide for themselves. The work of the two sexes is significantly different since "families are *constituted* for production primarily by the sexual division of labor."[5] But their work is equally necessary and valued, or nearly so.

The extensive literature on the tributary mode has relatively little to say about the systemic location of women. Karl Wittfogel, however, indicates that transition from a more egalitarian to a tributary mode is typically accompanied by shifts from female-based to male-based patterns of kinship and social organization, from a low-level agriculture dominated by women to an intensive agriculture organized by men, and from the extended family to the nuclear family.[6] Polygamy becomes systemic, but as a class phenomenon, a status symbol. In the extreme case of the ruling house this leads to the phenomenon of the harem. The accumulation of women is not just for sexual purposes: 1 Sam 8:13 refers to various kinds of "women's work." In one society that probably was close to the stage of development of early monarchical Israel Wittfogel quotes a figure of five percent of all the women in the population being concentrated under the personal control of the ruler.[7]

Feminist readings of Israel's transition to monarchy. In *Discovering Eve* Carol Meyers deals mainly with premonarchical Israel, using evidence from archaeology and comparative ethnology to build a picture of women's roles.[8] She largely accepts Gottwald's account of egalitarian Israel, and concludes that women enjoyed a substantial degree of equality and freedom within it. She analyzes the work that likely fell to women in the division of labor and believes it was no less important and valued than that which fell to men. The task of cooking, for example, was not just a chore but entailed control over the assignment of limited food re-

---

[5] Sahlins, *Tribesmen* 75 (emphasis in original).

[6] "The Stages of Development in Chinese Economic and Social History," in A. M. Bailey and J. P. Llobera, eds., *The Asiatic Mode of Production: Science and Politics* (London: Routledge & Kegan Paul, 1981) 114–119.

[7] *Oriental Despotism* (New Haven: Yale University Press, 1963) 240.

[8] *Discovering Eve: Ancient Israelite Women in Context* (New York and Oxford: Oxford University Press, 1988).

sources. Large family size in a pioneering society that desperately needs to build a population base is not, Meyers insists, a sign of women's oppression. The socialization and education of children, the adjudication of family and marriage law, and many other tasks critical to the life of the extended family would largely belong to women.

Meyers accepts the view that the activity of early Israelite women was largely confined to the private, domestic sphere. But according to her, comparative anthropology suggests that it is a modernizing error to assume that the private sphere was less important than the public. The public sphere would offer more overt prestige in such a society, but the private sphere would offer at least as much real power.[9]

Only in an epilogue does Meyers deal with the transition to monarchy. She argues that centralization based on exclusively male hierarchical structures would force peasants into wage labor, cause a decline in the household-based economy, and jeopardize old kinship structures, all to the detriment of women of the peasant class. Another consequence would be the appearance of a nonproductive type of upper-class urban woman. However, we should not exaggerate the effect of this kind of social change on village life. Though the village's economic situation would be negatively affected, its day-to-day life probably continued much as before.[10]

Naomi Steinberg provides support for the view that women tended to lose legal status as a result of the coming of monarchy, and suggests that this trend would not leave village women unaffected.[11] Her thesis is that Israel's monarchy sought to bolster the nuclear family at the expense of larger social units such as the kinship group or extended family. This was achieved partly by legislation, and we can find some of this in Deuteronomy 19–25, which concentrates on family law. Steinberg offers cross-cultural evidence that state systems as part of their program of centralization boost the nuclear family, which poses no political threat, while suppressing the larger social groupings that might become alternative power centers.

In feminist perspective the sharp point that Steinberg makes is that the laws in question are ones that have often been understood as pro-woman. For example the law in Deut 22:28-29, that a man who rapes an unattached woman must marry her and may not divorce her, does not work primarily to secure the status of the woman but to bolster the

---

[9] Ibid. 43–45; cf. 32–33.

[10] Ibid. 189–196.

[11] "The Deuteronomic Law and the Politics of State Centralization," in David Jobling, et al, eds., *The Bible and the Politics of Exegesis: Essays in Honor of Norman K. Gottwald on his Sixty-Fifth Birthday* 161–170.

nuclear family. (That the arrangement is advantageous to the woman is of course highly questionable on other grounds, for example psychological.) The effect of these laws is to bring both women and men under tighter control. Finally, Steinberg notes that the laws widen the distance between ruling and ruled groups since the ruling group is much less subject to them in practice.

Mieke Bal's *Death and Dissymmetry* is not only a new reading of the book of Judges but also a deliberate critique of the way biblical studies is structured as a discipline. The dominant approach to Judges, according to her, has privileged history over anthropology, the public over the private domain, and at a still more profound level culture over nature and change over continuity. Over against the "coherence" that this dominant approach has imposed on Judges, Bal proposes a "countercoherence." The conflict that most shapes the book is at the level of domestic, not national politics. It arises out of a transition in marriage patterns from a pattern in which the husband visits his wife at her father's house to one in which she comes to live at her husband's house.[12]

Bal's thesis, interesting as it is, is less important than her expansion of the scope of literary criticism of the Bible and her insistence that the choices literary critics make imply political choices. She draws not only on narratology and speech-act theory, recognized methods within literary criticism, but also on anthropology, psychoanalysis, film theory, and other methods. Her substitution of domestic conflict for national political conflict is intended not to reaffirm the public-private dichotomy but to subvert it. More radical than Meyers, she affirms that the two spheres are not separate. The domestic *is* the political.

Bal has virtually nothing to say about the transition to kingship. Nevertheless, her treatment has clear points of contact with our discussion. The process of transition that she herself is positing, in marriage patterns and sexual politics, can readily be seen in the light of Steinberg's investigations as one expression of political centralization.

For a literary-critical approach highly compatible with Bal's, but one that *does* pay direct attention to the transition to kingship, I turn finally to Regina Schwartz's treatment of sexual politics in the establishment of the house of David.[13] Schwartz discerns in modern biblical scholarship a powerful compulsion to present this transition as a smooth development (I have discerned such a desire in the work of the Deuteronomic historians [61–64, 103–104]). She prefers Michel Fou-

---

[12] *Death & Dissymmetry: The Politics of Coherence in the Book of Judges* (Chicago: University of Chicago Press, 1988) 6, 80–93, and *passim*.

[13] "Adultery in the House of David: The Metanarrative of Biblical Scholarship and the Narratives of the Bible," *Sem.* 54 (1991) 35–55.

cault's view of history as a series of violent ruptures, and she presents the transition to monarchy in these terms.

Schwartz's major point is that Israel's transition to kingship is literarily expressed, to a remarkable extent, by means of sexual scenes involving royal characters. Sexual rights over women confer political power, and conversely power can be expressed in terms of sexual rights over women. Like Bal, Schwartz denies any separation of public and private,[14] and she carries perhaps even further than Bal the suggestion that the very function of the "private" is to encode what is happening in the public domain. In the most overt way, for example, Absalom's taking over of David's harem is a claim to David's power.[15]

Schwartz concentrates mainly on David and three of his wives, Abigail, Michal, and Bathsheba. Her treatment of the first two of these particularly claims our attention, since their stories begin in 1 Samuel. Each is married to someone else, so that there is in each story a male as well as a female victim—Nabal, Paltiel, Uriah—over whom David gains power. Indeed, two of the three men die. The three episodes form a series, the consequences in each case underlining how the stories serve as paradigms of political power. In the case of Abigail no apparent guilt falls on David, and at least one child ensues (2 Sam 3:3). In the Michal episode David's guilt is not stressed, but Michal remains childless. Finally, David's extreme guilt over Bathsheba leads to the death of their child.

One part of Schwartz's discussion is extremely relevant to my suggestion that Israel's history writing is a search for a lost ideal [70–76]. Playing on the name Nabal (meaning "fool"), she suggests that David becomes himself a *nābāl* in the Bathsheba story (2 Samuel 11–12). In the scene immediately following that story Amnon is precisely so characterized for a similar act (2 Sam 13:13), and this must reflect back on David.[16] Likewise, when Tamar refers to rape as something "not done in Israel" our attention is drawn back to the contrast between David's taking of Bathsheba and Uriah's adherence to traditional ways (2 Sam 11:11). The transition to monarchy seems to trigger in the characters a nostalgia for some imagined premonarchic arrangements, including sexual arrangements.[17]

---

[14] Ibid. 45–46.

[15] Ibid. 46, referring to 2 Sam 16:21-22. Cf. Schwartz's similar treatment of Abner and Rizpah (2 Sam 3:6-11, p. 52).

[16] Ibid. 49.

[17] Ibid. 49–51. For rape as "folly in Israel" cf. Gen 34:7, Judg 20:6. See also Steinberg, "The Deuteronomic Law" 169 on the contrast between Deuteronomic law and the sexual practices of David's house.

Male scholarship tends to betray anxiety over clarity of method. Its tendency is also to separate literary claims from historical and other kinds of claims. In my own earlier work, particularly as a structuralist, I made this separation, and to an extent I still do.[18] But Bal and Schwartz freely intersperse literary with historical observations, and Meyers uses her anthropological findings as the basis for an extensive literary reading of Genesis 2–3.[19] And the findings from these approaches seem to converge. What should we make of this convergence?

None of the four scholars I have looked at takes a naïve view of literature. They do not claim that literature exists to reflect history, or that it does so reliably. But the way to combat such naïve views, they would affirm, is *not* to bracket out historical questions when pursuing literary approaches. These scholars would see any such attempt to create herme(neu)tically sealed "disciplines" as a continuation of the "divide and conquer" strategy of male-created academic traditions. Women's own struggles are too embedded in history for them to give up the resources history provides. But we have to find radically new ways of asking the historical questions.

Let me hazard one other conclusion. I have suggested that the Deuteronomic Historians write out of a context in which Israel has "forgotten" how fundamentally different Israel was before it had kings [75–76]. Even in the Extended Book of Judges there are very few passages with traces of egalitarian social ideals, but two of these are songs sung by *women*, Deborah (Judges 5) and Hannah (1 Sam 2:1-10). May it be that gender issues are less subject to the process of forgetting? Because women are largely excluded from the creation of the official national memory, may their issues tend to escape notice and be less rigorously censored? If this is so, the consequence may be that suppressed class issues will surface in the guise of gender issues. I will pursue this interrelatedness further after bringing the third frame of the triptych, race, into the discussion [306–308].

David's Women

Two wives of David, Michal and Abigail, play prominent roles in 1 Samuel. Both appear as strong initiative-takers, but their efforts really

---

[18] Even in this book I am more comfortable correlating the biblical writings with Israel's late postexilic history than with its ancient history [16–17].

[19] Meyers, *Discovering Eve* 72–121.

only help David in his rise to fame and power. Only in a very temporary and limited way (if that) do these women advance their own interests. Michal, in the beginning stage of what will be her tragic story, wins the sympathy of the reader. Abigail, on her way to eventual mere obscurity, becomes, as it seems to me, too caught up in the text's theological intricacies to win such sympathy.

Michal. David's first wife is Michal, the younger of Saul's two daughters. I shall deal with her briefly here, first since I find little to add to Cheryl Exum's fine account of her,[20] and also since we shall return to Michal in connection with David and the Philistines [227–230].

When David rises to military prominence and national popularity the fearful and jealous Saul offers him his elder daughter, Merab, as wife (18:17-19). This offer is, we are told, insincere. Saul hopes to buy David's service in the fierce fighting with the Philistines and hence to secure his death. For no clear reason, Saul does not carry through on his offer but gives Merab to another man.

There follows a superficially similar effort by Saul with his second daughter. But there is a crucial difference. This story begins with the statement that "Michal loved David" (18:20). Unlike Merab, who is given no active role, Michal (like Hannah) enters the scene as a narrative subject and gets the story going. Saul's role this time is reactive. Still, he hopes to use the situation to compass David's death, and hatches a specific plan to achieve this. He demands of David a brideprice the attempting of which must, Saul believes, be fatal. David, however, succeeds in obtaining the required goods, and Saul, his bluff called, sanctions the marriage (18:27). There is a second mention of Michal's love for David (v. 28).

Ominously, though, there is no mention of any reciprocating love on David's side. His response to Saul's offers is a double one: an obsequious denial of his worthiness to be Saul's son-in-law (18:18, 23) and a precipitate readiness to try against all odds to become just that. Maybe passion for Michal is part of his motivation. It would make a more agreeable story. But in the absence of any such indication it is easier to suppose that ambition was his motive. A reader who pursues the story of Michal to its end will doubt that David ever had any love for her.

[20] *Fragmented Women: Feminist (Sub)versions of Biblical Narratives.* JSOT.S 163 (Sheffield: JSOT Press, 1993) 16–60. Also excellent is Danna Nolan Fewell and David M. Gunn, *Gender, Power, and Promise: The Subject of the Bible's First Story* (Nashville: Abingdon, 1993) 146–149, 152–155. For a wide variety of perspectives on Michal see David J. A. Clines and Tamara C. Eskenazi, eds., *Telling Queen Michal's Story: An Experiment in Comparative Interpretation.* JSOT.S 119 (Sheffield: Sheffield Academic Press, 1991).

What for the woman is an affair of the heart is for the man a means of upward mobility.

Michal again takes the initiative in the next scene in which she appears. The woman who, in Saul's plotting, was to have been the cause of David's death now acts promptly to save his life (19:11-17). Having somehow learned of Saul's intention to kill David, she not only warns David of the danger (v. 11) but also assists his escape (v. 12) and carries out a plan of her own to cover up his absence (vv. 13-16). When accused by Saul of complicity, Michal, still quick-witted, claims that David threatened her with the words "Let me go; why should I kill you?"

Michal's whirlwind activity in this paragraph is a convincing enactment of her love for David. David, by contrast, has a passive role (the only thing he actively does is run away, v. 12). But we may wonder whether Michal has already begun to discern that her life does not really matter to her husband. When she invents David's threat to kill her (v. 17) she obviously does so to get herself out of a jam. Nonetheless, Saul accepts the idea as plausible. If David had gone about the court behaving like an ecstatic newlywed would Saul have been prepared to believe that David would threaten Michal's life under any circumstances? The story Michal invents has to be one that she thinks Saul will find believable, and this is the story she chooses.

Abigail. I have already looked at the story in 1 Samuel 25, but chiefly from Nabal's perspective [92–93]. We saw how the story is an allegory of the larger narrative, and especially of chs. 24 and 26, in which Saul pursues David and David spares Saul's life. In the allegory Nabal stands for Saul. Here I want to read the story at greater length from Abigail's perspective. The more I read it the more I dislike it, and I have tried to understand this subjective experience. In doing so I have discovered how the story fits into the deep currents at work in the closing chapters of 1 Samuel, and I shall be continuing here to build my picture of these chapters.

Abigail has several roles in the story. One is to predict David's future greatness (vv. 28-31), and in this respect it is she, not Nabal, who takes the place of Saul (see 24:20-21, 26:25), so that Saul is split into two. A second role, obviously, is to contribute to the theme of David's wife-getting. But Abigail has yet another role, which I believe—in part because the text struggles so hard to make it convincing—may be the most important. She is to be presented, like Michal, as a woman who keeps David from danger. But in this respect Abigail's story utterly lacks the simplicity and directness of Michal's.

I shall begin with a sequential reading. Understanding the problems in sequence will direct us to the cruxes in the narrative to be taken up later.

(25:2-22) There is a long prelude to Abigail's meeting with David. She is introduced by means of a direct contrast with her husband Nabal (v. 3). He is a fool by name and "surly and mean" by nature. She is introduced not only as "beautiful," which raises in the reader's mind the likelihood of a sexual relationship with David, but also (and first) as "clever," which raises less clear expectations but certainly makes us anticipate an active role for her.

Neither of these expectations is immediately gratified because Abigail is absent from the first part of the story (vv. 4-13). David sends servants to demand provisions from Nabal as a reward for his "protection" of Nabal's interests. Nabal, who seems to know nothing of this protection, gives the servants short shrift. He seems, rightly or wrongly, confident of his strength. On receiving Nabal's response David prepares for armed retribution.

This state of affairs is reported to Abigail by one of Nabal's workers (vv. 14-17), who has a definite point of view on the situation. He regards the protection arrangement with David as beneficial for Nabal's house, he sees David's victory in the threatened melée as a foregone conclusion, and he lays the blame for the crisis on Nabal's bad temper. Abigail's quick and active response suggests that she agrees with these assessments. Pointedly not consulting Nabal (v. 19), she collects copious provisions, sets up a meeting with David, and takes the provisions to him (vv. 18-20).

(25:23-31) On meeting David, Abigail is extremely deferential, beyond what one expects from a very prosperous lady meeting a bandit chief (vv. 23-24). Without waiting for him to speak she launches into a speech of remarkable length (vv. 24-31). After opening courtesies she lays the blame for the situation squarely on her husband, whom she describes in insulting terms (v. 25).

The core of the speech is in vv. 26-31, and it consists of several elements that are startling both individually and in their arrangement. I first offer an overview (in which the letters A–D connect related material from different parts of the speech):

A$_1$ YHWH has kept David from bloodguilt (v. 26)
B Wish that David's enemies "be like Nabal" (v. 26)
C$_1$ Petition that David accept the provisions for his men (v. 27)
C$_2$ Petition that David forgive Abigail's "trespass" (v. 28)
D Predictions of David's future greatness (v. 28-31)
A$_2$ David has been kept from bloodguilt (v. 31)
C$_3$ Petition that David "remember" Abigail (v. 31)

The importance of the theme of bloodguilt is shown by the way it recurs at the beginning and end of the speech. Although she piously says that YHWH has protected David from this danger (v. 26), Abigail is really stating her own motivation and pointing out what her prompt action has achieved. By averting a clash with Nabal *she* has kept David from bloodguilt—a danger so great that it could even have vitiated the future promised to him (v. 31).

Abigail's other statement in v. 26 is the oddest in her whole speech. What does she mean when she wishes that David's enemies may "be like Nabal"? Presumably she does not wish them to be "surly and mean." What she means is "dead"—she is using a conventional expression (cf. 2 Sam 18:32). But Nabal is not yet dead! What Abigail lets slip out, surely, is her wish that he were dead.

She next turns to making requests of David. In v. 27 she simply asks David to take the provisions and give them to his men, but no doubt she looks for his acceptance as a sign that he approves her entire initiative. She next asks that David "forgive the trespass of your servant" (v. 28). It is not obvious what this trespass is. Abigail does not blame herself for the problem: she has already put all the blame on Nabal. (In fact when you read the story in English, which unlike Hebrew does not specify the sex of the "servant," you are likely to suppose that she is asking David to pardon *Nabal's* offense.) The purpose of this petition seems to be merely to stress her deference.

The largest piece of Abigail's speech next follows: her predictions about David's future success. As v. 30 makes clear, she knows all about YHWH's royal promise to David. If we read this knowledge back into the earlier part of the story we gain a new understanding of her prompt action. Being assured of David's coming rise to national leadership, she could hardly doubt his ability to rout her husband's forces. This knowledge accounts also for her extreme deference. But Abigail goes beyond merely repeating promises to David of which the reader is already aware. She predicts that YHWH will give to David "a sure house" (v. 28), a term we will not encounter again before the great climax of 2 Samuel 7. She guarantees David full protection from his enemies (v. 29). She even predicts that he will do nothing bad in his lifetime (v. 28), surely the most extreme and glaringly false statement made about David in the whole Bible![21]

At the end of her speech Abigail returns to petition: "And when the LORD has dealt well with my lord, then remember your servant" (v. 31). The reader takes this to mean when David shall have become king.

(25:32-35) David's response to Abigail's speech is scarcely adequate to the great mouthful that she has addressed to him. He begins with

---

[21] On this speech see David M. Gunn and Danna Nolan Fewell, *Narrative in the Hebrew Bible.* Oxford Bible Series (Oxford: Oxford University Press, 1993) 69–71.

the bloodguilt theme (vv. 32-33), giving thanks for having been kept from this danger. Like Abigail, he gives the credit first to YHWH; but he also gives her the credit she modestly did not give to herself: "Blessed be your good sense, and blessed be you" (v. 33).

However, David's emphasis seems to lie elsewhere and to relate to something different from any of the elements of Abigail's speech.[22] He responds to her primarily as a petitioner (v. 35), but among her petitions he seems to respond directly only to the request that he accept her gift, and he does so by action, not word ("David received from her hand what she had brought him," cf. v. 27). His *words* (vv. 34-35) suggest that she has asked him not to attack Nabal's house. This is what the reader might have expected her to ask. But it is not among the things she actually did ask. Conversely, one petition that she *did* make is for the moment left hanging: that David remember her when he comes into his fortune.

(25:36-42) There remains the dénouement of the story. The events following Abigail's return home are swiftly told. She finds Nabal drunk and merry at his "kingly" party, and decides to say nothing immediately about her visit to David, but to keep it till morning (v. 36). Her news has a devastating effect on him—he "becomes like a stone" (v. 37). This sounds more like an incapacitating stroke than merely a powerful emotional response. His death ten days later is ascribed to a "stroke" from YHWH (v. 38), but this is surely just a conventional expression.[23] His effective death occurred when Abigail spoke to him.

While it would be too much to say that she devised a strategy for murdering her husband, her actions and words were carefully calculated to hurt him as much as possible. She brought him news that, in a culture of honor and shame, was sure to have a devastating effect. He had laid down a challenge to David but his wife had surrendered on his behalf, and even gone so far as to make a personal visit to his enemy. It is not obvious that Abigail needed to tell Nabal about her exploit at all. She chose to tell him, and she timed her news with care. We might think that it would have been even more effective for her to speak at the feast, in the presence of Nabal's peers, but she might have feared physical violence to herself, or simply that in his drunken state Nabal would not know what she was talking about. Instead she spoke to Nabal when he probably had a vicious hangover and felt as low as possible.

---

[22] Joel Rosenberg captures this inconsequentiality in the word "standoff" (*King and Kin: Political Allegory in the Hebrew Bible.* Indiana Studies in Biblical Literature [Bloomington, Ind.: Indiana University Press, 1986] 152).

[23] Like YHWH's "closing the womb" as a way of referring to barrenness (1:5-6).

That Abigail has murderous feelings toward Nabal fits into the pattern of their relationship as the story has built it up, from the contrastive introduction of the two characters (v. 3) through Abigail's intriguing with the servants behind Nabal's back (vv. 14-19) to her insulting him before David (v. 25). It agrees above all with her wish that David's enemies might be like Nabal, which can only mean a wish that Nabal might be dead (v. 26). We may guess that it is her meeting with David that brings the feelings into focus. She now consciously decides to try for a change of man. The sexual theme announced by the "beautiful" of v. 3 is at work not far from the surface. Abigail's last petition to David (v. 31) contains a *double entendre*. The time when YHWH will "deal well" with David, and when David should "remember" her, is perhaps not in the far future but in the immediate present! For David is quick to realize, when he learns of Nabal's death (v. 39), how well YHWH has dealt with him already. "Blessed be the LORD," indeed. Without risk to himself David has been avenged of an insult and acquired plentiful provisions. As a bonus the way is clear for him to have Abigail as well. Whether or not David feels love on this occasion (compare his relationship to Michal), he surely experiences a desire that reciprocates Abigail's own. There is no obvious political gain in marrying her: it is her he wants.[24] The emphasis in the account of their coming together is on haste, on both sides (vv. 40-42).

This distasteful story invites, I think, a critical rather than a recuperative feminist strategy [8–9]. Where Hannah's initiative benefited Israel as a whole and women in particular, Abigail's initiative does not. In the long run it does not benefit even herself. Her story is also overloaded, keeping too many themes and narrative intentions in play at once. I shall attempt to sort out the layers, using the Michal story from time to time as a point of contrast.

I begin with the sense of "David must win" that pervades the story. The narrator wants to abolish any doubt that David would have won if it had come to a battle with Nabal. Indeed, he works hard to keep the question from being asked. The only point at which the contrary possibility is even implicitly raised is in the description of Nabal's own attitude (25:10-11). The narrator trivializes this attitude by having none of the other characters take it seriously. He also uses the bloodguilt theme as a smoke-screen. Both Abigail and David are made simply to *assume* that David has been saved from bloodguilt, and to assume so is to assume that he would have won. But this is not so obvious. What if Nabal was right in thinking he had the measure of David?

---

[24] Perhaps there is material gain, though it is not clear that Abigail would command Nabal's wealth after his death.

Questions arise about this narrative strategy if we take seriously the Nabal–Saul parallel. In chs. 24 and 26, though Saul is momentarily in mortal danger from David, the larger context shows David still in mortal danger from Saul. In this regard the narrator seems to want to provide in ch. 25 not an allegorical parallel to chs. 24 and 26, but contrastive relief. In this story, at least, David is unambiguously "on top." If this positive message is then read back into the larger story the effect is to assure us that David must win in the end (despite his own continuing fears, especially in 27:1). But the exchange of meaning between text and context can go the opposite way and evoke the possibility that Nabal is right, that David is in mortal danger also in ch. 25. We will never know since it was never brought to the test, just as we will never know how David would have behaved if he had taken part in the last battle between Saul and the Philistines (ch. 29) [238–240].

This line of thought illuminates one aspect of Abigail's role. As we have seen, the text goes to great lengths to present her as saving David from danger, but the danger is not of the straightforward kind from which Michal rescued him. Rather it is a danger that seems to the reader to be suddenly plucked out of nowhere, that of *bloodguilt.* True, this is not the only place in the account of David's rise where this theme appears. It will recur in 2 Sam 3:28-29. But there it will be a matter of who gets blamed for a brutal murder *that has already happened.* Here it is a mere hypothetical possibility.[25] The reader of 1 Samuel 25 is justified in asking why David, who manages quite nicely to restrain himself from killing his enemy in chs. 24 and 26, cannot do so here without help. The suspicion arises that the entire theme of Abigail's saving David from bloodguilt cloaks another possibility: that she saved him from a beating, or worse, at Nabal's hands.

Abigail also takes on the role of predictor of David's future greatness. In chs. 24 and 26 this role belongs to Saul. In the allegory Nabal cannot assume it; someone has to, and the woman is available. But there are problems in how she performs the role. First of all, her predictions are overdrawn, going well beyond what Saul predicts. They overload the story and overwhelm the reader. What is the point of Abigail's knowing so much—knowing more about David's future than any other character in 1 Samuel knows, more than the narrator elsewhere knows, more, in fact, than will prove true?

The fundamental problem, I think, lies in the way the prediction theme gets mixed up with the sexual one. Abigail, like Michal, loves

---

[25] We could speculate that the theme has been conveniently imported from 2 Samuel 3 into 1 Samuel 25.

David and expresses her love in action. But we get very different impressions of the two women. I do not believe that the difference arises simply from a conventional preference in the text for a youthful love over a mature one. If Abigail were just a widow responding with unseemly haste to a favorable offer, especially after (if we accept her side of the story) a bad marriage, we would say "good luck to her!" But much more is going on than this. At a level not far below the surface the story casts Abigail in the role of a Bathsheba (2 Samuel 11), but one who is active rather than passive, desiring and working for the death of the husband who stands in the way of the desired marriage.[26] At this level guilt is laid on Abigail. The text works hard to offset this possibility by carefully presenting Nabal as a bad character who deserved all he got, and by lamely asserting that it was YHWH who actually killed him (v. 38). But my suspicion persists. Perhaps the danger from which Abigail *ultimately* saves David, by taking it on herself, is a guilt like the one he himself will later bear over Bathsheba and Uriah.

We can turn the screw another notch by recalling the earlier discussion of ch. 25 [92–93]. Piecing together the allegorical correspondence between Saul and Nabal, and David's taking in the same chapter another wife with the same name as Saul's (Ahinoam in 25:43), I suggested that what the chapter may really be "about" is David's stealing Saul's wife—with her active collaboration, the Abigail story would seem to say.

The effect of these dynamics on the way we read Abigail's predictions of David's future greatness seems to me profound. Instead of being a sudden divine inspiration they become a flagrant piece of flattery serving a selfish strategy. This accounts for their being so overblown in comparison to the predictions that other characters elsewhere make.

The further careers of David's first three wives. The footnote to the Abigail story in 25:43-44 claims our attention for another reason. At least to a modern sensibility any romantic reading of Abigail's story is deflated by David's taking another wife at the same time![27] It is a powerful narrative stroke to tell, in the same breath as these new marriages, of Michal's being given to another man (her passive role in v. 44 is in stark contrast to her initiative earlier). Women are already a commodity for David: trade one for two.

---

[26] On this comparison see Peter D. Miscall, "Literary Unity in Old Testament Narrative," *Sem.* 15 (1979) 40–41.

[27] Fewell and Gunn, *Gender, Power, and Promise* 157. They rightly refer to "Abigail, whose options are now closing."

After ch. 25 we hardly hear of David's women in the rest of 1 Samuel. Abigail and Ahinoam do share an adventure in ch. 30, one that savors much more of the ethos of Judges than of emergent monarchy. They are captured by a raiding party and have to be rescued by David and his men in a daring counterraid.

In 2 Samuel the theme of David's women develops rapidly. First, after David has been anointed king of Judah and has taken up residence at Hebron (2:1-4) Ahinoam and Abigail are joined by (at least) four other wives, and all six have sons (3:2-5). Here the biblical story of Ahinoam and Abigail ends. Abigail, whose debut in the story was so glamorous, is not kept in memory even by her son, for Chileab is never again mentioned either. The obscure Ahinoam in a sense does better, becoming the mother of David's firstborn, but perhaps she lives to wish that she had had (like Abigail) only an obscure son or (like Michal) none at all, for this firstborn, Amnon, will eventually be murdered by his half-brother Absalom in revenge for the rape of his half-sister Tamar.

Intertwined with all this, the drama of David and Michal plays itself out.[28] As part of his price for entering into negotiations to become the king of all Israel, David demands Michal's return. Her new husband Paltiel laments her departure and can scarcely be wrenched from her side (3:12-16). His is a passion that matches Michal's own for David. David never seems to reciprocate this feeling. He does not pretend that the return of Michal has anything to do with feeling: it is entirely a matter of power politics. Their only remaining interaction is tragic. In connection with the bringing of the Ark of God to Jerusalem Michal finds David's public behavior contemptible (6:20-23). David responds with utter rejection of Michal. After a final note that Michal remained childless she suffers, as Cheryl Exum puts it, narrative murder. The narrator simply removes her permanently from the story.[29]

David and polygyny. One particular marker of the sexual politics of kingship is royal polygyny, the habit kings have of taking many women. This theme will reach a famous biblical climax with Solomon's thousand wives (1 Kings 11:3). But even David's women are very numerous. We know of eight by name (Michal, Bathsheba, and the ones in 2 Sam 3:2-5), not counting Abishag (1 Kings 1:2-4), and we know there were others (2 Sam 5:13). The harem phenomenon is systemic in the tributary mode of production. Polygyny in such societies is not the norm for the whole population but a status symbol for the dominant class, especially the king [146].

---

[28] Ibid. 152–155.
[29] Exum, *Fragmented Women* 16–41.

David's polygyny can be correlated with his rise to royal power. That his marriage to Michal was monogamous is indicated by 1 Sam 25:43-44—had he had other wives before then, they would presumably be mentioned. In these verses he first moves into polygyny, but at the minimum level, as it were. This bigamy might be thought of as a relatively modest foretaste of future royal license.

Even so it stands in revealing contrast to the presentation of *Saul* in 1 Samuel as monogamous. Saul's monogamy is in fact a textual contrivance. We know that he had at least one other woman, but this information has been expelled from 1 Samuel—we find out about his secondary wife Rizpah only in 2 Samuel 21. This withholding of information looks like a careful piece of narrative work. If his supposed monogamy is yet another indication that Saul was never really a king this fits in with many other aspects of the portrayal of him in 1 Samuel.

Conclusion. I have not, of course, followed to its end the theme of David's women. For the purposes of this book I have already traveled far enough beyond 1 Samuel. The story will go on to David's rape of Bathsheba, a married woman, and his murder of her husband (2 Samuel 11), then to the sexual crimes of a new generation in the stories of Amnon, Tamar, and Absalom. It is not too much to say that the fundamental role of women in the Book of the Everlasting Covenant, and beyond, is to express the struggle of men for royal power.[30]

Perhaps the most chilling aspect of these stories of women as pawns in royal power struggles is the way they are processed as stories of women's love for men. These stories become a sort of commentary on the words of Gen 3:16: "Your desire shall be for your husband, and he shall rule over you." This claim that from the very creation women are condemned to desire their own subordination is turned in 1 Samuel (and beyond) into a desire *on the part of women* for a political system based on domination and subordination. Women are on the side of kingship; they work to bring it about as a consequence of their individual desire for David. But the farther we progress from story to story—Michal, Abigail, Bathsheba, Tamar—the more the deception is stripped away. What Michal and Abigail have been working for is a system that will bring no good to women. We saw this at one level in the anthropological studies of how state systems narrow women's options. We see it at another level in the tragic results for themselves of the initiatives of David's women.

---

[30] See Schwartz, "Adultery in the House of David."

Jonathan and Gender

. . . your love to me was wonderful,
passing the love of women (2 Sam 1:26).

So David addresses the dead Jonathan at the end of his great lament over Jonathan and Saul. The story of David and Jonathan, and these words in particular, assume great importance for gay rights activists, who find in them virtually the only positive presentation of male homosexuality in the Jewish Bible. Here is a man telling of his love for another man, comparing it with heterosexual love, and saying it is better. A reading of 1 Samuel that claims to be in touch with issues of ethics and human liberation can no longer overlook the central importance of the book for one of the urgent and vibrant discourses of our time.[31]

The validity and power of the gay reading. Nothing in the text rules out, and much encourages the view that David and Jonathan had a consummated gay relationship. The text does not force this conclusion on us; there are obvious cultural reasons why it would not. But it is at least as valid as any other.

There are issues in the text that the homosexual reading seems better able to explain than other readings, for example Saul's outburst in 20:30-34. Saul is infuriated that Jonathan has "chosen" David (v. 30). The reason Saul gives for his opposition is that David threatens Jonathan's succession to the throne, and this is why he sentences David to death. But this "reason" fails to explain the extremity of his fury against *Jonathan*. If Saul wants to help his son to the throne, impaling him on a spear will scarcely serve his end. It is fair to look for some unspoken cause of the irrational rage, and modern experience of irrational homophobia suggests that this may be the cause.

This possibility is strongly confirmed when Saul brings Jonathan's "choice" of David directly into the realm of the sexual (v. 30). The key words are "to the shame of your mother's genitalia." Is Saul as father desperately trying to transfer the blame for Jonathan's behavior to the mother? The idea that a gay man is a "mother's boy" is a commonplace of homophobia. The father tries to destroy the possibility that there is anything *in himself* that could have made the boy turn out like this.[32]

---

[31] My reading here is close to that of Fewell and Gunn, *Gender, Power, and Promise* 148–151.

[32] Fewell and Gunn (ibid. 149–150) read this incident in a generally similar way. They create a nice wordplay, I presume deliberately. They note that gay readings of David and Jonathan are often dismissed as "simply 'perverse'" (p. 149). They then highlight the words of v. 30, "You son of perversity and rebellion" (their translation,

The text is open to a gay reading, and this is no bland statement, for one can easily see ways in which it could have discouraged such a reading. The non-trivial, politically important claim stands that the Bible here shows itself able to say what it has to say through the dynamics of what appears to be a gay relationship.

Jonathan's role as a woman's role. But problems arise when one comes to ask *what* exactly the text says about the relationship. The answer is: Jonathan plays the same role that I have ascribed to David's women. The role of Michal and Abigail is to love David, to do practical things to save and help him, and to prophesy his coming kingship. Jonathan does all of this and more.

When he returns to the story in 18:1 (having been absent since ch. 14), the first thing mentioned about him is his passion for David. He acts to save David from Saul in 19:1-7 and in ch. 20. He foretells David's kingship in 20:13-16 and 23:17. And in each of these respects he is ahead of the women, beginning to exercise each function earlier in the story than they do. He is (in terms of narrative space) more in David's company than the women are. If these features, along with sex, constitute "the love of women" as David has experienced it, then Jonathan's love does indeed "pass the love of women." Randall Bailey suggests that the women of 1 Samuel are better men than their men.[33] Jonathan, in terms of the way the text exploits women's power, is a better woman than David's women.[34]

The women's love for David, as we saw, is not clearly reciprocated. He is not said to love Michal, and his later history with her suggests that he did not. To Abigail he is probably at least attracted, but he marries someone else at the same time he marries her and we hear nothing of the quality of their married love. Perhaps even more striking than David's failure to reciprocate women's love is his consistent failure to reciprocate Jonathan's. At least up to David's lament in 2 Samuel 1 virtually all the emotive language in this relationship, and most of the significant action, is on Jonathan's side.

A reading of the covenant between Jonathan and David. Jonathan "loved David as his own life" (18:1, 3, 20:17) and "took great delight in David" (19:1). There are no such expressions of David's feeling for Jonathan. David does, indeed, make reference to Jonathan's feeling for

---

p. 150). Readings that attribute "perversion" to biblical characters are "simply" perverse readings—even if the text itself joins in attributing the perversion!

[33] "Reading the Book of Samuel as a Message to the Exiles: A Hermeneutical Shift," *JITC* 18 (1990–1991) 104–106.

[34] "Jonathan is a woman, more woman than women are" (Fewell and Gunn, *Gender, Power, and Promise* 151).

him: "Your father knows well that I have found favor with you" (20:3; NRSV "that you like me"). While it makes sense in context for David to put it this way there is no reason why he could not speak of a mutual attachment. There seems to be an embargo in the narrative on suggesting that David cares for Jonathan.

As to actions, Jonathan hands over to David the robes and weapons that symbolize his official status as king's son (18:4). He energetically, and at first successfully, strives to maintain David's good standing at court (19:1-7). He wants to see justice done to David, but also, no doubt, he wants David near him. In ch. 20 he says he is willing to do anything whatsoever for David (v. 4), and goes on to save David's life at risk to his own.

The relationship is mostly worked out as a "covenant" between the two men, which we can read as analogous to a marriage agreement. Jonathan makes a covenant with David as early as 18:3, and later we get some impression of what its terms were. David, for example, understands the covenant to guarantee that Jonathan will protect him (20:8), while Jonathan sees it as binding David to be always loyal to Jonathan's house (20:13-16).

There are several points to be made about this covenant. Except for the very last reference in 23:18 it is entirely of Jonathan's making. This is how the narrator refers to it: "Jonathan made a covenant with David" (18:3, 20:16). But it is also how David refers to it: "You have brought your servant into a covenant" (20:8). The use of "your servant" here suggests an unequal covenant imposed by the stronger party, as does David's obeisance in 20:41. Jonathan is, after all, the king's son. Still, David's modesty seems like a ploy when Jonathan so clearly wants the relationship to be equal and mutual.

Tension develops between the covenant and the emotional relationship. We see this first in 20:8-9. David appeals to the covenant as a guarantee of his safety (v. 8). It is disquieting that he would appeal to this quasi-legal relationship rather than to Jonathan's subjective attachment to him, reaffirmed as recently as vv. 3-4. Jonathan's reply in v. 9 suggests that he feels slighted by David's rather businesslike appeal, as if to say "Haven't I done and said enough to convince you of my loyalty?" But a little later Jonathan himself seems to separate the emotional from the quasi-legal (20:13-17). Having sought a guarantee through covenant of David's loyalty to his house (vv. 13-16), he goes on to exact from David an oath, apparently separate from the covenant, whose basis is the emotional relationship: "Jonathan made David *swear again by his love for him*" (v. 17). This form of words is ambiguous, but it seems probable in view of the last part of the verse that it is *Jonathan's* love that is the guarantee of the oath.

At the end of ch. 20 the emotional and the covenantal seem at last to come together. For the first and only time the expression of emotion is mutual: they "wept with each other" (v. 41),[35] though even here David's homage to Jonathan strikes a discordant note. Finally, at their last meeting the two of them make a covenant *together* (23:18).

Conclusion. The sequence of Jonathan–David scenes creates a peculiar picture. On the one hand we have a covenant relationship in which Jonathan takes the lead because he is the more powerful party and that only at the end reaches apparent mutuality. On the other hand we have an emotional relationship in which Jonathan takes the lead because he is in love, and that again takes a long time to be expressed with anything like mutuality. The two levels relate uneasily to each other. Jonathan's love makes him want not just to equalize but actually to reverse the power relationship: as the powerful party making the covenant he appeals to it against the time when he (or his house) will have become the powerless party! When David appeals to the covenant Jonathan senses that this implies a slight on his love. David seems to be happiest relying on Jonathan as a powerful protector and suspicious of Jonathan's striving toward mutuality.

This reading of Jonathan is an alternative to my earlier reading [93–99]. There it seemed impossible to give any plausible account of Jonathan's motivation in abdicating his heirdom to David. Now it seems that the gender dynamic may have been exploited to provide the needed plausibility. If Jonathan can be cast in the image of the women who love and marry David, who serve David and assist his rise to power without expecting anything in return other than being married to him, this will solve the problem of motivation. To be the heir, and thus in a position to abdicate, he must be male. To have the motivation to do so he must (within the text's conceptual resources) be like the women who empty themselves for David. The answer: a gay relationship in which Jonathan takes a female role. But for this alternative reading to work, Jonathan will have to die. No "wifely" role can be imagined for him in David's household after David becomes king.

I return to where I began, the lament in 2 Sam 1:19-27. This is glorious poetry, meant to show David at his best. But the words are still problematic. They are spoken, after all, to one who is now dead, and prompt the reader to ask again why no such words are recorded as spoken by David to the living Jonathan. And even here there are still

---

[35] The textual evidence on which David is sometimes said to have wept more or longer than Jonathan—e.g., NRSV ("David wept the more")—is flimsy.

no words (or at best ambiguous ones) of *David's* love for Jonathan. David sings still of Jonathan's love for *him*.[36]

Hannah in the Context of Monarchy

The issues raised in this chapter bring us back to Hannah. We have seen how the powerful initiatives of David's women smooth his path to the kingship. We have seen in the individual stories of Michal and Abigail how their initiative brought no long-term good to them. And anthropology has shown us the same dynamic projected on a larger canvas: monarchy coopts women's services while diminishing their lives. Hannah is a woman of powerful initiative who does not live under monarchy, yet monarchy has coopted her services too—in the Deuteronomic text, in the process of canonization, and in the tradition of biblical interpretation.

Coopting Hannah. In the Deuteronomic text Hannah is certainly a key actor in the story of Israel's turn to kingship. Her initiative produces the leadership of her son Samuel, and Samuel will be Israel's king-maker. But this effect is just as ironic in her case as in Samuel's. For Samuel, to establish a king is to negate the traditional order of judgeship for which he stands. Hannah, as I have read her, also put forth her strength to restore that traditional order. This first level of cooption is part and parcel of the contradiction within the Deuteronomic mythic work. It is because the Deuteronomists are so desperate to affirm continuity between judgeship and kingship that Hannah gets turned into a forerunner of monarchy.

The second level is the canonical creation of the beginning of (1) Samuel, which makes Hannah's story into the beginning of a "book." This, I argued, encourages us to read her story forward rather than back, to look for clues to its meaning primarily in what follows it. Reading in this way tends to highlight any references to or hints of monarchy in the text. I suggested that for Christian readers Luke's rereading of Hannah's story (Luke 1–2) strongly confirms this forward-looking, monarchical reading [136–139].

The third level of cooption is in the work of biblical interpretation. Some readers find extensive indications of monarchical discourse in Hannah's story. I earlier argued against such readings, suggesting that

---

[36] Fewell and Gunn (*Gender, Power, and Promise* 150–151) provide a fuller reading of the lament along these lines.

such indications arise in the minds of the readers precisely because they are reading the story *as a beginning.*

Monarchy in Hannah's Song. There is, though, one undeniable moment of encouragement in the text for a monarchical reading of Hannah. It lies in the reference to the king at the end of her song (1 Sam 2:10). Her words are:

> YHWH will judge the ends of the earth;
>   he will give strength to his king,
>   and exalt the power of his anointed.

On the face of it these words invite the reader to see the whole song—and perhaps then the whole story—as looking toward monarchy. This seems to me perverse. To make my point I shall present and criticize one extreme "royal" reading of the song.

Polzin sees Hannah's song and David's song in 2 Samuel 22 as programmatically placed at the two ends of the Masoretic Book of Samuel,[37] and he proposes extensive parallels between these songs. 2 Samuel 22 (= Psalm 18) is ostensibly a meditation by David on his experience as king. Polzin's purpose in tracing the parallels is to suggest that the monarchical theme pervades Hannah's song rather than being confined to its final half-verse.

His alleged parallels relate much more to some parts of Hannah's song than to others. The parallels to the beginning and end of Hannah's song are compelling (1 Sam 2:1-2, 10, cf. 2 Sam 22:3-4, 32, 14, 29, 51).[38] For the central portion of Hannah's song (2:4-8), which is of particular interest to me, Polzin claims few parallels in 2 Samuel 22, and even some of these are far-fetched (e.g., 1 Sam 2:4, "But those who stumble have put on strength" and 2 Sam 22:40, "For thou didst gird me with strength for the battle"). There are just two strong parallels:

A. "[YHWH] brings low, he also exalts" (1 Sam 2:7)
   "Your eyes are upon the exalted to bring them down" (2 Sam 22:28)

B. "[YHWH] raises up the poor from the dust" (1 Sam 2:8)
   "I beat [my enemies] fine as the dust of the earth" (2 Sam 22:43)

I shall pay particular attention to these two parallels in my critique.

---

[37] *Samuel and the Deuteronomist: A Literary Study of the Deuteronomic History. Part Two: 1 Samuel* (San Francisco: Harper & Row, 1989) 31–35.

[38] I am unimpressed by the alleged parallels to 1 Sam 2:9 in 2 Sam 22:26, 34, 39, 29, but this is not important for my argument.

My basic problem with Polzin's reading of Hannah's song is that he ignores the contradiction between the closing words in 2:10 and the general tendency of the rest of the song. The central section (vv. 4-8) celebrates YHWH's liberation of the oppressed in terms compatible with a theology of revolution. Identifying herself with the oppressed, Hannah sings of how YHWH acts to reverse sociopolitical dichotomies, taking power from those who have it and giving it to the (militarily) weak, the hungry, the barren, the poor. Celebration of these reversals forms the substance of the poem. The voice we hear is one we have not heard clearly since Judg 5:6-11—another woman's song—the celebration of peasant power in Israel.[39]

How can such revolutionary sentiments be made to fit with a celebration of kingship? Not easily, but an attempt to make them fit has certainly been made in the literary process of creating the song. We cannot recover the details of this process, but someone has set out to make 2 Samuel 22 into an interpretive context for Hannah's song. There is a tendency in the text to "monarchize" the song and thus to coopt the power of a *woman's* voice on the side of monarchy.

In such a case what is to be our reading strategy? Polzin's is to accept the monarchizing tendency in the text and even to carry it further (for example by what I see as an exaggeration of the parallels with 2 Samuel 22). Mine is to be suspicious of the monarchizing tendency. I can illustrate the distance between us by looking at parallels A and B. The incorporation of the song into a monarchical context has worked strikingly well for the beginning and end of the song (1 Sam 2:1-2, 9-10). It has not worked well for the middle—the part that for me gives the song its essential quality as a celebration of social upheaval—except possibly for parallels A and B.

The parallel (A) between 1 Sam 2:7 and 2 Sam 22:28 is impressive at the verbal level. YHWH is in both cases the agent of the bringing down of the exalted. But words have very different values in different contexts. Hannah's song speaks of general social upheaval whereas David's speaks of a (highly mythicized) upheaval through which the king alone is rescued from his enemies.

The parallel (B) between 1 Sam 2:8 and 2 Sam 22:43 is less verbally impressive but even more revealing. YHWH raises the poor from the dust, while David (with YHWH's aid, it is understood) beats his enemies into the dust, indeed makes them dust. The parallel invites us to

---

[39] For a reading of the song in these terms see Norman K. Gottwald, *The Tribes of Yahweh: A Sociology of the Religion of Liberated Israel 1250–1050 B.C.E.* (Maryknoll, N.Y.: Orbis, 1979) 534–540.

think of these two processes as one: the way that the poor are raised from the dust is by the king reducing his enemies to dust. The fiction to be created is that kings are on the side of the poor. At the mythic level of 2 Samuel 22 they even *are* the poor. Polzin reproduces this piece of royal mythology: "The poor and downtrodden . . . are all Is-rael's kings . . . ⌐."[40] We know that tributary societies [145–146] were very adept at creating the fiction that the king is on the side of the poor. The best example in the Jewish Bible is Psalm 72.[41] The setting for the creation of the song in its present form is to be looked for in the work of the royal propaganda machine.

This parallel seems, though, to backfire. Read at the surface level it might be taken to equate the poor with David's enemies, which cer-tainly corresponds to the truth of the matter: royal systems create or in-tensify the distance between rich and poor. The curious comment that David hates "the lame and the blind" (2 Sam 5:8) takes on a certain conviction if read in connection with Hannah's celebration of the sal-vation of the oppressed! This is perhaps a foolish allusion, but my point is that one cannot get anywhere with such "parallels" unless one is ready to ask whether kingship tends to raise the poor from the dust or tends to beat them fine as the dust.

Strategies of reading. I read the way I do because I read on the side of those for whom 1 Sam 2:4-8 is a charter for their own liberation—the socioeconomically oppressed, including women. I simply cannot imag-ine readers from a South American base community (say) finding the songs of Hannah and David similar, or being persuaded that they are. Such readers are well aware of the claims of autocrats to be on the side of the poor! I, along with them, read with an eye to socioeconomic, gen-der, or other differences in the text. Readers like Polzin pay no attention to such differences, accepting without comment, for example, the text's strategy of paralleling the song of an obscure woman with that of a king.

In the tendency of the text Hannah is another woman coopted into promoting the kingship of David—not as one who directly assists him like Michal and Abigail, but as one who anticipates him from afar. Her song has been *made* into a celebration of kingship (though rather trans-parently and ineptly, I believe). The monarchical climax and other touches (including many of Polzin's parallels) enable monarchy even to claim as its own the concern for the poor and oppressed that fills the middle section (vv. 4-8), though this concern is the antithesis of how a

[40] *Samuel and the Deuteronomist* 33.

[41] David Jobling, "Deconstruction and the Political Analysis of Biblical Texts: A Jamesonian Reading of Psalm 72," *Sem.* 59 (1992) 95–127.

monarchy really functions. The canonization process carries the coop-tion further. The story in which Hannah takes the initiative and sings her song becomes a story of a new phase in Israel's history, the monar-chical phase.

Modern critics are therefore right to discern monarchizing tenden-cies in the text at a variety of levels. But to concentrate exclusively on these tendencies, to exaggerate them, to *buy into* them without any ref-erence to feminist and liberationist critique is simply to extend into the present the ancient work of coopting the Bible's women characters. To see one verse of Hannah's song as reversing the plain meaning of the rest of it, to see in her entire story *only* a "parable" of the coming of kingship,[42] is to trivialize the text, Hannah as a character, and the whole work of feminist biblical scholarship. It is also to become complicit in the Bible's destructive cultural effects.

Hannah in the Context of the Judges

In this section I hope to show that we read Hannah very differently if we read her not forward toward kingship, but backward into the book of Judges.

Feminist reading of the book of Judges. There is a strong link be-tween Judges and the development of feminist biblical interpretation. The remarkable current "desire" of biblical scholarship for this can-onical book [33–34] seems to me to be due above all to its appeal for certain styles of feminism as expressed in the work of Mieke Bal and others.[43] In the Feminist Companion to the Bible series the volume on Judges is scarcely shorter than the following one on Samuel and Kings, texts whose total length is about five times that of Judges.[44]

At the beginning of the Feminist Companion Athalya Brenner notes that "the book of Judges is replete with female figurations."[45] She

---

[42] Polzin, *Samuel and the Deuteronomist* 25–26 and the whole of his Chapter 1.

[43] Bal, *Death & Dissymmetry; Murder and Difference*. In Gale A. Yee, ed., *Judges and Method: New Approaches in Biblical Studies* (Minneapolis: Fortress, 1995), a primer on biblical method based on Judges, five of the seven chapters are by women with ob-viously feminist approaches.

[44] Athalya Brenner, ed., *A Feminist Companion to Judges*. The Feminist Compan-ion to the Bible 4 (Sheffield: Sheffield Academic Press, 1993); *A Feminist Companion to Samuel and Kings*. The Feminist Companion to the Bible 5 (Sheffield: Sheffield Academic Press, 1994).

[45] *Feminist Companion to Judges* 9.

goes on to caution that this does not mean that women are necessarily valued there or treated in any consistently positive way. The variety in the presentation of women in Judges is in fact enormous. They are often victimized, often brutalized, but the ones presented passively are outnumbered by those who powerfully assert themselves in the story—Achsah, Deborah, Jael, Samson's mother, Delilah, Micah's mother (ch. 17). Even the victims are not presented *merely* as victims. Some—Jephthah's daughter, the Levite's wife (see 19:2)—are at times active subjects. What makes Judges nearly unique in the Bible, and what creates its importance for feminist analysis, is the fact that throughout the book women are almost always an integral part of what is going on.

Bal bases her "countercoherence" for Judges on the situation of women in different forms of marriage [148]. She suggests that the book can be explained—at least as well as by any other theory—as the literary deposit of a social process whereby matrilocal was giving way to patrilocal marriage.[46] One of the foundations of her case is the Bible's use for certain married women—Abimelech's mother (8:31) and the Levite's woman (ch. 19)—of a Hebrew word different from the normal word for "wife." The word is *pīlegeš*, traditionally translated "concubine" but taken by Bal to be the normal term for matrilocal wife. Though Bal's thesis has not received general acceptance it is the most serious attempt to provide a definition of what Judges is fundamentally about that takes seriously the centrality of women in the book.

The correlation of kingship and polygyny I identified earlier in this chapter can be traced also into Judges. The basic ideology of judgeship seems to assume monogamous marriage. Jephthah rather strengthens than weakens this impression; he is driven from his father's house because he is illegitimate, the son of a woman other than his father's (one) wife (11:1-2). Neither the unrestrained treatment of sexuality in the Samson cycle nor the horrific treatment of it in Judges 19–21 departs from the norm of monogamous marriage.

---

[46] These are terms from anthropology. In matrilocal marriage the wife continues to reside in her father's house; in patrilocal marriage she moves to her husband's house. In reading Bal it is vital to note that she adjusts this standard terminology so that "patrilocal" refers to the wife remaining in her father's house and "virilocal" to her moving to her husband's house. In this adjustment "patrilocal" takes on the exact opposite meaning to what it has in general anthropology. Bal's usage makes the woman the point of reference, while the anthropological usage assumes the viewpoint of the child of the marriage. For the present discussion I keep the more customary anthropological terms.

The only exceptions to monogamy in Judges are linked, directly or indirectly, to the theme of kingship. Gideon had enough women to produce seventy-one sons, a fact we learn just at the moment that he rejects/accepts the kingship (Judg 8:22-31). The reference in Judg 5:30 to a man's winning several women as a spoil of war is in the context of a specifically royal oppression. Finally, some of the minor judges must be polygynous, given the great number of their offspring (10:4, 12:9, 14). But the system of minor judges stands in contrast to the main ideology of Judges, and indeed, in its concern with continuity adumbrates kingship [45–46].

Rereadings of Hannah. Hannah not only belongs to but plays a critical role in my Extended Book of Judges. As the initiative-taker in her story she is the cause of the restoration and glorification of judgeship in Samuel. Through her son she achieves the resolution of the twin scandals of her time, the Philistine occupation and "all the people doing what was right in their own eyes." I have suggested that the way her story is told invites us to think of her as *intending* to intervene in Israel's national situation [134–135]. It is fitting, given the prominence of women in Judges, that a woman plays so necessary a role in judgeship's restoration. Hannah fits right in with the powerful, resisting women of Judges. Here I show some more specific links.

As the mother of Samuel the judge, Hannah is directly related to two of the women in the book of Judges, the mothers of Samson (Judges 13) and Jephthah (Judg 11:1-2). Less directly she is related to the mother of Abimelech (Judg 8:31). Abimelech, though not a judge, is a national leader of the judges' time. All these three women are unnamed, so that in this respect Hannah stands in contrast to them.

It is natural to begin with the mother of Samson, for many parallels have been noted between her story and Hannah's. The accounts begin in almost identical fashion, with the introduction of a man who will become the father of the judge (Judg 13:2, 1 Sam 1:1). Both mothers are barren, and the sons are both to be Nazirites (which imposes conditions on both mother and child: Judg 13:4-5, 14; 1 Sam 1:11, cf. 14-15).[47] In each story the father becomes marginalized from the main action and is even made to look foolish, while the mother takes the initiative. But the stories differ in how they handle the mother's initiative. Hannah stands gloriously alone in moving her story forward. The initiative of Samson's mother, though it is powerfully affirmed by contrast to Manoah's ineptness, is enclosed in the typical annunciation framework.

---

[47] See Peter D. Miscall, *1 Samuel: A Literary Reading* (Bloomington, Ind.: Indiana University Press, 1986) 12–13.

This makes her initiative secondary to the initiative of God as expressed through the angel [138, 140].

What Hannah shares with the mothers of Jephthah and Abimelech is less clear. The most promising starting point is that, like them, she is in a relationship with a polygynous man. All three are marginalized by the ability of men to have multiple women and to discriminate between them on whatever ground the men see fit. Abimelech's story is created out of his mother's marginalization (probably as a matrilocal wife). Only the sons of Gideon's preferred (patrilocal) wives participated in rule after Gideon died (Judg 9:2).

Jephthah's mother is apparently even farther down the scale of preference, not even a *pīlegeš*, but a *zōnā* (11:1). The latter term typically means "prostitute." There is a problem, though, in understanding it this way in the case of Jephthah. The text states that "Gilead was the father of Jephthah." But if he were the son of a common prostitute how could his paternity be known? His story is so similar to that of Abimelech as to suggest that his mother, too, was a *pīlegeš*, or at least some category of woman with whom a man could enter into a long-term relationship allowing for certainty of paternity.[48]

There is no indication in Hannah's story that she is legally a different kind of wife from Peninnah. What is very striking, though, is her independence within Elkanah's household, and especially her assumption of complete control over her firstborn son. She assumes the right to make her own vow to YHWH regarding this child and to carry it out, and at no point is this right questioned. This freedom of the mother surely fits much better in the ethos of matrilocal than of patrilocal marriage. Thus it is not hard to imagine Hannah's story as that of a *pīlegeš*.

This is an interesting speculation. The text, however, seems to assume that Hannah was part of a regular patrilocal setup, a member of Elkanah's household, and this is what I assumed when I read her story in the last chapter. But a major point of my reading was that Hannah *resists* the constraint of her domestic situation. The story of Peninnah and Hannah effectively demonstrates the potential brutality of polygyny for the women caught up in it. Hannah's initiative is directed against this brutality.

In summary, the figure of Hannah as the mother of a judge has been created largely out of elements from the book of Judges. Her role

---

[48] Perhaps *zōnā* is meant to be an insult. It is interesting that it is the narrator who uses the term; Jephthah's brothers use the much more neutral "another woman" (11:2).

recapitulates and transcends that of Samson's mother and is filled out with indications from other Judges women.

Hannah's song in the Extended Book of Judges. Reading Hannah's song backward links it to the two other major pieces of poetry in the Extended Book of Judges. One of these is the Song of Deborah (Judges 5), another woman's song that celebrates the uprising of the peasants of Israel and the sweeping away of the vaunted power of kings. The other is the intensely antimonarchical fable of Jotham—a man's song, but one that finds its fulfillment in a woman's assassination of a king (Judg 9:8-15, 53-54)! Reading Hannah's song in relation to these passages focuses our attention squarely on its middle section. What Hannah celebrates is the social revolution that *gets rid of* kings, and the positive reference to the king in the final verse seems to have no business being there. Hannah's song—and her whole story—fit much more comfortably into the context of the book of Judges than into the framework of emergent monarchy in Israel.[49]

Once Again Ruth

We have already noted the impact of the placement of Ruth, in some canonical traditions, between Judges and 1 Samuel. In a feminist discussion the fact that Ruth is a woman's story focuses this impact.

Feminist exegetes are divided about Ruth. Some are enthusiastic about the book, seeing Ruth as a strong, independent character and her relationship to Naomi as an example of voluntary female bonding unique in the Bible. Others see Ruth and her book as subserving male agendas.[50] I am more convinced by the second option.

The cooption of Ruth. The canonical placement of Ruth can be thought of as another example of the cooption of women. I suggested earlier that this book provides an alternative route from the judges to King David, a route that avoids the complex currents of 1 Samuel [106–109]. Here I simply add that it is a *woman's* story that is pressed into service to achieve this painless transition. In particular, putting

[49] There are many narrative connections between Hannah's story and the end of Judges, for example men "from the hill country of Ephraim" (Judg 19:1; 1 Sam 1:1) and the frequent references to Shiloh.

[50] "It is the reader's task to determine whether this book affirms Ruth or ultimately erases her" (Amy-Jill Levine, "Ruth," in Carol A. Newsom and Sharon H. Ringe, eds., *The Women's Bible Commentary* [Louisville, Ky.: Westminster/John Knox, 1992] 79). Cf. Levine's whole introduction.

Ruth before 1 Samuel confirms the cooption of Hannah into the monarchical ideology. Her link to the women of Judges is weakened and her story stands in immediate proximity to the pro-David story of Ruth.

The tendency of the book of Ruth seems to me to duplicate the tendency we found in the narrative presentation of Michal and Abigail. The shape of the book as a whole allows women, both Ruth and Naomi, to take the initiative and make the plans—but only until the time comes for the real decision making. Then the men take over (contrast ch. 4 with chs. 1–3). And the result of the story is the birth of David. Long before David is even born, strong women put forth their strength so that he may become king!

Exegetical issues in Ruth. A few more specific points can be made. Bal has suggested that the conflict between two forms of marriage, matrilocal and patrilocal, is fundamental for understanding the book of Judges. It is of extraordinary interest, therefore, that the very first incident in Ruth marks a clear dividing of the ways between these two options. Naomi's two daughters-in-law make opposite choices in Ruth 1. Orpah's choice to stay in her own place rather than be associated with her late husband's family is an option for the matrilocal system—indeed, it is to her "mother's house" that she is said to return (1:8).[51] Ruth chooses the patrilocal, associating herself with her husband's family. Her bond to Naomi, which forms the backbone of the book and which is charmingly presented as her own free choice in the book's most memorable words (1:16-17), in fact valorizes a relationship—mother-in-law to daughter-in-law—on the success of which the patrilocal household depends.[52] The result of these choices is that Orpah disappears from the canonical story while Ruth becomes an essential link in it. By her choice she becomes the mother of Davidic kings.

The book of Ruth enacts a shift in the role of women. The relatively fluid situations in which the women of Judges live their lives is continued in the fluid situation in which Naomi and Ruth find themselves and the range of options that seems open to them, but through the very decisions that these women make the book moves toward the relatively more fixed position of women under patrilocality and monarchy.

---

[51] See Carol Meyers, "'To Her Mother's House': Considering a Counterpart to the Israelite *Bêt ʿab,*" in David Jobling, et al, eds., *The Bible and the Politics of Exegesis: Essays in Honor of Norman K. Gottwald on his Sixty-Fifth Birthday* 39–51.

[52] So it is a just historical irony that Ruth's words have traditionally been used, down to the present, to express the bond of patrilocal marriage.

A central issue in Ruth is the legal ownership of women.[53] Ruth's decision puts her under male ownership. The first question that must be raised about Ruth when she gets to Bethlehem is who owns her (2:5), and in ch. 4 the ownership of her is bound up with the ownership of land. Ruth is to "find security . . . in the house of [her] husband" (1:9). The message that a woman's safety lies in being securely owned within a legal system is powerfully reinforced by the juxtaposition of Ruth and the end of Judges. The stress on the legal acquisition of Ruth sharply counterpoints the lawless (though sanctioned) acquisition of women in Judges 21. More sharply still, Orpah's decision to go her own way is analogous to the decision of the Levite's wife to leave her husband's house (Judg 19:2). That decision led to the woman's rape and murder, and it is no surprise when a rabbinic text tells us that Orpah, too, was gang-raped on her way home [231].

Finally I note one of those serendipitous connections in which meaning so often is to be found. The LXX-Christian canon places Ruth 4:15 and 1 Sam 1:8 only a dozen verses apart, and sets up a micro-dialogue between them. Ruth is more to Naomi than seven sons, while Elkanah claims to be more than ten sons to Hannah. Taken together these two verses convey a message that neither alone adequately conveys: that the patrilocal system, summarized in the triangle of head of household, his wife, and his surviving mother, is more important than mere fertility, which any system achieves.

---

[53] For the legal issues see Steinberg, "The Deuteronomic Law."

Chapter 8

ALL THE WOMEN OF 1 SAMUEL

To conclude my section on gender I "go looking for women" in 1 Samuel.[1] What can we say about the presence of women in a biblical book *in its entirety?* My method is open-ended, reviewing all the women in (in some cases implicit in) the book in relation to a set of characteristics and themes that are rather *ad hoc* but have theoretical importance and enable a reasonably systematic presentation of the data. A measure of arbitrariness cannot be avoided, since some of the characters fall into more than one category.[2]

In dealing with the issue of government I discovered a feature specific to the canonical 1 Samuel, namely the surrogacy system (Chapter 5). As a conclusion to the present chapter I shall assess the role of women within that system.

Hypothetical, Absent, and Uncharacterized Women

In this section I look at women whom the text mentions (occasionally even by name) or whose existence it tacitly assumes, but who are

---

[1] This form of words is from Danna Nolan Fewell and David M. Gunn, *Gender, Power, and Promise: The Subject of the Bible's First Story* (Nashville: Abingdon, 1993) 18.

[2] My survey owes a good deal to Mieke Bal's proposal for analyzing narrative subjectivity in texts. Her scheme is conveniently summarized in Mieke Bal, *Death & Dissymmetry: The Politics of Coherence in the Book of Judges* (Chicago: University of Chicago Press, 1988) 248–249, and explained on pp. 34–38.

in no sense agents in the narrative. This broad statement covers a variety of *sorts* of narrative procedure, which I shall try to organize. I hope I have found all these women. In my first drafts there were several that I missed. If you find others, let me know!

The barren and the fertile. Sometimes the text evokes classes of women and refers to their situation. The first such example is in Hannah's song, "the barren" and "the one with many children" (2:5). The song celebrates social reversal in a variety of ways, but here it includes a reversal specific to women.

It is interesting that "the barren" and "the one with many children" are *singulars*. In this respect they differ from the comparable terms in the song. Verses 4-5a have plurals ("the mighty," etc.), and even "the poor" and "the needy" in v. 8, though grammatically singular, are construed as collective plurals (note "them" in the second couplet). Grammatically it would be equally possible to construe the female terms in v. 5b as collective plurals, but in fact the text insists they are singular, giving them singular verbs.

These singulars invite us to relate the two terms to the characters in the larger story, that is, to Hannah and Peninnah. The song wants to state a general principle yet it does so in such a way as to compel particularization. The application to Hannah is straightforward, though oddly she bears six rather than seven (Samuel plus the five in 2:21). But in what sense is Peninnah "forlorn"? I shall return to this question shortly.

Women under monarchy. A second example of this type is in 8:13, 16. If Israel were to have a king, Samuel says, the king would claim the services of Israel's women as well as its men for his own purposes. Various kinds of work are listed for these women. Sexual work is conspicuously omitted, though the sexual appropriation of large numbers of women is a major feature of monarchies [146]. We cannot assume that the activities specifically listed for women in Samuel's speech are the only ones that would involve them. Of the tasks listed in the male domain, at least agriculture (v. 12) would employ women in a major way. And of course women's lives would be affected by the exploitation of their men.

If one reads Hannah's song, as I do, as evoking the state of affairs under an ideal judgeship, this example provides a neat counterpoint to the previous one by describing how things would be under kingship.

Women entirely absent from the text. In the cases of women whose existence the text implies but whom it never mentions we have to assess the significance of the omission, and different readers may do so in different ways. The omissions I note here are of women associated with the leadership succession in 1 Samuel.

First, the wives of Eli and Samuel are not mentioned. This is so even though the relationship of these leaders to their *sons* is important in the story. When the story blames Eli, for example, for his sons' bad behavior (3:13) it shows no interest in any responsibility their mother might bear.

Second, despite the fact that the mother of a leader often becomes a significant character in the Bible,[3] Saul's mother is not mentioned and David's barely is (22:3-4). This inattention is troubling, since with characters of such importance we want to know about the influence of the mother.[4]

Saul's womenfolk: Ahinoam, Merab, Michal. Except for his mother, the women in Saul's life are mentioned and given names.[5] But when they are first mentioned (14:49-50) they do not become characters. They simply fill empty narrative slots: "Saul's wife," "Saul's daughters."

Saul's wife Ahinoam, though she has a name, will never become a character. But this does not mean that she altogether disappears. She becomes an absent presence again, this time anonymously, in the remarkable 20:30 [161–162]. Saul is here heaping blame on his son Jonathan for (as I believe) his homosexual relationship with David. Ahinoam (Jonathan's mother) is mentioned at least in the phrase "to the shame of your mother's nakedness."

According to the NRSV and other translations Ahinoam is also mentioned earlier in the verse: "You son of a perverse, rebellious woman." The Hebrew here can be read, and is probably better read, as "You son of perversity and rebellion." But if we follow NRSV Saul is clearly shifting the blame for Jonathan's conduct or character onto his mother: *she* is perverse and rebellious. We might think that Saul means merely what we mean when we say "You son of a bitch," intending to insult only the person addressed (of whose mother we may know nothing at all). But Saul *does* know Jonathan's mother; it was his knowing her that produced Jonathan. He is shifting the blame not from Jonathan (whom he blames copiously) but from himself. This is an all-too-familiar reaction of a father finding that his son is gay. For present

---

[3] Recall the mothers of judges [171–173]. Other examples are the "matriarchs" of Genesis (as well as Hagar), the mother of Moses, and Elizabeth and Mary in Luke 1–2.

[4] It is interesting that the larger canonical traditional in a certain sense remedies these two omissions by providing quasi-birth stories for both Saul and David [67, 106–109].

[5] Including his secondary wife Rizpah (2 Samuel 21).

purposes I just want to emphasize how a woman can take blame without ever even making an appearance as a character.

It does not make much difference which is the "correct" reading in 20:30. If we read "You son of perversity and rebellion" we simply transfer the dynamics I analyzed in the preceding paragraph from the producers of the text to its English translators. It is the NRSV's reading that many people know.

Saul's daughters Merab and Michal, unlike their mother, *will* become real characters and I will later look at them as such. But before they become characters they reappear once as an absent presence in a very significant way. Women often appear as ciphers in male transactions or male imaginings, and 17:25 provides a striking example. Some Israelites suggest that Saul "will give his daughter" as a reward for Goliath's slayer. This daughter has no name, is not even specified by any such term as "the elder." She is simply a category. This is what king's daughters are for, to be bestowed as a reward. They are interchangeable—and this, as we shall see, is how Saul will treat them even when they *do* become characters in the story.

Women and war. As a prelude to hewing Agag, Samuel refers (15:33) to the women whom Agag's wars have made childless (whose number Agag's own mother will now join). By its gender particularity this verse highlights the specific grief that war brings to women. War also makes fathers childless, but the two cases are not symmetrical. A man who became childless would probably have greater opportunity to have more children. If he had multiple wives he might still have children even if one of his wives lost all of hers. Childlessness means something different to a woman, whose social worth may be defined largely by fertility (cf. 2:5).

Enemy women become the property of the victors in war (see, for example, Judg 5:30). Often, however, wars mean total destruction and women are put to death (15:3, 27:9, 11; cf. 22:19). A further effect of war on women is that they are deprived of sexual intercourse while their men are bound by the rule of abstinence during warfare (21:4-5 [MT 5-6]).

Women in Groups

Most of the women in 1 Samuel appear anonymously in groups. Identification by group is not a gender-specific phenomenon. There are male characters who appear in groups (for example, the priests in ch. 22, though it is interesting that they form a hierarchy with a leader), but proportionate to their total presence in the text women are presented in groups more than men are.

The temple attendants. The first group is "the women who serve at the entrance to the tent of meeting" (2:22), of whom we are told only that the priests Hophni and Phinehas habitually have sexual relations with them. These women are subject to the authority of the priests, so that they cannot be considered as entering voluntarily into these liaisons. The women are victims of exploitation. Their routinized rape continues the theme of rape from the end of Judges. But though their situation certainly lacks the sheer horror of the story of the Levite's wife in Judges 19 it seems more sordid than the mass abduction of women in Judges 21, with which it can more easily be compared. Such a comparison again implies a contrast between judgeship and kingship [177]. What happens in Judges 21 is a violent effort—with at least some communal sanction— to deal with an intractable problem produced by anarchic conditions, and it involves the abducted women in the sort of rough and ready situation in which the women of Judges have often found themselves. The conduct of Eli's sons represents a move toward the conditions that characterize monarchy: men of hereditary privilege using women as they wish, without anyone's being able to check them.

At the level of plot, however, these women function in the opposite way, to move the story away from the brink of kingship and toward the restoration of judgeship. What is done to them becomes a main reason for the rejection of the hereditary priestly house. It assists the rise of Samuel and perhaps even provides one of Hannah's motives for intervening in public affairs [134–135].

The young women at the well. Arriving in Samuel's town, Saul and his servant meet some young women coming to draw water (9:11-13). Unlike the women at the tent of meeting these are active characters who are given a voice. Indeed, they have a lot to say for themselves (vv. 12-13). The text amusingly suggests a clamor of voices perhaps not unrelated to the presence of the handsome stranger; we should think of the many brief clauses in these two verses as spoken by different ones in rapid succession rather than as a long speech in unison.

These women are engaged in arduous labor, but they do not seem to be exploited. We could only say for sure if we knew about the entire organization of labor in their town, but the impression they give is of people *not* alienated from their work, people secure in their group identity and happily at home in their natural setting. They fit perfectly into the positive picture that Carol Meyers draws of women's work in premonarchical Israel.[6]

---

[6] *Discovering Eve: Ancient Israelite Women in Context* (New York and Oxford: Oxford University Press, 1988).

Singers of victory. The women who sing songs of victory (18:6-7) are fulfilling an expected social function (cf. Exod 15:20-21). Still, they are presented as taking an initiative and they clearly have the power to decide what words they sing. Their words will linger long in memory, at least in the memory of the Philistines (21:11, 29:5)! The narrator has them come out "to meet King Saul," which is doubtless their official function, but they come out at least as much for a sight of David, and it is David they praise in their song. Exceeding their brief, they become the first to announce publicly the transition from Saul to David. Their impertinence has its effect. Saul is in no doubt about the political implications of the song ("what more can he have but the kingdom?" v. 8), and this marks the beginning of his enmity toward David (v. 9).

Women abducted by the Amalekites. The last example is the women in ch. 30, wives and daughters of David's men (including David's own two wives). They with their children are abducted by the Amalekites and then daringly rescued by their husbands. These women are passive and voiceless in the storytelling. Their story brings into focus one of the specific effects of war on women: women whose men lose in war become the property of the men who win.[7]

Women in Pairs

1 Samuel has a striking tendency to present its women in pairs, two women sharing some role identity but with one developed into a major, the other only into a minor character: Hannah and Peninnah, Michal and Merab, Abigail and Ahinoam. We are familiar with paired female characters from other books of the Bible—Leah and Rachel, for example (Genesis 29–31), or Lot's daughters (Genesis 19).[8]

There is no such pairing in Judges (Deborah and Jael do not share an identity) or 2 Samuel (except that Abigail and Ahinoam continue briefly as a pair into that book; see 2:2), so that we might see this habit of pairing as another defining characteristic of 1 Samuel. The Christian

---

[7] I have deferred for later consideration two other groups of women. Those who attend the childbed (and deathbed) of Phinehas's wife (4:19-22) it will be convenient to discuss when we discuss her. The mediums whom Saul expelled from Israel (28:3, 9: the noun is of feminine gender) we shall look at in connection with the Medium of Endor.

[8] Also in Luke: Elizabeth and Mary in ch. 1, and Mary and Martha in 10:38-42.

canon, though, places an important example of the pairing of women in immediate juxtaposition to 1 Samuel. I am referring, again, to the book of Ruth. The pairing I have in mind is not that of Ruth and Naomi, who form a very asymmetrical pair, but that of Ruth and Orpah (Ruth 1). What makes this pair particularly interesting is that they have identical choices to make and choose in contrasting ways. Contrast is one of the potential uses of pairing.

Hannah and Peninnah. The two wives of one man, Hannah and Peninnah are introduced by a contrast: "Peninnah had children, but Hannah had no children" (1:2). They are contrasted also in Elkanah's affection. We are told that he "loved" Hannah, with the implication that he did not love Peninnah, or not as much (v. 5). Peninnah has a short life as a character (only up to v. 7). The account of the relationship between the two women shows it only as bad and appears to put the blame on Peninnah, who repeatedly chides Hannah for her childlessness (vv. 6-7). The story hints, however, that blame may attach also to Elkanah, since Peninnah's malice is a response to his favoritism [140–141]. At any rate, no blame for the situation is put on Hannah.

One of my students criticized me for failing, in my reading of Hannah, to take any adequate account of Peninnah, and thus for continuing the long history of favoritism that Elkanah and the biblical narrator began.[9] I plead guilty. There are really two parts to the reproach. First, I should have explored Peninnah's own situation more deeply. The text uses her to help account for Hannah's distress and then just gets rid of her.[10] I shall not now try to make Peninnah into a positive character or speculate at length on her situation (though these are directions other readers may take), but I do draw attention to the simplistic "wicked stepsister" characterization of her. In the history of interpretation Peninnah has certainly been "forlorn" (2:5)!

The other part of the reproach, to which I do need to make a response here, is that I do not take Hannah's attitude to Peninnah into account as I create my very positive picture of Hannah. For my student "Hannah is a heroine, but not a feminist heroine." To satisfy the definition of a feminist heroine Hannah would have to seek solidarity with Peninnah in their shared situation. Again, I agree with this critique.

---

[9] Danielle Duperreault, in an unpublished paper entitled "Methodological Problems for Feminist Exegesis: Three Brief Character Sketches of Minor Female Characters in First Samuel."

[10] Cf. Orpah in Ruth 1. These are further cases of what Cheryl Exum exposes as the narrative "murder" of women (*Fragmented Women: Feminist [Sub]versions of Biblical Narratives.* JSOT.S 163 [Sheffield: JSOT Press, 1993] 16–41).

One way of giving depth to the reading of Peninnah and Hannah is to look at them through the lens of Leah and Rachel, two women in an analogous situation (Genesis 29–31). The dichotomy of "bad" Leah versus "good" Rachel is present in their story too, in Jacob's attitude and—to a distinctly smaller extent—in the narrator's. Leah, like Peninnah, exploits her fertility to raise herself in the estimation of a husband who prefers his other wife. But unlike Peninnah, Leah is given a real subjectivity and her character is allowed to develop with some subtlety. Most of all, the two women work together on what really is a joint problem. In Gen 30:14-15 Rachel, rather than turning to God, turns to her sister, and the two women come eventually to speak with one voice (31:14-16). Hannah takes no such initiative and so must share in the responsibility for her estrangement from Peninnah [306].

Merab and Michal. Merab is even less of a character than Peninnah. Her entire story in 1 Samuel consists of being promised to one man, David, but given to another, Adriel (18:17-19). What is the point of telling about her at all? To show Saul's ill will to David? If this is the reason, then the procedure is remarkably redundant, given the much fuller expression of the ill will in the very next paragraph (vv. 20-29), not to mention the whole following narrative. It is also rather inept, since it is hard to create a story out of vv. 17-19 (does David do something significant in the way of being "valiant for" Saul and then come asking for Merab?) No, the point seems to be to set up, however slightly, a contrast between the sisters. This contrast can only reside (reading Michal's story back into Merab's) in Michal's *love* for David. Merab's problem is that she does not spontaneously love David. She does not get on the bandwagon with Michal—and later Abigail.

Merab's story has an epilogue in 2 Samuel 21. I have suggested that this passage is a dumping ground for material that belongs in 1 Samuel but that if put there would upset the theological work [106]. In 2 Sam 21:8 David takes a curious revenge on Merab. He includes her five sons by Adriel among the men he hands over to the Gibeonites so that they can take their vengeance on Saul's house. Since these grandsons by a daughter scarcely fit the category of "sons" of Saul that the Gibeonites demanded (v. 6) we may wonder if David does not conveniently use them to punish Merab for being denied to him, or rather for not loving him. In this story Merab is still denied a narrative role. She is not even allowed to share the tragic glory of Rizpah, the other bereaved mother in the story.

In an account full of irony the careers of the two sisters, Michal and Merab, repeatedly diverge, but then always come back together. Stage 1: Though married to David, Michal like Merab is given to another man (1 Sam 25:44). The contrast between the sisters is no contrast: loving David makes no difference. Stage 2: In 2 Samuel, David takes Michal back. But she will have no children (2 Sam 6:23), whereas Merab has children. The contrast seems now to favor Merab (shades of Peninnah and Hannah). Stage 3: David kills Merab's children—the contrast again vanishes.

The irony reaches a fitting conclusion in a textual problem in 2 Sam 21:8. David handed over "the five sons of Merab" to the Gibeonites. "Merab" is the reading in many ancient versions and in all modern translations, but the Hebrew text reads "Michal"! The Freudian nature of this slip is only too obvious. After their separate stories have run their course, after all the contrasts have been made between them, they become indistinguishable again. They are undifferentiated fillers of the category "daughter of Saul," just as they were when an anonymous daughter of Saul was to be the prize for Goliath's slayer (1 Sam 17:25).[11]

Abigail and Ahinoam. For this pair, as for the last, the issue is marriage to David. In this case the major character appears first and figures largely in the narrative before acquiring her twin as an afterthought (25:43). But their status will be reversed in 2 Samuel. Ahinoam's son (Amnon) will be a central character while Abigail's will be a nonentity (2 Sam 3:2-3).

The other feature of interest about Abigail and Ahinoam is that for a significant length of time (more than the "one year and four months" of 27:7) they live together and share all their experiences. Together they travel with David to Gath and later Ziklag (27:2-6). Together they undergo the rigors of an irregular life on the fringe of the desert, including being captured and rescued (ch. 30) and in the course of this ordeal presumably raped (they are in enemy hands at least for several days: v. 13, and are involved in a drunken orgy: v. 16). Yet the narrator shows no interest whatsoever in their relationship. We will never know what passed between them through all this time and experience.

The Other Women Characters

There are just two women in 1 Samuel who fall into none of the categories I have employed so far.

---

[11] Cf. the comments of J. Cheryl Exum, *Tragedy and Biblical Narrative: Arrows of the Almighty* (Cambridge: Cambridge University Press, 1992) 91.

The wife of Phinehas. 4:19-22 tells of the death in childbirth of the anonymous wife of Phinehas (and daughter-in-law of Eli). The news of the loss of the ark and of the death of her father-in-law and husband brings on her labor. Abruptly we are told that the birth will be fatal to her ("as she was about to die"), and the sequel suggests that the characters as well as the narrator know this. She is attended by some women (one of the anonymous groups I passed over in my earlier survey). They pronounce a formula specific to the situation of dangerous or fatal labor: "Do not be afraid, for you have borne a son" (v. 20, likewise in Gen 35:17). The mother does not answer, and the reader supposes that this is because she is too far gone. But she is capable yet of speech. She names her son "Ichabod," "Glory gone," and interprets this name: "The glory has departed from Israel, for the ark of God has been captured" (v. 22).

It is hard to enthuse over the role played by the attending women. Even if their little speech is purely conventional it seems gauche in view of the news that brought the labor on, news of the death of her husband as well as national disaster. Phinehas's wife pointedly ignores what the women say and moves to her own agenda. For her, to judge by her own words in v. 22, the only bad thing that has happened is the loss of the ark. The narrator is at pains to suggest she really did care about the death of the men, her father-in-law and her husband (in that order, vv. 19, 21), but she herself does not mention them. She knows that they were not worth much. Phinehas was an embarrassment of a husband and Eli was at best ineffectual. She knows too that the disaster is their fault. Dying, she laments the fate of the nation into which her son is born but not the death of her menfolk.

The story evokes the death of Rachel (Gen 35:16-20). Both the dying women give their sons sad names. Rachel's husband Jacob adjusts the name to something less negative. Phinehas has no opportunity to do the same.[12]

The Medium of Endor. The last woman, both in my survey and in order of introduction in 1 Samuel, is a character whose towering, or perhaps better abyssal stature ranks her in my estimation with Hannah. The importance I see her as having will not be exhausted by my reading here. She has a structural importance I will not be ready finally to assess until the conclusion of this book [303–307], but a surface reading of the story (28:3-25) makes her impressive enough.

(28:3) The story begins not with her, but with the group to which she belongs, the women mediums of Israel (v. 3). This again is a group I

---

[12] Fewell and Gunn, *Gender, Power, and Promise* 69–70 comment well on how the texts subsume the experience of these two women into their larger agenda.

passed over earlier in my survey. These women are paired with a male group, the "wizards," perhaps to make Saul's zeal for YHWH more impressive, but this should not distract us from the role of these women as a specifically female one. Their business is to call up the dead.

In an early example of media censorship "Saul had expelled the mediums . . . from the land." But where should they go? Are they not Israelites? An answer to these questions can be deduced from Deut 18:9-14. This passage enumerates many categories of practitioner of the occult arts, including those "who consult ghosts or spirits, or who seek oracles from the dead" (v. 11). The people referred to here, though, are *foreigners,* the inhabitants of the land who were expelled to make room for Israel. Indeed, it was on account of these practices that they *were* expelled (v. 12). The Deuteronomic text aims to render it unthinkable that Israelites should "learn" these practices (v. 9). They are foreign practices; they are part of what defines foreignness.

To be a medium (or a wizard, etc.) is therefore to be a foreigner and to be rightly expelled. The mediums cannot be Israelites for they have made themselves not Israelites by what they do. They have become "foreign women," which in Israel is the ultimate representation of the Other.[13] Here is a whole class of Israelite women who because of what they do (their profession, we would say) have been expatriated, "foreignized."

(28:4-8a) Saul wants supernatural guidance but is abandoned by YHWH. He seeks a medium woman. There is one at Endor.

Endor lies on the boundary between Israel and Philistia. Perhaps this woman is a Philistine, or of mixed blood [217]. Or perhaps when Saul expelled the mediums she retired strategically to the borderland, making herself foreign but still available, just in case.

Saul disguises himself and goes at night. We might be tempted to think that this is because he is entering enemy territory, but the text suggests that he does it to hide his action from his own people. This is not very kingly. Saul is still in the same bind he has always been, uncertain whether to submit to traditional law (formerly represented by Samuel) or to be a king and make his own rules (or "interpretations") [85–88]. A real king would reinterpret the Deuteronomic prescriptions about the occult to fit his needs. Kings, after all, keep a variety of religious practitioners at their disposal, just in case. If the official god will not speak, the king has the apparatus to get things done some other

---

[13] E.g., Claudia V. Camp, *Wisdom and the Feminine in the Book of Proverbs.* Bible and Literature Series 11 (Sheffield: Almond, 1985) 265–271; Exum, *Fragmented Women* 68–77.

way. Saul's shame about doing a kingly thing sets the tone for the story just as it sums up much of what we already know about him.

(28:8b-14a) The woman's story is in two parts separated by Saul's meeting with Samuel (vv. 14b-19 [89]). There is something odd about the storytelling, perhaps due to the text's difficulty in knowing how to handle so dubious a character as a medium. There is a basic, relatively unproblematic story but it is intersected by a theme that renders it incomprehensible, suggesting the possibility of a second, very different story.

In the relatively straightforward story the woman does not know who Saul is and is deeply wary of her anonymous visitor. "You know this is against the law," she says in effect (v. 9a). The peril is hers: there does not seem to be any penalty for *consulting* a medium, just for being one.[14] "By making this request you are putting me in mortal danger" (cf. v. 9b). Saul swears by YHWH that she will come to no harm (v. 10). The woman knows her job and goes about it initially (v. 11) without any of the ballyhoo we associate with spiritualism. She has the efficiency of a telephone operator: "What name?" And she gets the connection right the first time! Realizing now who Saul is, she reproaches him with setting a trap for her (v. 12). A second time reassured, she gets on with her job. But after her work is over she will reaffirm that she has "taken her life in her hand" (v. 21).

There are at least three problems with this reading. The first, if taken by itself, might be thought minor. How can the woman know that her visitor is in a position to protect her from the consequences of her lawbreaking? Perhaps she takes Saul to mean (in v. 10), "you can rely on my discretion," though his oath seems a bit strong for that. Perhaps she is won over by the very solemnity of the oath. Or perhaps she is just thinking about her fee, and takes a chance.

The biggest problem is, why does seeing Samuel make the medium recognize Saul (v. 12)? The first answer that comes to mind is that Saul is the only person who would call up Samuel, but this will not work, for by this reasoning she would have known it was Saul when he *named* Samuel as the one to be called up (v. 11).

The third problem is, why does the woman in vv. 13-14 resort to the professional ballyhoo she previously eschewed ("I see a god . . . an old man . . .")? Why, upon seeing Samuel, does she not simply tell Saul that the one he came to see is coming? Many readers have thought

---

[14] On reading this Gary Phillips confirmed a thought that had already crossed my mind, that the dynamics of this story have much in common with those of a meeting between a prostitute and a john.

that it is because she does not herself recognize Samuel and simply describes what she sees, but this would make her recognition of Saul at this moment even less explicable.

The recognition theme undermines the straightforward story and suggests that a different story is trying to find a voice. I have not found anyone who quite believes in my alternative story, and I believe in it myself only on certain days of the week. But it does solve all the problems, and it fits in with my impression of the medium in the last part of the chapter. Thinking about it will at least sharpen our reading of the text.

In my alternative reading the medium knows who Saul is from the start. Her first words are therefore of lightly mocking reproach: "Surely *you* know what Saul has done." In the "snare" that Saul has set (v. 9) he has himself been neatly caught (Ps 35:8). The woman is ready to accept Saul's oath that she will come to no harm, for she knows it is made by the one person who is able to guarantee it!

Still, she needs a safe and plausible way to reveal to Saul her recognition of him. This is where she employs professional technique. Exploiting the awesome ambience of a seance, she shouts out Saul's name in the profound moment when she sees Samuel, as if her recognition of Saul had come to her as part of the supernatural revelation. Continuing in the same vein, though she herself recognizes Samuel perfectly well she contrives matters so that Saul thinks it is he who does the recognizing (v. 14).

(28:20-25) The last part of the medium's story is as clear as the first part is complicated. Seeing Saul devastated by his experience, she simply ministers to him. She can do nothing for his spirit; he has chosen his own way and must follow it to its imminent end. But she sees and insists on remedying—lavishly—the urgent need of his body.

An assessment of the story. It is one of the major gains of the last decades that we are now open, as generations of our predecessors in biblical interpretation have not been, to a positive appreciation of this great woman. Particularly through a great deal of rereading of medieval Christian history we have moved past our kneejerk negative reaction to the term "witch." We have come to appreciate the role of women in religious institutions based on the agricultural cycle, institutions that have often been severely repressed in the name of biblical religion. We have come to see how they stressed domestic issues of special importance to women and how they emphasized healing.[15] We have begun to realize

---

[15] The medium acts as a healer to Saul at the end of ch. 28. We might speculate whether the function of a medium was connected to some women's healing tradition. For more on the medium as part of an alternative religious system see Jo Ann

that any sort of complete religious statement will have to do justice to "below" as well as "above," to the gods of earth as well as of heaven.

The Medium of Endor is a minister of religion, and a good one. She understands the need of the one who comes to her, she takes charge of the situation, she does what she can for him. In her technical capacity she efficiently performs the appropriate ceremony and gives Saul a satisfaction she realizes he must have even though it can do him no real good. In her larger capacity as minister to the whole person she insistently gets past his self-destructiveness, making him take the sustenance that in his desperation he would forego. All this she does for her bitter enemy, the one who would expel her and her colleagues from home and livelihood—with only the lightest, faintly humorous reproach.

Perhaps the most interesting aspect of 1 Samuel 28 is the attitude the narrator takes toward the woman. It is hard to find anything negative in it. The condemnation of the woman and of Saul for visiting her that dominates the history of interpretation has all been read into the text by the interpreters. For a narrator under the influence of Deuteronomy this woman should represent everything evil, everything that the religion of YHWH has expelled in order to be what it is. Yet when he writes of her religious function he does so objectively, indicating that she was competent, that she could do what she claimed to do; and at the end of the chapter he limpidly tells of her goodness.

The old religions can do what they claim. This by itself is no small admission. But perhaps there is more yet. The narrator seems to attach no blame to Saul for seeking help where he can get it. Saul has done what he could for YHWH, showing more zeal for this stern and capricious God than ever did him any good, ruining his reign by putting traditional religion ahead of being a king. Now that YHWH will not talk to him he seeks divine guidance elsewhere, and finds it. Perhaps there is no part of the whole passage so poignant as when Saul allays the woman's anxiety with an oath in the name of YHWH (v. 10): an oath by YHWH, in whose very name Saul expelled her and her kind! Yet she accepts it. This woman is no enemy to the religion of YHWH, and the religion of YHWH need not be an enemy to her. With this proposition I cannot see that the narrator disagrees.

If only we could persuade YHWH of it . . . .

Hackett, "1 and 2 Samuel," in Carol A. Newsom and Sharon H. Ringe, eds., *The Women's Bible Commentary* (Louisville, Ky.: Westminster/John Knox, 1992) 88.

Rachel: An Implicit Woman

On three separate occasions 1 Samuel evokes the story of Rachel in Genesis. I have mentioned two of these instances already. The story of Hannah and Peninnah recapitulates the story of Rachel and her co-wife, Leah, in the themes of barrenness and fertility and of the husband's unequal love. Phinehas's wife recapitulates Rachel's death scene. The third allusion to Rachel comes when Michal rescues her husband David from her father Saul (1 Sam 19:11-17). So also does Rachel deceive her father Laban to the benefit of her husband Jacob (Gen 31:19-42). This is a powerful structural similarity, but the clinching element is that both women's deceit involves objects called *teraphim*. Rachel steals her father's *teraphim*, while Michal puts the *teraphim* in the bed to look like David asleep.[16]

This is a remarkably mixed group of references. Their significance should be sought less, perhaps, in their particular content than in the importance of Rachel herself. She is one of the traditional matriarchs of Israel. More particularly she is the "mother" of northern Israel (see Jer 31:15) rather than of southern Judah to which David belongs. Most particularly she is the mother of Benjamin, Saul's tribe. Perhaps she is part of the memory of Israel's traditional order. At any rate, though never referred to she is one of the women of 1 Samuel!

The Issue of Anonymity

The namelessness of many of the Bible's women characters is often read as a failure to ascribe a real subjectivity to them. But this judgment has also been disputed.

The individual women of 1 Samuel tend to be named. For example, I compared Hannah with three mothers of judges in the book of Judges, all of them, unlike her, nameless. In fact, the only anonymous individual women are the wife of Phinehas and the Medium of Endor.

Adele Reinhartz has done a full survey of anonymous characters in both books of Samuel.[17] Her general conclusion is that anonymity is not gender specific—there are great numbers of anonymous male characters—and that it does not imply disparagement. I summarize

---

[16] *Teraphim* seem to be some sort of figures representing household gods. For details see the Bible dictionaries.

[17] "Anonymity and Character in the Books of Samuel," *Sem.* 63 (1993) 117–141.

her comments on the two anonymous women in 1 Samuel. Phinehas's wife differs from many anonymous characters in that she "does not contribute primarily to the portrayal of the named characters to whom she is related" (p. 127). She is given an independent, "prophetic" role. Reinhartz finds an appropriateness in this woman's anonymity, which is "a symbol of . . . national misfortune, of her death, and . . . of the moral barrenness of the house of which she is a part" (p. 127).

Reinhartz treats the Medium of Endor as part of a group that also includes the wise women of 2 Sam 14:1-24 and 20:14-22 (pp. 132–137). She gives impressive reasons why the anonymity here cannot in any way be seen as belittlement. These women are all portrayed in their professional identity. It is important that they are all known by *location*: one knows where to go for their services. They are in all likelihood anonymous even to the other characters in the stories. They all confront kings, and though they use "ostensibly self-deprecating language" (p. 135) they stand forth boldly, speaking at length and taking charge of the situation.

I believe Reinhartz is correct so far as 1 Samuel is concerned. Anonymity does not correlate with limited or negative development of female subjectivity. Conversely (as Reinhartz also suggests), having a proper name is no guarantee of fullness of character development. Peninnah, Merab, and the two Ahinoams, at least, are examples of named characters developed poorly, tendentiously, or not at all. The giving of a proper name can highlight its later removal: an example I noted earlier is "Saul's daughter" as the prize for Goliath's slayer (17:25), long after both Merab and Michal have been introduced by name.

Women and Surrogacy

I concluded my reading of the theme of government by showing how 1 Samuel as a whole is structured according to an implicit surrogacy system in which each leader is appointed during his predecessor's time and becomes his surrogate son (see Chapter 5). If this is such an important feature it is necessary to ask here what role gender plays in this system.

National leadership by a woman is a rare thing in Israel's history. Miriam is remembered as one of a trio of leaders from the time of Israel's beginnings (Mic 6:4). Deborah is one of the major judges (Judges 4–5). Athaliah is a reigning queen (2 Kings 11). We can mention also the prophet Huldah (2 Kings 22:14-20), but prophets are not *as such* national leaders. No system that Israel ever had or imagined gave women anything like an equal role in national leadership. The surrogacy system in 1 Samuel is no exception; the leaders it produces are all men.

Monarchy (at least some kinds of monarchy) will occasionally produce a reigning queen because of the failure of the male line. This is irregular, but it is systemic. In the other systems within our purview leadership is a matter of choice. In the theory of judgeship (and also at the time of Israel's beginnings in Exodus–Joshua) the choice is YHWH's, and this is no less the case with surrogacy. Occasionally, not often, YHWH chooses a woman. Perhaps in a few more generations of surrogacy the promising young person would have been a woman, but this does not happen in 1 Samuel. Unlike monarchy, surrogacy cannot run out of men.

If women are rarely leaders, what systemic roles *do* they play? In a monarchy the basic role of women is a simple but essential one. All that is *systemically* necessary is that one legitimate wife bear one viable male child (of course this does not preclude other roles from taking on great importance, for example the role of Queen Mother). An equally simple role is available in the surrogacy system, namely that the old leader's daughter marry the new leader. This is the son-in-law motif I traced earlier. But this possibility is never successfully actualized in 1 Samuel. It does not arise at all in the Eli–Samuel generation. In the Samuel–Saul generation there is a tantalizing hint of it [118–119]. In the Saul–David generation it actually happens, but the marriage fails. The surrogacy system is not, it seems, to be founded on this simple pattern, perhaps because that would make it too much like ordinary heredity.[18]

Still, mediation by women is part of the ambience of surrogacy in 1 Samuel. Though it is not in any obvious way necessary, it is consistently present. I have not, you must remember, suggested that leadership in Israel was ever actually transmitted through an official surrogacy system. My point is that 1 Samuel is structured *as if* such a system were in place. My surrogacy is a *literary* reality, and in its literary presentation some sort of mediation by women does seem to be a structural necessity.

Not only is there in each generation one individual woman (Hannah, the Medium of Endor, Michal) who mediates the leadership transition, there is also in each generation one *group* of women who assist the achievement of the transition. Eli's sons lose power in large part because of their treatment of the women temple servants (2:22); even as passive victims these women move the story toward its goal. The women at the well in 9:11-13, though they may have the negative func-

---

[18] The triangle of Jonathan, Saul, and David is really a transformation of the son-in-law motif, with Jonathan playing the daughter role. Perhaps it constitutes another sort of statement of the failure of the motif in 1 Samuel.

tion of signaling a failure of the son-in-law pattern of transition, also perform a positive function in bringing about the meeting between Samuel and Saul. Most powerfully of all, the women who sing victory songs (18:7) are the first to announce the transition from Saul to David.

However, these functions are very different from case to case, and it is hard to see consistent features. The individual women who mediate the generations in 1 Samuel are all strong initiative-takers, and this goes in part for the groups, but the temple women are an exception. It is as if the point were simply to ring the changes on the abstract category of "mediation." It is not possible to derive from these cases any *specific* structural roles for women. Hannah perhaps comes closest. She mediates the transition from Eli to Samuel from a definite structural position, and a position of some strength, that of the mother of the new leader. In my reading she works deliberately on Eli to get him to adopt her son into the temple service [132]. But even if this exemplifies a tendency in mothers to be ambitious for their sons, maternal ambition will hardly be part of the basis of the system.

The most divergent of the mediators from any imaginable norm is the Medium of Endor. Though she very powerfully mediates between Samuel and Saul she comes much too late to mediate the transition of power between them. This suggests, I think, that there is something fundamentally wrong with this transition, which of course is also the transition from judgeship to kingship. The only kind of mediation that will suffice now is mediation between the present and the lost past, between the living and the dead.

Just when the narrative is moving women toward the conventional role they will play in the monarchical system a woman appears who both marks some sort of failure in the transition to monarchy and opens up the possibility of a recovery of the past. The medium's role is not to move the story forward but to conjure up the past. She represents a different kind of link with the past than the official historical one—an unauthorized and occult link. That it is a *woman* who forges this link highlights the exclusion of women from the official history-making and also reminds us of what women in particular are losing in the transition to monarchy [305, 307].

Alice Bach has rightly suggested that the mere mediation of generations of men is not an inspiring role for women, and can easily co-exist with their denigration.[19] That women in some way mediate the

---

[19] "The Pleasure of Her Text," in Alice Bach, ed., *The Pleasure of Her Text: Feminist Readings of Biblical & Historical Texts* (Philadelphia: Trinity Press International, 1990) 37–38; she is referring to the beginning of monarchy.

generations of human societies is a truism, equally true of societies at the extremes of feminism or sexism. But the treatment of women's mediation in 1 Samuel, within the surrogacy system, has some very striking features that at least subvert the highly restricted roles that monarchy offers women.

Conclusion

While women characters are not so intrinsic to the action in 1 Samuel as they are in Judges or Ruth, they have a very significant presence in a great variety of roles. There are women active and passive, heroic and victimized. An argument can be made, I think, that 1 Samuel carves out a particular space for women (and the interplay with surrogacy is part of the creation of this space). Women are no longer, as in Judges, permanently on the front lines of a gender war of total violence. They are not yet, as in 2 Samuel, completely subsumed into the new royal order.

However, such an argument needs to be made with reticence. There is nothing exemplary or even satisfactory about women's situations in this book. If it is marked at each end by a woman of great narrative power, Hannah and the Medium of Endor, it is also marked at each end by a group of exploited women who lack power in their situations (the temple attendants in ch. 2, the women abducted in ch. 30). The variety of cases must continue to be investigated with a variety of feminist methods.

Part IV

RACE: "DO YOU NOT KNOW THAT THE PHILISTINES ARE RULERS OVER US?"

PROLOGUE

Class and gender, which defined Parts II and III of this book, are real issues. It is true that ancient discourses require significant work of translation before they are comprehensible in terms of what we call "class" and even that the category of gender cannot be simplistically transferred between ancient and modern.[1] But in both cases we have been dealing with matters that in their ancient settings had a basis in reality.

Race, which is the topic in Part IV, has no such real basis in the text of 1 Samuel or in its ancient contexts. A racial discourse can, as I shall show, be discerned in the way that 1 Samuel deals with the Philistines, but it is all in the imaginary register. There never was anything like a racial distinction, in our terms, between Israelites and Philistines: both groups belonged to what anthropologists call the "Mediterranean" type. The biblical tradition, however, often (not consistently) casts the Philistines as the utterly "other," as alien in a higher degree than any of the rest of Israel's neighbors. To this end the categories of a rudimentary kind of racialism are sometimes employed.

The term "Philistine" has enjoyed, and continues to enjoy, a quite remarkable afterlife. For several centuries (since about 1700, it seems), people in the West have been calling each other "Philistines" to enforce a variety of distinctions. Most recently it has tended to mean "the artistically illiterate," but this usage is relatively benign compared to some slightly older ones. In these usages there has been nothing racial at all; they have emerged in the internal discourses of Euro-American

[1] Sheila Briggs, "'Buried with Christ': The Politics of Identity and the Poverty of Invention," in Regina M. Schwartz, ed., *The Book and the Text: The Bible and Literary Theory* (Oxford: Basil Blackwell, 1990) 282–286.

197

populations. But they have connoted so strong a desire to impute otherness that they have been willing to borrow some of the apparatus of racialism, often in a rather bewildering mix with the apparatus of sexism and class distinction.

My method here is quite different from that of the earlier parts. Intertextuality, which I have employed as a method only briefly (reading 1 Samuel through the lens of the Gospel of Luke [136–139]), here becomes the methodological framework. My intertext is the modern discourse of "Philistines," or rather some formative parts of it, and it is with this "text" rather than the biblical text that I begin. Chapter 9, then, is an analysis of the modern discourse. In Chapter 10 I shall survey how 1 Samuel (with other parts of the Bible) presents the Philistines, and read two particular parts of 1 Samuel where the Philistines are important, using an intertextual method that highlights categories of interpretation suggested by the modern discourse. My methodological assumption here is that we can—and must—learn to read the Bible by listening to the odd ways in which we and our culture have unwittingly internalized it, a process of which the modern use of "Philistines" is a classic example.

The whole of Part IV is based on work that has been published jointly under my name and Catherine Rose's.[2] I shall note places where what I present derives from her original drafts.

---

[2] David Jobling and Catherine Rose, "Reading as a Philistine: The Ancient and Modern History of a Cultural Slur," in Mark G. Brett, ed., *Ethnicity and the Bible* (Leiden: E. J. Brill, 1996) 381–417.

Chapter 9

LATTER-DAY PHILISTINES

Edward Said subtitles a review article on Michael Walzer's *Exodus and Revolution* "A Canaanite Reading."[1] Writing as a present-day Palestinian, Said critiques the logic whereby Walzer applies the biblical "exodus" paradigm first to liberation in general and then to the politics of modern Israel. The problem lies not in the "exodus" paradigm as such, the release of slaves from their oppressors (Egyptians), but in the sequel to the exodus story, the conquest of Canaan. From a Canaanite perspective the conquest story tells how one's own people have to be dispossessed to fulfill a promise of liberation to another people; this is the position in which modern Palestinians are placed by the application of the exodus-conquest paradigm to the creation of the state of Israel. An analogous example is found in Robert Warrior's "Canaanites, Cowboys, and Indians."[2] Writing as a Native American in response to the white conquest of North America, Warrior likewise identifies with the Canaanites. Both Said and Warrior see the biblical Canaanites as a group whose narrative subjectivity the text has submerged. By highlighting the Bible's suppression of Canaanite subjectivity they are counteracting by analogy the ways in which their own groups' subjectivity gets submerged in current discourses.

---

[1] "Michael Walzer's Exodus and Revolution: A Canaanite Reading," in Edward W. Said and Christopher Hitchens, eds., *Blaming the Victims: Spurious Scholarship and the Palestinian Question* (New York: Verso, 1988) 161–178; Walzer, *Exodus and Revolution* (New York: Basic Books, 1985).

[2] "Canaanites, Cowboys, and Indians: Deliverance, Conquest, and Liberation Theology Today," *Christianity and Crisis* 29 (1989) 261–265.

There are, so far as I know, no current political groups that seek in a similar way to assert their interests through analogy with those of the biblical *Philistines*,[3] but we do most decidedly know of ways in which the *term* "Philistines" is used in current discourses with the intention of submerging the subjectivity of specific groups. I referred a moment ago, in the prologue, to the three-hundred-year history of such usages.

In due course I shall raise the question of my own relationship to groups who have been called Philistines and how this relationship directs my reading [243, 299–300]. But aside from any such direct interest of mine I would suggest that it is in general methodologically appropriate and necessary to restore the submerged subjectivities in texts, since such textual strategies of submersion will inevitably prove to be part of large cultural systems of exclusion. The more culturally important the text and the more prominent the group whose subjectivity the text submerges, the more vital is this work of analysis. The centrality of the Bible in our culture, and the prominence of the Philistines in the Bible, do not need to be argued. We may be confident that what the Bible does with the Philistines will be implicated in systems of exclusion in our own biblically shaped culture.

In this century "Philistine" has become one of those terms whose definition is vague, whose meaning everyone "just knows." But in earlier and still recent centuries it has had quite precise meanings that have shaped in complex ways our general sense *now* of what a Philistine is. I shall first deal briefly with the beginnings of the usage in Germany, and then more at length with the person most responsible for making "Philistine" a popular English word, the nineteenth-century writer and educator Matthew Arnold.

Germany

Student usage. The first consistent modern meaning of "Philistine" appears at the end of the seventeenth century among German students, to designate the non-student townsfolk. In the constitution of the German states students enjoyed enormous advantages over townsfolk. The town was dependent economically on the students, and the laws were biased in the students' favor. Students became heavily indebted to the townsfolk who sold and rented things to them. In student songs about

---

[3] It may, however, be more than a historical irony that Said's "Palestinian" community is linked etymologically with "Philistines."

the Philistines two themes stand out. One is utter *contempt* that sees townsfolk in their settled, conservative, small-town way of life as inferior and existing merely to be exploited in any way possible. The other is *indebtedness:* the students need the Philistines, and their extravagance may eventually give the Philistines power over them.[4]

The biblical basis for this usage is found in the character of Samson, with whose exploits the students strongly identified. A favorite theme is his use of foxes to devastate the Philistines' crops (Judg 15:4-5); students called themselves "foxes" and "fire-foxes."[5] The (probably apocryphal) story goes that this usage started when a clergyman took as the text for his burial sermon for a student who had died in a clash with townsfolk, "The Philistines are upon you, Samson!" (Judg 16:9, etc.)[6]

The divisive issue in this scenario is class. The privileged upper-class students despise the emerging middle class, but they also depend on it and to some degree are under its power. The students deal with this contradiction by a work of fantasy: they imagine their superiority and victory over the townsfolk. The work of ideology, according to Fredric Jameson,[7] is the production of such class fantasy, and I shall have much to say about such fantasy work. The students' projection of themselves as Samsons or foxes despoiling the Philistines is a way of fantasizing the real class conflict in which they are engaged. This ideological work includes various elements of perceived resemblance between Samson's situation and the students' own. The two key elements are the individual against the mass and the rebellion of youth against age. Samson's sexual prowess is a factor: sexual abuse by students of the town women is one of the things complained of by the townsfolk and celebrated in the students' songs.[8] The students also perceive a conflict between the spiritual or intellectual and the material: they see their transactions with the Philistines over material matters as a necessary evil, particularly annoying since their taken-for-granted intellectual superiority is not respected in these transactions.[9]

---

[4] For this summary see Ulrich Westerkamp, "Beitrag zur Geschichte des literarischen Philistertypus mit besonderer Berücksichtigung von Brentanos Philisterabhandlung" (Dissertation, University of Munich, 1912) 4–11.

[5] See William Harbutt Dawson, *Matthew Arnold and His Relation to the Thought of Our Time: An Appreciation and a Criticism* (New York and London: Putnam's, 1904) 98.

[6] See Westerkamp, "Beitrag" 13.

[7] *The Political Unconscious: Narrative as a Socially Symbolic Act* (Ithaca, N.Y.: Cornell University Press, 1981) 87 and *passim.*

[8] Westerkamp, "Beitrag" 6, 9.

[9] Samson does not seem to provide resources for this part of the fantasy.

What we have, then, is class fantasy fleshed out with a variety of specific features, and we will be able to trace these features in other historical usages of "Philistine." Before we move on it is worth underlining that this first consistent modern usage of "Philistine" portrays those using the term in a worse light than their opponents!

Romanticism and Brentano. A century or so later, with the rise of the Romantic movement, "Philistine" took on a broader meaning. The new usage still owed much to the students in that it continued to mock bourgeois conservatism and self-satisfaction. But the meaning now extended into the artistic and intellectual spheres as it expressed the rebellion of the Romantics against the stagnation they saw to be the result of the Enlightenment. The apparent triumph of reason had led, according to the Romantics, to smug self-satisfaction, an assumption that all human problems are on their way to being solved, particularly by technological domination over nature. All this is "Philistine."[10]

This phase in the development of the meaning of "Philistine" is associated above all with Goethe, but I shall look at it through the lens of a remarkable work by Clemens Brentano.[11]

In 1811 Brentano wrote "The Philistine Before, In and After History"[12] to provide an evening's entertainment for a dining club in Berlin of which he was a member, a club made up of intellectual leaders "mostly from the high Prussian aristocracy."[13] He produced it *ad hoc*, not intending it for publication. It is a parody of a pedantic work of historical scholarship, and to give it a mock appearance of "scientific" completeness Brentano includes a section on the biblical Philistines. It is lucky for me that he did, since the links he draws between Philistines ancient and modern give fascinating indications as to why this particular ancient term should have been chosen as a modern category.

The material on the biblical Philistines is in the section "In History." But before we consider this it is useful to look at the "Before History" section (pp. 198–201). Brentano presents a thoroughly dualistic view of creation. In the beginning the principles of Yes and No were united in the divine being. Then Lucifer, the No principle, tried to raise itself

---

[10] Ibid. 20–52.

[11] 1778–1842. Brentano is best known for his collaboration with Achim von Arnim on *Des Knaben Wunderhorn* (1805–1808), one of the most important early collections of German folk literature.

[12] "Der Philister vor, in und nach der Geschichte: Aufgestellt, begleitet und bespiegelt aus göttlichen und weltlichen Schriften und eigenen Beobachtungen," in Andreas Müller, ed., *Satiren und Parodien* (Leipzig: Reclam, 1935) 190–229. Unattributed page references in this section are to this work.

[13] Westerkamp, "Beitrag" 97.

above the Yes and was thrown to earth. Lucifer is, for Brentano, "the first Philistine or the idea of the Philistine" (p. 199). He fell from the Ideal into the Material, the Material being identified with the Philistine.

This was the first Fall. In a second Fall the Idea (Adam) was again overcome by the material (Eve), whence sprang the sin—likewise identified with the Philistine—on account of which God brought the flood. All in the greatest fun, then, Brentano has raised "Philistine" into a universal dualistic category connoting the materialism of the Enlightenment in its opposition to Romantic idealism.

Brentano's reading of the biblical Philistines begins, naturally, with Genesis. He notes (p. 202) the first actual use of the word, in the genealogy that includes the Philistines among Ham's cursed descendants (Gen 9:25-27; 10:14). Of the Philistines' relationship to Israel's ancestors in Genesis 21 and 26 he makes an interesting comment: "Even in their best period they stopped the Israelites' wells" (p. 204). The idea that the Philistines in this part of Genesis are different from and relatively better than those in Judges and Samuel will occupy us later [225–227].

Brentano naturally pays great attention to Samson, whom he admires for his constant warfare against the Philistines. He asserts that no Philistine can even comprehend such a hero's death, and he toasts all the heroes who have died fighting Philistines (p. 207). He has relatively little to say about 1 Samuel. He has some fun with the plague of hemorrhoids (1 Sam 5:6, etc.). Goliath he refers to as the "chief Philistine." On David's sojourn among the Philistines he ironically comments that the Philistines built their policy on the expectation that David would betray his own people, adding that modern Philistines are experts in political betrayal (p. 207).

Let us survey Brentano's themes. Although his usage goes beyond that of the students, it is still grounded there.[14] For example, Samson continues to be the most important biblical figure. Still apparent is the rebellion of youth against age, now writ large in the rebellion of the Romantics against the Enlightenment. The theme of the individual against the mass is also prominent. Brentano almost always refers to modern Philistines as a group who display predictable group traits. They are rarely considered as individuals, and one of the many things they themselves cannot grasp is individual talent and "genius." Very much clearer than in the student usage is the conflict of the spiritual against the material. Brentano raises the distinction between those

---

[14] In fact he seems to have drafted his parody already in 1799 when still a student; see Westerkamp, "Beitrag" 72–73.

who value "ideas" (his own group) and those concerned only for material prosperity and comfort (the Philistines) into a cosmic principle.[15]

The class situation is not so straightforward in Brentano as it was in the student songs. It is true that he keeps aristocratic company and often projects contempt for the middle class, and from our historical distance we can see that class did in fact continue to be the central issue: the Enlightenment attitude to the material world would, through the Industrial Revolution, soon redraw the class map of Europe. But from the Romantics' own perspective the struggle was mainly intergenerational. In the generation of the Enlightenment, they believed, Philistinism had taken over the universities and the arts as well as the political and social spheres. By the time of Matthew Arnold, as we shall see, the class issues would be clearer.

What is perhaps most interesting in Brentano is how the fantasy work extends itself into the areas of gender and race. I begin with *gender*. Brentano links Philistinism with some commonplace sexist themes, for example in his contrast of Adam as the spiritual with Eve as the material principle, or in his treatment of Delilah as a nagging woman (Philistine women are apparently worse nags than others). His most interesting treatment of gender comes, however, when he upholds the sanctity of marriage against the Philistines who, he claims, do not. In striking contrast to the students, who identify with the sexual side of Samson's prowess, Brentano even criticizes his hero on this point. By getting involved in "whoredom" Samson became a bit of a Philistine himself:

> . . . I call that kind of thing Philistinism, since to satisfy the most glorious human instinct disgustingly and conveniently, without passion, without sanctification by a priest or sanctification by valour, adventure and danger, is a Philistine thing . . . it is only because of Philistine attitudes that the protection of such sinful women can become established in a state (p. 206).

This is all complicated and confused. The Romantic notion that heroism can "sanctify" sex as well as marriage can would seem to get Samson off the hook, but Brentano has on this point an agenda more important than defending Samson. He needs both to idealize and to despise women and sexuality. "Philistinism" enables him to resolve

---

[15] A blurb I saw for a book on Romanticism refers to its "suppression of the female, the material, and the collective." *New York Review of Books* (12/5/94) 12. I shall turn in a moment to the female.

this dilemma. He can despise Philistine women as a means of idealizing those of his own class.

Perhaps even more interesting is his treatment of *race.* The absence of any racial difference between the German Philistines and their detractors does not prevent the theme of race from entering deeply into his fantasy. As we have seen, Brentano is quick to pick up on the Bible's own quasi-racial sense of Philistine otherness, expressed in Gen 9:25-27 and 10:14. The Philistines (as well as the Canaanites) belong, in this biblical account, to the branch of humanity based largely in Africa.[16]

Most revealing is the amazing interplay in Brentano of Philistines and Jews.[17] He shares the antisemitism of his time. The club for which he wrote his parody explicitly excluded from its membership both Jews and Philistines.[18] This pairing would seem to create a serious problem for his historical and biblical project, since to call other people "Philistines" is to put oneself in the position of an Israelite. This matter is so crucial for Brentano that he has to provide a theoretical basis for his procedure. The Jews, in crucifying the Son of God, gave up not only their election but also "the conflict with the Philistines." As a result Jews and Philistines, far from being opposites, have now come to "represent the two poles of perversity" (p. 204). Antisemitism enters smoothly into the details of his biblical reading. He calls the Judahites' handing over of Samson to the Philistines (Judg 15:13) "a truly Jewish reward" for his services, seeing no difficulty, apparently, in separating Samson from the Jews!

This *tour de force* brings the category of "Philistines" within the orbit of German antisemitism. To exclude both groups *as a pair* expresses, no doubt, a deep wish that the Philistines *were* racially different so that they might be more readily identified and shunned. Just such a wish was, in fact, overtly expressed by the Romantic philosopher Johann Gottlieb Fichte just a year after Brentano's satire and in exactly the same context, a speech to a dining club. Fichte worries about how one can be sure one is not a Philistine oneself. Differentiating oneself from a Jew is easy; it is just a matter of not being

---

[16] The use of Genesis 9 with a similar racist purpose is well known from recent South Africa. See Allister Sparks, *The Mind of South Africa* (London: Heinemann, 1990) 29.

[17] For an account of the complicated mythologies inhabiting German antisemitism and the difficulty in defining the term see Gavin I. Langmuir, *Toward a Definition of Antisemitism* (Berkeley, Cal.: University of California Press, 1990) especially 263–281, 301–352.

[18] Westerkamp, "Beitrag" 97.

circumcised. But no such mark distinguishes "Philistines." Fichte re-
cites a little poem that ends on a decidedly unsettling note. A person
who merely *thinks* about Philistinism, even to resist it, risks becoming a Philistine: "His Philistinism consists precisely in thinking that
he isn't one!"[19]

Through this discussion of racism, in its guise of antisemitism, we
have thus arrived at a fundamental anxiety over one's own *identity* vis-
à-vis the Philistines. This anxiety is easy to trace also in Brentano, for
example in the following telling passage (which also reveals something of the tone of the whole work):

> It needs particularly to be noted, that the outward marks . . . by no
> means suffice to make someone a Philistine; rather, it always depends on
> how, given these marks, he faces life. The very person who exhibits all
> the contrary marks can be a Philistine. . . . Ah, who can be sure that he
> is not himself already threaded on a string, and that, if ever the devil
> tightens the cord, he will not be hung with other Philistines like a row of
> onions around the neck of Satan's grandmother? (p. 212)

This quotation signals in effect the collapse of Brentano's whole
rhetorical strategy. That strategy consists of imposing a character on
the Philistines, of suppressing their own subjectivity. It allows absolutely no element of debate between equals. Part of the strategy is his
repeated assertion that Philistines *do not know what is going on,* that an
essential part of *being* a Philistine is an inability to grasp things. The
Philistines do not even know that they *are* Philistines! The correctness
of Brentano's own version of reality is established by the claim that the
"others," precisely because of who they are, are incapable of any ra-
tional version of their own. But in this quotation (as well as the one
from Fichte) the non-Philistine himself also does not understand what
is going on and becomes utterly unsure of his difference from the
Philistines.

Matthew Arnold[20]

A very sporadic use of "Philistine" is attested in English from about
the end of the seventeenth century: "Persons regarded as 'the enemy',
into whose hands one may fall, e.g. bailiffs, literary critics, etc.; for-

---

[19] Quoted by Westerkamp, "Beitrag" 99.
[20] This section is based on work by Catherine Rose.

merly, also . . . the debauched or drunken."[21] This suggests the same two general lines of meaning that we found in Germany: on the one hand a meaning related to the people themselves, that they are despicable; on the other a meaning based on one's relationship to them, that they may have *power* over one. But it is from the German usage, which he knows well, that Arnold actually borrows the term.

Class struggle in Arnold. "Philistine" is for Arnold quite specifically a *class* term. Writing in the context of the social upheaval brought about in England by industrialization and the introduction of universal male suffrage he uses the term as part of a strategy for quelling the conflict brought about by the growing political power of the middle and lower classes. He divides England into three classes: the aristocracy, whom he calls Barbarians, the middle class and organized labor, who are the Philistines, and the working class, or Populace.

However, Arnold refuses to locate *himself* and his project within class struggle. Rather he sees himself as representing an intellectual elite that is class-free and disinterested, in contrast to the various self-interests on which social classes are based. He distinguishes between the "ordinary self" and the "best self."[22] Our ordinary self, the self determined by our class, is "separate, personal, at war." Our best self is "united, impersonal, at harmony." To cultivate the best self is the task of education. The true elite transcend class conflict to claim their humanity: "So far as a man has genius he tends to take himself out of the category of class altogether, and to become simply a man" (5:130).

Arnold uses the term "Philistine" as part of a class fantasy that operates within a specific class struggle, namely a struggle for the "hearts and minds" of the Populace. Education is becoming universally available, and his aim is to keep it under the control of the educated elite to which he belongs. He wants to keep this critical work of educating the Populace out of the hands of the middle class, the Philistines. His strategy is by no means merely an idealistic one. Looking to the state as a center of authority that can rise above class politics and mediate social conflict, he is a strong advocate of public education under centralized control. In fact, he served for many years as Her Majesty's Inspector of Schools.

Arnold offers education to the Populace as a means of self-improvement, but the unstated price the Populace must pay for this improvement

---

[21] *The Compact Edition of the Oxford English Dictionary.* 2 vols. (Oxford: Oxford University Press, 1971) 2:2153.

[22] R. H. Super, ed., *The Complete Prose Works of Matthew Arnold.* 11 vols. (Ann Arbor: University of Michigan Press, 1960–1977) 5:134. Unattributed references in this section are to Arnold by volume and page (e.g., 5:134).

through education is domination by the intellectual elite. Claiming to eliminate class conflict, he in fact reinstates *aristo*cracy, rule by the best—the best people, the best ideas. As he puts it in the introduction to his essay *Culture and Anarchy* (which is here our main source), "the great help out of our present difficulties" lies in "getting to know, on all the matters which most concern us, the best which has been thought and said in the world" (5:233–234). This constitutes "culture," the term that sums up everything of which he approves.

Fantasizing the Philistines. Arnold summarizes the German use of "Philistine" as follows: "*Philistine* must have originally meant, in the mind of those who invented the nickname, a strong, dogged, unenlightened opponent of the chosen people, of the children of the light. . . . They regarded [the Philistines] as humdrum people, slaves to routine, enemies to light; stupid and oppressive, but at the same time very strong" (3:112). In contradistinction to the disinterested intellectual (the servant of the idea) who has extricated himself from narrow sectarian interests the Philistine is preeminently a member of a class and acts in that class's interest.

We can identify a number of key features in Arnold's fantasy. He sees the Philistine as provincial, narrow, and self-regarding, as worshiping mere externals, what Arnold calls *machinery*—size, power, numbers, wealth—while neglecting the idea, reason, and the good. The biblical image of the Philistines provides him with a portrait of people who have technological superiority while being *culturally* inferior. He describes the England of the industrial middle classes as "the very headquarters of Goliath" (3:111) where "the sky is of brass and iron" (3:113).

A key aspect of Arnold's profile is that the Philistine worships the freedom *to do as one likes*. This is the meaning of *anarchy*, which is the opposite of culture ("Doing as One Likes" is the title of a chapter in *Culture and Anarchy: Prose Works* 5:115–136). Arnold writes not long after the passage of the Second Reform Bill, which resulted in the "Philistines" forming a majority in Parliament. Their desire to do as they liked was now combined with the power to do just exactly that.

Despite his opposition to them Arnold acknowledges that the Philistines must be instrumental in the next stage of the development of England as a nation. The Industrial Revolution that has brought the middle and working classes to power has had the good effect of destroying feudalism in England. But he anxiously insists that though this is necessary, it is a passing phase. "Now, culture admits the necessity of the movement towards fortune-making and exaggerated industrialism, readily allows that the future may derive benefit from it; but insists, at the same time, that the passing generations of industrialists,—forming, for the most part, the stout main body of Philistinism,—are sacrificed to it" (5:105). This is another level of class fantasy. The Philistines are necessary at the moment but will be "sacrificed" to a better future. They are merely an *instrument* of a historical purpose that transcends them. This notion of instrumentality will be extremely important in our later discussion.

Arnold's class fantasy leads him deep into the politics of gender and race, and the two become interconnected. As in the case of Brentano a particular way of thinking about relationships between men and women is part and parcel of Arnold's use of the term Philistine. He characterizes the Philistine attitude toward women as crude and unrefined.

The Industrial Revolution changed the relationship between the sexes as well as between the classes, but throughout his work Arnold trivializes this change and plays down its depth. In *Culture and Anarchy* his examination of sexual politics is confined to discussion of a proposed parliamentary bill that would allow a man to marry his deceased wife's sister. The advocates of this bill argue for it on the basis that it does not contradict Levitical laws. Arnold depicts them as exhibiting "that double craving so characteristic of our Philistine . . . the craving for forbidden fruit and the craving for legality" (5:206). He goes on to deploy the rhetoric of racism as a persuasive strategy by characterizing advocates of the bill as having a "Semitic" attitude toward women:

> Who . . . will believe, when he really considers the matter, that where the feminine nature, the feminine ideal, and our relationship to them, are brought into question, the delicate and apprehensive genius of the Indo-European race, the race which invented the Muses, and chivalry, and the Madonna, is to find its last word on this question in the institutions of a Semitic people, whose wisest king had seven hundred wives and three hundred concubines? (5:208)

Arnold idealizes women as possessing spiritual influence even as he seeks to deny them material power. His discussion of marriage to in-laws is obviously cast in terms of male rather than female desire. Likewise in his discussion of divorce, in *God and the Bible* (7:225–229), Arnold expresses male rather than female motivation and interest. He characterizes John Stuart Mill, who argued for legalizing divorce as well as for extending economic and political rights to women, simply as an advocate of adultery. He never takes up Mill's argument for the enfranchisement of women or places the discussion of marriage in the larger context of Mill's concern for women's equality. Mill's advocacy of free love becomes in Arnold's account a crude and regressive desire for unlimited sexual expression.

Arnold employs a nature/culture, animal/human framework in his discussion of sexual relationships. He sets up a contrast between nature-polygamy-polytheism and culture-monogamy-monotheism. He links the first set of terms to the biblical image of the "strange woman." Mill's proposal to change marriage laws he portrays as a threat to monotheism and civilization that leads us back into the dark age of unbridled ecstasy symbolized by the Witch of Endor (see 7:221). These allusions to the biblical "other" belong to the same set of ideas as the Philistine "craving for forbidden fruit," and it is no surprise when Arnold refers, in the course of this discussion, to a biblical Philistine (Abimelech in Genesis; see 7:218).

We have just seen how Arnold could deploy "Semitic" as a racial category in his idealizing of women. In fact he uses throughout his work a whole web of ethnic categories in which his category of "Philistine," though it has nothing ostensibly to do with race, becomes enmeshed. His equation of Philistine attitudes with Semitic values points up the latent antisemitism that runs throughout his work. (He makes the same curious link between Philistines and Jews that we discovered in Brentano.) He adopts the ethnological theory that there are two major cultural and linguistic groups, the Indo-European (Aryan) and the Semitic, and argues that Indo-European values are more natural to the English Saxons than Semitic ones.

This set of attitudes also gets displaced, in an ethnographically curious but revealing way, onto Celtic culture. In a series of lectures on this subject Arnold depicts the Saxons as Philistines and the Celts as children of the light! He emphasizes the impact of Celtic culture on English literature. The sentimental Celts, with their flights of fancy and quickness of perception, have added a much-needed leaven to the culture of the steady-going but dull Saxons. However, just as he idealizes women while refusing to take their demands for political and economic power seriously, so too he ascribes a spiritual force to Celtic culture while refusing to grant it material power (3:298). He ends his lectures with a proposal to undermine Philistinism "through . . . the slow approaches of culture, and the introduction of chairs of Celtic" (3:386). The study of Celtic culture would provide the Philistine Saxons with the opportunity to acquire culture through the disinterested study of things outside themselves.

This ethnic farrago of Celts, Saxons, Indo-Europeans and Semites, further mixed up as it is with gender issues, is hard now to take seriously, but it forms an integral part of Arnold's pressing of the cultural claims of the literary establishment in its struggle with the Philistines.

Finally, Arnold reveals (like Brentano) anxiety about his own identity vis-à-vis the Philistines. That he does so in a jocular way does not at all diminish the sense of unease. In *Culture and Anarchy* he describes himself as someone who, while being "properly a Philistine," has been converted to culture:

> I myself am properly a Philistine. . . . And although, through circumstances which will perhaps one day be known if ever the affecting story of my conversion comes to be written, I have, for the most part, broken with the tea-meetings of my own class, yet I have not, on that account, been brought much the nearer to the ideas and works of the Barbarians or of the Populace (5:144).

"For the most part . . . ." To what extent is Arnold's castigation of the emergent middle class inhabited by unsureness of his own separation from it?

Conclusion

In this chapter I have approached the Bible from an unusual but, I would argue, logical and necessary direction. What we have been exploring is part of the Bible's legacy to western culture in the form of the recent history of one particular biblical word, a word that is also very important in 1 Samuel. The next step is to ask how this modern history may guide our reading of the ancient text. The emphases we have discovered in recent European uses of "Philistine" highlight, as I shall show, aspects of the portrayal of Philistines in 1 Samuel that, if we came at them only from directions authorized by more traditional biblical studies, we might overlook or underestimate. But the demonstration of this needs to be the work of a separate chapter.

Chapter 10

THE BOOK OF THE PHILISTINE ASCENDANCY

I shall argue in this chapter that the Philistine theme, like the theme of leadership through surrogate fatherhood and sonship (see Chapter 5), defines 1 Samuel in a particular way. Two facts make this claim immediately plausible. First, by the simple measure of quantity the Philistine presence is more pervasive in 1 Samuel than in any other book of the Bible. Second, the end of 1 Samuel precisely marks the point of division between the Philistines' dominance over Israel and their subsequent insignificance in 2 Samuel [101–102].

The Philistines are a significant presence in two other books, Genesis and Judges, and we must pay considerable attention to these books. Much but by no means all of what 1 Samuel says about the Philistines is in direct continuity with Judges. The relation to Genesis, on the other hand, seems to be largely one of contrast. But reading 1 Samuel through the eyes of Genesis will enable us to discover unexpected things about the Philistines.

In terms of the Philistine presence 1 Samuel can be conveniently divided into four sections: (1) the wars involving the house of Eli, the ark of God, and Samuel, in chs. 4–7; (2) Saul's Philistine wars in various parts of chs. 13–20 (also 23:27–24:1)—I shall sometimes call this the "middle section" of 1 Samuel; (3) material on the Philistines and the fugitive David in chs. 21, 27–30 (also 23:1-5); (4) the Philistine triumph in ch. 31.

The preceding chapter established a large number of categories under which we could read various modern discourses about "Philistines." It is these categories that will now lead us through 1 Samuel. The modern discourses represent some sort of processing, perhaps at an unconscious level, of the Bible. Our method here is to read the modern discourses back into the Bible, in the hope of identifying how the

Philistines may have functioned, again perhaps at a largely unconscious level, in the creation of the ancient text.

We will find a good use for nearly all of the categories, but the one most dominant in the organization of this chapter will be fantasy. We saw how the modern discourses of Philistines served largely to create class fantasies as a means of holding at arm's length real class struggles. We also found how such fantasizing came up against a definite limit as Brentano and Arnold found it impossible to sustain the lines of division between their own in-groups and the despised Philistines. In this chapter we shall see how Israel too uses the Philistines to fantasize their own situation, but how in 1 Samuel the limits of this fantasy work are reached and a realistic view of the Philistines asserts itself more and more.

We begin with a lengthy survey of the treatment of the Philistines in 1 Samuel, emphasizing fantasy but noting where it reaches its limits. We then briefly contrast the fantasy and reality work, exposing them as alternative and conflicting textual currents (related respectively to Genesis and Judges). The chapter concludes with two close readings. The first reading, of the brideprice episode in 18:17-29, shows fantasy in its freest flight. The second, of David with the Philistines (chs. 21, 27–30), shows reality asserting itself in a bitter battle with fantasy. In this section fantasy and reality are so intertwined that it requires reading of some subtlety to discover what may be going on.

Fantasizing the Philistines

Students read the Philistines. Since students were so influential in establishing the modern discourses of Philistines it seems appropriate to solicit their views. So I asked the seminary students in a course on 1 Samuel to put themselves in the position of Israelites and give their view of the Philistines, deliberately using a rhetoric analogous to that of sexism or racism: "Philistines are . . ." (cf. "women are . . . ," "blacks are . . ."). I encouraged them to take into account also Genesis and Judges to the extent that they were aware of these books' treatment of Philistines.

The answers ranged widely. There was some emphasis on sheer otherness, defined particularly in religious terms: Philistines are sacrilegious, polytheistic, and hence excluded from the people of YHWH. Their lack of circumcision was seen as a focus of this otherness; one student equated it with "having no morals." Many stressed force and cruelty, perceiving the Philistines as powerful, arrogant, oppressive, brutal, barbarous toward defeated enemies and (in the incident of the wells in Genesis 26) capriciously destructive. A few used extreme adjectives: "bestial," "subhuman." Several students found the Philistines "war hungry," assuming them to be always the initiators of conflict. In adversity they were seen mostly as fearful and confused, but sometimes as brave (1 Samuel 4).

Perhaps most interesting were the students' suggestions about the Philistines' intellectual capacities. Some found them "stupid, simpleminded," but others found them shrewd, in getting rid of the ark of the covenant (1 Samuel 6) and in keeping Israel disarmed. Despite all these negatives some students noted that the Philistines *were* after all culturally superior and usually victorious.

These answers can all be supported from the biblical text but they stress the negative side heavily. It seems fair to surmise that the students were reading the biblical Philistines through eyes conditioned by the negative uses of "Philistine" from much later times, and to this day.

Class, race, and gender. In the preceding chapter I concluded that the modern use of "Philistine" belongs fundamentally to *class* discourse. It is the response of an elite, particularly an intellectual elite, to an emergent middle class.

In the biblical presentation it is ethnicity rather than class that on the face of it defines the relations between Israelites and Philistines (we shall return to the ethnic issues). But there are traces in the Philistine traditions that encourage class analysis, and recent developments in biblical studies have made us more sensitive to these traces.[1] 1 Samuel 4:9 refers to Israelite *servitude* to the Philistines. The Philistine monopoly on iron (13:19-22) makes better sense as a class difference than an ethnic one; it indicates that the Philistines had better access to material resources than the Israelites. It has been suggested that the Samson cycle should be read as resistance literature generated by an oppressed class in their struggle against a culturally superior oppressor,[2] and the same possibility exists for 1 Samuel.

---

[1] I refer to the trend associated above all with Norman K. Gottwald. See for example "A Hypothesis about Social Class in Monarchic Israel in the Light of Contemporary Studies of Social Class and Social Stratification" in his *The Hebrew Bible in Its Social World and Ours* (Atlanta: Scholars, 1993) 139–164.

[2] J. Cheryl Exum, *Fragmented Women: Feminist (Sub)versions of Biblical Narratives.* JSOT.S 163 (Sheffield: JSOT Press, 1993) 90–91, with reference to Susan Niditch, "Samson as Culture Hero, Trickster, and Bandit: The Empowerment of the Weak," *CBQ* 52 (1990) 608–624.

It is interesting that while the Israelites' special name for the Philistines, the "uncircumcised," suggests ethnicity (see below), the Philistines' special name for the Israelites, "Hebrews," is likely a class indicator. "Hebrew" is almost certainly linked to the Akkadian *"apiru,"* which is a designation for disenfranchised and disadvantaged groups.[3] *Apiru* bands often hired themselves out as mercenaries, just as David's band hires itself to the Philistine king Achish (ch. 27). In 1 Samuel "Hebrew" is used five times by the Philistines (4:6, 9; 13:19; 14:11; 29:3).[4]

A *racial* (or quasi-racial) difference between Philistines and Israelites is expressed in the Bible in two ways. The first is the Philistines' descent from Ham (Gen 10:14), which Brentano, we recall, strongly emphasized. They belong, in this primitive ethnology, to a quite different section of humanity from Israel, a section that is cursed through its ancestor (9:20-27).

The second indicator is the epithet "uncircumcised." The use of this term suggests one particular way in which the Philistines are *more* different from Israel than Israel's other neighbors (who mostly shared the custom of circumcision). It is always a slur—the Philistines do not use it of themselves. It works to suppress the subjectivity of the other, especially as it reduces a person to a physical trait and probably to a physical function, the sexual. It is important for our analysis that this physical difference between Israelites and Philistines is bound up with the difference between the sexes.

A theme we shall later take up is that of the individual Israelite hero who battles a multitude of Philistines. All these heroes refer to the Philistines as "uncircumcised"—Samson (Judg 15:18), Jonathan (1 Sam 14:6), and David (17:26, 36)—and this physical feature provides the entire point of one of the hero stories (18:20-29) [230–231]. In 31:4 Saul also uses the term in a way that suggests a link with Philistine cruelty and barbarity. But it is not found either in 1 Samuel 4–7 or in the accounts of David with the Philistines in chs. 21, 27–29.

The developing biblical tradition heightens the sense of difference from the Philistines in another important way. The LXX translation of

---

[3] E.g., Norman K. Gottwald, *The Tribes of Yahweh: A Sociology of the Religion of Liberated Israel 1250–1050 B.C.E.* (Maryknoll, N.Y.: Orbis, 1979) 419–425. In an unpublished paper ("The Politics of 'Hebrew' in 1 Samuel") John L. McLaughlin argues that "Hebrew" is never an ethnic designator in 1 Samuel, but always connotes social class.

[4] It is also the term by which the Egyptians tend to refer to the Israelites in Exodus. It should be noted that in 1 Samuel it is also used once by Saul (13:3) and once by the narrator (14:21).

"Philistines" throughout 1 Samuel, and for the most part in Judges, is *allophuloi* ("strangers" or "others").[5] The odd effect of this is that in the LXX the Philistines sometimes call themselves "strangers" (e.g., 1 Sam 4:9). In Genesis, however, the LXX uses the neutral transliteration *phulistiim*. We shall return to the significance of this switch.

Gender enters the modern discourses in a two-sided way. The women in groups designated as Philistine are portrayed as despicable while the women of the in-group are idealized (and seen as needing protection from Philistine influence). The German students are contemptuous of the townswomen and their contempt takes the form of sexual exploitation: they identify with Samson's sexual prowess. With Brentano it is just the opposite. Philistinism is a culture of whoredom, of degraded women who degrade those who consort with them: even Samson incurs blame. But this very degradation enables Brentano to define by contrast an ideal Romantic version of femaleness. A similar ideal inspires Arnold to some of his heights of rhetoric ("the delicate and apprehensive genius of the Indo-European race, the race which invented the Muses, and chivalry, and the Madonna," and so forth).[6]

It is ironic, in view of these stereotypes, that among the first incidents involving Philistines in the Bible we find the entry of both Sarah and Rebekah into the household of King Abimelech (Genesis 20; 26:1-11). If we ask who, between the patriarch of Israel (Abraham, Isaac) and the Philistine king, espouses a high ideal of womanhood in these stories there can be only one answer!

In Judges, Samson's encounters with Philistines and with women overlap almost exactly, and the stereotypes that generate these stories at some level conflate women and Philistines.[7] Both represent the Other in relation to Israel's patriarchal and xenophobic mindset. The Philistines succeed in defeating Samson only when a woman helps them. Their means of fighting is womanish in the conventional sexist sense of using deceit rather than force. The sign of Israelite identity that most serves to exclude Philistines, circumcision, is a male sign that therefore also excludes women.

The prototype of the Philistine woman Other is, of course, Delilah. As woman and Philistine she displays a variety of "bad" characteris-

---

[5] To be precise Codex Alexandrinus uses *allophuloi* throughout Judges, while Vaticanus does so except on six occasions when it uses *phulistiim*, the last of which is 14:2.

[6] R. H. Super, ed., *The Complete Prose Works of Matthew Arnold*. 11 vols. (Ann Arbor: University of Michigan Press, 1960–1977) 5:208.

[7] See Exum, *Fragmented Women* 61–93 for the following points.

tics such as materialism, deceit, and oversexedness. Delilah as *femme fatale* still pervades today's popular culture to an extraordinary degree.[8] In some respects she has a counterpart in the Medium of Endor [186]. Neither woman is ever actually said to be a Philistine, but their respective locations, "the valley of Sorek" (Judg 16:4) and Endor, place them near the boundary between Israel and Philistia, giving scope for anxiety about how foreign they really are. In the case of the medium there is another aspect of Philistine otherness: traffic in the occult. The only other reference in 1 Samuel to practitioners of the occult is to Philistine diviners (6:2), and the same connection is made in Isa 2:6. It is no coincidence that Arnold chooses the Medium of Endor to symbolize the "dark age" of unbridled ecstasy (i.e., of free sexual behavior) before the "cultural conquest" that introduced marriage. She is one of the few women in 1 Samuel who wield public power. But Arnold might just as well have used Delilah as his example.[9]

Philistine topics and traits. In its most general terms the view of the Philistines we found in the modern data is a double one. They are both figures of fun and figures of fear. In Arnold's words they are "unenlightened" and "stupid," but also "very strong."[10] The German students regard the townsfolk as figures of fun and are confident of their ability to outwit them, but they are also aware of the Philistines' power over them. The emphasis in Brentano is heavily on ridicule, but Philistine power emerges clearly in his discourse.[11] With Arnold the strength of the Philistines, the threat they pose to national life, has become central, and the element of satire and making fun has considerably receded.

Both aspects are found in the Bible. In fact, it is their combination that supports the hypothesis of resistance literature.

Lampooning of the Philistines as *figures of fun* is at its clearest in Judges. They are simpleminded and easily deceived. Samson's Philistine opponents are made to look foolish by their inability to deal with him in combat. Sometimes they can temporarily get the better of him by shrewdness and deceit, but they are finally outsmarted.

---

[8] J. Cheryl Exum, *Plotted, Shot, and Painted: Cultural Representations of Biblical Women.* JSOT.S 215 (Sheffield: Sheffield University Press, 1996) 175–237.

[9] The other place in 1 Samuel where gender is exploited in relation to the Philistines is the brideprice story (18:20-29) [227–231].

[10] Arnold, *Prose Work* 3:112.

[11] E.g., "Der Philister vor, in und nach der Geschichte: Aufgestellt, begleitet und bespiegelt aus göttlichen und weltlichen Schriften und eigenen Beobachtungen," in Andreas Müller, ed., *Satiren und Parodien* (Leipzig: Reclam, 1935) 218–223, referring to Philistine control of the German theater.

The element of lampoon is much slighter in 1 Samuel. Polzin suggests that an Israelite audience would be amused by the Philistines' ignorance of Israel's history in 4:8.[12] They believe that Israel is polytheistic and that the plagues of Egypt happened in the wilderness. I find this suggestion dubious. 1 Samuel 5:7 and 6:6 show that the Philistines know the truth about these matters. When they ascribe polytheism to the Israelites they are doing no more than the narrator often does (e.g., Judg 10:6).

In ch. 5 there is an element of ridiculing the Philistines but it is not easy to assess its extent. There is something comic about Dagon's falling over during the night when no one is looking. The comic aspect of the plagues depends on the traditional translation "hemorrhoids" (5:6, etc.), which is far from certain (NRSV has "tumors"). There may also be a humorous suggestion that the Philistines are not quick on the uptake. The overturn of Dagon fails to convince them the first time and they frantically pass the ark between three cities before finally getting the point. But the suggestion of lampoon should not be exaggerated. It is not clear that the second city, Gath, wants the ark at all. The NRSV translation suggests bravado on the part of the Gittites: "Let the ark of God be moved to us" (5:8). But this translation follows the LXX version; the MT says that it was the lords of the Philistines who decided on the move to Gath. The third city, Ekron, definitely does not want the ark (v. 10). The Philistines are not so very slow and stupid.

In fact, ch. 6 suggests the opposite. The response of the priests and diviners to the problem posed by the ark is very interesting. It is hard to find any mockery here. These Philistine theologians are willing to admit the power of Israel's god over their own, but they are pragmatists: they require a test to decide whether Israel's god is behind their disasters or whether these happened "by chance" (6:9) [295–296]. They devise and carry out such a test (vv. 9-12). This seems not a bad strategy. They are calling the bluff of the god of Israel. If he exists and is powerful he will prove it by taking the ark back, saving the Philistines further trouble. If not, then the Philistines win the theological debate and perhaps keep the booty.

The other possible foundation for a stereotype of the Philistines as stupid and gullible is the character of Achish, King of Gath, around whom David's history with the Philistines revolves. To a first reading Achish seems very gullible. But we shall later, through a lengthy reading, cast grave doubt on this first impression. Suffice it to say for

---

[12] *Samuel and the Deuteronomist: A Literary Study of the Deuteronomic History. Part Two: 1 Samuel* (San Francisco: Harper & Row, 1989) 58.

now that even if Achish is sometimes gullible there are always other Philistines who quickly put him right. They certainly are not *all* gullible.

The stereotype of Philistines as *figures of fear* is again only one part of a mixed picture. It is symptomatic that in their very first appearance in 1 Samuel (4:1) the tradition hesitates over whether they are the aggressors. They are so in the Greek version: "In those days the Philistines mustered for war against Israel, and Israel went out to battle against them" (so NRSV). But the Hebrew version omits the reference to the Philistines altogether, making Israel the aggressor (so the old RSV).

The impression given of the Philistines in this war (4:5-10) is frankly an odd one, but by any account it is far from a stereotype. At the beginning of the war they are despondent because of the presence of the ark, but they rally, and then . . . simply win! The brevity with which their victory is announced in v. 10 oddly collapses the great buildup of Israelite confidence and Philistine fear in vv. 5-9. There is nothing here of the arrogant boastfulness with which Philistines are elsewhere portrayed (14:11-12, 17:8-10). I am reminded of the British mythology that grew up around the Zulu wars in the late nineteenth century. From a perspective of supreme confidence the British saw "the natives" as demonstrating a mixture of ignorant awe and desperate courage, and even idealized them up to a point. The only problem with this mythology was that more than once (most famously at Isandhlwana in 1879) what the British had to record was not a victory but an unaccountable defeat.[13] Just this patronizing admiration, deflated by a surprising disaster, seems to me to be the tone of 4:5-10. This passage constitutes an important moment in the movement from fantasy to reality.

It is the middle section of 1 Samuel that most emphasizes the fearsomeness of the Philistines. Their overwhelming numbers and the great fear they instill appear already in 13:5-7. This theme is resumed in 13:17-18. Modern translations completely miss the ominousness of the Hebrew: "The Destroyer with three heads came out. . . ." Though it is being used as a technical military term for "company" (so NRSV), "head" preserves connotations of its literal meaning, and the word "destroyer" is the same as the destroying angel of the Passover (Exod 12:23). The terror-inspiring quality of Goliath is of course similarly stressed (e.g., 17:11).

---

[13] I shall later read 1 Samuel in relation to a novel that has the Zulu wars as its background [259–264].

The later part of the book is mostly able to express Philistine power without resorting to such expressions of brutality or grotesqueness. As the Philistines get ready for their triumph over Saul and Israel their power seems simply to be taken for granted. For David their country is a place of refuge where Saul's power cannot reach (21:10, 27:1-4). At the very end, however, in recording their final triumph (ch. 31) the text returns to the stereotype. The Philistines are again cruel and barbarous in warfare, as witness their treatment of Saul's corpse (31:9-10).

We move now to more specific topics from the modern discourses, and begin with *the opposition of nature to culture.* Samson represents nature over against Philistine culture, for example in the free growth of his hair versus Delilah's hairdressing. The same opposition can be found in the battle between David and Goliath. Goliath, decked out for battle in a massive weight of "bronze" and "iron" (17:5-7) contrasts starkly with David, who refuses any armor at all (vv. 38-39) and fights with stones, natural objects (v. 40). Goliath's grotesquely metallic appearance may be linked with the Philistine monopoly on iron (13:19-22)—he is a fantasized version of Philistine technological superiority.[14]

We found this nature-culture opposition particularly in the Romantics, who set a cult of nature over against a stultifying middle class culture. Arnold, though he uses the term "culture" in a different sense, must admit the Philistines' technological superiority as he mocks their want of culture. His reference to industrial Britain as the "headquarters of Goliath," where "the sky is of brass and iron," makes a fascinating link, at the fantasy level, with the metallic Goliath [208–209]. His obsession with the terms "mechanical" and "machinery," which he uses to describe Philistine worship of mere "externals"—size, power, numbers, wealth—fits in the same context.

A closely linked issue is Philistine *materialism.* People enjoying technological superiority are typically charged with being materialistic, and this runs as a steady current through the modern discourses about Philistines. For this there is not much in the way of a biblical basis. Delilah has been accused of commercialism (Judg 16:5), and in other places Philistines assume that monetary tribute is the right way to expiate an offense—not only in 1 Samuel 5–6 (the capture of the ark) but also in Genesis 20 and 26 (the offenses against the Israelite matriarchs).[15]

---

[14] We could extend the metallic theme to the Philistine chariots of 13:5: Israel apparently possesses no chariots in 1 Samuel.

[15] The compensation is not clear in Genesis 26, but Isaac becomes rich immediately following the incident (vv. 12-14).

Modern Philistines are, in both the German and the English data, usually presented as an undifferentiated group. Prominent In Germany is the theme of the struggle of the individual (often youthful, often a solitary "genius") against the mass of Philistines.

This theme of *the individual and the collective* is equally prominent in the Bible. The Philistines there are very often an undifferentiated group, and even when they speak or act as individuals there is a good deal of stereotyping. In Judges the only individualized Philistines are Samson's bride-to-be (14:15-17), her father (15:1-2), and Delilah (if she is a Philistine). The two women speak and act in virtually identical ways, for the same purpose, and only at the instance of a (male) Philistine collectivity. The father-in-law has only one brief speech. There are no Philistines in the middle section of 1 Samuel who take on individual identity except Goliath. But though Goliath does speak in his own voice (17:8-10, 43-44) his words do not differentiate him from the Philistine collectivity: they consist entirely of the kind of empty taunt we find elsewhere (1 Sam 14:11-12; Judg 16:23-25).

Against Philistine collectivity is set Israelite individuality, especially in the recurring theme of the hero who successfully battles a multitude of Philistines. This begins in Judges with Shamgar (3:31) and Samson, and recurs in 1 Samuel 13–20. First the hero is Jonathan, who already in 13:3 defeats a whole garrison. He continues the hero in 14:6-15. (It is a relatively small number of Philistines that he and his attendant overcome, but the initiative leads to a general panic.) Later the hero is David. His triumph over Goliath (ch. 17) represents a simple transformation of the pattern of individual versus collective, replacing multitude with magnitude. The later exploit in 18:25-27 is decidedly David's own even if he has the assistance of "his men." It is made clear that these stories of Jonathan and David are *youthful* exploits (cf. similarly Samson).

On the other hand significant differentiation sometimes occurs within the Philistine collectivity, and some Philistines are developed as individual characters. In 1 Samuel 5 the inhabitants of each Philistine city form a separate agent. The five "lords of the Philistines" are differentiated from the general populace (5:8, 11; 6:12). The priests and diviners in ch. 6 are a separate group who take initiative in the narrative. In general chs. 5–6 present the Philistines in no monolithic way but allow for significant interaction among them. The same goes for chs. 21, 27–29. Achish (who with the possible exception of Abimelech in Genesis 20, 21, 26 is the most strongly drawn individual Philistine in the Bible) interacts with other Philistines—his servants in 21:10-15, the Philistine commanders in ch. 29—as well as with David.

Deeper currents (1): Instrumentality. My intertextual reading so far has dealt for the most part with features at the surface level of the ancient and modern discourses. In two aspects of his treatment of modern Philistines, though, it seems to me that Matthew Arnold instinctively plumbs greater depths, responding to features at what I have called the mythic level of the text. These are instrumentality and anarchy.

Arnold highlights a central biblical theme when he presents his "Philistines" as a class that is necessary at the moment but will disappear in the movement to a better future, will even be "sacrificed" to that future [208–209]. This view, which I called "instrumental," is underlined by the way Arnold, through his deployment of ethnological theories, makes one race serve the interests of another.[16] In 1 Samuel and its context the Philistines participate in two different plot movements that fall respectively within the Extended Book of Judges and the Book of the Everlasting Covenant. In each the text suggests that they are simply instruments for achieving specific narrative goals.

In their first appearance in 1 Samuel the Philistines take part in a plot about warfare that moves from defeat (ch. 4) to victory (ch. 7) for Israel. This sequence is related to the larger narrative at two levels. First, ch. 4 provides the fulfillment of the curse on the house of Eli (see especially 2:34). In the war Hophni and Phinehas (and as a consequence, Eli) die. Second, on a larger scale the sequence relates to Samuel's judge cycle. We see this overtly in ch. 7, but the logic of the judge cycles is made to embrace ch. 4 as well. Earlier I analyzed these issues at length [50–57], concluding that the appearance of the Philistines is really a reappearance; they have been *the* foreign enemy since Judges 13 (and present as an enemy even since Judg 10:7). Samuel's defeat of them (1 Samuel 7) makes him the greatest of the judges; each of the other judges defeated an enemy that arose only during his or her own lifetime, but Samuel defeats an age-old enemy. Thus the Philistines are instruments not only in the removal of Eli but also in the establishment of Samuel.

However, this incorporation of the Philistines into the logic of the judge cycles is not achieved without narrative strain. We discern the strain in the treatment of territoriality. According to the judge theory the Philistines ought to have been *occupying* Israel before their defeat in ch. 7, and this is what ch. 7 itself unambiguously implies. But chs. 4–6 (except for 4:9) imply a situation in which the two peoples are occupying adjacent territories, and ch. 6 supposes a definite boundary.

---

[16] This instrumentality can be traced also in the German material, in a crass form among the students—the townsfolk are a nuisance but an absolutely necessary one—and in a cosmic form in Brentano, where the Philistine "idea" is part of the eternal battle of good and evil.

This tension is related to the alternative readings of 4:1. The Hebrew version makes the Israelites the aggressors while the Greek gives this role to the Philistines [219]. The latter fits better into the judge theory: the Philistines have in principle been occupying Israel since Samson's time (4:9) but since they have been so long absent from the text their control needs to be reaffirmed. An Israelite offensive is harder to interpret, though we could see it as part of the parodic treatment of Eli's judgeship [51]. This "judge" (4:18) starts a war of national liberation but, in line with the unsatisfactory nature of his whole judgeship, the war ignominiously fails. It seems to me that we do best not to try to choose between these two options: the divergent traditions in 4:1 point precisely to a hesitation over how a crucial moment in the story is to be remembered.

Within this already complicated plot movement is set the story of the ark in chs. 4–6. An interesting possibility is to see the Philistines' possession of the ark as a metonym for the occupation of territory: in possessing the ark they occupy the very heart of Israel. But the main function of the ark story is surely more obvious: to show that Israel's God is under no kind of human control. The Philistines cannot hold the ark, but it proves no easier for the Israelites to handle.

In ch. 7 the Philistines are seemingly banished from the story, "sacrificed" (to use Arnold's term) to the future they have opened. But this conclusion proves premature since they are needed for another job, to assist the transition from Saul to David, and against narrative logic they are almost immediately reintroduced in order to do this. At least up to ch. 20 this new instrumental role of the Philistines is even clearer than the old. What I earlier said of Jonathan [95–96] could equally well apply to them: there is hardly any reference to them that does not directly serve David's rise.

The Philistines are brought back into the text as early as 9:16, the divine promise that Saul will save Israel from them. This promise will never be fulfilled by Saul (though it will be spuriously remembered as a promise made to *David*—2 Sam 3:18—and duly fulfilled by him). The Philistines return as an *agent* in the middle section. Here Saul's own performance against them is spotty at best, but Jonathan and then David are built up as heroes in the Philistine wars. David's career is boosted, at Saul's expense (18:7), by his defeat of Goliath, and in the brideprice episode (18:20-29) a plot by Saul to use the Philistines against David again only serves to advance David's career.

A case can be made for the same Philistine instrumentality beyond ch. 20. The Philistines distract Saul when he is on the point of capturing David (23:26-28), they provide David with a refuge from Saul (ch. 27), and they prevent him from compromising himself by fighting on their side against Israel (ch. 29). Finally the Philistines directly open the way for David by killing Saul and his heirs in battle (ch. 31).

I believe, and shall demonstrate later, that this view of the last part of 1 Samuel considerably simplifies a very complex situation. But as we move into 2 Samuel the Arnoldian process of "sacrificing" the Philistines to historical progress is unconcealed. They go without warning from a position of utter dominance at the end of 1 Samuel to being little more than a footnote in the account of David's triumphs (2 Sam 5:17-25; 8:1; cf. again 3:18). Their instrumental work has been done and the text has no further use for them. They do not need, like the Canaanites, to be literally exterminated. They are exterminated textually.

Deeper currents (2): Anarchy. For Arnold there is perhaps no more essential mark of a Philistine than the desire "to do as one likes." Its importance is indicated by his including "anarchy" (along with "culture") in the title of his major work on the Philistines. It is because of self-centered desire that his Philistine class lacks the social discipline that makes for state coherence.

There is a curious ambiguity in 1 Samuel 1–7 as to what Israel's most fundamental problem is. At one level the problem is the Philistine occupation, an active issue since ch. 4, but a reality, according to the logic of the judge cycles, since way back in the book of Judges. But in a different register the problem is anarchy, everyone "doing what is right in their own eyes" (Judg 21:25).

Both of these problems are, in different ways, connected with the lack of a king and serve as background to the people's request for a king in ch. 8. On the one hand the people want a king (among other reasons) so that he may fight their battles (8:20), and historical scholarship has usually concluded that the Philistine threat was indeed the cause of the appearance of monarchy in Israel. On the other hand the verse just quoted from Judges directly links *anarchy* to the lack of a king. But these two problems, Philistines and anarchy, are not narratively connected in 1 Samuel.

It is tempting to read these two problems as representing, within the biblical text, external and internal aspects of the same situation: national demoralization and religious apostasy. Such a reading brings us squarely into the logic of Arnold's view of the Philistines of his time. He simply equates what the Bible juxtaposes, Philistines and anarchy. He sees powerful state control (cf. kingship in Israel) as the only remedy, and the formula he uses for anarchy, "doing as one likes," is so similar to "doing what is right in one's own eyes" that it is hard to believe he did not have the biblical formula in mind. Once more Arnold seems to be in touch with the deep currents of the biblical text.

Fantasy and Reality: Alternative Views of the Philistines

As in Brentano and Arnold, so also in the Bible the Philistines seem uniquely available for fantasy work, and it is fantasy that I have emphasized so far in this chapter. Israel, like the modern authors, uses the Philistines as a means of achieving by contrast a sense of its own identity. Some biblical texts direct toward the Philistines a fear and hatred hardly paralleled in statements about any other group. They are those who have power over us and they are those who are wholly other than we, and this combination gives them an archetypical awfulness. This anxiety needs to be resolved precisely through fantasy, whether this takes the form of lampooning the enemy or of telling about youthful heroes who routed them (often both are found at once).

But just as reality overtook both Brentano and Arnold as they reached a point where they could not be sure of their own difference from the Philistines, so the biblical picture is far from consistent. There too a more realistic sense of the Philistines inhabits the fantasy work. It is now time to explore further this double face of the Philistines.

The split picture of the Philistines in 1 Samuel. With some exceptions in detail it is generally true to say that the elements of fantasy and stereotype are concentrated in 1 Samuel 13–20 and 31. We have found them to be much less present in chs. 4–7 and in the accounts of David and the Philistines in chs. 21, 27–29. In these latter sections we have found no consistent lampooning. At least some Philistines appear as shrewd rather than stupid, and I shall later present reasons to doubt even Achish's gullibility. The picture of warfare in these sections is also generally free of the stereotypical features: the Philistines do not exhibit great aggressiveness or brutality. The general picture seems to be of Israelite and Philistine armies confronting each other on a realistic basis, with victory going sometimes to one side, sometimes to the other, but with the Philistines having the edge and gradually increasing their power. It is noteworthy that the victories by individual heroes against absurd odds seem to have no lasting impact on this realistic picture. Despite these spectacular setbacks the Philistines are always still there, always getting a bit stronger.

What we have in 1 Samuel's treatment of the Philistines, I suggest, is a fantasy level sharing much in common with the highly fantasized accounts in Judges (3:31; chs. 14–16), superimposed on a level much closer to the literary conventions of realism.

The Philistines in Genesis. The "realistic" picture of national rivalry is very much closer to what we find in the other biblical book (aside from Judges) where Philistines are fairly prominent, namely Genesis. There the upshot of the relationship between the Philistines and Israel's ancestors is the establishment of a treaty (made in 21:22-34, tested and perhaps even broken, but reestablished in ch. 26). The making of this treaty follows considerable conflict in which the Israelites are arguably the aggressors (at any rate they are the newcomers). There is nothing here of the Philistines as uncircumcised or of their false gods—indeed, Abimelech appears as a God-fearer who readily acknowledges YHWH. Given the pattern of deceit that pervades accounts of Philistines both ancient and modern it is interesting that the treaty excludes "false dealing" (21:23).

The Bible often expresses ideology through geography, as different geographical spaces are assigned different values.[17] In terms of ideological geography the Philistines are a different kind of enemy from the Canaanites. The Canaanites inhabit space that is supposed to be Israel's, and this problem is to be solved by their extermination or expulsion to some other place. The Philistines, on the other hand, are invaders from the outside. They have their own space, which is not (at least in Judges and 1 Samuel) claimed by Israel. They wish to establish themselves in Israel's space and must be expelled from it and confined to their own.

This is consistent with a paradigm in which Israel and the Philistines are rival claimants, by conquest, for the territory of the Canaanites, a paradigm strikingly parallel to the standard historical view that the exodus Israelites and the Philistines arrived in Canaan at much the same time (ca. 1200 B.C.E.).[18] But this is not the view of the Deuteronomic History, which sees Israel as conquering the land and becoming established there under its judges *before* the conflict with the Philistines. Genesis stands in an interesting relationship to these views. It concedes to the Philistines a greater antiquity in the land than Israel, but it establishes a division of the land by treaty.

Genesis versus Judges. To read 1 Samuel in continuity with Judges is to highlight the fantasy elements in the portrayal of the Philistines. To read it through the eyes of Genesis is to raise the possibility of a much more realistic picture of the relations between Israel and the Philistines. Judges is literarily nearer at hand and its influence has been more strongly felt in both ancient and modern times.

---

[17] "[Biblical] geography is simply a visible form of theology" (Jon D. Levenson, *Sinai and Zion: An Entry into the Jewish Bible* [New York: Harper Collins, 1985] 116). For typical studies see David Jobling, *The Sense of Biblical Narrative: Structural Analyses in the Hebrew Bible II.* JSOT.S 39 (Sheffield: JSOT Press, 1986) 88–134; Elizabeth Struthers Malbon, *Narrative Space and Mythic Meaning in Mark* (San Francisco: Harper & Row, 1986).

[18] This paradigm gets encouragement from Amos 9:7: "Did I not bring up Israel from the land of Egypt, and the Philistines from Caphtor . . . ?"

There is early evidence, however, that Jewish commentators saw and feared the possibility that 1 Samuel would be read through the eyes of Genesis. A rabbinic source discusses the issue of whether Israel should have been obliged, later, to keep the Genesis treaty. It answers "no," on the grounds that the Philistines of Judges and Samuel were *an entirely different people* from the Philistines of Genesis![19] This need to separate the Philistines of Genesis from those of the later narrative is confirmed by the LXX's translations of Hebrew *pᵉlištim* ("Philistines"). Whereas in 1 Samuel and mostly in Judges it uses the pejorative *allophuloi*, "strangers" [215–216], in translating Genesis (and all the books up to Joshua) it uses the neutral transliteration *phulistiim*.

Having now defined the levels of "fantasy" and "reality" I offer in the remainder of this chapter two extended readings, in these alternative modes, of David's relations with the Philistines.

Reading Fantasy: The Episode of the Brideprice[20]

Nowhere in 1 Samuel do we find a more elaborate fantasizing of the Philistines than in 18:17-29. After Saul fails to carry through on his offer of Merab, his older daughter, to David as wife, Michal, his younger daughter, falls in love with David. Saul agrees to this match but specifies as a brideprice "a hundred foreskins of the Philistines," thinking by this to bring about David's death. David, however, secures two hundred foreskins, and marries Michal. The elements of gender, race, and class, as well as other topics we have explored in this chapter, are here found in a rich soup, nicely blended so that the flavors enhance one another, and it is hard to say where one element ends and another begins. This is fantasy work of a very high order!

Entering the world of the Other: David in contrast to Samson. The episode of David and the brideprice invites comparison and contrast with the first episode in the career of Samson (Judges 14). Both Samson and David are entering into marriage, the world of the woman Other, for the first time. The similarities extend into detail, notably the theme of conflict between prospective father-in-law and son-in-law. Samson and David share the experience of being promised a wife who

---

[19] *Midrash Tehillim* on Psalm 60 (William G. Braude, ed., *The Midrash on Psalms*. 2 vols. [New Haven: Yale University Press, 1959] 1:513).

[20] The original idea for this reading, as well as most of the writing in our earlier joint work, came from Catherine Rose.

is then given by her father to someone else. But the main point of comparison for our present purpose is that both stories involve the Philistine Other. Samson seeks a Philistine woman; David gets an Israelite woman by killing Philistines. Women and Philistines function together as the Other against whom male Israelite identity is defined [216–217].

The outcomes of the episodes for the two heroes are, however, starkly contrasted. The basic difference lies in their desire, or lack of it, for the Other. Samson sees the doubly Other, the Philistine woman, and wants her (Judg 14:1-3). From this desire flow all his subsequent troubles. David does not apparently desire Michal; she loves him (1 Sam 18:20, 28) but he is never said to love her [151–152]. He refers to his potential marriage only in terms of becoming son-in-law to Saul (vv. 18, 23). Nor is there any suggestion (at least at this stage of his career) of his desiring the Philistine Other. He wants triumph over the Other, not incorporation into it.

Exum suggests that the grid underlying the representations of women in biblical patriarchy is a dichotomy of mother and whore.[21] The image of the whore, who is the "strange woman," is particularly well personified in the foreign woman, and none is more foreign than the Philistine. This same grid is employed, as we have seen, by both Brentano and Arnold, and in both cases the Philistines are implicated. Arnold portrays advocates of "free love" (like John Stuart Mill) as having fallen victim to the wiles of the "strange woman," and lifts up the Madonna, the Lady (of medieval chivalry), and the Muse, images of women whose spirituality is related to their sexual unavailability and confinement, as figures that represent a proper appreciation of women. Likewise Brentano's contrast between the mores of the Philistine system and those of his own society is expressed in terms of female sexuality: the Philistine culture is "whorish." Exum suggests that underlying the mother/whore dichotomy is a male fear of women's sexuality and an attempt to control it. Just so do Arnold and Brentano depict the Philistine as a man who does not control women but is subject to a desire for them.

It may seem that Samson and David are set on their respective careers by the contrasting kinds of women they encounter. At the mythic level, though, it is surely the converse that is true: women become defined for the two heroes by the heroes' own attitudes toward them. In desiring the Other, Samson turns himself into a Philistine (as Brentano recognizes) and women become for him thereafter whores (Philistine, of course) who exploit and humiliate him. For David, on the other

---

[21] Exum, *Fragmented Women* 68–72.

hand, who does not desire them (or as long as he does not desire them) they become nurturing mothers. Earlier I showed how the primary function of David's women (especially Michal and Abigail) is to assist his rise to power [150–160]. To this end the women must be presented as full of initiative and resource, as strong narrative subjects. But they do not exercise these strong qualities to their or other women's advantage. Their stories will end, in the kingdom they helped establish, in obscurity or disgrace. It is not a son of Michal or Abigail who will inherit David's throne but the son of Bathsheba, a passive woman,[22] perhaps the first woman David sees and desires.

We are back, of course, to the theme of instrumentality. As in Arnold, the Other exists to serve the purpose of the in-group, and retains importance only as long as it serves this purpose. The conflation of women and Philistines reaches its deepest level in their being co-instrumental in David's story. The attempted reduction of the Philistines to the function of instrument in David's rise, which I identified earlier in this chapter, only mirrors the instrumentality of his women.

It has been compellingly suggested that the next scene in which Michal appears after the brideprice episode (19:11-17) symbolically enacts her "motherhood" of David.[23] Michal warns David of Saul's intention to kill him and helps him escape. The means she uses is to "let David down through the window," that is, to enable his passage from inside to outside, from the dangerous confinement of Saul's court to his life as a separate agent. The symbolic connection to the birth process is easy to see. This suggestion gains in force if we put it next to Mieke Bal's reading of the death of Samson (Judg 16:28-30).[24] Samson, having found no mothering women, must give birth to himself by forcing apart pillars of stone. But the result is a stillbirth. It is hard to imagine a more graphic expression of the contrast between the two heroes.

Another way of thinking about these issues is in terms of male bonding. In contrast to Samson, who separates himself from male-identified Israel and refuses bonding with his bridal companions, David valorizes male bonding.[25] David thinks of marriage to Michal as "becoming Saul's son-in-law"—in other words, he defines his relationship to a woman in terms of his relationship to a man! The modern

[22] In 2 Samuel 11 though not in 1 Kings 1–2.

[23] Exum, *Fragmented Women* 47.

[24] *Lethal Love: Feminist Literary Readings of Biblical Love Stories* (Bloomington, Ind.: Indiana University Press, 1987) 62.

[25] Exum, *Fragmented Women* 52–53.

discourses of Philistines, of course, grow out of and valorize male bonding. The ones we have examined are all directly the product of the male university and they provide evidence of the fantasizing of women, in both positive and negative terms, that was a necessary concomitant of women's exclusion from the university.

Race, circumcision, and gender. The denial of subjectivity to the Other reaches an extreme in the brideprice story when the Philistines are reduced to foreskins. What David does, in effect, is to circumcise the uncircumcised. The mark of "racial" otherness is expunged and the Philistines are, in a sense, incorporated into Israel—but only when they are dead. (Was there any actual necessity to kill these Philistines?) The Philistines are not given any narrative presence: David's encounter with them happens "off stage." The way the Philistines disappear from this text as the dangerous other prefigures the way they cease to play a significant role in the biblical text after David's ascent to the throne (2 Samuel). By circumcising the Philistines, David removes "the other" as a threat to the Israelite male community.

The brideprice episode contains echoes of Genesis 34, the story of the rape of Dinah. In the Genesis story (see vv. 13-17) Jacob's family make an insincere offer to the Hivites and use circumcision as a ruse. The offer is first of all of Jacob's daughter Dinah to the Hivite prince in marriage, but it is extended into an offer of kinship between Jacob's family and the Hivites. The price demanded is that the Hivite men agree to be circumcised. They are, in effect, to give up their foreskins as a brideprice, to open the way for the royal marriage and for general intermarriage. But this incorporation into the community of Israel does not (and in the larger biblical ideology cannot) happen. Circumcision becomes just a prelude to killing. The intertextual links—the insincere offer of a daughter and an alliance, the excision of foreskins as a brideprice—suggest that 1 Samuel 18 may be inviting the reader to imagine the possibility of alliance between the Philistines and Israel only to reassert the impossibility of such a union.[26]

That the circumcision of the Other occurs, in both stories, in connection with the giving of women confirms again the importance of this mark of "racial" difference as also a gender mark, and deepens the complicity of the racist and sexist strategies. Howard Eilberg-Schwartz

---

[26] Gary Phillips has suggested to me the possibility of an intertextual reading with Acts 10, with its theme of the incorporation of the Gentiles (referred to as *allophuloi* in v. 28) into Israel and its treatment of the problem of circumcision. This is an interesting possibility, but since I have already moved enough into Lukan territory I prefer to leave it to the interested reader.

suggests that circumcision signified to the Israelites fertility and secure genealogy.[27] It was a way of establishing kinship ties between men and descent through the father rather than the mother. If this is the case, then from the Israelite point of view a community that does not practice circumcision is female-defined. David's circumcising of the uncircumcised is of a piece with his determination to define rather than be defined by women.

The interconnection of the themes of race, gender, and circumcision attains a remarkable pornographic extreme in a rabbinic story that relates directly to the brideprice episode.[28] According to this midrash Goliath was descended from Orpah, Ruth's sister-in-law, as a result of rape. As Orpah returned home after choosing not to accompany Naomi she was raped by a hundred Philistines and a dog. The hundred Philistines are derived from 1 Sam 18:25-27 and the dog comes from Goliath's words in 17:43, "Am I a dog?" (If Goliath is the resulting child, presumably the dog was the father.) One of the goals of this fantasy, no doubt, is to subject Orpah to a punishment similar to that of the Levite's wife (Judges 19), for a similar "offense"—removing herself from the patriarchal household [174]. In terms of our present discussion the important goal is to have David and Goliath descend in parallel lines from Ruth and Orpah. The effect is to present the difference between an Israelite and a Philistine as a difference between two kinds of female behavior.

Class fantasy. Class issues in the brideprice episode may seem insignificant beside the spectacular deployment of the issues of gender and race, but they are present. In the context of Israel's subservience to the Philistines the story belongs to the genre of fantasized resistance literature whereby an oppressed class tries to come to terms with its impotence to do anything about its oppression. But the story alludes also to class stratification *within* Israel. David is a familiar fairy-tale hero. He presents himself as one who is socially insignificant (18:18) and even "poor" (v. 23). To become son-in-law to the king would mean for him an enormous rise in class status. He does not belong to a class that could offer Saul an adequate brideprice in goods. At this level our text, like other "rags to riches" fairy tales, is a piece of class fantasy on behalf of the poor, by means of which they imagine an improvement

---

[27] *The Savage in Judaism: An Anthropology of Israelite Religions and Ancient Judaism* (Bloomington, Ind.: Indiana University Press, 1990) 141–176; see also Exum, *Fragmented Women* 124–128.

[28] See Midrash Rabbah on Ruth 1:14 (H. Freedman and Maurice Simon, eds., *Midrash Rabbah*. 10 vols. [London: Soncino, 1939] 8:38–39).

in their own status within the monarchical system. In reality the result of David's actually becoming Saul's son-in-law, and later king, is that the poor have a new and worse oppressor.

However, what David *does* give Saul for a brideprice complicates the class picture by bringing in the Philistines. The foreskins can serve as a brideprice in lieu of material goods since they symbolize the breaking of the power of a class oppressor at a still higher level than Saul.

Gottwald posits a "two-tier" tributary system in postexilic Israel under which the peasant had to pay taxes at two levels: to the internal national system (based on the Temple) and to the imperial power (Persia) [16–17]. This complex system opens a space for a Nehemiah, for example, to gain popular support by claiming to represent the interests of the peasant against the demands of the imperial Persian power while in fact having no possible means of changing the system.[29] It is instructive to read the brideprice story against this background. David improves his position in the internal Israelite system through a fantasized victory over the supreme imperial power. If I am right that the Deuteronomic History reached its final form when Israel lived within such a two-tier system this reading takes on great importance, since it implies a veiled admission that the Philistines are in the position of supreme overlord.

It is not farfetched to draw a parallel between this complex situation and the one in which Arnold finds himself. He offers education to the lower class as a means of its self-improvement, but the hidden price is domination by the intellectual elite that he himself represents. Like David, Arnold can be seen as a figure who escapes class disadvantage to establish himself as a leader in a new system of domination, but the power *from* which he offers salvation, the Philistines, the emergent middle class, is quickly growing and will win out in the long run.

Reading Reality: The Philistines and the Fugitive David

Twice David goes as a fugitive to the Philistine king Achish of Gath. The first account (21:10-15)[30] is brief and obscure. We cannot tell, for example, whether David goes openly or clandestinely. At any rate, he

---

[29] Norman K. Gottwald, *The Hebrew Bible: A Socio-literary Introduction* (Philadelphia: Fortress, 1985) 432–434.

[30] Verses 11-16 in the MT. I shall use the English versification.

soon leaves. A long time (at least a long narrative space) then passes before his second visit. In this interval he has one encounter with the Philistines, worsting them in a brief engagement (23:1-5). When David arrives for the second time in Achish's court it is with the large following that he has in the meantime gathered, including a household of his own (27:2-3). He enters Achish's service but deals with him deceitfully, pretending to fight against Israel when in fact he is fighting against desert tribes (vv. 8-12).

As war looms between the Philistines and Israel, Achish appoints David to high rank (28:1-2) and plans that David and his men will fight on the Philistine side, but in ch. 29 the lords of the Philistines will not accept this, fearing that David may switch to Israel's side in the war, and they remain unmoved by Achish's protestation of David's loyalty. So David is not involved in the war.

These accounts are not at all transparent to read. I think (as I so often do) that the text is simply overloaded with contradictory ideological currents. As I have previously argued, this makes it only the more important to discern what the currents are. In terms of our intention in this chapter to assess the text's view of the Philistines we find ourselves in a more than usually vicious hermeneutical circle: as we try to derive an assessment of the Philistines from the story we find that our understanding of the story depends on how we think the Philistines are being assessed.

I call this section "Reading Reality" in order to sharpen the contrast with the last section, "Reading Fantasy." In fact reality does not hold sway here to anything like the extent that fantasy dominated the bride-price story. Fantasy is alive and well in these accounts of David with the Philistines, in the text and in existing interpretations of it, but it is locked in bitter battle with a realistic reading. If it is possible to speak of a winner, it is reality that wins—or perhaps reality wins with a bit of a nudge from me.

Where can we begin so as to get a handle on the issues? I have not been able to make sense of David's first visit to Achish when I read it by itself,[31] so I prefer to read first the account of his second visit, in the hope that this will clarify the options for reading the first visit. It is not that the second visit is without its obscurities, but it is unarguably a story of David's practicing to deceive, and he weaves a tangled web. Whom does he deceive, and how? Does he perhaps deceive himself?

---

[31] "21:11-16 is very concise and leaves very much open" (J. P. Fokkelman, *The Crossing Fates [I Sam. 13–31 & II Sam. 1]. Narrative Art and Poetry in the Books of Samuel, Volume II* [Assen/Maastricht: Van Gorcum, 1986] 362).

1 Samuel 27:8-12 seems at first to provide a solid basis for understanding. It suggests that David, obliged to be absent from Israel, does not waver in his allegiance to his own people. He uses all his wits not only to keep out of trouble during his enforced absence but even to advance his reputation at home.

Such a view would seem to imply, however, that the lords of the Philistines are right: had David taken part in the battle he would have gone over to the Israelites (ch. 29). This we can never know, and to second guess what might have happened under circumstances not narrated is to become ourselves enmeshed in David's tangled web. If David had changed sides, would Israel then have won? What, in that case, would have been David's position, or Saul's? No plausible story emerges.

"Nothing better"? I believe that the text works to repress a story in which David intends, at least from 27:1, to switch his allegiance permanently to the Philistines. Such a story is incompatible with the main current in the larger narrative, that of David's inevitable rise to kingship. It fits well, though, with certain undercurrents in the larger narrative. Stage one of my strategy will be to undermine attempts at a straightforward reading. Stage two will be to establish a basis for my counterreading. Stage three will be to raise the question of what opposed ideologies generate these opposed ways of reading the text.

The place to begin, I believe, is 27:1. In this verse David speaks in *internal monologue:* "David said in his heart" (NRSV) or, more naturally, "thought to himself." In internal monologue one tells the truth. David truly thinks that there is "nothing better for me than to escape to the land of the Philistines," and he acts accordingly.

Of course he may be wrong in his assessment, or he may change his mind later. We must also remember that we have only the narrator's word for it that this *is* what David thought to himself, and we have often seen that the narrator's view does not always make for a coherent reading. Still, this is what the narrator—the same narrator who tells of David's inevitable rise to kingship—understands David truly to think about his situation at this moment in the story.

This observation has consequences. Suppose we sense a contradiction between 27:1 and 27:5-12 (David's deceit of Achish). If we are to find coherence in the story we must resolve the contradiction, and if v. 1 records David's true intention we must resolve the contradiction in favor of this verse. Unless we can discover a reason to think that David changes his mind between v. 1 and v. 5 we must bring vv. 5-12 into line with v. 1, not the other way around.

David's words to himself in 27:1 come at an odd moment. He has just heard from Saul's mouth a speech of total contrition and an invitation to return: "Come back, my son David, for I will never harm you again . . . I have been a fool, and have made a great mistake" (26:21). From his youth up, when he was anointed, David has been bombarded with promises and reassurances of his future kingship, and these have been coming thick and fast in the chapters just before 27: from the heir to the throne (23:17), from Abigail (25:30), from Saul himself (24:20).

Suppose that David accepts Saul's invitation. We can imagine a story in which Saul and his family are thoroughly reconciled to the transition of power: "Come back to court as the acknowledged heir apparent." Such a story fits perfectly, of course, into the surrogacy pattern (note again Saul's "my son David"). This story could even include the ongoing conflict between David and Saul's house in 2 Samuel: perhaps not all of Saul's family accepts the abdication by Saul and Jonathan. This story could dispose of the Philistines as easily as 2 Samuel in fact will dispose of them (with more plausibility, if Israel's forces were united).

But this narrative way is not taken. The David of 27:1 places no confidence in Saul's words. He takes them to mean the exact opposite of what they say. He places no reliance even on the manifold promises of kingship. Perhaps the canny David anticipates that the manic-depressive Saul will turn back to his murderous mood, or, as I suggested earlier, perhaps the deep-structural dynamics of the Saul-David relationship preclude a narrative reconciliation [90–93].

Suppose, as a second narrative option, that David decides to wait it out until Saul dies or some other decisive event occurs. He might retire to Moab, where he has lodged his parents for safety (22:3-5). This would generate a story in which David watches the war between Saul and the Philistines from a safe distance, confident, probably, of a Philistine victory and intending to gather his forces thereafter.

Any of these stories would be considerably simpler than the one we have. By having David take refuge in Philistia the narrator forces the Philistines into a peculiar double narrative role. They must bring about the death of Saul and his sons and they must provide David with a refuge from Saul for the last crucial part of Saul's life.

The first role is simple enough, and in fact it is the same in all the scenarios I have considered. It *must* be the Philistines who dispose of Saul, perhaps to rule out any thought that David did so himself. The urgency of this plot function is shown by the Philistines' amazing disappearance after they have done the job. And the narrative is willing to pay a price for its insistence on this function: David's coming to power by the agency of foreigners takes some of the shine from the theme of David as king through divine promise and his ability to win every heart.

But why the second plot function? Why flee to Philistia and not to Moab or elsewhere? The narrative is in a jam from which it tries to escape by suggesting that David was knowingly playing a deceptive game with the Philistines. But this will not work at all, for a wide range of reasons.

First, what on earth can be the basis of David's confidence that he will be able to defeat the triumphant Philistines after Saul is dead? Perhaps he relies on all those promises of future kingship. But why could he not rely on them when Saul invited him back to court? As I have argued, this is a question the text cannot answer at all. It just cuts the knot by "forgetting" the Philistines in 2 Samuel.

Second, even on the most generous allowance for the possibility that David is pursuing a cynical strategy, he advances the Philistine cause. He removes from Saul's and Israel's side in the warfare the considerable force that he personally commands.

Third, and most important, David adopts a strategy in which the vital decisions are out of his hands. There is simply no way he can strategize, however cynically, about whether to be part of the battle. Even if he intends, once in the battle, to join Saul's side he makes his ability to do so dependent on Philistine decisions (and loses the gamble). He takes other risks too. What if Achish does not grant his request to move away from Gath (27:5)? What if Achish repulses him altogether, or worse? (In 21:12 David is in fear of Achish.) For all its attempts to cling to YHWH's faithfulness and/or David's cleverness, the text, when it sends David over to the Philistines, gives power over the narrative outcome to them.

Finally, what is the point of it all? What is to be gained by such a complex textual strategy? Why *must* David seek refuge with the very foreigners who *must* kill Saul? I have identified much easier narrative means that could have been adopted to the same end.

These problems with conventional readings encourage me in my insistence that David, in 27:1, believes that going over to the Philistines is the *best* available option. The one who so carefully avoided the dangerous desire for the Other (Philistine or female) now sincerely offers his service to the Philistines. Speaking the truth to himself in a narrative world of options, he sees "nothing better."

Is this decision so surprising? Consider David's options within the text's realistic view of the Philistines. He is a proven soldier; he commands a force that will give him bargaining power anywhere. He has fallen out with Israel's king, whose star he sees waning. Why not offer his services to the coming power? Who knows what rewards they may offer for loyal service after he has helped them get rid of Saul?—or what rewards he may be in a position to demand when he has further established himself? Might not this even be a more plausible way to the throne of Israel—as a king in some sort of treaty with the Philistines—than the one the text finally opts for?

David, in this reading, goes over to Achish king of Gath intending to serve him even against Saul. This is his "best case scenario." Nothing better! It remains to consider how such a reading can explain the text at a more detailed level than I have attempted thus far, and to this task I now turn.

David's second sojourn with the Philistines. Having made his decision in 27:1, David takes his considerable following (two wives and six hundred men with their families) to Gath. "David stayed with Achish" (27:3) suggests the passage of some significant time. David's decision is immediately justified at one level, since Saul ceases to pursue him (v. 4; cf. v. 1).

In the remainder of ch. 27 the narrative in its fantasy mode works hard to undermine the impression that David's decision, and his move, are permanent. We learn that David's stay in Philistia is quite brief: sixteen months (v. 7). This casts doubt on the expectation created by v. 1. The placement of this time notice is odd, but it presumably refers to all the time spent in Gath *and* Ziklag (through 2 Samuel 2). In v. 6 the narrator reminds us, by means of a learned aside about the history of Ziklag, that David is still on track to become king of Judah.

Above all the story wants to convince us that David followed a deliberate strategy while in Philistia. He was biding his time and being extremely careful to do nothing to hurt his reputation in Israel. To this end he systematically deceived Achish, on whose gullibility the story's credibility depends. Stage one of David's deceit consists of getting out of Achish's immediate reach. He gives no real explanation why he should live away from the capital: his words vaguely express humility (v. 5). He has his reasons, which will immediately become clear, and he is keeping them from Achish. Achish gives David control of Ziklag, an outlying Philistine town.

Stage two involves lying to Achish directly. David spends his time in Ziklag attacking tribes on the fringes of the southern desert (v. 8) but he tells Achish that it is Israelite groups he is attacking (v. 10). The narrator seems not to scruple over the wholesale slaughter in which David must indulge in order to cover his tracks. He displays, however, some anxiety about his story through certain unnecessary touches: giving the information about the slaughter twice (vv. 9, 11), reassuring us that this was all David *ever* did while in Philistia (v. 11). The narrator claims that Achish is duly taken in: Achish is convinced that David has burned his boats and is now bound to his service (v. 12).

Is Achish really deceived? It is easy to tell a story in which he is not. When he receives David's service he knows he has a tiger by the tail, for David's men constitute a formidable fighting force. Such a retinue makes David more valuable to him as a vassal, but he does not necessarily want them on his doorstep. Perhaps having them in Ziklag rather than Gath seems to Achish a welcome breathing space. In this reading the move to Ziklag might even be suggested by Achish.

As to David's elaborate deceit while in Ziklag, it is hard to believe that a king's spy system would not be on top of the situation. Achish knows what is going on. David's banditry does no more harm to Philistine than it does to Israelite interests. The Philistines will be quite content to have the desert fringe tribes thinned out, and Achish keeps getting the booty, wherever it may happen to come from (v. 9). Perhaps Achish understands that David's loyalty is a precious but fragile flower and wants to play him along gently.

But even if such a reading is plausible, you may say, is it necessary or even useful? Why not suspend our disbelief and go along with the text's picture of deceitful David and gullible Achish? I would reply to this in two ways. First I would rest on my earlier argumentation, culminating in my reading of 27:1. David's words in this verse constitute a fundamental problem for the straightforward reading. If David had spoken them to *Achish* as part of his strategy of deceit they would fit perfectly with the rest of the chapter. But he spoke them *to himself.* If he changed his mind later, why did the text omit to inform us of this? Given this omission, can we any longer talk of a "straightforward" reading?

Second, the tension in ch. 27 is in continuity with all that I have proposed in this chapter about alternative depictions of the Philistines in the registers of fantasy and realism. The text invites reading in both of these two registers, and this constitutes a conflict within the text itself. Against the realistic indication of 27:1, vv. 5-12 want to revert to the fantasy story. I am impressed by the ways in which a reading in each mode can maintain its own logic, down to details. The more gullible Achish is, the more David would want to (pretend to) serve him in the fantasy story but the less he would want to in reality. In fantasy kings can be hoodwinked by simple strategies, but not in the real world. And only in fantasy is it all right to wipe out large numbers of people simply to achieve narrative goals (vv. 9, 11; cf. for example 18:27).

The transactions in 28:1-2 and ch. 29 are firmly in the register of reality. The Philistines disagree among themselves about David. The very possibility of their disagreement, I have argued, is a real world element since it rules out the fantasy representation of the Philistines as an undifferentiated herd.

Achish wants David, whom he has now permanently attached to himself (28:1-2), to fight on the Philistine side against Israel. But the lords of the Philistines are not prepared to allow this.[32] The difference is really over a point of interpretation. The lords have heard a troubling Israelite jingle that goes "Saul has killed his thousands, but David his ten thousands" (29:5). These words of Israel's women (18:7) have traveled far. Ten thousands of whom? Philistines, of course. The only message the lords of the Philistines can hear in this jingle is: David is very bad news for Philistines. (Perhaps the event recounted in 23:1-5 confirms this message.) Achish, who knows David personally, hears a different message in the words: David is a formidable warrior whom it is good to have on one's own side. But the lords share the view that Achish has been gullible in his dealings with David. They apparently have power to impose their will on Achish, for he must reluctantly dismiss a protesting David (29:6-11).

Before this disagreement among the Philistines the fantasy reading was at its wits' end. It retains plausibility only thanks to the Philistine lords. David has agreed to fight on the Philistine side (28:2). The words he uses, "Then you shall know what your servant will do," are of course a little trick of the narrator to keep the story's options open. But will there be any options, once David is in the battle, that will enable an acceptable story to be told? I have argued not. The fantasy reading can only bite its nails until relief comes from the Philistine lords. David will not have to fight. David's inevitable rise to kingship is left intact. Achish's gullibility is left intact. But it has to be admitted that those other Philistines are smart people!

Are they, though? What if the David they send home is one who has truly thrown in his lot with them?—or one whose still uncertain mind would have been made up in the battle itself, that his best course lay in loyalty to the Philistines? We will never know, for the realistic story of David and the Philistines ends with 1 Samuel. All that remains for the lords of the Philistines is a victory brief and hollow, whose fruits, when the story gets fully back into fantasy mode in 2 Samuel, will be instantly lost.

Too late the lords will discover that Achish was no fool. He was a Philistine pragmatist like the priests and diviners of ch. 6. Just as the priests and diviners put YHWH to the test, so Achish wanted to put David to the test, and he rated Philistine power high enough that he saw no great danger in doing so. If only the lords had listened! David might

---

[32] It is unclear whether the people who confront Achish are the same as "the lords of the Philistines" in chs. 5–6. The same word is used in 29:2, 6, 7, but in vv. 3, 4, 9 a different word is used (NRSV "commanders"). There seems to be no point to this difference and Achish apparently uses the words interchangeably.

then have pursued a glorious Philistine career and attained the goals he envisaged in 27:1. Who is to say that, rather than being a gullible idiot needing to be corrected by wiser heads, Achish was not the most far-sighted of Philistines, who would have prevented his people's defeat by Israel had he not been surrounded by smart people?[33]

David's first sojourn with the Philistines. David, as we have noted, came once before to Achish (21:10-15). He came for refuge from Saul. He came alone, having at that time neither household nor retinue.[34] The text is not easy to understand. My intention here is to see if my findings from chs. 27–29 help me to read ch. 21.

The reading that seems to be invited is one in which David wants to enter Achish's service but to do so incognito. Achish's servants blow his cover (21:10-11). Gullible Achish being put right by others makes us think, naturally, of ch. 29, and alerts us that we are in fantasy mode. Now that Achish knows who he is, David becomes afraid and pretends to be a madman (vv. 12-13). Gullible Achish believes this farce (vv. 14-15).

Such a reading is not without problems even in its own terms. Why is it to Philistia that David goes for refuge, with Philistine blood on his hands? (What has he done with the telltale sword of Goliath from v. 9?) He seems to assume that his life will be forfeit if his identity becomes known. But does he really think he can avoid exposure? What, even if all should go well, are his long-term intentions? The later story in chs. 27–29 will provide answers to such questions, but this first story provides none.

These questions relate to the general framework of the story. Others arise as we read into it. The clever servants are not so clever if they expose David's identity to Achish in David's own presence; but how, otherwise, does David know that he has been unmasked (v. 12)? And why would Achish, if he thought of David as the most dangerous of enemies, let him go, mad or sane? Achish gives no indication of coming to terms one way or another with the exposure of David's identity. He acts neither to do away with a powerful enemy nor to gain a

---

[33] Most surprisingly, Achish is a king. The surprise is because no other Philistine king is mentioned in Judges or 1 Samuel. But Achish cannot be a real king, certainly not an absolute monarch. At the crucial moment he must submit to the will of the "lords." (It is unclear if he is one of their number.) Is there anything that this might imply about kingship, about Israel's move toward it? If Achish had been a real king would Israel ever have had King David? These waters become too murky even for me, but you may care to swim in them some more!

[34] I assume that David's "young men" in the preceding story (vv. 4-5) are a figment invented to deceive the priest Ahimelech. There is nothing in the account of his time with Achish to suggest he was accompanied.

powerful servant. Even the circumstances of David's departure are made ambiguous: he "left there and escaped" (22:1). Has he escaped by the skin of his teeth by his clever ruse or simply decided to go away because whatever he came to do has become impossible?

I cannot escape the impression that this story exists simply to set up Achish as a gullible character so that we will read him that way in the later, much more critical sequence. This story does not really know why David seeks refuge with a Philistine. It relies on the reader getting caught up in a sort of Scarlet Pimpernel excitement over the hero passing incognito in the very palace of the enemy, and not asking.

But once again an alternative reading in the realistic mode beckons. As in ch. 29, Philistine attitudes in this story turn on the interpretation of the jingle about Saul's thousands and David's ten thousands (the servants quote it in 21:11). The impression on which the fantasy story relies is that any Philistine who knew who David was would want to kill him. But why should not shrewd Achish see the situation as already one of opportunity? Perhaps he even knows who David is before the servants tell him. The question he will certainly ask himself is, why has David come? For refuge from Saul, but perhaps also to find a new master. What service such a one would be capable of rendering!

It does not work out because David panics and makes a fool of himself. He is not confident of his position; he has not yet thought the thing through (27:1!). He could have put his situation before Achish from the beginning, or he could have done so after being "exposed." He might have persuaded Achish (who might have needed little persuading) that he was estranged from Saul and Israel and sincerely wanted to enter Achish's service. Instead he behaves like a fool (as well as a madman). Achish has no use for such a one yet, but perhaps he already sees the future potential. It perhaps seems quite natural to a Philistine king that an ambitious young Israelite would prefer the prospect of leadership in imperial Philistia to uncertain power in defeated Israel. Let David go for now and establish himself more firmly (it is interesting that David begins to build his fighting force directly after this incident). Let him divide Israel even further. Later he may become a real prize.

Conclusion: Reality Ascendant

The Philistines in 1 Samuel: Concluding comments. If 1 Samuel stages a long battle between Israelites and Philistines it also stages a battle between two views of the Philistines. If in the first battle the

Philistines win, in the second reality wins (though only momentarily in both cases). These two victories are one and the same.

One side of Israel's view of the Philistines is a fantasy of difference and superiority. It entrenches itself in the book of Judges and in the middle section of 1 Samuel. A history of ordinary warfare with a troublesome but ordinary neighbor is turned into a myth whereby the hero David can establish the Israelite state only by the absolute suppression of the Philistine Other. To this end all the resources of fantasy are marshaled.

Yet Israel has another, deeper memory of the Philistines. It recalls a neighbor with whom its ancient ancestors in Genesis had some tiffs that were resolved into a reasonably comfortable coexistence. The threat that this memory poses to the myth of Philistine otherness is clearly shown in the efforts of the rabbis and of the LXX translators to deny that the Philistines in Genesis were even the same people as in Judges and Samuel [227].

In 1 Samuel this neighbor has grown very great. 1 Samuel knows, or comes to know, that the Philistines are in the ascendant. It knows the answer to the question once posed to Samson, which I have borrowed as the title of this part of my book: "Do you not know that the Philistines are rulers over us?" (Judg 15:11). Yes, we know it! Israel in 1 Samuel is increasingly under foreign dominance, exploitation, and occupation, and this is the real political context for its move to "kingship." The relentless Philistine advance toward the end of the book renders the earlier stories of individual Israelite heroes merely pathetic. If, as I have suggested, even Israel's great king begins at the end of 1 Samuel to merge his identity with that of the dominant Philistines, how can Israel hold on to its sense of utter difference?

This narrative work on the Philistines defines 1 Samuel as surely, I would claim, as does the surrogacy pattern of government. From the beginning of the book the text works to supplant the fantasized view of the Philistine enemy in favor of a more realistic view, and the book ends at the precise moment when this work is complete. 1 Samuel is the Book of the Philistine Ascendancy.

Back to the future: The modern discourses. In the development of both the German and the English discourses of the Philistines it is biblical *fantasy* that is most at work. On the German side Samson holds center stage, while Arnold moves more to Goliath. The alternative realistic view in the Bible is scarcely at work on the surface of these discourses. Brentano, merely for sake of completeness, comments on the Philistines in Genesis, but since he can find little negative to say about them he lamely concludes that this was their "best period."[35]

---

[35] Brentano, "Der Philister" 204.

It seems safe to say that if Genesis and the beginning and end of 1 Samuel were our only sources for the Philistines their name would never have become a modern cultural slur. It is nonetheless interesting (though here I can only sketch the process) to read back the realistic view of the Philistines into the modern discourses. This view can be linked to all the symptoms we found of anxiety over identity and difference. The conflict between Arnold's elite and the emergent English middle class over the "hearts and minds" of the lower classes seems entirely like a territorial dispute between claimants who are equal in principle. To fantasize this struggle Arnold works desperately hard, and in this work the biblical Philistines are his main tool. But neither he nor Brentano is ultimately confident of his difference from the Philistines, even though they both urgently need this sense of difference in order to establish their own position.

Moreover, like Israel in 1 Samuel these modern despisers of the Philistines are engaged in a losing battle. Both German Romantics and classically trained English intellectuals try to mythicize a tide they cannot stem, whose flood we in many ways see still with us. The growth of the English industrial middle class, which Arnold tried vainly to impede, led through various vicissitudes to the social democratic state of the period after World War II. In this period I was given access to educational opportunity that someone of my class would not previously have enjoyed. I owe much to the Philistines!

Part V

COMING TO TERMS WITH
1 SAMUEL

PROLOGUE

1 Samuel has held me captive. For more than two decades I have been trying to write my way out of this text, but have really only written myself farther in. Whenever I have felt ready to move on, 1 Samuel has bought some more hours of my time to continue the analysis. But the fact that you are reading this means that I have at some level terminated the analysis and written it up. What do I take with me from this engagement; what do I have to offer to my patient reader? As I *get out* of 1 Samuel, escape its toils, what do I *get out* of it at the level of meaning?

Not, certainly, an "answer." It would be the worst of taste as well as the worst of scholarship to present a text so rich in contradiction in a way that claims finally to be beyond contradiction. What I shall try to do in conclusion is to present the contradictions in some new light or to move them to some new level.

In three major sections of this book (Parts II to IV) I have dealt with the categories of class, gender, and race. In each case we have seen 1 Samuel negotiating issues of otherness and difference, but the dynamics have proved different in each case. The category of *race* has provided a typical example of how a text deconstructs itself. Deconstruction teaches us that contradictions emerge in a text at the points where the mindset generating the text tries to establish its difference from its Other. Israel's sense of identity depends on its difference from the Philistines, but this difference becomes more problematic the more it is affirmed.

Something quite different occurs with the category of *gender*. In an important sense this is *our* concern, a product of our interests rather than the text's. The producers of 1 Samuel, I suggest, have no such conscious investment in establishing a particular relationship between women and men as they have for Israelites and Philistines. They mostly *assume* a relationship within the framework of a routine patriarchy. But this does not diminish the importance of the observations about gender that we—as trained and committed readers—are able to make. These observations probe the "unconscious" of the text. Some of the women of 1 Samuel threaten the boundaries patriarchy tries to set. Hannah does so, and perhaps the Medium of Endor (about whom I still have a good deal to say) does so even more.

The category of *class* provides a different case again. The text is intensely concerned with the issue that underlies this category, the issue of government and how government determines the lives of people, but it operates without the tools of class analysis. By this I do not mean merely that it lacks *our* tools (Marxist or otherwise). I mean also that it makes little use of the tools we know from other parts of the Bible (Deuteronomy, some of the prophets) to have been available to Israel. Class differs from race and gender in another important respect. Although each of these three categories manifests itself mainly in terms of a binary opposition (Israelite/foreigner, male/female, judgeship/kingship) the text does not automatically identify itself with either term of the opposition judgeship/kingship. Both systems lie in the distant past. (I have suggested that this is one reason why 1 Samuel mysteriously evokes a third system of government that I have called surrogacy.)

The categories of class, gender, and race have entered our discussion not in separation but in increasingly complex interaction with each other. Elements from each, and from all in combination, will reappear in new and unexpected ways in this final part.

It has been my particular concern to show how the very creation of 1 Samuel as a "book," the determination of its beginning and end, is caught up in the negotiation of the contradictions the text addresses. I have treated at some length the beginning of 1 Samuel (and the significance of Ruth), and will not have much more to say about this. But the issues at the end of 1 Samuel will need some more pulling together. As to government, the end of the book shows Israel kingless and David in the most ambiguous situation vis-à-vis the kingship. As to race, the Philistines play a startlingly different and diminished role in 2 Samuel as against 1 Samuel. As to gender, the powerful figure of Hannah at the beginning of the book is balanced at the end by one no less powerful, the Medium of Endor. It remains to ask how these separate elements may be connected in some sort of total view of the ending of 1 Samuel.

In the interest of maintaining the tension and contradiction I offer not one "total" reading of 1 Samuel, but two. To maximize the contrast I call them "tragic" (Chapter 11) and "comic" (Chapter 12), and this will do as a generalization, but you will find the tragic not wholly tragic, and the comic not wholly comic. Indeed, someone whose perspective differed from mine might be inclined to reverse the two terms!

In fact this contrast is an apples and oranges affair, since both my methods and my aims are very different in the two chapters. In Chapter 11, starting from the frequent designation of Saul as a tragic figure, I suggest that 1 Samuel is a tragic book, the focus of Israel's sense of a past irremediably lost [19–20]. The Other with which I confront 1 Samuel in this chapter is the literary, artistic, and philosophical tradition of the West. I read Israel's and 1 Samuel's tragedy intertextually through the lenses of other texts, modern and postmodern, that are shaped (as no western text can avoid being) by the Bible.

The Other with which I confront 1 Samuel in Chapter 12 is the variety of methods that have recently been used to interpret it and the rest of the Bible, the methods I reviewed in Chapter 1. My intention here is to turn inside out the notion that the Bible (like other books, but perhaps more so) determines the methods that can or ought to be applied to it. The consequence of this notion has most often been to authorize methods that produce orthodox and conservative results. If the Bible is read in orthodox ways it is found to authorize orthodox methods. I shall show that if the Bible is read subversively it is found to authorize subversive critical methods.

These linkages are examples of what I have called "transference," the reproduction in the interpretation of the text of the dynamics in the text itself [23–24], and transference provides my entire methodological framework in this final chapter. For this reason I begin the chapter with a personal, and for a long time unconscious, experience of 1 Samuel that I now believe to be the origin of my obsessive attention to this book. This experience has enabled me to discern dimensions of meaning in 1 Samuel that I would not otherwise have seen. So the work of reading has had for me a happy ending, and I hope also for you, if in any way I am able to broaden your horizons of biblical engagement. It is in this sense that Chapter 12 is "a comic reading of 1 Samuel."

Chapter 11

THE DEAD FATHER:
A TRAGIC READING OF 1 SAMUEL

In this chapter I shall explore the nature of the tragedy in 1 Samuel and why this book stands in a special relation to tragedy. I shall take two main approaches. First I shall summarize my view of the creation of the Deuteronomic History and 1 Samuel and relate the tragedy *in* the book with the tragedy in the circumstances of its creation. Then I shall use four intertexts to try to tease out some dimensions of this tragedy.

The Tragedy of King Saul

Exum's view of Saul as a tragic figure. It is a commonplace of biblical scholarship that if the Bible has a figure comparable to the tragic heroes of Greek drama that figure is King Saul. In the most recent and, for me, the best treatment of biblical tragedy J. Cheryl Exum in principle accepts this standard view.[1] Contrasting Saul with other characters who in some measure present tragic dimensions, especially Samson, she suggests that only Saul[2] can be called a fully developed tragic character.

Drawing on Greek, Shakespearean, and modern tragedy Exum is guided not by any tight generic definition but by "tragic vision," a cluster of characteristics of which the essential are "hostile transcendence," human guilt, and the human struggle against fate. The tragic hero *does* bear guilt, but experiences, because of the ambiguity or outright enmity

---

[1] *Tragedy and Biblical Narrative: Arrows of the Almighty* (Cambridge: Cambridge University Press, 1992). Unattributed page references in this section are to this book.

[2] And Job, whom she excludes because she is treating only narrative parts of the Bible.

of transcendent forces, a fate out of proportion to the guilt. Against this fate the hero hopelessly struggles. Exum rejects the common notion that biblical tragedy is impossible because the Bible's God is just. The Bible often presents divine involvement in human affairs that is not, by any comprehensible standards, on the side of justice (pp. 1–15).

Saul fits this picture, for he is certainly presented as in some way guilty. Wherein his fault lies in 1 Samuel 13, the first account of his rejection, is not clear. (He was instructed to wait seven days for Samuel's arrival, and did so—but he still did not wait long enough!) Clearer is his guilt in failing to kill the Amalekites in ch. 15, though even here he protests his essential obedience with great conviction. His guilt in seeking the life of David or in killing the priests (1 Samuel 22) is unambiguous.

Still, it is impossible, and this is the tragic point, to explain Saul's fate in terms of his guilt alone. YHWH's treatment of Saul is at best ambivalent. YHWH promises him victory over the Philistines but fails to deliver it. Saul strives to do YHWH's will as best he sees it but can never get YHWH to answer his appeals. His descent into failure and madness is marked by frustration: he is doomed always to do the wrong thing. He is guilty but not wicked. His punishment is out of proportion to his guilt, and forgiveness is mysteriously withheld from him. Though it does not work out in any automatic way, the reader knows that his fate is predestined (pp. 16–42).

The tragic dimension of a text is not, for Exum, confined to the tragic hero. *Events* may also be called tragic, and so may characters who, though they do not fit the definition of the tragic hero, are caught up in tragic events (Jephthah is a particularly good example: pp. 45–69). In the Bible, Exum claims, women are particularly easily cast as tragic victims (p. 12). She extends her analysis of the tragic along these lines in two chapters that deal with the fates of the houses of Saul and David. Beginning with Saul's own children, Jonathan and Michal, the fate of everyone connected with his house is determined by the need for the divine rejection of Saul himself to be carried through to its conclusion (pp. 70–119). That Jonathan, Michal, Abner, or Ishbosheth might be saved through their attachment to David is built up as a possibility only to be in each instance rejected. In the last and perhaps most poignant stage of the working out of the curse, in 2 Samuel 21, the most that Rizpah can do (shades of Antigone) is to secure burial for Saul's last male descendants, while the deity withholds comment on this practice of human sacrifice (pp. 109–119).[3]

---

[3] Of great interest, but going beyond my purpose here, is Exum's contrasting treatment of the house of David. David himself is by no means a tragic character,

Exum's treatment of tragedy, and of the tragic Saul, is of profound value for what I want to say in this chapter. Her sophisticated literary method is compatible with my own. I admire her concern for "the repressed and unconscious dimension of texts" (p. 13) and her resistance to facile generalizations about the Bible. Perhaps of most importance to me methodologically is her idea of a "tragic reading" of a text. This moves "tragedy" out of the often sterile definition of genre and into the area of a radical reader-response criticism. Tragedy becomes a tool for reading texts rather than a label to be attached to certain texts. Exum also exemplifies the issue-sensitive, political style of scholarship I have advocated and tried to practice in this book.

My only problem with Exum's account follows from what I said earlier about plot and character in biblical narrative [6–7]. I see the development of character as circumscribed by the necessities of plot. It seems to me, therefore, that Exum's approach of dealing first with tragic characters and later with tragic events needs to be reversed. At the very end of her book she suggests that the entire Deuteronomic History (from which she has taken all her examples) is "the tragedy of the nation" (p. 180). I fully agree. But such a recognition leads me to ask: what does it do to the tragic dimensions of *characters* that they belong to a tragic *story* that covers very much more than their lifetime?[4] For example, if "YHWH has an ambivalent attitude toward kingship" (p. 35), must this fact not be basic to the working out of his "hostile transcendence" toward any particular king?

Why, in the long tragedy of Israel's history, is it precisely Saul who is the uniquely tragic character? In what follows I shall suggest an answer to this. 1 Samuel, I believe, lies at the center of a tragic sense of Israel's past in the Deuteronomic History precisely because it is the book that tells of the greatest tragedy, the transition to kingship, the abandonment of Israel's premonarchical ideal [70–76]. Of necessity this tragedy is expressed in the character of Israel's first king. It is in the plot that the tragedy is primarily to be sought, and only secondarily in Saul the character.

---

yet "there is no question the *story* is a tragic story." There flow from David's sin the deaths of his own children and other consequences far beyond (pp. 120–149; quotation on p. 121).

[4] The question deserves theoretical discussion going well beyond the Bible. Exum mentions the tension between the *Iliad* as the tragedy of Hector and as a "part of epic cycle that keeps on going" into the *Odyssey* (p. 156). Another example is Shakespeare's sequence of historical plays, whose tragic ingredient Exum also mentions (pp. 3, 154).

Samuel as a dead father to Saul. 1 Samuel is, I have suggested, very precisely "the Book of Samuel and Saul," and the transition from one to the other is the book's main story [110–111]. This transition is at the same time Israel's transition from one form of government to another, from judgeship to kingship. In Samuel's relationship to Saul kingship is born out of judgeship; or perhaps we had better say, using the conceptuality of the surrogacy system, that kingship is "adopted" by judgeship.

For those for whom 1 Samuel is part of a sacred history this close relationship between Samuel and Saul creates a comforting sense of historical continuity between judgeship and kingship. But in my reading this comfort is thoroughly undermined by Samuel's deadness. Even before Saul appears Samuel ought according to the logic of judgeship to be dead. Since it is so important I summarize and somewhat extend the evidence for Samuel as a dead person living on [58–59, 69–70, 77].

First, his death is fully staged on two separate occasions. In ch. 7 he is presented as reaching the appropriate end of a judge's life. Having established external peace and internal justice, he judges Israel "all the days of his life." According to the pattern of the other judge cycles he should now "die and be buried." But he lives on. Again in ch. 12 he is presented as coming to the end of the life of one of the great ones of Israel. Like Jacob, like Moses, like Joshua he delivers a long valedictory speech. Now he should like them be "gathered to his fathers." But he lives on.

Second, things happen in Samuel's subsequent lifetime that we have been told will not happen. 1 Samuel 7:13 tells us that the Philistines leave Israelite territory and that they will create no further trouble "all the days of Samuel." Yet they are back in force by ch. 13, and 9:16 suggests they never left. The statement that "Samuel judged Israel all the days of his life" (7:15) implies paramount leadership and is not compatible with the simultaneous reign of a king.

Third, when Samuel does finally literally die the notices of the event (25:1, 28:3) are extraordinarily brief for a figure of such immense stature. This makes better sense if he did his real dying earlier, with proper fanfare.

Fourth, Samuel does not stay dead. He briefly returns to life when Saul summons him through the Medium of Endor in ch. 28. Is it mere coincidence that the figure who has shown a unique reluctance to die, who has twice survived his "logical" death, should be the only figure in the Jewish Bible to survive as a character after his actual death?

Finally, it is worth adding one other aspect of Samuel's survival, though at a quite different level. Most canonical traditions, by giving the name "Samuel" to a book or books, bring the ongoing story almost as far as the death of David under the aegis of Samuel.

Samuel's quasi-deaths in chs. 7 and 12, and his living on thereafter express views of Israel's past that are contrary, even incompatible. The quasi-deaths are Samuel's death *as a judge*, which is also the death of judgeship. For monarchy to begin, judgeship must end. These forms of government are in polar opposition. Kingship can establish itself only by killing judgeship. This, to borrow the terms I used in the last chapter, would be the "reality" view. Samuel's living on expresses the alternative view, in the register of fantasy, that kingship emerges organically out of judgeship. As supreme representative of kingship's opposite, Samuel should die before kingship begins. To enact the organic emergence of kingship out of judgeship he must survive this death.

At one level, then, Samuel is dead before Saul ever meets him. It is to a dead father that Saul must relate. It seems to me the peculiar genius of 1 Samuel that it allows this suppressed but necessary truth to break through directly to the surface in ch. 28. Even at the cost of breaking all the Deuteronomic rules about traffic with the dead, this scene must be staged. Saul *must* speak to a dead Samuel.

Perhaps he never talked with any other kind. Even in the continuity of the surrogacy relationship, even in the warmth that occasionally developed between them there is a persistent sense of Samuel as a father who is *not available* to Saul. As soon as Saul has become king Samuel comes to him later than he promised (10:8), too late to prevent tragic consequences (13:8). The past that Samuel represents, the old order, is not available when it is needed. In ch. 15 Samuel is torn in two, desperately willing to abide by Saul but not able to. The message of rejection is the only message he can bring. It is especially poignant that when Saul makes contact with the really dead Samuel, in ch. 28, Samuel's words do not differ from his words when alive—they even include direct quotation (15:28; 28:17). The dead past is fixed; its message does not change.

Saul, Israel's first king, occupies the point in the story at which a sense of historical continuity is most necessary and at the same time most impossible. This is why he *must* be a tragic figure.

The Loss of a Living Past

Wieseltier and the Jew out of time. Judaism, according to Leon Wieseltier, "is based on a revelation that is over."[5] The sense of being

---

[5] "Leviticus," in David Rosenberg, ed., *Congregation: Contemporary Writers Read the Jewish Bible* (San Diego, New York, and London: Harcourt Brace Jovanovich, 1987) 27. Unattributed page references in this section are to this article.

born "out of time" is a fairly common topic of Jewish literature but Wieseltier expresses it with particular power. "The faith of the Jew is premised upon the denial of contemporaneity with revelation" (p. 27). It is a religion that is different now from what it was in a time long gone and irrecoverable, when God spoke and acted in the world. To have a written record of that other time but not to have the time itself is the fate of the Jew. "Coming too late, the Jew detests time" (p. 27).

Judaism has provided compensation in two ways. One is the powerful development of tradition, which "holds a consolation for the loss of immediacy." The other is a form of future-directedness, messianism, which claims that "What has been lost in time will be made up in time" (p. 28). These strategies have worked, if anything, too well. For the most part "the Jew is supremely willing to wait, to live in the interim" (p. 29).

Nonetheless there is the recurrent phenomenon of the "impatient" Jew, the one who wants to experience the real religious action in her own time. "It should be possible to read the Bible not only for what it tells about tradition, but also for what it tells about experience" (p. 29). But eventually such a one finds it "hard to read [the Bible] without a feeling of metaphysical jealousy," which becomes "the characteristic emotion of the impatient Jew" (p. 30).

This religious sense of a lost past that has power over us but that in a fundamental way we cannot partake of is by no means confined to Judaism. As Wieseltier himself says, it is characteristic of the Western religions based on revelation. In Christianity it manifests itself in various means by which people try to achieve contemporaneity with Jesus. Its particularly profound expression in Judaism is no doubt related to the extreme ancientness of Judaism's time of revelation, a time of (as Wieseltier says) often embarrassing religious "primitiveness" but also of enticing mystery.

Biblical history writing as writing of loss. There is a first level of tragedy in 1 Samuel that corresponds simply to Wieseltier's sense of belatedness. The Deuteronomists already come too late, and their history expresses the loss of the very past it records.[6]

I think of the building of the canon of scripture as a process whereby Israel tries to come to terms with its existence simply by talking about its past. This is a communal self-analysis through many generations, for

---

[6] This requires an adjustment of Wieseltier's emphasis. He sees the whole Bible (with the exception of Esther) as simultaneous with the time of divine presence and activity, ignoring the long period over which the Bible developed and the consequent distance between the time of writing and the time written about.

canon-building is a *long* process.[7] Israel produces and endlessly modifies a "national text," reclaiming some bits of the national "self," suppressing others, reading the pieces in this order and that. The urgency of this canon-building lies, as Wieseltier indicates, in a sense of the loss of the past, a sense of fundamental disconnectedness from it. What has been lost is a time when relationships were different, when the presence of God was different.

Nevertheless, the Deuteronomic History is a text that at least continues to urge the past as meaningful, in a context where others expressed radically different attitudes to the past. It shares the postexilic time frame with the "Priestly" parts of the Pentateuch (P) and Ezekiel, texts that downgrade or even suppress the very same past that the History urges as meaningful.[8] It may be roughly contemporary with Qoheleth, which claims in a quasi-philosophical way that there is nothing at all to be learned from any past.[9]

Rejecting such alternatives, the Deuteronomic History tells, in a time when such people have ceased to be, of judges and kings and prophets. It claims that what the past records about such figures is of critical importance in creating the sense of identity needed to live in the present. It works from a fundamental contradiction: the past must have been good since it is our past, but it must have been bad since it gave rise to the intolerable present.

Most of all, though, it speaks out of an epistemological doubt. The History is haunted by the sense that it cannot tell the truth about the past precisely because the past is lost. Polzin, we recall, doubts whether in 1 Sam 8:11-18 Samuel is reporting accurately what God told him to

---

[7] I am very much in agreement with the recent tendency to see the Bible as a direct historical source only for the later centuries of Israel's history: e.g., Philip R. Davies, *In Search of "Ancient Israel."* JSOT.S 148 (Sheffield: Sheffield Academic Press, 1992); Niels Peter Lemche, *Ancient Israel: A New History of Israelite Society.* The Biblical Seminar 5 (Sheffield: JSOT Press, 1988).

[8] According to P the only past that defines the nature of Israel is a prehistoric, quasi-mythic past before Israel's arrival in Palestine. For example, P conceptualizes the historical Jerusalem Temple in terms of a mythic "tabernacle" (Exodus 25–27; 35–40) that Israel carried around with them in the desert. Note also the extreme denigration of Israel's past in Ezekiel 20.

[9] Frank Crüsemann is close to my point of view when he sees Qoheleth as the product of a consciousness that no longer believes that human behavior makes any difference, for good or bad. Divine guarantees of the meaningfulness of experience are no longer valid. See "The Unchangeable World" in Willy Schottroff and Wolfgang Stegemann, eds., *God of the Lowly: Socio-Historical Interpretations of the Bible* (Maryknoll, N.Y.: Orbis, 1984) 57–77.

say.[10] Writ large, this is the doubt of the historians and canon-makers. Do the voices of the past report God's word faithfully? It is a doubt so devastating that all possible means must be used to keep it from coming to the surface.

Why 1 Samuel in particular? It is surely no coincidence that the text of 1 Samuel so richly provides metaphors for the Deuteronomists' situation as I have described it. Like Samuel, Israel has lived on beyond its history, beyond its exilic "death." Like Samuel coming to meet Saul in 1 Samuel 13 the past always comes too late. Like Saul, Israel continues to call up the dead but continues to get only the same message. As Saul must make do with a dead father, so Israel lives with all the dead fathers of the past. 1 Samuel is a prototype of the first, most general level of Israel's tragedy. The book functions as a metaphor of belatedness.

However, 1 Samuel is a prototype of tragedy also at another level. It is implicated in specific ways in the shift that Wieseltier discerns between the lost primal time and the belated present. First, the immanent divine activity in the world that characterized the primal time undergoes a definite change in 1 Samuel, with ch. 12 marking the turning point. Up to that point the divine frequently irrupts into human affairs. The ark stories in 1 Samuel 4–6 are full of such divine activity, and it is found also in the divine call of Samuel, in the spirit of YHWH coming on Saul (11:6), and especially in the miracle with which YHWH responds to Samuel's prayer in 12:18. After ch. 12 there is very much less of it. After his reign really gets under way in ch. 13 Saul seems to inhabit a less God-filled world. This is part of his tragedy.[11]

Second, Wieseltier pinpoints "a reduction of divinity by textuality" as another aspect of Israel's belatedness (p. 30). In place of the living presence is put the written record, the Bible itself. The Deuteronomists substitute a *record* of the past for the real past. This is no more than a platitude: all historians must inevitably do so.[12] But it takes on special significance in regard to 1 Samuel when we consider that what makes

---

[10] *Samuel and the Deuteronomist: A Literary Study of the Deuteronomic History. Part Two: 1 Samuel* (San Francisco: Harper & Row, 1989) 82, 86–87 [64].

[11] Jerome Charyn, "I Samuel," in Rosenberg, ed., *Congregation* 98–105. Divine irruption does, of course, reappear from time to time in the Deuteronomic History, for example when Uzzah is struck dead for touching the ark (2 Sam 6:6-7) or in the conflict of Elijah with the prophets of Baal (1 Kings 18:36-39).

[12] "To write is perhaps to bring to the surface something like absent meaning" (Maurice Blanchot, *The Writing of the Disaster*, translated by Ann Smock [Lincoln: University of Nebraska Press, 1995] 41). Written in the wake of the Holocaust and Hiroshima, Blanchot's book is a profound commentary on the issues of this chapter.

the written record both possible and necessary is . . . monarchy! It is
the state system that refuses to trust the living memory and invents the
text. The coming of monarchy is the beginning of Israel's belatedness,
of its living with a text rather than with experience.

Samuel—along with Saul—marks the very point of rupture. Samuel's being dead yet still living is a parable of Israel's sense of the past
(and of the religious sense of the past in the whole western tradition).
The sharpness of this rift with the past is intolerable. The characters
Samuel and Saul, and the book 1 Samuel itself, are created to give a
sense of naturalness and continuity to the transition, to foster the illu-
sion that Israel can reach back behind the rift to the ideal that is lost.
But as we have seen, the characters and the book thus created merely
replicate in their own structures the irreducible rift.

The question of guilt. Exum is clear about the necessity in tragedy
of the element of guilt, though the guilt is never sufficient to justify the
punishment.[13] Wieseltier (in understandable reaction against a Christian
obsession with guilt) plays down the element of guilt when speaking of
the belated Jew. "Fate without sin is punishment by duration. You are
not guilty, you are merely late" (p. 30). But it seems to me that a certain
guilt does inhabit Israel's remembering of its lost past. If 1 Sam 13:8-15
is a parable of how the past always comes too late to help it is also a parable of how the past nonetheless still lays blame on the present.

Israel's sense of guilt in relation to the past comes first from the
sense that the past represents an ideal from which the present has
fallen, sets a standard that the present cannot maintain. But this guilt
has an unreal quality, since the ideal against which the present is to be
measured is an ideal that has been lost. Israel senses a standard it cannot maintain because it does not know what the standard is, because
the standard belongs to a lost past. In Blanchot's words, Israel's loss is
a "lost loss."[14] 1 Samuel 13:8-15 continues to work uncannily as a parable of this situation: Saul is convinced of his guilt though he has no
idea what it is! Israel's work of national remembering has to be done
in the presence/absence of the divine Father who was present but is
now absent, except that He remains present to make sure we get it
right, to blame us if we don't. Wieseltier is right in principle but wrong
in practice. No guilt attaches to merely being late in time, but time still
finds a way to blame us!

This false guilt serves to cloak a more real guilt that inhabits Israel's
national self-analysis, a guilt with which the Deuteronomists were out

---

[13] E.g., *Tragedy and Biblical Narrative* 40.
[14] Blanchot, *Writing of the Disaster* 41.

of touch but that we are in a better position to identify. It is guilt over the systematic exclusion of certain voices from the work of remembering. The official memory has become the domain of an elite (class), of men rather than women (gender), and of people who define themselves by a narrow ethnic purity (race). But in each case the official memory— that is, the text of the Bible—shows traces of the suppression of other voices, of the voice of the Other. It is precisely these traces that I have tried to reveal in Parts II–IV of this book. In the last chapter I shall sum up all these findings from another perspective [301–305].

H. Rider Haggard's Nada the Lily

The bulk of this chapter consists of a series of intertextual readings that draw out different aspects of the tragic sense of 1 Samuel I have been discussing. The first two intertexts are novels. I begin with a book that, like Ruth, is "female" in the sense of having as its title the name of its main woman character.

After spending a brief period in his youth as a colonial agent in Natal and the Transvaal, H. Rider Haggard returned to England and became a prolific author of romantic novels. He is best known for books like *King Solomon's Mines* and *She*, in which Englishmen undertake incredible quests into the interior of Africa. The Africans they encounter are frequently of the "noble savage" variety. I was a devotee of Haggard's books as a teenager, and they contributed greatly to my first impressions of Africa.

Nada the Lily,[15] published in 1892, though it has many of the same adventure-story trappings, is profoundly different both in intention and in formal features. It recounts, albeit in a highly romanticized way, the history of the first two Zulu emperors, Shaka (reigned 1816–1828) and Dingaan (1828–1843).

The book takes the conventional form of a story within a story. The enclosed story is the Zulu history as told by Mopo, Shaka's steward and one of his assassins. The historical elements are interwoven with a tragic story, of Haggard's own invention, of the love between Mopo's daughter Nada and Umslopogaas, whom Shaka believes to be Mopo's son but who is in fact Shaka's own son. The tragic plot at the personal level highlights the sense of tragedy in the Zulu political history. This

---

[15] H. Rider Haggard, *Nada the Lily* (London: George G. Harrap & Co., 1925). Unattributed page references in this section are to this book.

story (in sharp contrast to Haggard's better known works) includes no European characters.

The frame story (pp. 15–21, 288), on the other hand, has a European protagonist. A white man is trading in winter between Natal and Pretoria. He has two ox-wagons and a number of black hired hands. One night there is a heavy snowstorm in which the oxen stampede and are lost. In the resulting perplexity the head of the hired men makes a suggestion: "At the kraal yonder . . . lives a witch-doctor named Zweete. He is old—very old—but he has wisdom, and he can tell you where the oxen are if any man may . . ." (pp. 16–17). Professing skepticism, the white man follows this suggestion. Zweete correctly says where the oxen are. The white man is delayed for some days and during this time Zweete tells him the main story. At the beginning Zweete reveals himself as Mopo, and on the last page he dies.

Biblical analogies. This is unmistakably a retelling of the story of Saul's search for the donkeys in 1 Samuel 9–10. It follows the Bible so closely that Haggard must intend the allusion. Common to the two stories are lost animals, the consulting of a sage at the suggestion of a servant (1 Sam 9:6-10), and the sage's successful location of the animals (v. 20). In both stories the lost animals are merely a pretext for a more important agenda (in 1 Samuel the anointing, in *Nada* the telling of the Zulu history).[16]

There is, though, one complication to this parallel, and it lies in Zweete's first words to the white man: "You do not believe in me and my wisdom; why should I help you? Yet I will do it, though it is against your law, and you do wrong to ask me . . ." (p. 17). The parallel here is not to the biblical story of the donkeys but to that of the Medium of Endor: "Surely you know what Saul has done, how he has cut off the mediums and the wizards from the land. Why then are you laying a snare for my life to bring about my death?" (28:9). Though this is the only parallel to 1 Samuel 28, it is very close. It is confirmed by the reference to Zweete as a *witch*-doctor, for tradition has called the medium the Witch of Endor.

In order to tell *his* story Haggard not only alludes to the story of Samuel and Saul but neatly encompasses it by evoking the first and last times that Samuel and Saul were together. While I feel sure that Haggard's allusion to the donkeys story is deliberate, I do not imagine that all the links I shall explore between his situation and the biblical

---

[16] The parallels extend to some smaller details. In both stories it is necessary to bring an appropriate gift to the sage, and both sages know about the loss of the animals without being told.

story are consciously made. Rather, aspects of Haggard's world triggered his "biblical unconscious."

Up to a point the intertextual relations can be explored in terms of historical analogy. At the simplest level Mopo corresponds to Samuel and the Zulu kings to the first Israelite kings. Shaka transformed Zulu society quickly and violently from a relatively egalitarian traditional order to an imperialist monarchy in much the same way that historians see Saul and David as doing. Like Samuel, Mopo is a maker and breaker of kings. There are plenty of suggestions in *Nada* that Mopo, like Samuel, remains loyal to the traditional order of things. Like Samuel he lives on beyond his time.

A second set of equations is more complicated but likely brings us nearer to the heart of the matter. *Nada* itself has very little to say about black-white relations, but Haggard deals with them in a revealing way in an introduction. To understand these dynamics one must know something of the history not of the first Zulu kings but of the much later time of the frame-story (around 1880). In 1877 the British annexed the Boer republic of the Transvaal, and Haggard claims in his introduction that they did so to save the Boers from imminent massacre by the Zulu (p. 6).[17]

The sense of identity among the Boers was based on the Bible to a remarkable degree, and more on the Jewish Bible than the New Testament.[18] They saw themselves as a new Israel. Forced (as they saw it) out of the Cape Colony by British restrictions, they had set out like the Israelites on their great treks to the interior. In this Boer mythology the black inhabitants of the land were naturally assigned the role of the Canaanites whom God would thrust out before the chosen. This belief structure held up well through the middle part of the nineteenth century as the migrating Boers were able to carve out living space for themselves. But the rise of Zulu imperialism created a threat to the Boers on a different scale from that presented by the other black tribes.

Haggard's view of this political situation corresponds closely to the standard historical view of Israel's transition to kingship. Israel's old egalitarian order was adequate to deal with the threats posed by foreign nations in the period of the judges, but the Philistines constituted

---

[17] The threat was a real one, but Haggard oversimplifies the forces in play. See Edgar H. Brookes and Colin de B. Webb, *A History of Natal* (2nd ed. Pietermaritzburg: University of Natal Press, 1987) 124–135.

[18] Allister Sparks, *The Mind of South Africa* (London: Heinemann, 1990) 22–33; Donald Akenson, *God's Peoples: Covenant and Land in South Africa, Israel and Ulster* (Ithaca, N.Y.: Cornell University Press, 1992).

a new kind of enemy, highly organized militarily and necessitating central organization on Israel's part in order to resist them. Likewise, Haggard suggests, though the old Boer republican order may have been sufficient to meet old threats, the Boers' only safety in the face of the Zulu threat lies in coming under the protection of British imperialism. Haggard makes use, with only slight adaptation, of the Boers' own biblical "equations." "Israel" is now whites as a whole, perceived as sharing a common interest. The enemies of "Israel" are still the blacks, but the Zulu are a special case. Black Canaanites in general have become Zulu Philistines in particular. Racism, obviously, is an essential ingredient of the second set of equations: "Philistines" are once again marked by racial difference.

These two sets of biblical analogies (the Zulu as Israel, the whites as Israel) are, of course, entirely incompatible with each other, but this is no reason to doubt that both may be fully operational in Haggard's biblical unconscious.

The anxiety of history. These analogies, revealing as they are, do not tell the whole intertextual story. Perhaps indeed they leave the main issue untouched, namely the deep _anxiety_ Haggard betrays over his whole enterprise of telling about the past. His forcefully stated intention is to preserve a Zulu history that, he believes, will be lost if he does not tell it. He makes strong claims for the correctness of his account (pp. 9–12). He even projects his voice (from England, where he is writing) as the voice of the Zulu who (as a result of defeat in the Anglo-Zulu wars of the late 1870s) "are no more a nation" (p. 6).

This anxiety carries over into the frame story of _Nada_, the story of how Mopo told the Zulu story to the white man. Haggard describes Mopo's storytelling as follows:

> This man, ancient and withered, seemed to live again in the far past. It was the past that spoke to his listener, telling of deeds long forgotten, of deeds that are no more known (p. 18).

The hyperbole of the last sentence serves as the vehicle for an illogicality. If the things are "forgotten" and "no more known" how can Haggard write about them?

The anxiety relates in a particular way to the situation of a white man telling a black people's story. It is no accident that in the frame story a white "Saul" encounters a black "Samuel," for part of what is being recounted is the transition in Africa from black to white regimes. The most overt message is that the telling of black history must be entrusted to white people since blacks are not capable of preserving it themselves. Mopo dies at the moment he has finished telling his story.

This means that any further retelling of it, its very survival as a story, must lie in the hands of the white man. Such cultural salvage work is apparently a part of "the White Man's burden."[19]

The most extraordinary expression of this claim is found in Haggard's treatment of his character Umslopogaas. All the authorities on Zulu life and history that Haggard adduces in his preface are white: missionaries, colonial administrators, and the like. But his daughter and biographer tells us that he had an African informant—named Umslopogaas! "From him Rider heard many a tale. . . . Many of these . . . were written down . . . in . . . *Nada the Lily*."[20] It could hardly be more specific: for this very book Haggard was heavily dependent on an African source. Not only has he suppressed this fact in the preface but he has made Umslopogaas into the hero of *Nada*. Haggard's strategy is to banish his African informant from real life into fiction. It is hard to think of a more brutal way of insisting that this is a white man's telling. The white must be the teller and the black the told!

But again the frame story betrays the anxiety. Another part of the description of Mopo's storytelling is as follows:

> It is not all written in these pages, for portions may have been forgotten, or put aside as irrelevant. Neither has it been possible for the writer of it to render the full force of the Zulu idiom nor to convey a picture of the teller. For, in truth, he acted rather than told his story (p. 18).

There is a double message in these sentences. On the one hand there is a claim that the white man's story is an improvement on the original, even that the black man could not tell the story at all without white mediation. On the other hand there is a sense of something irretrievably lost in the telling.

The deepest symptom, I believe, of Haggard's anxiety is the *double* allusion to 1 Samuel and the double identity of Mopo. Mopo, as we saw, is not only Samuel but also the medium (witch) who calls up Samuel's ghost. The illicitness of Saul's consulting the medium carries over to the white man's hearing and retelling Mopo's story: "it is against your law, and you do wrong to ask me" (p. 17). The white concern with black history, if on the one hand it is a colonial duty, is on the other hand a sort of trafficking with the dead, with a past that is dead. In a single character, Mopo, the antitheses come together: Samuel the worthy representative of the glorious old order, and the medium who

[19] Rudyard Kipling, *Complete Verse* (New York: Doubleday, 1989) 321–323.
[20] Lilias Rider Haggard, *The Coat That I Left* (London: Hodder and Stoughton, 1951) 55–56.

illicitly brings Samuel back from the dead. In making the witch-doctor an essential link in his fictive chain of informants Haggard reveals his sense of a dark side to his glorious enterprise of making the Zulu past live.

It is no surprise, in light of our earlier exploration of quasi-racial dimensions in 1 Samuel [214–217], that gender enters the picture at this point. The female witch of 1 Samuel becomes a male witch in *Nada*, and despite the designation "witch" Haggard is able to preserve Mopo as a consistently positive character. The negative aspect of witchcraft he displaces onto the female, for within the body of the book he gives the most harrowing descriptions of the activity of female witches in the old Zulu society (pp. 64–74).

This, however, is only one side of the infiltration of racial by gender concerns. Haggard gives his book the name of its main female character though she is scarcely important enough to justify this. The tragic Nada is extraordinarily light-complexioned for an African.[21] The finding of whiteness in black Africa is an obsession of Haggard that in other books takes the form of the discovery of a white nation in the center of the continent. Of the Zulu in particular he speculates that they are not really black at all, but related to the Arabs.[22]

One of Haggard's strategies—among many—for dealing with his anxiety is, then, the erasure of racial difference. Cutting across his sense of the replacement of an old black order by a new white one is his desire somehow to find the white already in the black, to make the black white. Hence Mopo, his Samuel character, representative of the old order, becomes father to a child who is in effect white. Both this strategy and the opposite one—of exaggerating what is dark in darkest Africa (the "black arts" of the witches)—are projected onto the female.

Haggard's project, like the Deuteronomists', involves the burden of history, the responsibility to preserve history, and the problem of identity. His strategies bear an often uncanny resemblance to those of the Deuteronomists. It is no surprise, then, that his creative mind calls up episodes from 1 Samuel to provide his narrative framework.

---

[21] Mopo, whose daughter she is, speculates that she may have Portuguese blood on her mother's side (p. 58). Haggard's description of Nada is of an African whose features show unusual European characteristics. Publishers of the book have not been so restrained. The dustjacket of a 1963 reprint, still in circulation in 1996 through the Boston public library system, depicts her simply as a fair-skinned European!

[22] "The origin of the Zulus is a mystery . . . but it is thought they sprang from Arab stock, and many of their customs and ceremonies resemble those of the Jews" (quoted in Haggard, *The Coat That I Left* 36).

Donald Barthelme's The Dead Father

My second intertext is another novel, but of an utterly different kind: a surrealist work of the 1970s by Donald Barthelme.[23] Nevertheless, there are things it shares with Haggard as well as with Wieseltier. Anxiety in dealing with the past is neither a specifically Jewish nor a specifically religious phenomenon. It is characteristic of Western culture (as this has been shaped, of course, by the Bible).[24]

Outline of the novel. This novel shares with *Nada the Lily* the shape of a book within a book. In the framework story (which in this case, however, constitutes most of the book) the Dead Father is being transported to his burial, which happens at the very end. The Dead Father has a double existence in the story. He is a regular character who has more or less normal interactions with the other characters, but at the same time he is a massive statue-like figure that requires a large crew to haul it. These two identities come in and out of focus in an apparently random way.

The other main characters are Thomas, the leader of the expedition, and Julie, his lover. Of less importance are another pair of male and female characters, Edmund and Emma. The story is interspersed with a series of "commentary" dialogues between the two female characters that seem to have the same sort of function as the theological summaries in the Deuteronomic History [28–29].

In the course of the journey to the Dead Father's burial Thomas and Julie are given a book called "A Manual for Sons." This is the book within the book. The whole text is given, and Thomas and Julie read it.

The power of the father. The central issue of the whole book is the power of fathers. The "Manual" stands in complete contrast to the main story over this issue. In the main story the power of the Dead Father is a joke. It seems that he was once powerful: people often humor him by recalling his former greatness. But by now he is entirely under the control of the other characters. The younger generation has patiently and successfully rid itself of the father's authority and his burial will merely set the seal on this overthrow.

The "Manual for Sons," by contrast, deals with the extreme anxiety of sons before the very real power of their fathers. This power only

---

[23] *The Dead Father* (New York: Farrar, Straus and Giroux, 1975). Unattributed page references in this section are to this book.

[24] "To acknowledge how literature acts upon men—this is perhaps the ultimate wisdom of the West; perhaps in this wisdom the people of the Bible will recognize itself" (Emmanuel Levinas, quoted by Blanchot, *Writing of the Disaster* 141).

grows greater after the father's death, when "his fatherhood is returned to the All-Father, who is the sum of all dead fathers taken together" (p. 144). The father is harder for the son to deal with in
memory than in life.

> Fatherless now, you must deal with the memory of a father. Often that
> memory is more potent than the living presence of a father, is an inner
> voice, haranguing, yes-ing and no-ing—a binary code, yes no yes no yes
> no yes no, governing your every, your slightest movement, mental or
> physical. At what point do you become yourself? Never, wholly, you are
> always partly him. That privileged position in your inner ear is his last
> "perk" and no father has ever passed it by (p. 144).

Yet the son inevitably becomes a father in his turn, so that oppressive
fatherhood tends to reproduce itself for ever. Even if a new generation
revolts against it, the best that can be hoped for, according to the "Manual for Sons," is a gradual diminution of fatherhood. "Your true task, as
a son, is to reproduce every one of the enormities touched upon in this
manual, but in attenuated form. You must become your father, but a
paler, weaker version of him" (p. 145). The "Manual" ends:

> Begin by whispering, in front of a mirror, for thirty minutes a day. Then
> tie your hands behind your back for thirty minutes a day, or get some-
> one else to do this for you. Then, choose one of your most deeply held
> beliefs, such as the belief that your honors and awards have something
> to do with you, and abjure it. Friends will help you abjure it, and can be
> telephoned if you begin to backslide. You see the pattern, put it into
> practice. *Fatherhood can be, if not conquered, at least "turned down" in this
> generation*—by the combined efforts of all of us together (p. 145; empha-
> sis in original).

The point of the whole book seems to lie in the contrast between this
very guarded optimism and the high optimism of the frame story. Indeed, it is doubtful if "optimism" is at all the right word for the "Manual." If radical change depends on "the combined efforts of all of us
together" such cooperation seems unlikely to happen soon.

Is the dead weight of the past something to be simply tossed away,
with perhaps an amusing ceremonial charade, as in the frame story?
Or is it so entrenched that it will scarcely yield its hold even bit by bit,
as in the Manual? Modern consciousness seems to me to be caught in
this very bind. It confidently thinks it is casting off the past even as it
continues anxiously to repeat the past's gestures.

The women in the novel. There is a powerful feminist current in
The Dead Father. It is expressed primarily in the running commentary

provided by the long and frequent dialogues of Julie and Emma. The work of commenting on the essentially male process of replacing the father by the son is given to the women characters. And it is Julie who makes the final comment on the "Manual for Sons": she throws it in the fire after reading it. The brief interaction as she does so nicely repeats the whole novel's hesitation over the power of the dead father:

> Seems a little harsh, Julie said, when they had finished reading.
> Yes it does seem a little harsh, said Thomas.
> Or perhaps it's not harsh enough?
> It would depend on the experience of the individual making the judgment, as to whether it was judged to be too harsh or judged to be not harsh enough.
> I hate relativists, she said, and threw the book into the fire (pp. 145–146).

When I first introduced this reading of *The Dead Father* at a colloquium Mieke Bal, who was present, suggested that the role of the women in the book is a parable of the impact of feminism on biblical studies: to insert a critical female voice into the sequence of the male generations [272–273].

Barthelme and the Bible. The "Manual for Sons" is certainly in some sense the Bible. Biblical allusions are frequent in it, including advice on what to do if your father tries to impale you on a javelin (p. 120; 1 Sam 18:10-11, 19:9-10)! The Manual also clearly states that fathers can be texts, or texts fathers.

> Many fathers are blameless in all ways, and these fathers are either sacred relics people are touched with to heal incurable illnesses, or texts to be studied, generation after generation, to determine how this idiosyncrasy may be maximized. Text-fathers are usually bound in blue (pp. 122–123).[25]

Barthelme clearly recognizes how basic the Bible is to the problematic sense of the past that is the theme of his novel, and that characterizes the whole Western tradition.

At the colloquium Bal again applied Barthelme's words to the changes currently going on in biblical studies (to which she has contributed as much as anyone): "Slightly better is all you can hope for." Our aim must be to repeat the gestures of traditional biblical scholarship a little less in each generation. I try to do so here, but already I see the generation following me refusing *my* gestures!

---

[25] The NRSV I have used in preparing this book is bound in blue.

"David Playing the Harp for Saul"

The painting and the generational split. Bal has herself contributed to the understanding of 1 Samuel as in a special sense a document of the loss of the past. In her treatment of the paintings of the Rembrandt school she devotes a long section to "David Playing the Harp for Saul."[26] This painting portrays the figures of Saul, filling the whole left half, and David, much smaller in the bottom right. Saul is a figure of kingly power yet he seems lifeless, lacking any sense of action or communication. David too, though he is playing his instrument, shares this sense of indrawnness. He also has been "contaminated" with whatever it is that is troubling Saul. But what is most striking is the total vertical split between the two figures. They are not at all looking at each other, and they are separated by a heavy curtain (which also covers one of Saul's eyes, giving him a one-eyed appearance).[27]

There is nothing in this painting that suggests to Bal the main feature of the relationship between Saul and David in the biblical text, namely their rivalry.[28] Rather what seems to be expressed is "the loss of a unity" (p. 355). What Bal observes in this painting corresponds closely to my earlier discussion of surrogate fathers and sons [111–125]. In fact, Bal uses the language of "father" and "son" for Saul and David without comment throughout her reading. The surrogate father-son relationship has become split. Continuity between the generations has been broken.

I have already identified one generational split—between Samuel and Saul—as being of fundamental importance in 1 Samuel. It is extremely interesting that Bal (and Rembrandt) confirm this split, but with a displacement from the Samuel-Saul to the Saul-David generation. This displacement does not matter much. The potential for 1 Samuel to serve as an exemplar of Israel's tragic relation to the past exists in either case.

---

[26] *Reading "Rembrandt": Beyond the Word-Image Opposition.* The Northrop Frye Lectures in Literary Theory (Cambridge: Cambridge University Press, 1991) 355–359. Unattributed page references in this section are to this book. This is the painting that appears on the cover of Exum, *Tragedy and Biblical Narrative.*

[27] Investigation has suggested that the two panels of which the painting is made may once have been separate.

[28] Bal refers to a "tension between the verbal and the visual stories" (p. 356). It would be irrelevant to respond that at this point in the text of 1 Samuel no rivalry has yet developed. The visual artist would want to convey a total sense of the Saul-David relationship rather than being confined to an accurate correspondence with the written text.

Art and melancholia. Discussing this painting among others, Bal presents a general thesis about art that is suggestive for the case I am trying to make. Her main theme is narcissism and its importance for the theory of art. For Freud narcissism is "the most general element in the formation of the subject" (p. 326). Psychoanalysis has recently begun to shift its main focus from castration (the Oedipus complex) to narcissism. In the Oedipal tradition, which long dominated psychoanalysis, masculine identity is taken as primary and is constructed as a lack: the son's lack of the power of the father. Feminine identity is then constructed—derivatively from and in opposition to the male—as a lack within a lack. From the perspective of narcissism, by contrast, the identity of both genders is constructed as a single lack: "the lack of wholeness," "the self perceived as not whole." The sense of this lack begins with the child's first perception of separation from the mother. This primary loss is repeated in all later experience of loss, and programs how loss will always be experienced (pp. 346–347).

With help from the work of Sarah Kofman, Bal develops from this psychoanalytic base a theory of art. Narcissism is the basic impulse in artistic creativity. However, it also has a negative side, which is Bal's main topic in the chapter in which she deals with Saul and David. The negative side is what Freud understood as "melancholia, or failed mourning" (p. 329).[29] Melancholia is first of all an illness, a clinical condition; but since mourning is always, given the absoluteness of each individual's primal loss, to some extent failed mourning, "melancholia" in a more general sense is part of the human condition. Art is one of the main responses to it.

According to Kofman "the process of art is melancholic mourning." Art, both the creation and the observation of it, is an "attempt to escape from the elusiveness of all things." But the beauty itself that the artist and the viewer seek proves elusive, so that artistic beauty becomes the supreme example of the very lack it is supposed to fill. Art is both the cure for melancholy and the focus of our experience of it. "The viewer is compelled to relate to the object and to suffer from the melancholic inability to relate by which the work contaminates him or her." "Beauty, the ultimate resource for sufferers of loss, constitutes loss by its elusiveness" (p. 349; see also pp. 347–348 for this paragraph).

Hence the experience of the work of art is an experience of "both similarity and difference." The work combines the representation of

---

[29] With reference to Sigmund Freud, "Mourning and Melancholia," in James Strachey, ed., *The Standard Edition of the Complete Psychological Works of Sigmund Freud.* 24 vols. (London: The Hogarth Press, 1953–1974) 14:243–258.

what is with the evocation of "what it is not; something else." "The effective work of art will present an object *lost by definition*," so that our experience of it is that we are "not simply looking at one thing, but rather that something is happening on another level" (p. 349; my emphasis).

Saul has frequently been thought of as suffering from a mental disease, and melancholia is the favorite possibility. I have suggested that his tragic situation as a character expresses a sense of tragedy that the creators and readers of the biblical text share. The melancholia is not only Saul's but also theirs. The preceding discussion provides new ways of expressing this possibility.

In the text of Samuel, Israel fails adequately to mourn its lost past. An essential phase, according to Freud, of unsuccessful mourning is a manic jubilation,[30] and we can perhaps observe this in the indecently hasty shift, in 2 Samuel, back to euphoria over kingship and King David. It is supremely ironic that this shift should be achieved by a mourning song—famous for its beauty—namely David's eulogy over Saul and Jonathan in 2 Samuel 1. This lament closes the books on a "bad" kingship and opens the way for a "good" one. But as Bal reads Rembrandt's picture (and it is the same message we read in Barthelme), "the father's lack does not shift power to the son" (p. 357). Saul's loss cannot be made into David's gain. Rather "the split between father and son embodies the melancholic paralyzing mournfulness"—for both men—"of the loss of unity" (p. 358). It is a loss of unity with the past, the past before there was *any* kingship, and a consequent melancholy that will pass down through Israel's generations.

Though no mourning can be adequate to Saul's and Israel's situation there is, I believe, a better attempt at mourning in 1 Samuel 28. It is a further indication of the appropriateness of the ending of 1 Samuel that the book includes this, but excludes David's less adequate mourning in 2 Samuel 1. In 1 Samuel 28 Saul and Israel confront the inaccessibility of the dead past in its emblem, Samuel, who is dead. Saul enacts the absolute loss and impotence of the mourner (v. 20), and he is attended by a woman skilled in mourning, in ministering to the mourning.[31]

Bal reads "David playing the harp for Saul" in a chapter called "Blindness as Insight," and her concern is first of all with the problems of sight in the picture. One of Saul's eyes is covered and there is a general failure of sight in both figures, Saul and David. They cannot see, cannot look at each other. Bal defines tragedy, including Saul's, in

---

[30] Ibid. 253–258.
[31] For "mourning women" in Israel see, for example, Jer 9:17.

terms of the "insight" that comes only through "the acceptance of not-being-able-to-see" (p. 348).

Bal has a particular interest in paintings, such as biblical ones, that exist in relation to a written text.[32] When she reads biblical paintings she does not neglect the further level of complication that lies in "the deeply antivisual culture of the ancient Hebrew texts." This cultural taboo is one response to a deep awareness of the ambiguity of sight, its "attractions" and "dangers" (p. 328).

There is some indication in 1 Samuel that visuality is one of the things that belong to Israel's lost past: the loss of visuality is yet another level of the story 1 Samuel tells. Samuel was a "seer" (9:9, 11, 18-19), but in the same breath that it tells us this (9:9) the text also tells us that "seers" are something Israel *once* had but has no longer. They have been replaced by "prophets"—the visual has given way to the verbal. But at the end of the book the Medium of Endor *sees* the ghost of Samuel (28:12-14; note how this professional ability to see confirms the link between Samuel and the medium intuited in the double identity of Mopo in *Nada the Lily*). There is no indication that Saul is able to see Samuel; rather he relies on the medium's description. She preserves the lost power of seeing; his is only the insight that comes through acceptance of not-being-able-to-see.

Israel came to value literary above visual artistry. But literary artistry is also an approach to beauty, and what Bal has to say about the melancholia intrinsic to art may carry over to literature as well, including biblical literature. There has recently been a great flowering in our awareness of the uniqueness and power of biblical narrative. The "poetics" of this narrative, its subtlety, its sense of command, its ability to express a distinct view of the world have been celebrated by recent readers, above all Meir Sternberg. In 1 Samuel it is Robert Polzin who most insists on our recognizing these qualities. Though I often question their claims in detail, I too find the narrative power of 1 Samuel compelling (more so, perhaps, even than that of the books around it).

Still, I read 1 Samuel as a book unequal to the task it sets itself, and Bal's theory of art helps me pull together this double experience of literary power and impotence. All this great artistry—like Rembrandt's in his different sphere—is an expression of and compensation for irretrievable loss. To tell of Samuel and Saul with such literary power seems to bring them back—but they are brought back only as the more irrevocably gone (cf. Wieseltier). This inadequation between the means

---

[32] See the subtitle of her book: "Beyond the Word-Image Opposition."

to be used and the task to be done is what lies, I think, behind the manifold symptoms in 1 Samuel of the text confronting its own failure—the contradictions, repetitions (Freud's "compulsion to repeat" comes to mind when one reads 1 Samuel), hesitations over critical points. My main disagreement with Sternberg, Polzin, and others is over their need to read these textual features—often quite implausibly—as part of the artistry rather than as symptoms. In the face of fundamental uncertainty about the past, biblical narrative tries to maximize the past's claim to truth. It does so mainly by developing the astonishing narrative competence that Sternberg and others analyze. But this competence is in the end a compensation for a real lack of control over what the past has bequeathed. In fact, in terms of Bal's theory of art the more artistically successful biblical narrative is the more it focuses a sense of failure and loss.

The patient in psychoanalysis often demonstrates extraordinary creativity and control. He is so intensely focused on himself that he unearths bits of his past that he was not consciously aware of, makes startling connections, and sometimes produces a discourse of compelling conviction that the con man, or the author, might envy. The analyst will note this, even be glad of it, but will not equate it with the patient's coming to truth about himself, or even with making sense. This convincing discourse still serves, the analyst knows, to conceal the self from itself as well as reveal it. Writ a million times larger, this is the situation of the Deuteronomists and of Israel's other self-analysts down the generations.

I suspect that it is out of this dynamic that the tendency has developed to read the Bible in small pieces. In liturgy, for example, the Bible is offered to the faithful in brief, well-honed "readings" (or "lessons"). For it is at this level, I would speculate, that biblical storytelling works best in the sense of carrying conviction through the power of its literary form. When one looks at the *whole* story one is more aware of majestic but necessary failure.[33]

Gender. Bal's treatment bears profoundly on issues of gender. The shift in psychoanalysis from castration to narcissism she celebrates as a shift also from obsession with the father to attention to the mother. "The force of primary narcissism is aimed not against the father but against the mother" (p. 327). Narcissism is common to both sexes, but

---

[33] My conclusion here is similar to that of Lévi-Strauss at the end of his immense work on Amerindian mythology. See Claude Lévi-Strauss, *The Naked Man*. Introduction to a Science of Mythology, Volume 4; translated by John and Doreen Weightman (London: Jonathan Cape, 1981) 625–695 [5–6].

this does not mean that it plays out the same for men and women. Bal's analysis therefore always pays attention to gender difference both in the thematics of the paintings and in their affective reception.

Referring to the group of paintings that includes "David Playing the Harp for Saul" she notes that "the woman, the mother, is absent from this work" (p. 358). But at a deeper level the mother is, after all, present "not so much as a figure, but as the framework, the background, the ground upon which the self emerges" (p. 359). Just as the mother "frames" the development of the self in narcissism, so she frames paintings of the transitions between generations of men. This framing by the mother is also, as I shall show, a defining feature of 1 Samuel [306–308].

Specters of . . .

My final intertext is Jacques Derrida's *Specters of Marx*.[34] Here more than anywhere I find someone who pioneers the trails of the book I have wanted to write. I cannot do justice to Derrida's endlessly patient and subtle argument, but I hope to show that the possibilities his work opens up for our reading of 1 Samuel are many and—haunting!

"Something has been attempted, but it has failed."[35] Derrida writes in the wake of the universally announced "death" of communism, particularly the fall of the "Marxist" (he generally puts the word in quotes) regimes of Europe in the late 1980s and early 1990s. With reference to the European Community he notes how Europe, in a frenzy of celebration, is conceiving "great unifying projects" (p. 5) now that the menace is out of the way. Interestingly, he invokes a Freudian topic we found also in Bal, manic jubilation as a phase of unsuccessful mourning. Just such a euphoria he recognizes in the celebration of the end of communism (p. 68). Derrida also notes a new eagerness to accept Marx as a philosopher, even as an essential philosopher in the great tradition, now that he no longer threatens to change the world (pp. 31–32).

---

[34] *Specters of Marx: The State of the Debt, the Work of Mourning, and the New International,* translated by Peggy Kamuf, with an introduction by Bernd Magnus and Stephen Cullenberg (New York and London: Routledge, 1994). Unattributed page references in this section are to this book.

[35] Martin Buber, *Kingship of God,* translated by Richard Scheimann (New York: Harper & Row, 1967) 83.

Derrida fully accepts the tragedy of the way communism actually worked out in the Soviet system. Indeed, he finds the debate over the recent "end" of communism and the new framing of the question "Whither Marxism now?" to be old hat. Already in the Paris of the 1950s, he says, during his intellectually formative period, the failure of the Soviet approach and the need for utterly new thinking under the rubric of Marxism were apparent.

Derrida devotes much attention to the work of Francis Fukuyama as a major example of the literature spawned by the "death" of communism.[36] Fukuyama's major thesis is that we are seeing in our time the fulfillment of the whole history of human striving, in the form of universal liberal democracy and market economics. He puts the death of communism forward as the primary evidence for the correctness of this thesis.

I discussed Israel's lost ideal first in reference to Buber, who saw early Israel as seeking an ideal theocracy but being unable to maintain it—the shift to monarchy was for him the tragic fall. I then referred to the view of Gottwald and others that what was lost when monarchy arose was *an egalitarian order of society* [72–75]. If this is so, then what Israel mourns is a death analogous to the death of communism—the death of the vision of a social order radically different from the one we know. The failure in the Deuteronomic History to mourn the loss of the past, the enthusiastic rush into the substitute ideal of the Davidic monarchy, looks very like the "manic jubilation" that, for Derrida, has marked the celebration of the end of communism.

Hauntology. In the midst of the triumph over the death of communism and Marxism Derrida discerns also a deep worry over whether they are really dead, whether they may not reemerge. Europe's dread has not really gone away.

This brings him to the guiding category of his whole book, the *ghost* or *specter.* He begins his argument with the opening words of Marx and Engels' *Communist Manifesto* of 1848: "A specter is haunting Europe—the specter of communism. All the powers of old Europe have joined into a holy hunt against this specter" (pp. 4, 37–40).[37] Derrida suggests that this "Holy Alliance" of European powers is not much different now from that of 1848. Once again Europe finds "its great unifying projects" inhabited by this ghost, "as powerful as it is unreal"

[36] *The End of History and the Last Man* (New York: The Free Press, 1992).

[37] Karl Marx and Friedrich Engels, "The Communist Manifesto," in Emile Burns, ed., *The Marxist Reader: The Most Significant and Enduring Works of Marxism* (New York: Avenel Books, 1982) 22.

(p. 13). What if Marxism were to take subtle new forms for which our techniques of recognition are not adequate, and infiltrate again?

But is there not an obvious difference between the specter celebrated by Marx and feared by his contemporaries and the specter still haunting Europe in the post-communist present? What is feared now is the *return* of something that we have already known (a ghost, after all, is what something becomes when it is dead). But Marx's specter in 1848 was of something not yet born. It was only a *future* possibility on the horizon. How, before it acquired any real historical manifestation, could communism have been a ghost that haunted Europe (pp. 37–40)?

Derrida raises this issue but argues that there is no real difference. Marx is but one testimony—albeit a testimony of unique power—to something that *always* haunts humanity. This something is a day of justice, a day when the structures of "right or law"—stemming from the repetitive cycles of human vengeance—are transcended. "And is this day before us, to come, or more ancient than memory itself?" (p. 21).

We cannot tell, precisely because our "time is out of joint" (p. 22; Derrida uses *Hamlet,* particularly the ghost of Hamlet's father, as another intertext throughout his book). We are so removed from that day that we cannot say whether it is past or future. From our perspective the day is always desired as something to come. If we locate it (as many religions and mythologies do) in the past, this is not in order to celebrate its past existence, which would merely intensify our sense of loss and distance. Rather it serves to evoke the return of that day as a future possibility.

It is this hoped-for future, which is also perhaps a lost past, that haunts us in the specter of Marx, whether in 1848 or in 1997. In a move typical of his style Derrida here introduces the concept of "hauntology" (a play on "ontology"), which he sees as representing the limit of all philosophizing in the western ontological tradition. All the classical philosophical thinking about "what is" has inevitably been inhabited by "what haunts." The thing that haunts is that which "is" not, that which is beyond observation and experience but is nevertheless *there.* "Therefore 'I am' would mean 'I am haunted.' . . . The essential mode of self-presence of the *cogito*[38] would be th[is] haunting obsession" (p. 133).

Samuel, as I have everywhere insisted, stands for the old order that is lost. In him it dies and yet will not die: it reappears in the form of his ghost. This parallel becomes uncanny when Derrida says of Marx, "He too has died, let us not forget, and more than once" (p. 114). How these uncanny parallels haunt the work of reading! Elsewhere Derrida says:

[38] The reference is to Descartes' famous *Cogito ergo sum:* "I think, therefore I am."

"The founder of the spirit of a people . . . always has the figure of a . . . ghost-survivor" (p. 146). If Samuel cannot be called the founder of Israel's spirit or consciousness he is at least its refounder.

It is on Saul, as we have seen, that the burden of Israel's tragic loss of the past chiefly falls—hence his universal reception as a tragic character. Derrida's intertext of *Hamlet* adds much to the picture here. It provides the generational relationship since Samuel's ghost, like Hamlet's, is the ghost of the father. It provides the context of monarchical succession. Perhaps most of all it enables us to see Saul's problem as the problem of his *time*. "The time is out of joint. O cursèd spite/ That ever I was born to set it right."[39] Like Hamlet, Saul is the one born to compensate for an earlier crime, "the crime of the other" (p. 21). He endeavors to maintain old Israel, to be a king in the framework of the old covenant [66–68, 85–88], but he cannot do it, for he bears in himself the divine punishment for Israel's having asked for a king at all.

According to Norman Gottwald the egalitarian paradigm that survived from the time of Israel's beginnings was "able to produce that extraordinarily self-critical Israelite prophetic movement which aided the survivors of the wreckage of the Israelite states in later times to form various kinds of truncated quasi-tribalized social forms in dispersed communities as well as in a restored Palestinian community."[40] In the light of Derrida I find myself saying "yes" and "no" to this suggestion of Gottwald's. Israel does seem in a special way to be haunted by the egalitarian possibility, but does this possibility belong to the past or the future? This is what is undecidable. Do the prophets really remember an egalitarian Israel that the historical books have mostly forgotten? Or do they, rather, replenish—even essentially create—Israel's "memory" through their own praxis?

What is it that haunts Israel? What is Samuel's ghost the ghost of? At a profound level Israel does not know what it has lost, because it has lost it. Buber is right that the Bible sometimes conjures up a lost ideal, but canonically, in the space where we expect the ideal society to appear we get instead the book of Judges, which seems less than ideal. If the time of the judges is the best ideal the past can offer, the canon implies, then good riddance to it! But if not that, then what exactly was Buber's ideal? This is the question to which the prophets offer an answer, and Gottwald too, and also Marx and Derrida (Jews both)! By these testimonies Israel, and we, continue to be haunted.

---

[39] *Hamlet* I, v, 188–189.

[40] *The Tribes of Yahweh: A Sociology of the Religion of Liberated Israel 1250–1050 B.C.E.* (Maryknoll, N.Y.: Orbis, 1979) 699.

Laying the ghosts? Derrida approaches the tragic split in Marxism in this century, and the line that leads to Stalinism, through Marx's own obsession with specters. Through a rereading of Marx's basic texts he shows how ambiguous Marx was about the metaphor of the specter, how he failed to come to terms with the ghosts he himself conjured.

It is not only in the *Manifesto* that Marx employs this metaphor. In his *Critique of Political Economy* exchange value, and even money itself, are specters.[41] But, argues Derrida, Marx hates these "ghosts" and tries to be rid of them. He always looks for a precise dividing line in economics between specters and reality. With incomparable insight and power Marx conjures up the ghosts that spook the western tradition, but in doing so he spooks himself (p. 139). So he tries to get rid of these economic "ghosts" by putting them on a "scientific" basis. It is out of this quasi-scientific impulse in Marx, Derrida further argues, that there arises Marxism's "rush[ing] headlong" toward an ontology (p. 91) and away from a hauntology, with tragic consequences in this century.

Derrida deals with another extraordinarily interesting sequence in which Marx looks at the historical antecedents of the socialist revolution and at ways in which the reformers and self-styled revolutionaries of his own day relate themselves to this past.[42] Marx tries to make a distinction between the "spirit" and the "ghost" of revolutions past (especially the French Revolution). The *spirit* gives energy to revolution whereas the *ghost* produces only a parody of revolution. Derrida sees this dubious distinction as encapsulating Marx's ambiguity about the past. At the end of his argument Marx, exasperated at the pointless discussions of the past that drain the energy of his contemporaries, abandons the distinction. He comes to the point of completely denying the usefulness of the past: "The social revolution of the nineteenth century cannot draw its poetry from the past, but only from the future."[43]

Marx's exasperation at such a moment is with the way that the past's hold on the present sometimes limits possibilities for the future. The past creates a dilemma that can be illustrated from a passage in Second Isaiah:

> Thus says the LORD,
>> who makes a way in the sea,
>> a path in the mighty waters . . .

[41] *Specters of Marx* 45–47, with reference to Marx, *A Contribution to the Critique of Political Economy* (Moscow: Progress Publishers, 1970) 107–148.

[42] *Specters of Marx* 111–114, with reference to Marx, *The Eighteenth Brumaire of Louis Bonaparte* (Moscow: Progress Publishers, 1967) 10–13.

[43] Marx, *Eighteenth Brumaire* 12–13; Derrida, *Specters of Marx* 114.

> Do not remember the former things,
>   or consider the things of old.
> I am about to do a new thing . . . (Isa 43:16, 18-19).

The prophet "remembers former things" as he evokes the Exodus, that piece of the past that haunts Israel most of all. It is hard for the prophets, it seems, to express *any* hope for YHWH's intervention in the future without evoking the exodus. But having remembered, Second Isaiah's audience is then called on immediately to forget! Too much remembering must not be allowed to limit the imagination of new activity of YHWH to the parameters established by the exodus.

Through his treatment of Marx, Derrida provides us with resources for dealing with the similarly paradoxical picture the Deuteronomic History paints. The History fails to give us anything like an adequate picture of an old egalitarian society. Rather the egalitarian ideal can be said to *haunt* Israel's memory of its past. "The time is out of joint." Israel is so far removed from the day of YHWH that it cannot say whether that day is past or future! The Deuteronomic History is contemporary with other voices—Ezekiel, Qoheleth, etc.—that in different ways have ceased to believe in a past that is lifegiving [256–257]. The History itself, in the toils of the past's unfathomable ambiguities, has the utmost difficulty in locating a lifegiving past. But it insistently tries to do so. As a result it preserves for Israel and for others, even if in a faint and conflicted way, the haunting egalitarian ideal; and so social revolution today can continue to draw its poetry from the biblical past as well as from the future.

Messianism and Zionism. Everywhere in Derrida's book there surfaces the issue of messianism in its various forms. Any discourse of messianism evokes inevitably my discussion of Israel's turn to kingship, which is my whole book. For it is in the anointing of David, in the exact middle of 1 Samuel, that messianism has its beginning. At the risk of oversimplifying we can say that for Derrida messianism takes two forms. Christian messianism looks to a future that is in principle already known, Jewish messianism to a future that is radically unknown.

Derrida finds the European Holy Alliance against communism, whether in its mid-nineteenth-century or its late-twentieth-century manifestation, to be based on a Hegelian form of Christian messianism in which history is inevitably directed toward an "end." Fukuyama represents for Derrida a particularly crass form of this way of understanding history. Fukuyama's announcement of "the end of history" assumes a full comprehension of where history *must* be going. Derrida is particularly devastating in his treatment of what counts, for Fukuyama, as evidence for his thesis. Fukuyama fluctuates opportunistically between empiricism and idealism, latching on to events like the "death" of communism as proof while shrugging off the vast amount of evidence the world daily provides to contradict his optimistic view (pp. 56–75).

Derrida's own messianism is of the Jewish kind, in which the Messiah remains radically in the future, his/her/its lineaments still unknown and undelineated in any system. In fact, Derrida prefers the term "the messianic" to "messianism," since the latter usually indicates some particular religious understanding of the future. Accepting that Marxism is also a messianism, Derrida insists that it is of this Jewish kind, at least to the extent that it avoids the "scientific" temptation (p. 89).

His hope is for the "democracy to come" (pp. 65–66), the day of justice. He defines his whole project of deconstruction as a way of keeping history open against all efforts, like Hegel's, to organize the future (pp. 74–75). Given that the present is out of joint any future that we project based upon it will inevitably share its evils. The future has a chance of being good only if we leave it radically open. What Derrida means by "the messianic" is simply giving ourselves over to this future, living with disjointedness without any guarantee of coherence to come (p. 29).

Out of this aspect of Derrida's book emerges a particularly haunting connection with my discourse in this book. In an extraordinary parenthesis covering four pages (58–61) he juxtaposes Fukuyama's understanding of the new liberalism and capitalism as a "Promised Land"[44] with the current situation in the biblical Promised Land, Palestine. Of all the counter-evidence that the politics of our time sets against Fukuyama's cheap optimism—and facile borrowing of biblical metaphor—none is so powerful as that which comes from the Middle East. Derrida's words are surprisingly forceful: "The war for the 'appropriation of Jerusalem' is today the world war. It is happening everywhere, it is the world, it is today the singular figure of its being 'out of joint'" (p. 58).

There is an uncanny link between Derrida's argument and the dilemma in which David finds himself at the end of 1 Samuel [234–241]. Should David seek a future with the Philistines? or should he take the course that brings him to kingship and to Jerusalem? In 2 Samuel Jerusalem will win out and the Philistines lose, in every sense. Does David really have an option? His anointing in 1 Samuel 16 seems to determine all that follows. It sets the narrative on a course that must

[44] *The End of History* xv.

inevitably lead to David's kingship. Like Fukuyama's, so David's history moves to its necessary end. Its course has many vicissitudes, but from the perspective of the anointing these can only be retarding devices to heighten the dramatic interest. David cannot really give up on messianism. He has to carry through the promise of his anointing. The very peculiar verse 1 Sam 17:54 will seem in retrospect like a parable of David's future. He takes the severed head of Goliath to Jerusalem even though Jerusalem is not yet an Israelite city. It is a sort of deposit on the future. In the end David will proceed to Jerusalem by the dismemberment of the Philistines and by the rejection of his own Philistine option.

Still, at the end of 1 Samuel he seems to have a real choice. What he says to himself in 27:1 implies a choice: he intends to do the best he can in the situation as he reads it, and at that moment the best is to join the Philistines [234]. The placement of the end of 1 Samuel seems to focus the reader on the reality of David's choice.

For David to opt for the Philistines would be to give up on the messianic, or at least on a certain form of it. It would be to give up on what is, in Derrida's terms, a Christian form of messianism, the kind that knows the end from the beginning. It would be to opt for the other kind of messianism, what Derrida sees as the Jewish kind—doing the best one can in the face of a future that is radically open.

Whether David has a real choice will, from another direction, be the theme of my final chapter. To conclude my intertextual reading here I simply note how David's choice parallels the choice that faces the state of Israel. David's choice is Jerusalem and empire or living with the Philistines. Modern Israel's choice is between the Greater Israel of the Zionists and coexistence with the Philistines' etymological relations, the Palestinians. I am not unmindful of the peril for me as a Christian of advocating for Jews a turn from what a Jew (Derrida) defines as a Christian form of messianism to what he defines as a Jewish form! But I cannot shirk the question when the stakes in Derrida's "world war over the appropriation of Jerusalem" are so high for all of us.

Living with the lost ideal. Derrida insists that we need to go on living with the memory of Marx (p. 13). The historical project inaugurated by Marx is unique "in the whole history of humanity, in the whole history of the world and of the earth" (p. 91), and we are all unavoidably heirs to it.[45]

---

[45] Derrida declares his own debt when he says that his project of deconstruction "would have been impossible and unthinkable in a pre-Marxist space" (*Specters of Marx* 92).

The lost ideal of Marx's historical project not only provides an *analogy* for Israel's lost ideal. The two also stand in direct historical continuity. The specter of Marx is the specter of Samuel, for Samuel stands for the very biblical past that produced Marx, and Derrida's reading of him. Derrida's book is therefore not just a fundamentally important document of our time but also an essential tool for the reading of 1 Samuel.

Chapter 12

OTHER GODS: A COMIC READING OF 1 SAMUEL

Personal Introduction

This final chapter had its beginning in a totally subjective experience. For a long time I have been haunted by a few words from 1 Samuel, just part of a verse, and a feeling that they apply particularly to me. I had recognized this haunting and decided to refer to it in this way long before Derrida's treatment of haunting appeared. The words are these:

> " . . . for they have driven me out today from my share in the heritage of the LORD, saying, 'Go, serve other gods'" (1 Sam 26:19).

Like biblical David (of course I am myself "David"), I am exiled geographically. In fact I am doubly so—first from England to North America, and then, after I had begun my career in the United States, from there to Canada. But it is not primarily in relation to *this* exile that the words from 1 Samuel have a hold on me. Much more they come to me as a commentary on the way my scholarly career has developed, my espousal of "postmodernism" and the great tumult of methods it has fostered. (Post)structuralism, feminism, psychoanalysis, and so on, the approaches I surveyed in Chapter 1: these are the "other gods" that have claimed my service. In my identification with the biblical words there is undoubtedly a measure of guilt. I am guilty of apostasy from the historical criticism in which I was trained. I am aware of disapproval or incomprehension on the part of my mentors toward the way I have taken.

Yet despite this element of guilt my visceral response to the words is a positive one. I am glad of the directions in which I have been "sent" and the kind of career and colleagues they have given me. I think of it as a methodological liberation. I take the notion of "sending" seriously. I see my part in the development of new methods in biblical studies very much as a mission. The question, though, is: who did the sending? If I understand myself as the object of the words quoted, whom do I understand as their subject? I would like, as a Christian believer, to think that it is God who has sent me on this mission. But this seems difficult in view of the plural subject: "*they* have driven me out."

We need to take such experiences seriously. Those of us who are brought up with the Bible (and this includes everyone who is a product of Western culture) are *enmeshed* in it in ways that are often unconscious or semi-conscious. We need to find ways of examining these strange associations, these "hauntings"—ways of bringing them to the surface. One reason why we need to come to terms with them in our scholarly work is that they operate at a level far deeper than our intentional scholarship. They *inhabit* our scholarship, so that we may be playing out internalized biblical scenarios just when we think we are being most objective. It is this dynamic I have been trying to probe through the psychoanalytic category of *transference* [23–24], and this will be the chief approach I will pursue throughout this chapter. If for Freud dreams are the "royal road" to the individual unconscious,[1] for me transference is the royal road to the "biblical unconscious." So deeply is the Bible inscribed within us that the processes by which we read it are simply the rehearsal at another level of what we find in it.

1 Samuel has captured and held my attention for so many years. By a very large margin it is the book I have studied most and about which I have written most. This text, more than any other, has accompanied my pursuit of the "other (methodological) gods." Do I hear the words in 26:19 as words about myself because I am obsessed with the book, or did I become interested in the book because I was already hearing those words that way? I do not remember. It does not matter. It is not a real question. The unconscious traffic between text and reader is a two-way street.[2] The methods I use obviously tend to determine what

---

[1] "The interpretation of dreams is the royal road to a knowledge of the unconscious activities of the mind" (Sigmund Freud, *The Interpretation of Dreams*, translated by James Strachey. The Pelican Freud Library, Volume 4 [Harmondsworth, Middlesex: Penguin Books, 1976] 769).

[2] Recall the strong words of Mieke Bal: "Whether the motivation originates in the painter's [or writer's] irretrievable psyche or in the viewer's [or reader's] unacknowledged response is utterly beside the point" (*Reading "Rembrandt": Beyond the Word-Image Opposition*. The Northrop Frye Lectures in Literary Theory [Cambridge: Cambridge University Press, 1991] 359).

I find in 1 Samuel. Is there, conversely, something about this particular book that has pointed me in these particular methodological directions? When I identify with 26:19 is my mind merely grabbing at some free-floating words as a means of self-understanding?—or am I also entering in an unconscious way into the dynamics of the text of which those words are a part? Is my gut reaction to the words something that can inform my scholarly reading as well as vice versa?

In this chapter I want to set up a conscious relationship between the text and my experience of it. I want to see if I can use the experience I have been describing *as a way of reading the text,* as a way of getting perspective on 1 Samuel. This text of tragedy has played a major part in my personal drama of comedy (in the classic sense of a story that moves from the negative to the positive). It has accompanied what I see as my methodological liberation. Perhaps my experience will lead in the direction of a comic reading of the book.

Over the last several chapters I have been developing a reading of the final chapters of 1 Samuel and particularly of David's role there. Here I summarize and conclude that reading, beginning with a close reading of 26:19 and moving out from there. I put aside at this point the rhetoric of direct self-disclosure, but if you want to look for a *double entendre* in what I shall say about biblical David you will probably find it.[3]

1 Samuel 26:19 and the Ending of the Book

The problem of the subject. My main personal difficulty with 26:19 was deciding who could be the *subject* of the sending. This problem leads, I believe, to the most productive interpretive issue in the verse. Let us look now at the whole verse (which I arrange by lines, to clarify the argument):

> "If it is the LORD who has stirred you up against me,
> may he accept an offering;
> but if it is mortals,

---

[3] Once again Derrida has led the way in showing how auto-psychobiography can function in scholarly work. See Geoffrey Bennington and Jacques Derrida, *Jacques Derrida. Religion and Postmodernism,* translated by Geoffrey Bennington (Chicago: University of Chicago Press, 1993). See also Jill Robbins, "Circumcising Confession: Derrida, Autobiography, Judaism," *Diacritics* 25 (1995) 20–38. I make no attempt to imitate Derrida, but if his is a "circumfession" my self-disclosure will have to be an "uncircumfession" (the significance of this will emerge).

may they be cursed before the LORD,
for they have driven me out today from my share in the heritage of the
     LORD,
saying, 'Go, serve other gods'."

David is speaking to Saul. Someone has stirred Saul up against
David, but David does not know who. The subject is the problem.
David juxtaposes two possibilities as to who it might be: "the LORD" or
"mortals." He posits these two options at the same logical level ("if . . .
but if") and considers them in turn, but he draws out the second option—not the first—into a logical proposition: *If* mortals have "stirred
you up," *then* they have "driven me out." These hypothetical people are
the cause of David's expulsion, so that they can be considered the
agents of it: "they have driven me out." But this raises the question of
why the first option should not be drawn out into an analogous proposition. If YHWH has stirred Saul up against David, has *he* not—by the
same logic—driven David out? Thus the verse logically evokes, though
it rhetorically suppresses, the possibility that it is YHWH who has driven
David out and even told him to "Go, serve other gods."

Looking back from 26:19. This unthinkable possibility that the text
nonetheless obliquely "thinks" and that I must also unconsciously
have "thought" in the process of finding myself in this verse is not, in
point of fact, really unthinkable. If we look simply at the words of
26:19 it is arguable that the "YHWH" option gets more support from the
story to this point than the "mortals" option. It is hard to find any
people in 1 Samuel who stir Saul up against David, despite David's assertion in 24:9 that there are such people. The best candidate would be
Doeg (22:9-10). On the other hand, it is clearly stated more than once
that YHWH stirs up Saul against David (18:10-12; 19:9-10).

The dominant assumption among commentators is that in the latter part of 1 Samuel YHWH acts behind the scenes to move David's career along its indirect but inevitable course to the kingship. But in fact,
aside from the anointing, it is *humans* who promote David's progress
(though they often say that it is YHWH who is doing it: 20:16, 22-23;
24:19; 25:28-31, etc.) YHWH's thoughts and actions remain mostly in
mystery. Stirring up Saul against David is one of the few things YHWH
actively does.

Despite the frequent predictions of David's coming kingship we
have seen symptoms in the text of doubt over its inevitability. Saul's
fluctuation between pursuit of David and reconciliation with him in
chs. 24 and 26 makes problematic *his* recognition of David's coming
kingship (24:20). Abigail's predictions in 25:28-31, I have suggested,

are exaggerated to such an extent as to make one wonder if the hyperbole does not cloak anxiety about David's future [156–157]. This story simply assumes that David would win if he were drawn into a battle with Nabal's forces. But Nabal seems to believe that he can defend himself from anything David can throw at him. We have no way of knowing whether this judgment is realistic or foolish since it is not put to the test. In terms of the allegory between Nabal and Saul this doubt confirms the doubt in the larger narrative.

David with the Philistines. It is David himself who expresses this doubt most clearly, and he does so only a very few verses after 26:19—in 27:1, which I have discussed at length [232–241]. There is surely a profound connection between these two verses. In 27:1, at a moment when everyone, including Saul, is rallying around him, lavishing him with royal expectation, David decides that Saul will inevitably kill him one day and that he had better go to the Philistines. This makes a lot more sense if we imagine David thinking (or perceiving at a level deeper than thought) that it is YHWH who is stirring Saul up against him, YHWH who is sending him away (26:19). In 27:1 David pieces it together. YHWH is sending him to the Philistines. The "other gods" of 26:19 will be the Philistine gods. David at this point makes a conscious decision in line with YHWH's will as best he can understand it.

Within 1 Samuel, David will not in any evident way alter this decision. I have argued against the common view that David's entire strategy with the Philistines was one of deceit, that he was feigning allegiance to them and simply biding his time. This view is hard to reconcile with 27:1. David's allegiance to the Philistines was not put to the final test since he was not allowed to participate in their final battle with Saul (ch. 29). We can no more know how he would have acted in that battle than we can know whether he would have beaten Nabal if it had come to a fight.

A dimension has been added to the theme of David and the Philistines by the insertion into their story of Saul's meeting with the Medium of Endor (28:3-25). I have begun to argue that the medium is the pivotal figure for our understanding of the end of 1 Samuel, that she represents at a deep level an alternative option for Israel's perception of its relationship to the past. I will conclude this argument later in the chapter [303–305]. For the present I simply recall the possibility that the medium is a Philistine [217]. If she is, then the option she represents is a Philistine option and the placement of her story at the point where David is considering *his* Philistine option is profoundly apt.

The end of 1 Samuel. The impossible possibility that it is YHWH who drives David out to serve other gods is related to the choice of an end point for 1 Samuel. The end of the book, when it is remarked on at all, is usually read as the end of the tragedy of Saul. The point that it marks in the fortunes of David or of Israel is rarely commented on: the interpreters are anxious to read on into 2 Samuel for the fulfillment of the promises to David. But 1 Samuel ends at a moment in David's career that is uniquely ambiguous [101, 279–280].

He has no fixed abode and has surrounded himself with a motley crew. He has not begun to take charge of the situation (as he firmly does already in 2 Samuel 1). His adherence to Israel is unclear since his immediate loyalty seems to be to the Philistines. There are other ways too in which David is "unfixed" at this point. His sexual identity is unclear and he is not yet a father. 2 Samuel 1:26 will celebrate his homosexual side but also put it firmly behind him. Soon thereafter he will indulge in a veritable orgy of royal heterosexuality and procreation (2 Sam 3:2-5). All this, however, lies still in the future at the end of 1 Samuel.

Something analogous can be said about *Israel's* situation at the end of the book. Israel has at this moment no king, so that the entire question of kingship *might* be reopened. If Israel were now to *abandon* kingship it would not be the first time. Its first experiment with kingship, in the person of Abimelech, came to an end (Judges 9), and we recall the studied similarity between Abimelech's death and Saul's (Judg 9:54, 1 Sam 31:4-5) [101]. The issue of kingship is in any case moot, since Israel is at this moment fully under the control of the Philistines and its immediate future is life under foreign occupation.

In Regina Schwartz's terms Israel's identity is, like David's, not yet fully "mapped."[4] The end of 1 Samuel is one of the points at which different possibilities present themselves. Perhaps even now there could be a real work of national mourning, a "cry to YHWH," instead of an "inevitable" passage into a monarchical future.

Of course the reader "knows" how these things will turn out. He knows that YHWH is for David, but definitely against "other gods." He knows that David is destined to be king and will become king. He knows that Israel will become an independent, even an imperial nation, while the Philistines will somehow be removed from the story. I note one more haunting moment in the "orthodox" continuation of the 1 Samuel story. In 2 Sam 5:21, during his brief Philistine wars, David finds the abandoned Philistine "idols" and takes possession of them. What else are these than the "other gods" of 1 Sam 26:19 whom

---

[4] "Adultery in the House of David: The Metanarrative of Biblical Scholarship and the Narratives of the Bible," *Sem* 54 (1991) 50–51.

David then believed he would be serving? These Philistine gods, which symbolized his alternative future and the possibility of a different story, now go into the trophy room of the king next to the head of Goliath.[5]

Will this all necessarily be so? In this book I have complained a good deal about a narrowness of interpretation due to overinsistence on reading the beginning of 1 Samuel *as a beginning*. Regarding the ending my complaint has been the converse, of a narrowness of interpretation that results from *not* taking it *as an ending*! I have in various ways (of which this section has been a summary) pressed the question of why the canonical book ends just where it does. Why does it end at the moment when the reader is not sure what will become of David and of Israel, when it is logically possible to doubt all of the fulfillments that will happen in 2 Samuel, when such doubts are even encouraged. 1 Samuel 26:19 evokes, in my reading, the strange possibility of a divine Yes to David's and Israel's ambiguous situation as the book ends. It evokes the possibility of a quite different continuation of the story from the one that 2 Samuel provides.

Transference and the Divine Narrator

According to Gabriel Josipovici, one of the most perceptive of the Bible's recent readers, biblical scholarship can be a tragic or at any rate a futile business. The Bible resists our attempts to read it because it is "too vast, too varied, too ancient." There is one characteristic of the Bible that, however, helps us: "it is actually *about* many of the critical and hermeneutical issues" that arise when we try to read it.[6] This is simply another way of expressing the concept of transference.

Transference is a two-edged sword. In this section I shall show how it can function on behalf of what I facetiously call "narrowtology," a form of narrative criticism that limits the options in biblical interpretation. In the next section I shall respond with some subversive transferential possibilities.

---

[5] Which is already in Jerusalem before David conquers the city—see 1 Sam 17:54. Also in the trophy room, perhaps, will be one or two hundred desiccated Philistine foreskins (1 Sam 18:27), the brideprice Saul owed back to David when he gave Michal to another man.

[6] *The Book of God: A Response to the Bible* (New Haven and London: Yale University Press, 1988) 27; emphasis in original.

Omniscient narrator, receptive reader. Recent literary work on 1 Samuel[7] has laid heavy stress on the role of the "omniscient" narrator [142]. This approach is exemplified, among those who have written books on 1 Samuel, by Lyle Eslinger and Robert Polzin,[8] and also by Robert Alter and Meir Sternberg.[9] The biblical narrator, according to this view, claims full control of everything that is going on in the narrative, claims to know even the secret thoughts of the characters, including God (this is what is particularly meant by "omniscient"), and claims to be fully aligned to God's point of view. Biblical narrative draws a fundamental contrast between this privileged point of view and the limited or false points of view of the characters. The characters can be only what the narrator lets them be.

As a description of the conventions of biblical narrative this seems to me, though not wholly satisfying, to contain a large measure of truth. I have suggested a reason why biblical narrative needs to give this appearance of being so fully under control [271–272]. It would be unfair to suggest that these readers promote a simplistic notion of the traffic between the narrator and the reader. The strategies by which the narrator directs the reader are of great subtlety and (especially in Sternberg's version) designed to take account of different levels of reading competence.

However, I have a problem with the corollary that is usually drawn: that our reading of the Bible must be constrained by the claims the narrator makes, that readings are only valid if they lie within the parameters defined by the narrator. The work of discovering meaning in the Bible becomes identical with acquiring "competence" in following the narrator's directions for appropriate reading.[10] The reader can only read more or less well; reading *differently* is disallowed.

---

[7] For a review see Robert Polzin, "1 Samuel: Biblical Studies and the Humanities," *RStR* 15 (1989) 297–306.

[8] Eslinger, *Kingship of God in Crisis: A Close Reading of 1 Samuel 1-12.* Bible and Literature Series 10 (Sheffield: Almond, 1985); Polzin, *Samuel and the Deuteronomist: A Literary Study of the Deuteronomic History. Part Two: 1 Samuel* (San Francisco: Harper & Row, 1989).

[9] Alter, *The Art of Biblical Narrative* (London: Allen & Unwin, 1981); Sternberg, *The Poetics of Biblical Narrative: Ideological Literature and the Drama of Reading* (Bloomington, Ind.: Indiana University Press, 1985). Both of these books include readings of portions of 1 Samuel.

[10] David M. Gunn, "Reading Right: Reliable and Omniscient Narrator, Omniscient God, and Foolproof Composition in the Hebrew Bible," in David J. A. Clines, Stephen E. Fowl, and Stanley E. Porter, eds., *The Bible in Three Dimensions: Essays in*

In the case of Sternberg, it has been suggested, this becomes a quasi-theological claim. The narrator's claim to speak with the voice of God *must* be translated into a convention under which the narrator rules reading.[11] This is an instance of transference as I have defined it: between the relationship of God to human characters *in* the text and the relationship of narrator to readers in the *reading* of the text. The effect is to ascribe to the narrator the authority of God: I recall Eslinger's statement that the narrator is "the author and finisher of our reading."[12]

"Everyone doing what is right in his or her own eyes." Obviously such an approach excludes alternative ways of reading, often with a great show of rhetorical force. I quote at length two important lists of exclusions by prominent literary readers.

> By foolproof composition I mean that the Bible is difficult to read, easy to underread and overread and even misread, but virtually impossible to, so to speak, counterread. Here as elsewhere, of course, *ignorance, willfulness, preconception, tendentiousness*—all amply manifested throughout history, in the religious and other approaches—may perform wonders of *distortion*. No text can withstand the kind of methodological *license* indulged in by the rabbis in contexts other than legal, or by critics who mix up their quest for the source with the need to *fabricate a new discourse*. Still less can it protect itself against being yoked by *violence*, in the manner of the christological tradition, with a later text whose very premises of discourse (notably "insider" versus "outsider") it would find incomprehensible. Nor can it do much to keep out *invidious assumptions* about Israelite ethics and culture. . . . In a hermeneutic and *moral* as well as a theological sense, interpretation may always be performed *in bad faith*.
>
> Short of such *extremes*, biblical narrative is virtually impossible to counterread.[13]

> [We stress] the role of the critic as someone who helps make possible *fuller readings of the text*. . . . An orientation of this sort seemed to us particularly appropriate . . . because at this moment in cultural history there is *an urgent need to try to learn how to read the Bible again*. Certain varieties of contemporary criticism are not represented here because we think they are not really concerned with reading in the sense we have

---

Celebration of Forty Years of Biblical Studies in the University of Sheffield (Sheffield: Sheffield Academic Press, 1990) 53–64.

[11] Mieke Bal, *On Story-Telling: Essays in Narratology*, edited by David Jobling (Sonoma, Cal.: Polebridge Press, 1991) 59–72; Burke O. Long, "The 'New' Biblical Poetics of Alter and Sternberg," *JSOT* 51 (1991) 71–84.

[12] *Kingship of God in Crisis* 75.

[13] Sternberg, *Poetics of Biblical Narrative* 50; my emphasis.

proposed. For example, critical approaches mainly interested in the origins of a text in ideology or social structure are not represented here; nor is Marxist criticism . . . or psychoanalytic criticism. Given *our aim to provide illumination,* we have not included critics who use the text as a springboard for *cultural or metaphysical ruminations,* nor those like the Deconstructionists and some feminist critics who seek to demonstrate that *the text is necessarily divided against itself.*[14]

The methods I have used in this book are excluded, on the face of it, more explicitly by Alter and Kermode than by Sternberg, but Sternberg's category of readers "in bad faith" is potentially a large one, and would likely include practitioners of some of the approaches mentioned by Alter and Kermode.

The transference between this battle over interpretation and the dynamics at the beginning of 1 Samuel is irresistible. What the literary readers rhetorically evoke is a scene of interpretive anarchy in which every interpreter "does what is right in his or her own eyes" (Judg 21:25). They heap together long lists of undesirable approaches not merely to pronounce them undesirable but to create the impression of a mishmash of perverse possibilities. They do so in the name of singleness of interpretation. This is overt in the case of Sternberg. He insists that the text, diverse as it is, expresses a single, though complex, ideological perspective.[15] Alter and Kermode, on the other hand, claim that their book is "pluralist," "eclectic," and not "doctrinaire."[16] But the section I quoted assumes a singular "cultural need" (why should *everyone equally* "need to try to learn how to read the Bible again"?), and if the Bible is not "divided against itself" it is hard to see how interpretation can be plural in any productive sense. In the face of anarchy these readers look for a king in the Israel of biblical studies (Judg 21:25 again).

Kingship and anarchy are political terms and they alert us to Alter and Kermode's specific exclusion of readings that grow out of overt political commitments. These authors seem to sense—correctly—that the text can preserve its traditional authority only if it is protected from political inquiry. For political reading exposes not only the text but also the academic and religious institutions in which it has received its

---

[14] Robert Alter and Frank Kermode, eds., *The Literary Guide to the Bible* (Cambridge, Mass.: Harvard University Press, 1987) 5–6; my emphasis.

[15] Note his use of the term "ideology" in this singular sense throughout *The Poetics of Biblical Narrative.* Polzin uses the term in the same way in *Samuel and the Deuteronomist* [12–13].

[16] Alter and Kermode, *Literary Guide* 6.

authorized interpretation to the voices that have been silenced in its production and interpretation—largely silenced, but not completely.

A perfect poem for the lower classes.[17] Do these literary readers reject Philistine reading as well as anarchic reading? To answer this I shall tell a long transferential story that begins again with Matthew Arnold, for whom an anarchic reading and a Philistine reading would have been one and the same [208].

In Arnold's project of educating the great mass of the population the Bible has an important role to play. He aims to use the Bible in order to present human history as a connected whole, with a coherence beyond sectarian interests and class conflict. The Bible is particularly fitted to this task of "civilizing" the newly enfranchised masses because they know it already. It is a part of popular culture. Arnold writes: "If poetry, philosophy, and eloquence, if what we call in one word *letters*, are a power, and a beneficent wonder-working power, in education, through the Bible only have the people much chance of getting at poetry, philosophy and eloquence."[18]

Seeking to present the Bible in a way that reduced the impression of contradiction and fragmentariness, Arnold looked for "some whole, of admirable literary beauty in style and treatment."[19] To this end he produced a reader based on Isaiah 40–66. His understanding of biblical education as a way to reduce class conflict is clear from the hopes he expresses for this reader:

> Whoever began with laying hold of this series of chapters as a whole would have a starting point and lights of unsurpassed value for getting a conception of the course of man's history and development as a whole. . . . There are numbers whose crosses are so many and comforts so few that to the misery of narrow thoughts they seem almost driven and bound; what a blessing is whatever extricates them and makes them live with the life of the race.[20]

John Henry (the future Cardinal) Newman applauded Arnold's intention but had problems with the choice of Isaiah, since the messianic passages might lead to disputes over dogma. Writing to Arnold, he made a countersuggestion: "If I was obliged to throw out some alter-

---

[17] Some of this section was originally drafted by Catherine Rose.

[18] R. H. Super, ed., *The Complete Prose Works of Matthew Arnold*. 11 vols. (Ann Arbor: University of Michigan Press, 1960–1977) 7:503.

[19] Ibid. 506.

[20] Ibid. 72.

native for popular education, I should recommend the 1st book of Samuel; which is a perfect poem, epic or tragedy. . . ."[21]

It is rather droll that Newman should recommend to Arnold, the great scourge of the Victorian Philistines, the part of the Bible that most treats of the ancient Philistines. In fact Newman's words, in their context, summarize all the points I shall raise in what follows: the desire of a threatened intellectual class to take control of general education; the assumption that the Bible can make a major contribution to education designed to erase class difference; the choice of 1 Samuel as especially apt for this project; and the reference to its artistic perfection.

Saving the masses. Arnold's project, in a word, is to save the masses from the Philistines. He wants to take responsibility, over the head of the Philistine middle class, for the religious education of the lower class. He believes that this can happen only in a strong statist political framework.

There is surely here a strong transferential link between Arnold and one of the voices in Judges and 1 Samuel—the voice for which the adoption of kingship in Israel, the move to a strong statist system, is a way of saving the mass of Israelites from the Philistines. As I have shown, the "Philistines" can be thought of in a literal way as a foreign oppressor, or as an externalization of the anarchic tendency in Israelite society ("everyone doing what is right in his or her own eyes") [224]. In a different way we can find the same logic of appeal to the masses over the heads of other interests in Brentano. His life's work was to bring folk literature to prominence in German national life as a way of overcoming the modernizing influence of the "Philistine" Enlightenment.

It seems to me that the selfsame pattern also characterizes the long section I quoted from Sternberg and to which I now return. He is here introducing his key idea of "foolproof composition," which he puts forward as a (even the) foremost characteristic of biblical poetics. This quality in the Bible insures that the unskilled or unlearned reader will not be led astray in his reading. The Bible is so composed that the simpler message he derives from it is not different in principle from the "plenary" understanding that more accomplished readers can derive.[22] "Foolproof composition" ensures that a *less skilled* reading will not be a *wrong* reading.

Sternberg is making a gesture, then, to ordinary readers of the Bible. He makes this gesture, though, over the heads of various "counterreaders." Given that counterreading is "virtually impossible" it is quite

---

[21] Ian Ker, Thomas Gornall, et al., eds., *The Letters and Diaries of John Henry Newman*. 31 vols. (Oxford: Oxford University Press, 1973–1984) 26:95–96.

[22] *The Poetics of Biblical Narrative* 56.

astonishing how many readers he includes in this category—all aggadic readers (that is, the producers of rabbinic commentary on biblical narrative), a great many Christian readers, and various readers "in bad faith."

Alter and Kermode make a gesture similar to Sternberg's, for they aim to appeal to a wide audience of nonspecialist readers and their exclusions are designed to increase the appeal. Predictably they invoke Arnold as a model, though now a scarcely attainable one—from their perspective, a lost ideal.[23]

Philistine readers. The recent use of the term "Philistine" for the artistically incompetent seems to hover not far from this gesture of Sternberg. The Bible is for him the supreme pinnacle of literary art: "Scripture emerges as the most interesting as well as the greatest work in the narrative tradition."[24] Those who resist seeing it this way would therefore presumably be artistic Philistines, and in fact there are a couple of indications that the bad readers over whose heads Sternberg gestures to the ordinary reader of the Bible may precisely be *Philistines*.

First, I omitted from my quote from Sternberg (note the lacuna) his only specific *example* of bad faith reading. He quotes (as "a relatively mild specimen") the following words from the biblical critic Bruce Vawter: "[The Bible develops] the sort of themes that would appeal to rough humor and rouse the chuckles of the fairly low audience for whom they were designed, who doubled with merriment at the thought of the 'uncircumcised'."[25] This is a bit complicated. Sternberg does not explicitly call Vawter a Philistine, but the fact that Sternberg's sole example of reading in bad faith directly evokes the Philistines (the uncircumcised) strikes me as no more a coincidence than Newman's recommending of 1 Samuel to Arnold. To put words in Sternberg's mouth, his complaint about Vawter is that to accuse the ancient Israelites of taking a Philistine attitude to the Philistines is . . . Philistine!

The second indication, from elsewhere in Sternberg's book, takes us back to the text of 1 Samuel. He refers to "all qualified observers, pointedly excluding unbelievers like the afflicted Philistines or waverers like Gideon."[26] Sternberg is referring here not to *readers of* the Bible but to *characters in* it, who observe events and are more or less "qualified" to draw the right conclusions from those events.[27] But in Stern-

---

[23] *Literary Guide* 3.

[24] *The Poetics of Biblical Narrative* 518.

[25] Vawter, *On Genesis: A New Reading* (Garden City, N.J.: Doubleday, 1977) 359.

[26] *The Poetics of Biblical Narrative* 162.

[27] He uses as a positive example Abraham's servant in Genesis 24, who draws from his encounter with Rebekah the right conclusions about God's will.

berg's transferential method there is hardly a distinction between the qualification of biblical characters to interpret right, based on their belief, and the qualification of readers of the Bible to interpret right, based on their good or bad faith.

Sternberg's "unbelievers like the afflicted Philistines" is a reference to 1 Sam 6:9. Here the Philistines, afflicted with plagues, consider the possibility that their sufferings may be "by chance" rather than being a punishment from YHWH [218]. Their "unbelief" consists, for Sternberg, precisely in their holding open an explanation of their experience that differs from the narrator's.[28]

Sternberg's argument here is much illuminated by Polzin's treatment of this same verse, 1 Sam 6:9.[29] Polzin's treatment of the Philistines in 1 Samuel 4–7 is marked by an ambiguity reminiscent of the way Brentano and Fichte make fun of the Philistines while worrying about whether they are Philistines themselves [205–206]. On the one hand he sees the presentation of them as prejudicial: "the fairly comical struggles of the Philistines," the "almost playful picture" of them as "misguidedly ignorant."[30] On the other hand he finds a powerful tendency to draw parallels between Israel and the Philistines.[31] This ambiguity provides the context for Polzin's treatment of 6:9.

> What the Philistine sorcerers say about God's "heavy hand" is relevant as the reader ponders the nature of the intricate compositional connections between chapters 4–6 and their literary context. The text offers two alternatives: the intricacy happened "by chance" or "it is *his* hand that strikes us" (6:9). Is the narrative hand "crude"—what critics usually mean when they write *redactional*—or "careful"—what I mean when I write *authorial*?[32]

I hope my preceding discussion has prepared you to see how revealing this quotation is. The transference that I noted earlier between the

---

[28] *The Poetics of Biblical Narrative* 105.

[29] Polzin prefaces his treatment of 1 Samuel 4–7 with part of a quotation from Matthew Arnold that I also have used: "Philistine must have originally meant, in the mind of those who invented the nickname, a strong, dogged, unenlightened opponent of the chosen people, of the children of the light" (*Samuel and the Deuteronomist* 55) [208]. It is not clear what Polzin intends by this epigraph since he never refers to it afterwards.

[30] Ibid. 4, 58.

[31] E.g., ibid. 55. The contrast can be observed on a single page: compare "as humorously ridiculous a light as the narrator can devise" with "God's heavy hand against Israelite and Philistine alike" (ibid. 65).

[32] Ibid. 56–57; emphasis in original.

relationship of God to human characters _in_ the text and the relationship of narrator to readers in the _reading_ of the text is precisely accomplished by Polzin here! There is no more room for ambiguity. God's "hand" is expressly the narrator's "hand"; _ergo_ the narrator is God. The question whether every textual phenomenon represents the conscious will of the narrator becomes _the same as_ the theological question of whether everything that happens in the world is due to the will of God. Readers who reject Polzin's (or Sternberg's) view of the omniscient narrator put ourselves in the place of the Philistines, rejecting the evidence of the work of God!

The constraint that this threatens to put on the reading of the Bible is staggering. The text of the Bible lies beyond the reach of real critical questioning because the biblical narrator does, because the biblical God does. It is only by making such an implausible and appalling assumption that Sternberg can exclude such a range of "counterreaders," and Alter and Kermode such a variety of methodological options, from the reading of the Bible. Thereby they rule out _a priori_ questions that many people are now urgently putting to the Bible—just such questions of class, race, and gender as I have pressed here.

The philosophical stakes are also high. 1 Samuel 6:9 evokes a whole history of _empirical_ approaches to reality, a history with which the term "Philistine" is tightly bound up. Both Brentano and Arnold are locked in bitter struggle against a commonsense empirical approach to the world, one that is increasingly disinclined to accept the claims of "high" culture.[33] "When is a plague just a plague?" ask the biblical Philistines. "Isn't the rainbow just a meteorological phenomenon?" ask Brentano's Philistines.[34] In the same vein some of us who are unimpressed by extreme claims about the narrator's skill and control of "his" material ask, "When is the biblical narrator's 'skillful use of repetition' just the same word being used twice?"

1 Samuel Reading Itself Subversively

The message of the preceding section is that if we read the Bible out of a frame of mind that fundamentally assents to it the text of the Bible

---

[33] We can make a useful link here to Derrida's critique of Fukuyama, who in the process of arguing for a new world order based on Eurocentric high culture shrugs off the empirical evidence contrary to his case [278–279].

[34] Clemens Brentano, "Der Philister vor, in und nach der Geschichte: Aufgestellt, begleitet und bespiegelt aus göttlichen und weltlichen Schriften und eigenen

will be found to undergird that style of reading. This can become, as it does especially in Sternberg and Polzin, such a closed circle that the possibility of breaking out of it seems nonexistent, or perhaps we should say heretical. In this section, though, I hope to show that if we read the Bible subversively the text of the Bible will be found to undergird this style of reading too. Such are the ways of transference. I shall here identify the elements in 1 Samuel itself that have suggested to me lines of resistant reading, reading against the grain.[35]

Polytheist reading. The possibility of a *polytheist* reading is suggested by my discussion at the beginning of this chapter of the "other gods" whom David has been driven out to serve (26:19). As "David," I find myself compelled to try such a reading!

At a recent conference on biblical studies and theology I tried to introduce into current "god-talk" the polytheistic option.[36] The response was that I must be joking. Polytheism, it seemed, was something simply outside the conference's discourse. Such is the power of religious and cultural tradition that "polytheism" has scarcely become the name of any vibrant discussion in biblical studies or theology.[37] Yet I believe it is needed. Can we really get a single account of reality from looking (to put it very roughly) at the user-friendliness of the created world, at the working out of human history, and/or at the impulses of the individual psyche?

One reason why I raised the issue at the conference was that I had noticed in its proceedings a prevalence of "poly" words understood in a positive sense. Among many examples were "polyopsis," "polycontextual," and "polydox." One way of reading the postmodern scene is

---

Beobachtungen," in Andreas Müller, ed., *Satiren und Parodien* (Leipzig: Reclam, 1935) 201.

[35] Judith Fetterley, *The Resisting Reader: A Feminist Approach to American Fiction* (Bloomington, Ind.: Indiana University Press, 1978); Terry Eagleton, *Against the Grain: Essays 1975–1985* (London: Verso, 1986).

[36] A book of the conference has appeared: Cynthia Rigby, ed., *Power, Powerlessness, and the Divine* (Atlanta: Scholars, 1997).

[37] But see recently Regina M. Schwartz, *The Curse of Cain: The Violent Legacy of Monotheism* (Chicago: The University of Chicago Press, 1997). One prominent theorist who leads the way in discussing what polytheism might imply for us now is Michel Serres. "Cross-breeding—that's my cultural ideal. Black and white, science and humanities, monotheism and polytheism—with no reciprocal hatred" (Michel Serres with Bruno Latour, *Conversations on Science, Culture, and Time.* Studies in Literature and Science, translated by Roxanne Lapidus [Ann Arbor: University of Michigan Press, 1995] 28; this book is the easiest introduction to Serres' work). These words, in which Serres calls for a radical questioning of the lines of division

in terms of the failure of myths of singleness. Words and texts are plural rather than single in meaning. The individual human psyche is a network of impulses producing no stable, single "person"; we can all truly say, "My name is Legion; for we are many" (Mark 5:9). Results are plural in relation to causes (in chaos theory). And so on.

In a postmodern worldview the "poly" (or "multi") words tend to intertwine with and corroborate each other, over against the corresponding "mono" (or "uni") words that together express a still-dominant worldview that sees the world in terms of unity. As one example recall how Arnold set a nature-polygamy-polytheism complex in contrast with culture-monogamy-monotheism [210]. It makes sense, in a context full of all these poly words, to ask also about polytheism. The alternative would be to cast "God" as the last bulwark of a mono world.

In a general way we have in the major religions of the world a division between those that imagine divine power as single and those that imagine it as plural,[38] but the recent history of the encounter between monotheism and polytheism has been shaped above all by the colonial domination of polytheists by monotheists.[39] On this uneven playing field the dominant discourse of monotheism has been able to suggest that there is something disgraceful about polytheism. It is salutary to recall Derrida's "world war" over Jerusalem, the focus, for him, of what is out of joint in our world [279]. This is a war that involves precisely the three great monotheisms of the West, Judaism, Christianity, and Islam. Is monotheism the world's fundamental problem? At least it seems high time to listen to the wisdom of polytheism.

The Hebrew Bible knows of significant divine plurality. To take but one example, Prov 8:22-31 posits relationship within the divine, even

---

that bedevil current culture, would be commonplace were it not for the unexpected inclusion of "monotheism and polytheism" among the lines of division. He calls for a theology based on the multiplicity of angels rather than the singleness of God: "My philosophy is more like a heaven filled with angels, obscuring God somewhat" (p. 118). The vision of space filled with angels seems to him the most adequate response to the infinite criss-crossing of multiple electronic messages with which our ethernet is filled.

[38] This has been on my mind since I heard Gayatri Chakravorty Spivak talk about the polytheistic experience (based on some research in her native village in India). Without touting polytheism as a cure for the world's ills she suggested that the West needs the polytheistic experience.

[39] On the relationship between colonialism and monotheism see David Jobling, "Globalization in Biblical Studies/Biblical Studies in Globalization (a response to articles by D. J. A. Clines, R. Rendtorff, and R. S. Sugirtharajah)," *Biblical Interpretation* 1 (1993) 96–110.

male-female relationship: YHWH and HOKHMAH (Sophia, Wisdom). Must we conceive of this relationship as one of total harmony and agreement? How are real human relationships, for example between the sexes, helped if we conceive it that way? May we not hear YHWH muttering, between the lines of Proverbs 8, something like "Women creators! Never could stick to a blueprint"? And Sophia answering, "For God's sake lighten up!"

So far as 1 Samuel is concerned a polytheist hermeneutic enlightens the places where YHWH's role appears as a plural one.[40] One obvious example is the depiction of YHWH in the kingmaking in chs. 8–12 as both rejecting kingship and demanding that a king be installed [61–62]. The Deuteronomic contortions to make YHWH's role coherent fail to conceal at such a point that there is conflict at the very heart of things. My favorite example, though, is again 26:19. The YHWH who sends his chosen one out to "serve other gods," who allows the peculiarly open situation in which David and Israel find themselves at the end of 1 Samuel, is himself an "other god" from the jealous god who demands monotheism and who keeps the course of history strictly to a plan (the "inevitability" of David's rise to the kingship).

Philistine reading. I have already presented my Philistine reading of 1 Samuel in Part IV of this book ("Reading as a Philistine" is in fact the title of the essay in which much of the work in Part IV was first published),[41] and I will here merely underline a couple of points and add one or two others.

A Philistine reading of 1 Samuel commends itself first of all because if things had stayed as they were at the end of the book the Philistine reading of the events is the only one that would have survived. This trivial remark is given depth if we recall yet again Derrida's discussion of the "world war" over Jerusalem and my linking of this with the situation at the end of 1 Samuel [279–280]. Whose reading will survive this world war, or will anyone's? A Philistine reading, so strange are the ways of history and etymology, helps remind us of the necessity of a Palestinian reading.

A Philistine reading will overlap with a polytheist reading since the Philistines are generally presented as polytheists (see the "gods" or "idols" in Judg 10:6; 1 Sam 6:5; 17:43; 31:9; 2 Sam 5:21), and it is surely the Philistine gods that David finds himself sent to serve (26:19; 27:1).

---

[40] The usual Hebrew word for god, *elohim,* is grammatically plural.

[41] David Jobling and Catherine Rose, "Reading as a Philistine: The Ancient and Modern History of a Cultural Slur," in Mark G. Brett, ed., *Ethnicity and the Bible* (Leiden: E. J. Brill, 1996) 381–417.

Even more will it overlap with an anarchic reading (see the next section) via Matthew Arnold and also by means of the irresistible pun between uncircumcised and uncircumscribed. The Philistine's lack of the physical mark means that he has not been brought under the law. Likewise I have offered readings uncircumscribed by any canons for the "lawful" literary reading of the Bible.

Finally, there is the current use of "Philistine" to mean artistically incompetent. David Gunn takes powerful issue with the view of Sternberg that I looked at earlier in this chapter, that competence in understanding literary artistry is the main factor in reading the Bible well. "No amount of 'competence'," says Gunn, "is going to settle substantial questions of meaning."[42] To agree with Gunn, as I do, is to range oneself, from the high literary point of view, with the Philistines.

Is this mere empty word-play? Word-play it is, certainly, provided we realize that word-play is word-work, entering into the work that words do in their "unlimited semiosis" [10–11]. But it is by no means empty. "Philistine" is the name for an extraordinarily complex space into which one may choose to enter to see what view of the world is available from there. This is one of the things I have tried to do.

Anarchic reading. The possibility of an *anarchic* reading arises, as we have seen, not in 1 Samuel itself but in the words immediately preceding it in the Deuteronomic History: "All the people did what was right in their own eyes" (Judg 21:25). This situation is presumably thought of as continuing at least into the beginning of 1 Samuel—indeed, it well describes the wicked priests (2:12-17, 22), and also Hannah (1:23) [306–307].

In the last section I discussed the transferential relationship between this anarchy in Israel and the current "anarchic" scene in biblical interpretation. On both sides of the analogy those who claim to see anarchy misrepresent the opposed point of view. In the text the monarchist voice at the end of Judges perceives in the absence of a king only anarchy. This "anarchy," however, is only one option within a variety of biblical assessments of the premonarchical period. The unspoken assumption behind this voice is that letting things get out of control (whose?) is bad. People are acting freely, doing what they want, and they do a lot of bad things. Implication: they need a king; a king would be good for them, would "save them from themselves." Forget the bad experience with Gideon and Abimelech. Forget the ideal of YHWH as Israel's king.

What about the anarchy in current biblical interpretation? Is it just a "free-for-all"? No and yes. I do not concede that we are now in a situation where anything goes in reading the Bible. Most of the new

---

[42] Gunn, "Reading Right" 55.

readings emerge from a commitment to the text at least as profound as that of the orthodox literary readers. On the other hand I *do* affirm a scene of biblical reading that is and is becoming "free for all": a scene, that is, in which different readers express their various freedoms— freedoms often new and hard-won. I trust that we can leave the question of *responsible* freedom to them. For they have communities to which they are responsible—often in a much more obvious way than academics do. I anticipate that implausible readings will not survive long. But while I see different readings apparently giving life to these different communities, I am not prepared to worry much about the question of plausibility.

Trafficking with the dead. Josipovici gives a number of examples of his principle that the Bible "is actually *about* . . . the critical and hermeneutical issues" involved in reading it,[43] ending with this:

> And may we not see in Saul's desperate calling up of Samuel from the dead, and in the irony of the old prophet's ghost being able to tell Saul only what he already knew, an image of those scholars who would penetrate behind the veil of the Bible's words to the truth beneath, only to find there what they knew already?[44]

With uncanny accuracy Josipovici goes to the very passage, 1 Samuel 28, that is the focus of my final transferential remarks on 1 Samuel and the problem of the past.

The idea I explored in the last chapter, that the Bible is literature of loss, is not a new one. Regina Schwartz, for example, has demonstrated how the Bible itself testifies to its creation as "a process of loss and recovery, forgetting and remembering."[45] But Schwartz, and also Wieseltier [254–258], point to a general process of loss without being specific about just what got lost in the process. What *in particular* has been lost or suppressed in the production of 1 Samuel and the Deuteronomic History, and by what means might it be restored to consciousness?

I have assumed that the History continued to develop well into the postexilic time when Israel was incorporated into the empires of

---

[43] *The Book of God* 27.

[44] Ibid. 28.

[45] The Bible and Culture Collective, *The Postmodern Bible* (New Haven: Yale University Press, 1995) 125, referring to Schwartz, "Joseph's Bones and the Resurrection of the Text: Remembering in the Bible," in eadem, ed., *The Book and the Text: The Bible and Literary Theory* (Oxford: Basil Blackwell, 1990) 40–59. This whole section of *The Postmodern Bible* (pp. 125–128) is relevant.

Persians and Greeks. What, in a time of imperial subjugation, are the *usable memories* of the past? David's dilemma at the end of 1 Samuel seems to me to speak to this question, but in a way that reveals a deeply divided consciousness.

The course that David actually pursues in 2 Samuel highlights the memory of Israel's old imperial glory, as if to say to the postexilic audience: We are now the subjects of an empire, but once we were ourselves the imperialists—and may be again when God chooses to fulfill the promises to David. The course that David, at the end of 1 Samuel, thinks he *might* pursue is a very different one. To try to prosper as a servant of the Philistines is to address the problem of how to live well and successfully in a world defined by aliens. Now the word to the postexilic audience is: We have long been politically subordinate and there is no sign that God intends to alter this—so let us make the best of it.

This latter message is in fact strongly conveyed in other parts of the Jewish Bible: in the story of Joseph in Genesis, and in the books of Daniel (1–6) and Esther.[46] It is plainly a message of the utmost relevance. But in the books of Samuel it recedes almost to the point of invisibility behind the alternative message of David's inevitable rise to power. In the treatment of the Philistines memories of coexistence with dominant aliens are forcibly displaced by memories of imperial power.

Even more deeply buried is a third kind of memory, the memory of a just society without domination from outside or inside, Buber's Kingship of God. Undoubtedly Israel's monarchy, while it lasted, labored hard to expunge this memory. It is, indeed, part of the very system of monarchy to enforce the forgetting of what preceded it. The royal propaganda of the ancient Near East projected kingship as eternal and changeless. According to the Sumerian King List, for example, "kingship was lowered from heaven" by the gods at the beginning of time.[47] Non-monarchical human society is thus rendered unthinkable. That Israel's monarchy indulged in similar propaganda is shown particularly by the book of Psalms.[48]

The Deuteronomic History refuses this notion. It insists that monarchy in Israel *had a beginning*, and we should not underestimate how radical an affirmation this is. But the memory of what preceded

---

[46] Among the deuterocanonical books see also Tobit.

[47] "The Sumerian King List," translated by A. Leo Oppenheim, in James B. Pritchard, ed., *Ancient Near Eastern Texts Relating to the Old Testament* (Princeton, N.J.: Princeton University Press, 1955) 265.

[48] See my "Deconstruction and the Political Analysis of Biblical Texts: A Jamesonian Reading of Psalm 72," *Sem* 59 (1992) 95–127.

monarchy has become so distant as to be almost lost. So the History is ambiguous about how to assess the premonarchical time, projecting it more as an anti-ideal than an ideal, putting monarchy forward as an alternative ideal.

What is our means of access to this past? I have suggested in this book that it is through critical reading of a text that is resistant to our reading. Critical reading evokes a past different from what the Bible wants to let us know about or even itself remembers.

The Deuteronomists, and the Bible in general, would like to preserve an access to the past that is unproblematic, open and above board. It would like to see the past as an unbroken continuum extending into the present. We have seen the Deuteronomists striving for the appearance of continuity particularly in their treatment of Samuel as both judge and kingmaker [61–64]. But history insists on breaks and ruptures, and we have seen the Deuteronomists' hopes for continuity founder on the stubborn fragmentariness of the story they tell.[49]

The hope for continuity is expressed especially by the sequence of male generations, the links between father and son. My aim has been to show that this sequence is precisely what fails. Real fathers are in 1 Samuel consistently estranged from their sons. The hope for continuity therefore gets displaced, I suggest, onto generations defined by *surrogate* fathers and sons [111–125]. Up to a point this works. We have seen how elements of real continuity link Eli, Samuel, Saul, David. But all of these links finally fail. Even surrogate fathers become estranged and unavailable. The series of intertexts I used in the previous chapter all, in various ways, emphasize this failure of continuity. Taken as a whole the text of 1 Samuel and my intertexts highlight the figure of the dead father as an expression of failed continuity.

The Medium of Endor enters the text as a mediator between male generations, but a strange mediator, since it is with a dead father that she brings Saul into contact. Her story implies an admission of the failure of the authorized historical continuity between present and past, but at the same time it asserts the possibility of reestablishing the broken continuity by other, unauthorized means. The past cannot be told, cannot be preserved as a resource by relying on the authorized continuity of the male generations. To be available, the past must be searched for in hidden places—in the depths of the national psyche, we might say, and not just in its official records. To preserve the past as a resource for the present is to traffic with the dead.

---

[49] On this issue see especially Schwartz, "Adultery in the House of David."

I want to stress again how extraordinary it is that the Deuteronomic History would introduce a character like the Medium of Endor in such a positive way. She is a member of a class of religious practitioners who must be expelled from official Israel. Indeed, her place is not merely outside Israel, but outside of acceptable human character as the Bible can otherwise conceive it. Nowhere else in the Bible is such a person allowed to be a character at all. Surely had the writers so wished they could have told of Saul's last misdeed with little circumstantial detail about the woman, leaving the reader to draw the appropriate negative conclusions about her (or preferably not to dwell on her at all). Why build her up into a person of professional skill and high human qualities? It is playing with fire! The only explanation is that the text at this juncture has need of her, desires her. There is more to this incident than meets the eye, or than my earlier reading probed [185–189].

The timing of her appearance is equally revealing. Just when David has been sent to serve other gods we come to the story of this woman who belongs, within the text's dominant logic, to the realm of the "other gods." As symbol of an alternative means of access to history she appears at exactly the moment when David is enacting Israel's alternative history.

Will it be possible to maintain control of Israel's alternative memories? What danger might they pose for the stability of the present? The Deuteronomic History, I have surmised, owes some of its characteristics to a sense of guilt that the national work of remembering that it enshrines has not been fully "national" at all, that certain voices have been excluded. The medium embodies all these exclusions and conjures up all the dangerous memories.

The first potential danger is to the sociopolitical order of the postexilic period and the status of its elite. The person the medium raises from the dead is Samuel the judge, representative of the possibility of an egalitarian, non-imperial order. The authorities of postexilic Judah have no use for such memories. They want no such prophetic voices: they have recently announced that the voice of prophecy is dead! If such memories have to be evoked, let them be evoked as dead and gone—like Haggard praising the old Zulu order, but only as a thing of the past, like the new Europe praising Marx the philosopher now that his power to change the world is gone [273]. The Kingship of God has become a dangerous, occult memory.

The second danger is the confusion of identity. The Medium of Endor is found in close proximity to the Philistines who loom so large in 1 Samuel [217]. She lives on the border between Israel and the Philistines, she practices the Philistine arts, she may be herself a Philistine. Textually, too, she is juxtaposed to the Philistines. She appears at the time of Philistine dominance over Israel, at the time when David has gone to serve the Philistines, on the very eve of Saul's last battle.

Israel's official memory is of how all this danger passed, how David moved to his destiny and the Philistine Other simply disappeared. This official memory supports the narrow ethnic identity that postexilic Israel is trying to take on. But what if a truer contact with the past were available only by breaking open this narrow identity? What if Israel's authentic past were one that only the Philistine, the most utterly Other, could call up, a past in which the other may not have been so very other? We are reminded of Haggard, establishing white imperialist identity by claiming that only whites can preserve black history, while at the same time pathologically searching for the white within the black, seeking an escape from racial difference while triumphantly affirming it [264].

The third aspect of the dangerous memory of the Medium of Endor is that she is a woman. The access to the past that is an alternative to the authorized continuity of male generations, and that from the perspective of authority belongs to the realm of the occult, is the work of a woman. So threatening is this to Haggard that he makes the medium, in effect, into a man, and conflates her with Samuel himself [264]. I will return to a feminist reading of the medium in the next section.

I announced at the beginning my hope of breaching the boundary between biblical studies and therapy, noting that psychoanalysis is a practice of healing before it is a literary method [23–24]. I like to borrow and extend Itumeleng Mosala's challenge that we liberate the Bible so that it may liberate us[50] by adding that we need to heal the Bible so that it may heal us. In this chapter my entire methodological framework has been psychoanalytic, and the idea of healing—of myself, of the text, of biblical studies—has throughout been close at hand.

Saul, who is the figure of Israel's tragedy, turns to the Medium of Endor out of absolute need when all else has failed, and so far as he is capable of receiving it he finds healing. The Deuteronomists too, I suggest, turn to the medium when all else has failed—all the hopes that official historiography can create a satisfying relationship to the past. They sense that she points a way to heal Israel's atrophied and distorted memory, which is the memory of all of us who share in the biblical culture of the West.

---

[50] *Biblical Hermeneutics and Black Theology in South Africa* (Grand Rapids: Eerdmans, 1989) 175.

Framing by the Female

For my own career the most important of the new reading communities that have recently appeared in the field of biblical studies is the community of feminist readers [7–9]. The preceding rereading of the Medium of Endor completes my feminist work in this book, and I take this opportunity for a self-critical look at this work as a whole.

One response to my reading of Hannah, particularly from women students, has been to ask why I so much *need* Hannah to be a positive character [8]. There are some contingent reasons having to do with the setting in which I first presented that reading. I wanted among other things to provide an example of the continuing force of a recuperative feminist approach. (This is not the approach that I usually stress in my work.) But such reasons, I have come to think, do not get close to dealing with the force of the question. Why *must* Hannah be a strong, positive figure for me?

The question was put to me by people who found certain aspects and actions of Hannah to be anything but admirable. Their critique stressed two points. First, there is no sense of mutuality and solidarity between her and Peninnah, no awareness that their problems are two sides of one coin [182–183]. Second, we have to ask whether Hannah is not complicit in child abuse. She thrusts her son, at a tender age, away from the care of a family and into a temple system she knows to have been tolerant of gross personal abuses. Of his experience there we know little except that he in some sense prospered, but the one incident in his upbringing that we do know of (3:2-18) is not reassuring. He is subjected to a night of terror during which he becomes the channel of an appalling divine oracle, followed in the morning by severe grilling and threats from a scared old man.

I read Hannah the way I did because I perceived great strength in her character and was appalled at how some of the most skilled male literary critics were unable to come to positive terms with it, how they were obliged either to deny or to trivialize it [140–141]. My wish to counteract these readings led me into a measure of sentimentality that, I now think, made me actually underestimate Hannah's strength. For the critiques just mentioned, pointing out an insensitive and even brutal side to Hannah, only emphasize her singleness of purpose. The most radical aspect of my reading, I believe, is that she consciously sets out to change her world and succeeds in doing so. She does what seems best to her (1 Sam 1:23, Judg 21:25)! The result of her initiative is that Israel defers monarchy for a generation or two, rediscovers a basis for national life without monarchy.

Such a powerful sense of purpose, as Danna Fewell has suggested to me, is not likely to make her a desirable mother by conventional standards. Hannah could even be said to sacrifice Samuel to her purpose, perhaps with lasting psychological effects [70].

This critique of Hannah, if it makes us like her less, brings her closer, I think, to the stature of the Medium of Endor—my first portrait of whom was also not free from some sentimentality [185–189]. When I wrote about Hannah I had not begun to consider the significance of the medium, but I must already have been intuiting the importance of these two women *together* for understanding 1 Samuel. They both point us to the lost memory of egalitarian Israel. Hannah does it by acting to reestablish judgeship through Samuel and by celebrating egalitarian Israel in her song (2:4-8). The medium does it by controlling access to Samuel and hence to the past for which he stands. In relation to the fundamental transition from judgeship to kingship, both are *epochal* figures.

And these women frame 1 Samuel! The final clue for me came with Mieke Bal's insight into how male accounts of history as the succession of male generations are framed by the mother whose exclusion was the condition for the creation of the male accounts [272–273]. The excluded female comes back to haunt the structures of exclusion. The creation of 1 Samuel as a canonical book seems to me to be an extraordinary example of this process. The process of developing an authorized male account of Israel's past produces a "book" that occupies the central position in that account and that is defined by female figures.[51] This is why I "needed" Hannah (and the medium) to be positive figures.

Josipovici's insight that the Bible manages to be *about* the very processes by which we undertake to interpret it corresponds to my most basic conviction as an interpreter of the Bible. He shows no sign of awareness of any brand of feminist reading of the Bible,[52] but my identification of the framing of 1 Samuel by the female or the mother provides a signal example of his principle. I was led to perceive this phenomenon by my immersion in feminist biblical scholarship over many years. Without that immersion I would never have noticed. The recent history of biblical scholarship has likewise been "framed by the female." It has been shaped by the new presence of large numbers of

---

[51] Further along the same lines I have explored the importance of a woman's book, Ruth, as an introduction or even an alternative to 1 Samuel, and of the repeated allusions in 1 Samuel to Rachel, the mother of Israel [106–109, 190].

[52] Which is perhaps why he fears that scholars may be finding in the Bible "only . . . what they knew already"! (*The Book of God* 28).

women readers who have made feminist questions unavoidable. The arrival of feminist biblical criticism in full force has done more than anything else to redefine the relation of current biblical studies to the past that it inherits.

Israel's official memory is shaped by the systematic exclusion of certain voices, notably those of women. Likewise the tradition of "authorized" biblical interpretation that we inherit. My concentration in this book on the women characters and the feminist issues in 1 Samuel has been an attempt to reverse, in a small way, the exclusion of the female from that work of remembering that we call biblical scholarship.

Conclusion: The Bible Abiding our Question

I dip one last time into Matthew Arnold. His sonnet on Shakespeare begins: "Others abide our question. Thou art free."[53] There is, for Arnold, some mysterious quality in Shakespeare that exempts him from the critique we bring to bear on other poets. To make such a claim plausible Arnold in effect applies to Shakespeare language the Bible uses for God ("Planting his steadfast footsteps in the sea, Making the heaven of heavens his dwelling place" [cf. Ps 77:19; Deut 10:14]).

"And behold, something greater than Shakespeare is here" (cf. Luke 11:31). The Bible would seem to have an even higher claim to exemption from critique. This, in essence, is what readers like Sternberg, Alter and Kermode, and Polzin want to give it. Their dazzling technical achievements finally are just an elaborate way of exempting the Bible from "abiding our question."

In the end it is a theological matter. Is the freedom of the Bible, and the freedom of the God whom some of us still think to find in, around, under, against the text of the Bible, a freedom that must be preserved by protecting the Bible and the biblical God from critical questioning? What sort of freedom would it be that could be preserved only by destroying the freedom of the reader, or the believer?—that could be preserved only by excluding the participation of those who are just entering the discourse, out of a history of being suppressed by gender or class or race privilege?

Thus I have tried to affirm the "anarchy" in current interpretation, the ferment of new reading methods that perhaps can be summarized

---

[53] *The Poems of Matthew Arnold 1840–1867* (Oxford: Oxford University Press, 1922) 58.

under the category of the "postmodern." I have affirmed the questioning of all the assumptions the text makes and all the assumptions that all kinds of interpretive orthodoxies make. I have tried not to create a new orthodoxy, though of course it is to one's own faults that one is most blind. I have insisted on the counterreading that Sternberg declares impossible. Whenever the text gets into its "inevitable" mode (the inevitable movement toward the kingship of David is the prime example) I have resisted this inevitability.

In doing so I have tried wherever possible to follow what Phyllis Trible calls "the clue within the text."[54] This is not the only option. The questions the Bible must abide are not only the ones that it raises itself. It is a matter of personal style but it is also, I think, a little more than that. In the scene I inhabit, the question of the "authority" of the Bible is still raised in utmost seriousness, and it is important to be able to show the range of understandings of its own authority to which the Bible proves itself open: a very wide range, but not indefinitely wide. The Bible (and of course I would say the same of any other text) must also have the freedom to question our readings of it.

Biblical scholarship as it emerges into the postmodern is, like modern consciousness in general, caught in Barthelme's bind [265–267]. We cannot avoid repeating the gestures of patriarchy, of outmoded power structures, even as we resist them. "Slightly better is all you can hope for." I have written this book to do my part in the "turning down" of patriarchy, to repeat its gestures a little less in my generation, but I am very much aware of how much I still repeat—especially when I see the generation following *me* already finding a certain quaintness in my efforts to be radical. The Bible *can* be read "otherwise," in ways that will make it a significant partner in the discourses of the third millennium, but no one can predict what these ways will be. As Derrida says, trying to program the future is just what makes revolution go wrong.

---

[54] *God and the Rhetoric of Sexuality*. Overtures to Biblical Theology (Philadelphia: Fortress, 1978) 1–5.

FOR FURTHER READING

I have written this book in the conviction that literary theory and the reading of texts must be kept always in dialogue with each other. "Literary theory" is understood here in a broad sense to include anything relevant to the way we read texts. The following suggestions for further reading include both theoretical writings and works on the text of the Bible. I have naturally given preference to works on the whole or part of 1 Samuel, but have included works on other parts of the Bible when these illuminate the work of reading in ways that the 1 Samuel literature does not.

LITERARY THEORY

Eagleton, Terry. *Literary Theory: An Introduction.* Oxford: Basil Black-well, 1983.

Jameson, Fredric. *The Political Unconscious: Narrative as a Socially Symbolic Act.* Ithaca, N.Y.: Cornell University Press, 1981.

THEORY AND THE READING OF THE BIBLE

The Bible and Culture Collective. *The Postmodern Bible.* New Haven: Yale University Press, 1995.

Jobling, David. "Writing the Wrongs of the World: The Deconstruction of the Biblical Text in the Context of Liberation Theologies," *Semeia* 51 (1990) 81–118.

McKenzie, Steven L., and Stephen R. Haynes, eds. *To Each Its Own Meaning: An Introduction to Biblical Criticisms and Their Application.* Louisville: Westminster/John Knox Press, 1993.

Yee, Gale A., ed. *Judges and Method: New Approaches in Biblical Studies.* Minneapolis: Fortress Press, 1995.

FEMINISM AND THE BIBLE

Bal, Mieke. *Death & Dissymmetry: The Politics of Coherence in the Book of Judges.* Chicago: University of Chicago Press, 1988.

Meyers, Carol. *Discovering Eve: Ancient Israelite Women in Context.* New York and Oxford: Oxford University Press, 1988.

Rutledge, David. *Reading Marginally: Feminism, Deconstruction and the Bible.* Biblical Interpretation Series 21. Leiden: E. J. Brill, 1996.

Trible, Phyllis. *God and the Rhetoric of Sexuality.* Overtures to Biblical Theology. Philadelphia: Fortress Press, 1978.

SOCIAL SCIENCE AND THE BIBLE

Eilberg-Schwartz, Howard. *The Savage in Judaism: An Anthropology of Israelite Religions and Ancient Judaism.* Bloomington, Ind.: Indiana University Press, 1990.

Gottwald, Norman K. *The Hebrew Bible in Its Social World and in Ours.* Semeia Studies. Atlanta: Scholars Press, 1993.

Steinberg, Naomi. "The Deuteronomic Law and the Politics of State Centralization" in David Jobling, Peggy L. Day, and Gerald T. Sheppard, eds., *The Bible and the Politics of Exegesis: Essays in Honor of Norman K. Gottwald on his Sixty-Fifth Birthday.* Cleveland: Pilgrim Press, 1991, 161–170.

PSYCHOANALYSIS AND THE BIBLE

Halperin, David J. *Seeking Ezekiel: Text and Psychology.* University Park, Pa.: Pennsylvania State University Press, 1993.

Jobling, David. "Transference and Tact in Biblical Studies," in Timothy K. Beal and David M. Gunn, eds., *Reading Bibles, Writing Bodies.* Biblical Limits. London and New York: Routledge, 1997, 208–218.

Rashkow, Ilona N. *The Phallacy of Genesis: A Feminist Psychoanalytic Approach.* Louisville: Westminster/John Knox Press, 1993.

LITERARY APPROACHES TO THE BIBLE

Alter, Robert. *The Art of Biblical Narrative.* London: Allen & Unwin, 1981.

Bal, Mieke. "The Bible as Literature: A Critical Escape," in eadem, *On Story-Telling: Essays in Narratology,* ed. David Jobling. Sonoma, Cal.: Polebridge Press, 1991, 59–72.

Josipovici, Gabriel. *The Book of God: A Response to the Bible.* New Haven and London: Yale University Press, 1988.

Long, Burke O. "The 'New' Biblical Poetics of Alter and Sternberg," *JSOT* 51 (1991) 71–84.

Sternberg, Meir. *The Poetics of Biblical Narrative: Ideological Literature and the Drama of Reading.* Bloomington, Ind.: Indiana University Press, 1985.

LITERARY READINGS IN 1 SAMUEL

Eslinger, Lyle M. *Kingship of God in Crisis: A Close Reading of 1 Samuel 1–12.* Bible and Literature Series 10. Sheffield: Almond, 1985.

Exum, J. Cheryl. *Tragedy and Biblical Narrative: Arrows of the Almighty.* Cambridge: Cambridge University Press, 1992.

Gunn, David M. *The Fate of King Saul: An Interpretation of a Biblical Story.* JSOT.S 14. Sheffield: JSOT Press, 1980.

Miscall, Peter D. *1 Samuel: A Literary Reading.* Bloomington, Ind.: Indiana University Press, 1986.

Polzin, Robert. *Samuel and the Deuteronomist: A Literary Study of the Deuteronomic History. Part Two: 1 Samuel.* San Francisco: Harper & Row, 1989.

Rosenberg, Joel. *King and Kin: Political Allegory in the Hebrew Bible.* Indiana Studies in Biblical Literature. Bloomington, Ind.: Indiana University Press, 1986, 99–199.

FEMINIST READINGS IN 1 SAMUEL

Bach, Alice. "The Pleasure of Her Text," in eadem, ed., *The Pleasure of Her Text: Feminist Readings of Biblical & Historical Texts.* Philadelphia: Trinity Press International, 1990, 25–44.

Brenner, Athalya, ed. *A Feminist Companion to Samuel and Kings.* The Feminist Companion to the Bible, 5. Sheffield: Sheffield Academic Press, 1994.

Exum, J. Cheryl. *Fragmented Women: Feminist Subversions of Biblical Narratives.* JSOT.S 163. Sheffield: JSOT Press, 1993, 16–93.

Fewell, Danna Nolan, and David M. Gunn. *Gender, Power, and Promise: The Subject of the Bible's First Story.* Nashville: Abingdon Press, 1993.

Hackett, Jo Ann. "1 and 2 Samuel," in Carol A. Newsom and Sharon H. Ringe, eds., *The Women's Bible Commentary.* Louisville: Westminster/John Knox Press, 1992, 85–95.

Schwartz, Regina M. "Adultery in the House of David: The Metanarrative of Biblical Scholarship and the Narratives of the Bible," *Semeia* 54 (1991) 35–55.

THE DEUTERONOMIC HISTORY

Noth, Martin. *The Deuteronomistic History.* JSOT.S 15. Sheffield: JSOT Press, 1981.
McCarthy, Dennis J. "II Samuel 7 and the Structure of the Deuteronomic History," *JBL* 84 (1965) 131–138.

GENERAL INDEX

INDEX OF SCRIPTURAL REFERENCES

Note: Biblical books are listed below in the order in which they occur in the Hebrew canon. The order differs in most English translations.